COPYRIGHT BEYOND LAW

The form of graffiti writing on trains and walls is not accidental. Nor is its absence on cars and houses. Employing a particular style of letters, choosing which walls and trains to write on, copying another writer, altering or destroying another writer's work: these acts are regulated within the graffiti subculture. *Copyright Beyond Law* presents findings from empirical research undertaken into the graffiti subculture to show that graffiti writers informally regulate their creativity through a system of norms that are remarkably similar to copyright.

The 'graffiti rules' and their copyright law parallels include: the requirement of writing letters (subject matter) and appropriate placement (public policy and morality exceptions for copyright subsistence and the enforcement of copyright), originality and the prohibition of copying (originality and infringement by reproduction), and the prohibition of damage to another writer's works (the moral right of integrity). The intersection between the 'graffiti rules' and copyright law sheds light on the creation of subculture-specific commons and the limits of copyright law in incentivising and regulating the production and location of creativity.

Copyright Beyond Law

Regulating Creativity in the Graffiti Subculture

Marta Iljadica

• HART •
OXFORD • LONDON • NEW YORK • NEW DELHI • SYDNEY

HART PUBLISHING
Bloomsbury Publishing Plc
Kemp House, Chawley Park, Cumnor Hill, Oxford, OX2 9PH, UK

HART PUBLISHING, the Hart/Stag logo, BLOOMSBURY and the Diana logo are trademarks of Bloomsbury Publishing Plc

First published 2016
Paperback edition, 2019

A catalogue record for this book is available from the British Library.

Library of Congress Cataloging-in-Publication Data

Names: Iljadica, Marta, author.

Title: Copyright beyond law : regulating creativity in the graffi ti subculture / Marta Iljadica.

Description: Oxford [UK] ; Portland, Oregon : Hart Publishing, 2016. | Includes bibliographical references and index.

Identifiers: LCCN 2016029282 (print) | LCCN 2016029539 (ebook) | ISBN 9781849467773 (hardback) | ISBN 9781509902026 (Epub)

Subjects: LCSH: Copyright—Art. | Public art—Law and legislation. | Law and art. | Graffi ti—History. | Street art—History.

Classifica tion: LCC K1460 .I45 2016 (print) | LCC K1460 (ebook) | DDC 346.04/82—dc23

LC record available at https://lccn.loc.gov/2016029282

ISBN: HBK: 978-1-84946-777-3
PB: 978-1-50992-794-4
ePDF: 978-1-50990-201-9
ePub: 978-1-50990-202-6

Typeset by Compuscript Ltd, Shannon

SHOUT OUTS

Thank you

Michael Cooper, for that throw-away comment; Tanya Aplin and Penny Green, for brilliant supervision; the graffiti writers and street artists (this is your book), and everyone I met during fieldwork, for the privilege of seeing a different world; my examiners Fiona Macmillan and Andreas Philippopoulos-Mihalopoulos, for thought-provoking comments; Maurizio Borghi, John Coggon, Mark Jordan, Daniela Simone, Eleonora Rosati, Sophie Stalla-Bourdillon and Mark Telford, for comments on different parts of this book; Kathy Bowrey, Debora Halbert and participants at the International Society for the History and Theory of Intellectual Property workshop in Paris, 2013, for engagement with a paper incorporated here; and Paul Scott, for unwavering support, encouragement and thoughtful comments on each and every chapter.

To my family—*hvala vam za sve.*

A NOTE ON PICTURES

There are no reproductions of graffiti in this book. The pages that follow argue that graffiti is copyright protected. But whether or not that is correct, this book is about a creative process and its attendant norms; it seeks to demonstrate that much of creativity and many of the pleasures of creation and belonging exist beyond copyright. Copyright does not reach, and cannot speak to, these pleasures. So, rather than seeing here examples of graffiti creativity outside the cultural and spatial context in which they reside, I invite you to walk the city; to seek out graffiti writing (and street art, too). See the names repeating. See the forms that graffiti creativity takes (and those it doesn't) and the places in which it is found (and those in which it isn't). None of this is an accident.

CONTENTS

Panel III: Copying

Panel IV: Reputation

Panel V: Interactions

Introduction

Graffiti breaks every rule but within itself still has rules. (Anon29)

The form of graffiti writing on trains and walls is not accidental. Nor is its absence on cars and (most) houses. Graffiti writing has rules. Employing a particular style of letters, choosing which walls and trains to write on, copying another writer, altering or destroying another writer's work: these acts are regulated within the subculture. This book is based on empirical research into graffiti writing and it aims to identify and explain these norms ('graffiti rules'). At the same time this book applies United Kingdom (UK) copyright law to graffiti creativity in order to highlight parallels between copyright and the graffiti rules and, in so doing, to ask what the convergence and divergences in the regulation of creativity in the intellectual commons might reveal about how creativity ought to be regulated by copyright and where copyright falls short of what creators need. The discussion below provides a brief overview of some of the themes running through the analysis both of the applicability of copyright to graffiti, and the nature of the graffiti rules.

Commons, Creativity and Norms

The title of this book, *Copyright Beyond Law*, draws attention to the interaction between copyright and the graffiti rules in the sense that graffiti creativity is beyond copyright—because copyright cannot account for crucial aspects of the *process* of producing graffiti in such a way as to recognise the importance of pleasure and community belonging to those who produce it—but also because the alternative normative framework that is produced to support the creative process is a form of regulation that stands apart from, that is beyond, legal rules. In other words, a normative framework exists within the graffiti subculture which both mirrors and exceeds the regulatory potential of copyright in regulating creativity internally within the subculture but falls short of addressing uses by non-writers outside of it. Addressing the limitations of copyright in the context of copyright-like rules offers the prospect of imagining an alternative copyright law. In particular, the auto-positioning of graffiti writers against copyright law raises questions about the boundaries that exist, or ought to exist, within the propertised and public domains within the intellectual commons.

The graffiti rules examined in the forthcoming chapters operate in the context of two important, and distinctive, regulatory features within the graffiti subculture as compared to copyright: that the protection of individual creative efforts is a means of further enriching the graffiti subculture's intellectual commons (what one graffiti writer called the 'library of style') but also, that the regulation of graffiti creativity effectively collapses the distinction between the physical and intellectual commons in regulating both the content and reproduction of works, and the location of works. Thus while letters are free for all to use, choices about the combination and style of the letters, and *where* the final work is placed are circumscribed. This is one example of how the conception of a stylistic 'commons' is embedded in the graffiti rules notwithstanding the highly individualistic motivations of graffiti writers to simply 'get up' (be visible in urban space) in order to gain fame and respect from fellow writers. Alongside the constraints placed on graffiti writers regarding appropriate placement the framework of norms identified in the empirical work suggests the existence of a graffiti-specific 'bounded commons' within the broader intellectual commons (as it is understood in copyright literature).

Taking into account public space also means recognising and respecting territories. Graffiti, especially tagging,[1] originated in its modern form in 1960s Philadelphia although it is more commonly associated with the writer Taki183, who began writing his tag around New York City in the 1970s, and the train writers of the New York subway system who were immortalised in the book *Subway Art*,[2] the documentary film *Style Wars*[3] and other media in the early 1980s. The subculture was transplanted to London in the 1980s and the first wave of writers emulated the style of their American counterparts. Crucially, this included adopting the concerns over acceptable (and unacceptable) behaviour that emerged in this period in the United States (US) and which gave rise to the graffiti rules.

As the following chapters suggest, territory—graffiti occurs in a specific city neighbourhood at a specific time—is highly relevant to the interface between the physical and intellectual commons. The intellectual commons always 'touches' a particular material, whether it is a wall or train, but graffiti writing, and the graffiti rules themselves, must also be understood as a global practice that is the product of a particular historical process. As such graffiti writing might be seen as a creative practice that is regulated by a set of norms that are transnational in their existence but highly dependent, in their specific application, on territory: day-to-day

[1] A tag is graffiti writer's name or signature written in one colour.
[2] M Cooper and H Chalfant, *Subway Art* (London, Thames & Hudson, 1984).
[3] T Silver and H Chalfant, *Style Wars*, Public Art Films, 2007 (released 1983).

interpretation of, and adherence to, the graffiti norms will take into account the 'scene' of the particular city in which effect is given to them.

Copyright law grants certain economic and non-economic (ie moral) rights to the creators of original literary and artistic works including the right to reproduce their work. In the UK as in the US, Australia and elsewhere, graffiti writing is a potentially illegal activity. In the UK graffiti writing may constitute criminal damage and/or anti-social behaviour. This makes graffiti writers' auto-positioning against copyright to create within a 'bounded commons' unsurprising. Graffiti writers will not usually avail themselves of copyright protection[4] in order to seek compensation when their works are reproduced. So although copyright likely subsists in graffiti works (eg a five-letter piece using a particular combination of angles and colours) it is largely irrelevant to the motivations of graffiti writers. Indeed, even if graffiti writers wished to enforce their copyright, by revealing both their 'tag' and their real name they may be at risk of prosecution for criminal damage. Graffiti creativity thus flourishes without reference or recourse to copyright.

Moreover, the operation of copyright raises broader questions about the intellectual commons and the public domain, a problem that intensifies when considering that graffiti creativity is fundamentally a spatial practice that calls into question not only the appropriateness of the rules regulating creativity and their impact on protecting and preserving culture in the intellectual commons but *also* the physical commons of the everyday, public street or train network.

Outline of Chapters

To analyse the existence of an alternative normative framework this book draws broadly on the legal literature on copyright and creativity as well as the sociological literature on graffiti writing. In particular, it draws upon and contributes to the small but growing body of literature on non-legal intellectual property norms within specific communities, which asks how and why some creative communities create their own rules in situations where their creative outputs are either unprotected or insufficiently protected by copyright law, or where copyright law is simply ignored even though it may apply. Chapter ten considers the expectations graffiti writers have about how their creativity ought to be used by those *outside* of the subculture—especially in the context of non-writers photographing and sharing graffiti, and of third party commercial exploitation—while the copyright chapters (four, six and eight) consider how copyright would apply to

[4] Although this, too, appears to be changing at least in the US, eg *Jason Williams, et al v Roberto Cavalli S.p.A., et al* CV 14-06659, 2015 US Dist LEXIS 34722.

graffiti creativity and its uses *within* the subculture that is, in regulating how works are created, shared and copied, and disputes dealt with amongst graffiti writers. The application of copyright is then contrasted with the operation of the graffiti-specific norms for regulating creativity. This in turn identifies the specific challenges that graffiti creativity poses to the application of copyright law as well as pointing to the limitations of copyright law more generally in regulating creativity within the intellectual commons including, amongst other things, preserving the public domain within the broader intellectual commons.

The book is divided into different Parts or 'panels'.[5] The first panel provides the context for the graffiti rules and copyright rules as well as an overview of methodology. Chapter one provides a brief history of graffiti writing. It explains the structure of the graffiti subculture including conceptions of respect, hierarchy, visibility and style. These concepts help to explain some of the similarities and differences between graffiti rules and copyright law and the question of why graffiti writing flourishes in the absence of copyright protection. Chapter two provides an overview of the justifications for copyright protection in the context of the relationship between copyright, creativity and the public domain and introduces the concept of a graffiti-specific 'bounded commons'. It then examines the existing empirical studies of non-legal normative frameworks for the regulation of creativity with a view to adding this book to that literature. Chapter three explains how the empirical research on which the book is based—semi-structured interviews with graffiti writers and street artists—was conducted. The role of the methodology chapter is to provide a 'behind the scenes' look (matched by a somewhat colloquial, first person narrative in contrast to the rest of the book) at the fieldwork as a whole. It offers reflections on the process of data gathering to identify the source and scope of the ensuing analysis in the empirical chapters.

The book's second, third and fourth panels identify, based on the fieldwork data, a set of graffiti rules and also examines them in relation to the analogous copyright rules. The argument is made that graffiti writers recognise, though do not necessarily enforce, norms that demonstrate striking similarities and telling departures from copyright rules. In each of the copyright law chapters, copyright law is applied to graffiti creativity as it is produced, and experienced, within the 'bounded commons' of the graffiti subculture while the empirical chapters show how graffiti creativity is *actually* regulated within the subculture given that graffiti writers forgo copyright protection. The empirical chapters also draw attention to the parallels, albeit imperfect, between the graffiti rules and copyright.

The second panel examines the relevance of form and placement to creativity. Chapter four considers the subject matter and fixation requirements for

[5] A graffiti writer's term for a section of a train, namely a train carriage on which to write. *Subway Art* is more specific in defining a 'panel piece' as '[a] painting below the windows and between the doors of a subway car': Cooper and Chalfant (n 2) 27.

copyright protection, the necessity of qualification and fixation and immorality and public policy considerations. The chapter asks, in particular, whether graffiti creativity is a literary or artistic *work* in which copyright subsists. Chapter five then examines what 'graffiti writing' means in the graffiti subculture. It considers the importance of writing letters (a concern analogous to the subject matter requirement in copyright law) as well as the critical importance of *where* graffiti works may or may not be placed based on distinctions made between public and 'personal' property.

The third panel considers the rules regarding the copying of creative expressions. Chapter six examines the originality requirement in copyright law and, in particular, whether graffiti creativity qualifies as an original artistic work for the purposes of UK copyright law. It also examines infringement, including reproduction and communication to the public. The expectation that a graffiti writer will create their own style that draws upon the shared cultural history of graffiti but is not copied from another writer is considered in chapter seven. This chapter considers the parallel between graffiti writers' preoccupation with 'being original' and the originality requirement and the infringement of copyright through the reproduction of a work.

The fourth panel is broadly concerned with the protection of a creator's reputation. Chapter eight examines the moral rights of graffiti writers especially attribution, the right against false attribution and the integrity right. It considers, in particular, whether graffiti writers could claim that the alteration of their work was prejudicial to their honour or reputation. Chapter nine considers the prohibition within the subculture on damaging or destroying another writer's work as analogous to the moral right of integrity. As with copyright law, alteration is perceived as damaging to reputation but unlike copyright law, the assessment of damage to reputation is the result of a process of negotiation that takes into account the broader context of the work including its relative aesthetic merits and the graffiti writer's place in the subculture's hierarchy. This chapter also considers 'going over' as a sanction for breaking the graffiti rules discussed in the preceding empirical chapters.

Chapter ten broadens out the scope of the inquiry in relation to both the graffiti rules and copyright law to encompass the reproduction and dissemination of graffiti writing by non-writers. It examines the fieldwork data that cover the expectations graffiti writers have of third parties, that is, how graffiti writers think their work *ought* to be treated. The discussion then moves to a broader discussion of copyright law and how it takes into account the public placement of works. The two approaches—the graffiti rules and copyright law—are then contrasted in order to consider what the graffiti subculture's approach may contribute to the potential reform of copyright law, in particular the contours of new copyright exceptions that make the public placement of works a key factor in determining the acceptability of the reproduction and dissemination of works.

Finally, the Conclusion draws together the common threads in the discussion of the similarities and differences between the copyright rules and graffiti rules to argue that copyright law and the graffiti rules share common concerns with the development of culture. The study of the regulation of creativity within the graffiti subculture reveals what a copyright law that considered creativity as a process—a process central to belonging to a community, experiencing pleasure and, whether intended as an act of political resistance or not, producing an alternative regulation of space—would be.

Panel I

Context

1

Graffiti History and Development

> I think the graffiti movement throughout the world has tried to emulate [the golden era of the New York graffiti] movement and hasn't swayed much from those original aesthetics or rules or kind of, yes, street rules that are associated with that scene. You bomb the system, you tag trains, you paint pieces on trains, you vandalise public property. … And also … the rules handed down through generations of writers: this is how it was, this is how it should be. (Anon4)

Introduction

Drawing on sociological accounts of graffiti writing, this chapter provides an overview of the history of graffiti, the London scene, and the structure of the graffiti subculture all of which are important to understanding the operation of the graffiti rules. The rules—and this is something the graffiti rules have in common with copyright—are the product of particular social contexts that reflect, or seek to embody, certain justifications for the protection and regulation of creativity.[1] The discussion in this chapter will help to ground the analysis of the graffiti norms in subsequent chapters especially chapters five, seven, nine and ten which consider the empirical data and also chapter two which addresses the literature on creativity, the intellectual commons and the public domain, and other examples of alternative frameworks for regulating creativity.

This chapter has two parts. The first part considers the definition of graffiti writing and its historical development. The second part examines certain elements of the subculture: motivations and identity, fame and hierarchy, visibility, placement and style, and the relationship between illegality and the graffiti rules.

Historical Development

This part considers the definition of graffiti, the origins of graffiti writing and the evolution of the London/UK scene as an example of a transplant of graffiti culture

[1] Graffiti writers are concerned with safeguarding original styles while eg copyright law is concerned with original literary and artistic works. See Berne Convention for the Protection of Artistic and Literary Works, Paris Act of 24 July 1971, as amended on 29 September 1979, 828 UNTS 222.

from the US. Understanding this background is relevant because it demonstrates that the graffiti rules described here are the product not only of a collection of individual justifications for how and why graffiti creativity ought to be protected within the subculture but that the rules also crystallise the practices of graffiti writers at the inception of the subculture. Graffiti history is necessarily a series of impressions dependent on imperfect documentation,[2] as indeed is any history. Therefore, the information from secondary sources is supplemented with observations from graffiti writers contained in the interview data.[3]

Defining Graffiti Writing (and Street Art)

The use of walls as a medium for artistic expression has a history that can be traced back thousands of years to the paintings in the Lascaux[4] and Chauvet caves.[5] An article on the metaphorical significance of walls to art published in 1979 (oblivious to the contemporaneous evolution of graffiti writing in Philadelphia and New York) argues that walls and other surfaces have also been used for political slogans[6] and protest,[7] declarations of love, hate speech and the marking of gang territory.[8] These types of 'graffiti' are not relevant here. The remainder of this section considers the definition of graffiti writing vis-a-vis street art including highlighting the crucial element of graffiti culture: the tag.

This book distinguishes between graffiti writing and street art, a distinction drawn by many of the research participants. A major element of graffiti culture is the promulgation of a name, specifically tagging (writing a graffiti name). Tagging 'encompass[es] place, style and purpose'.[9] This goes to the heart of any definition of graffiti—and, as discussed below, distinguishes it from street art—because graffiti writing is a practice: the way the work is created and where it is placed are both crucial. It cannot be discussed simply in terms of its finished products: the 'tag', the

2 On the difficulties of writing a history of graffiti see R Gastman and C Neelon, *The History of American Graffiti* (New York, Harper Design, 2010) 15.

3 The anonymised interview data are referenced within the text in the form of Anon[number] (referring to a research participant).

4 RP Bezanson and A Finkelman, 'Trespassory Art' (2010) 43 *University of Michigan Journal of Law Reform* 245, 257.

5 eg L Mullen, 'Cave Art and the Origins of Typography' (2008) 15 *Visual Communication Quarterly* 6.

6 The political significance of text and images can be seen in areas of conflict eg I Edwards, 'Banksy's Graffiti: A Not-so-simple Case of Criminal Damage?' (2009) 73 *Journal of Criminal Law* 345, 351.

7 Distinguishing between political graffiti, protest graffiti, graffiti art, tagger graffiti, gang graffiti and toilet graffiti: R White, 'Graffiti, Crime Prevention & Cultural Space' (2001) 12 *Current Issues in Criminal Justice* 253, 254–55.

8 Examples may be found in London in hastily written postcodes such as 'e5'. See eg on graffiti and gangs in Los Angeles: SA Phillips, *Wallbangin': Graffiti and Gangs in L.A.* (Chicago and London, University of Chicago Press, 1999).

9 TE Bowen, 'Graffiti Art: A Contemporary Study of Toronto Artists' (1999) 41(1) *Studies in Art Education* 22, 24.

'throw-up' (usually a large, two-coloured rendering of the tag in block or bubble letters) or the 'piece' (large, complex work of many colours which may include figurative elements).[10]

Graffiti is usually created in urban public space. Its visibility in turn means that it affects communities rather than just the owners of a property on which graffiti is found.[11] As such it has some affinity with public art in the form of murals[12] but is different from artistic production commonly associated with the art market (ie works created to be sold). Graffiti writing and street art as it is understood today is the latest incarnation of the artistic drive to alter and decorate walls; to make the creator present in space. Yet with graffiti writing, it is not only walls but also trains that are important as surfaces. Train writing marked a shift away from the static medium of the wall to embrace the danger and movement of the train that took a writer's name out of his/her neighbourhood and around the city (and later, between cities).[13] Writing on trains remains the pinnacle of achievement for graffiti writers.[14] Graffiti writing must therefore be considered as a point in a process of moving through the city to create works and, importantly, to create these works as part of a community of creators.

However, the lines between graffiti writing and street art are blurred. One participant referred to himself as a 'Graffiti writer slash artist. Graffiti writer slash graffiti artist' (Anon15). Broadly speaking, graffiti refers to the writing of letters while street art refers to more figurative work including stencils, paste ups (wheat paste posters) and large scale murals. Indeed, the earliest graffiti writers simply called themselves 'writers' and their work 'writing'.[15] The terms 'graffiti writing'[16] and 'graffiti art'[17] were rarely used. Participants in the fieldwork—the data largely consist of interviews—were hesitant to draw a bright line between graffiti and street art though the extent to which they were prepared to do so depended on the extent of their own identification as writers or artists. Graffiti writers who identified closely with the graffiti writing subculture tended to draw a clearer line, focusing on lettering and execution.[18] Some writers identify specifically as

[10] A related form is the 'production' which combines pieces with a background: R Kramer, 'Painting with Permission: Legal Graffiti in New York City' (2010) 11(2) *Ethnography* 235, 243.

[11] M Halsey and A Young, 'The Meanings of Graffiti and Municipal Administration' (2002) 35(2) *Australian and New Zealand Journal of Criminology* 165, 167.

[12] Baca referred to in Bowen (n 9) 25.

[13] See J Ferrell, 'Freight Train Graffiti: Subculture, Crime, Dislocation' (1998) 15(4) *Justice Quarterly* 587.

[14] See generally N Macdonald, *The Graffiti Subculture: Youth, Masculinity and Identity in London and New York* (Basingstoke, Palgrave Macmillan, 2001) 110–17.

[15] Gastman and Neelon (n 2) 5.

[16] ibid.

[17] eg The United Graffiti Artists exhibition held in City College, New York on 2 December 1971: A Caputo (ed), *All City Writers* (Bagnolet, France, Kitchen93, 2009).

[18] eg '[M]y focus is around letters, lettering' (Anon15); 'So the purists say it's graffiti writer…' (Anon2).

taggers[19] meaning that they exclusively, and often prolifically, write their names in their own, individual style.

Many of the participants recognized that the lines between graffiti and street art are blurred. While graffiti works are usually made free hand with a spray can and are composed of letters these works may well also include elements such as cartoon characters or pictorial representations of a kind that are common to street art which may also be made free hand with a spray can (but the practice also encompasses ordinary paint, stenciling, stickers and the like). A good example of this blurring (brought up by a few participants in interviews and in the course of informal discussions) is the London crew[20] Burning Candy. The crew combines a street art aesthetic with a graffiti sensibility. The crew—made up of several members[21] each with their own distinct avatar including a trident, clothes peg, crocodile, owl and monkey face—take risks to create their works in difficult to reach places and so gain the respect of graffiti writers and crews for their daring and visibility. It is irrelevant in terms of the respect they gain that they also produce prints and participate in gallery shows. Although not, strictly speaking, writers since they usually use figures rather than letters, they might be described as 'graffers'. As one writer put it:

> [I]f you're Burning Candy crew, those guys do shit super high up in the air what they call the heavens. ... nine storeys up, gigantic, high-traffic, 24/7. I mean they're real graffers, those guys live the graff life ... (Anon20)

This suggests that graffiti writing is distinguished not only by the use of letters or its style but also how it is done: illegally, in dangerous yet visible places. Indeed alongside the writing of names, illegality, as the history and structure of the graffiti subculture demonstrates, is one of the defining aspects of graffiti practice and may explain why graffiti writers eschew copyright laws in favour of the internal regulation of their creativity. Furthermore, what the above interview excerpt suggests is that there is another element to the definition of graffiti—the authenticity that comes from the practice of creating graffiti—that cannot be evident from simply looking at the substance of the graffiti work. Of course much street art is also placed on walls without permission but the thrill associated with illegality does not appear to be a motivating concern.

Finally, both graffiti and street art are distinguished from what is commonly referred to as 'public art', for example, sculptures in public squares and parks.[22]

[19] eg 'Mister Ed is, was, and always will be a tagger. Not a graffiti artist, but a constant, untamed, and uncontrollable vandal' in Paul 107 (ed), *All City: The Book About Taking Space* (Toronto, ECW Press, 2003) 51.

[20] A crew is a group of creators who will eg share works and collaborate on large pieces that incorporate individual tags.

[21] Listed as Tek33, Goldpeg, Rowdy, Dscreet, Cyclops, LL Brainwashed, Cept, Rowdy and Mighty Mo in a short documentary video posted to youtube referring to them as street artists: pure evil charley, *Burning Candy: The Wall: 3 Minute Wonder*, 9 November 2009 www.youtube.com/watch?v=K--S_GoctnM.

[22] See eg H Hein, 'Symposium: Public Art' (2008) 54(1) *Art Criticism* 1.

The academic discussion over public art is often concerned with how such art might represent the public.[23] By contrast, graffiti writing is discussed, inter alia, in terms of crime, marginality, the reclamation of space, or otherwise as a challenge to the aesthetic and/or social ordering of space.[24] This literature often acknowledges a wider social unease with graffiti writing (and less so with street art as Banksy's continuing popularity indicates)[25] that has led to its close identification, in both political discourse and some case law relating to criminal damage with dirt, disorder and disease.[26]

Origins of Graffiti Writing

There are a multitude of personal accounts of the origins of graffiti writing, most of which will never be known due to the ephemeral nature of the work and the anonymity of its creators. Still, graffiti history remains important for writers. As one participant put it:

> Yeah, I don't know, I wasn't there. This is the funny thing ... In the early 70s I wasn't even born so I know about the 70s through documentation and my interpretation—and also you know the kind of, the rules handed down through generations of writers: that is how it was, this is how it should be. (Anon4)

This section provides an account of the historical development of graffiti writing from its origins in the 1960s in the US with a particular focus on the period of New York graffiti train writing in the late 1970s and early 1980s (since this period was referred to by numerous participants as significant). It then considers the transplantation of graffiti writing to other countries, specifically the UK. Attention is paid to the evolution of the London scene, including the distinction between old

[23] eg B Hoffman, 'Law for Art's Sake in the Public Realm' (1991) 17(3) *Critical Inquiry* 540.

[24] For different approaches to the subject of graffiti in a variety of disciplines see eg White (n 7); R Schacter, 'An Ethnography of Iconoclash: An Investigation into the Production, Consumption and Destruction of Street-art in London' (2008) 13(1) *Journal of Material Culture* 35; AM Brighenti, 'At the Wall: Graffiti Writers, Urban Territoriality, and the Public Domain' (2010) 13(3) *Space and Culture* 315; J Ferrell, *Crimes of Style: Urban Graffiti and the Politics of Criminality* (Boston, Northeastern University Press, 1996); J Ferrell, 'Urban Graffiti: Crime, Control, and Resistance' (1995) 27 *Youth and Society* 73; GJ Snyder, *Graffiti Lives: Beyond the Tag in New York's Urban Underground* (New York, New York University Press, 2009); LL Hanesworth, 'Are They Graffiti Artists or Vandals—Should They Be Able or Caned: A Look at the Latest Legislative Attempts to Eradicate Graffiti' (1995) 6 *DePaul Journal of Art and Entertainment Law* 225; Halsey and Young (n 11); A Sheon, 'The Discovery of Graffiti' (1976) 36(1) *Art Journal* 16; D Ley and R Cybriwsky, 'Urban Graffiti as Territorial Markers' (1976) 64(4) *Annals of the Association of American Geographers* 491; PJ Craw, 'The Mural as Graffiti Deterrence' (2006) 38(3) *Environment and Behavior* 422; L Rosewarne, 'Visual Terror: Graffiti and Outdoor Advertising as Street Harassment' Refereed paper, Australasian Political Science Association Conference, October 2004, www.adelaide.edu.au/apsa/docs_papers/Others/Rosewarne.pdf.

[25] On Banksy see Edwards (n 6).

[26] In *R v Austin and Ors* [2009] EWCA Crim 394 eg the Court quoted the sentencing judge: 'This type of offending sickens members of the public who have their travelling lives blighted by this sort of criminal damage': [24].

school and new school graffiti writers. This is important because identification as new or old school helps to account for some of the different perspectives on, and adherence to, the graffiti rules identified in later chapters.

Two issues are especially relevant to the origins of graffiti. The first relates to practice and style: many works are called graffiti but are not graffiti *writing*; many different people may create what is popularly considered to be graffiti but they are not graffiti *writers*. Second, the documentation (eg in books and other media) of the history of graffiti writing as the origin of current practices is crucial; for the graffiti rules discussed in this book may be viewed as the crystallisation of practices or rituals of early graffiti writers that were documented in key texts at the time.

Graffiti writing as it is defined above originated in the US before spreading to Europe, Australia and elsewhere. The first, or rather best-known, example of graffiti that contained both the elements of the signature and visibility was the ubiquitous Second World War slogan 'Kilroy was here', which was sometimes accompanied by a cartoon of a person peering over a wall.[27] It was first written by a former sign painter James J. Kilroy on ships bound for the war but appears to have then been taken up by servicemen and written within and outside the US.[28] This was not an example of graffiti writing in terms of style but the repetition of a signature and the drive to place it in numerous visible spots had something in common with what was to come.

In the mid- to late 1960s someone going by the name of Cornbread began writing in Philadelphia,[29] and Julio204 and Taki183 began writing in New York.[30] The first graffiti writers in the 'true' sense, working independently of each other, may not have been following in Kilroy's footsteps yet if 'Kilroy was here' was an example of a graffiti signature that servicemen took up as belonging to everybody,[31] Cornbread and Taki183 gave birth to modern, *individualised* graffiti where one tag (signature) referred to one person and the tag was thus an extension of the writer's personality. Placing the tag, making it visible, was not an expression of patriotism as with the 'shared' Kilroy name but rather the simple assertion: 'I am …'.[32] Taki183, while working as a messenger, wrote his name not just in his own neighbourhood but on walls all over the city. He was therefore perhaps the first graffiti writer to go 'all city'.[33] This is significant because it is a starting point in the development of the major concern, alongside style, of graffiti writing: visibility. The expression 'all city' is a way of saying a writer is very prolific and is able to get

[27] Gastman and Neelon (n 2) 38.

[28] ibid 40.

[29] Alongside other Philadelphia graffiti writers, see J Stewart, *Graffiti Kings: New York City Mass Transit Art of the 1970s* (Abrams, NY, Melcher Media/Abrams, 2009) 13–16.

[30] For a timeline of graffiti writing 1967–89 see Caputo (n 17) 4–11.

[31] ibid 41.

[32] Macdonald (n 14) 66, figure 5.1. Or, perhaps, after Descartes, 'I write therefore I am': F Braun, *Children of the Can: 25 Years of Bristol Graffiti* (Bristol, Tangent Books, 2008) 11.

[33] M Cooper, *Tag Town* (Arsta, Dokument Forlag, 2008) 8.

up in a variety of different places in such a way as to remake the graffiti writers' 'map' of the city.[34]

Visibility was linked to fame from the early days of graffiti—the more visible you were the more likely you were to be considered a 'king' (highly respected writer) in the graffiti subculture.[35] Taki183 (the 183 referred to the number of his street in New York) became visible enough to capture the attention of journalists and he was written about in *The New York Times* in 1971.[36] The article 'TAKI 183 spawns pen pals' has been 'alternately credited and blamed'[37] for the rise of writing on trains. By 1971 'getting up' (being visible in urban space) was already a crucial part of the graffiti writing subculture.[38] Whilst the article likely helped to popularise graffiti writing it was not the only reason for the emergence of the subculture.

The history of graffiti writing began on walls but moved to trains in 1970s New York. The rise of writing on trains was followed by a determined effort to remove graffiti as New York City declared a 'war on graffiti'.[39] For example, train yards were fortified, and a concerted effort was made to remove graffiti from trains[40] and in 1989, the New York City Transit Authority could declare that New York trains were free from graffiti.[41] This marked the end of the era of piecing (the creation of pieces) on trains in New York.[42] The 'Buff' as this period of graffiti removal was called, had the unintended consequence of encouraging bombing (placing numerous tags) on walls and vehicles and discouraging piecing.[43] Yet, thanks to documentation by the photographer Martha Cooper and documentary maker Henry Chalfant and others,[44] the train writing of, amongst others, Futura, Seen and Dondi influenced a new generation of graffiti writers. Norman Mailer captured the excitement of watching a train covered in graffiti go by in the 1970s in his essay 'The Faith of Graffiti':[45]

> [T]he look of New York and afterward the world might have been transformed, and the interlapping of names and colors, those wavelets of ego forever reverberating upon

[34] J Ferrell and RD Weide, 'Spot Theory' (2010) 14(1–2) *City* 48, 56.

[35] See eg Ley and Cybriwsky (n 24) 493.

[36] 'Taki 183 Spawns Pen Pals' *New York Times* 21 July 1971. Interestingly the article explains the existence of the Taki 183 tag in the context of the Kilroy graffiti. For academic reaction at the time see ibid 494.

[37] Gastman and Neelon (n 2) 57.

[38] ibid 51.

[39] For an excellent account of the criminalisation of graffiti and the political and social discourse on graffiti as a social problem see J Austin, *Taking the Train: How Graffiti Art Became an Urban Crisis in New York City* (New York, Columbia University Press, 2001).

[40] ibid 210, 219.

[41] Caputo (n 17) 11.

[42] ibid 11. For an account of the 'retaking' of the trains see Austin (n 39) 207–26.

[43] ibid 232–34.

[44] See especially M Cooper and H Chalfant, *Subway Art* (London, Thames & Hudson, 1984) and the documentary: T Silver and H Chalfant, *Style Wars*, Public Art Films, 2007 (released 1983).

[45] Mailer took the phrase 'the faith of graffiti' from a graffiti writer, Cay 161, who referred to the name or tag in this way: Austin (n 39) 49. See also eg reference to 'benching' in the context of observing graffiti on trains in 1980s New York: P Cavalieri, *From the Platform: Subway Graffiti, 1982–1989* (Atglen PA, Schiffer Books, 2011) 17.

> one another, could have risen like a flood to cover the monstrosities of abstract empty techno-architectural twentieth century walls... The kids painted with less than that in view, no doubt. Sufficient in the graffiti-proliferating years of the early Seventies to paint the front door of every subway car they could find. The ecstasy of the roller coaster would dive down their chest if they were ever waiting in a station when a twelve-car train came stampeding in and their name, HONDO, WILDCAT, SABU or LOLLIPOP, was on the front! Yes, the graffiti had not only the feel and all the superpowered whoosh and impact of all the bubble letters in all the mad comic strips, but the zoom, the aghr, and the ahhr, of screeching rails, the fast motion of subways roaring into stations, the comic strip comes to life.[46]

This brief account of the origins of graffiti matters because, as indicated above, the graffiti rules regulating creativity within the subculture may be viewed to a certain extent as the crystallisation of nascent rules or practices of the early New York writers: 'That is how it was, this is how it should be' (Anon4). The shape of these rules and practices was captured in the prominent texts and/or glossaries: *Subway Art*,[47] *Spracyan Art*[48] and *Getting Up*.[49] These books not only provide an historical account of the origin of graffiti writing but are also part of the process whereby graffiti writing was popularised outside the US (discussed further in the next section). Several participants identified *Subway Art* in particular as highly influential.[50] The book contains numerous pictures of train pieces, references the key figures in the scene (or at least those who the authors were able to access) and provides a brief history of graffiti writing and the structure of the subculture. It also contains a glossary of key terms.[51] The photographs of graffiti were especially important in influencing the further development of graffiti styles.

A few historical elements that were documented in these texts deserve mention here because these elements demonstrate that the phenomena described in subsequent chapters have always been a part of graffiti culture. What this book adds to existing accounts of rules and practices within the graffiti subculture is to reveal them to be, in regulating creativity, analogous to existing copyright rules. First, in the early days of graffiti train writing (when the trains were not cleaned) space to write on the outside of train carriages was at a premium and the respect afforded to individual writers and the nature of the work itself governed whether another writer would go over the work or not.[52]

[46] N Mailer and J Naar, *The Faith of Graffiti* (New York, icon !T, 2009) 13–14.

[47] Cooper and Chalfant (n 44).

[48] H Chalfant and J Prigoff, *Spraycan Art* (London, Thames & Hudson, 1987).

[49] C Castleman, *Getting Up: Subway Graffiti in New York* (Cambridge, Massachusetts, The MIT Press, 1982).

[50] At a special screening of *Style Wars*, Roundhouse, Camden, Sunday 14 November 2010 in London there was a post-screening discussion with the maker of the documentary and one of the authors of *Subway Art*, Henry Chalfant. A man in the front row put his hand up and said words to the effect of 'Thank you. *Subway Art* is the bible' (field notes 2010).

[51] Cooper and Chalfant (n 44) 27.

[52] Going over is discussed in chapter nine.

Second, this period in graffiti writing was characterised by crews working together to create pieces on trains.[53] Ferrell, for example, describes how writing as part of a crew is a collective artistic endeavor allowing individuals to '[build] alternative communities... form deep social bonds as their members share time and resources'.[54] This is broadly analogous to joint authorship in copyright law. Third, the first references to biting (copying) originated in this period and the term is still used to voice concerns over the originality of a writer's style. The originality rule has its analogues in the notions of originality and infringement in copyright law. Finally, it is worth noting that the creative content of the work immortalised in the documents from the period have become creative touchstones for present day graffiti writers. The styles from this historical period are so familiar as to make any copying—where a writer attempts to pass a style off as their own—obvious. As these styles were transplanted to other cities and towns across the world, the attendant practices and modes of thinking were transplanted as well. In particular, the nascent rules relating to going over, biting, etc—even though these were the consequence of the specific constraints of writing on trains—began to apply to writing on walls and not just trains. This particular rule finds its analogue in the moral right of integrity (discussed in chapter nine).

Transplanting the Subculture

As graffiti writing disappeared from the New York subway it reappeared on freight trains throughout the US[55] and on subways and train lines around Europe and elsewhere.[56] In Europe, a sort of Grand Tour of other countries' rail systems became part of the graffiti subculture.[57] Dissemination of the documentation of the New York scene as well as music and travels by New York graffiti writers also helped to spread the subculture to different cities.

Graffiti writers remain divided as to whether graffiti originated in tandem with hip hop culture in the US (that is, whether graffiti is one of the four elements of hip hop alongside emceeing, dj-ing and breakdancing).[58] Some participants

[53] An example of a book documenting this period is Cavalieri (n 45).

[54] Ferrell, 'Urban Graffiti' (n 24) 84.

[55] Ferrell (n 13).

[56] See generally T Sjostrand, *Subway World: Graffiti on Trains* (Arsta, Sweden, Dokument Press, 2009). The book celebrating subway systems across the world and including maps. See also eg magazines: *Keeping the Faith 2*, Spring 2011; *Fatbucks Magazine*, Issue One (no date).

[57] These exploits are often recorded in the numerous graffiti magazines and blogs. The concept is also mentioned in T Rychlicki, 'Legal Questions About Illegal Art' (2008) 3(6) *Journal of Intellectual Property Law and Practice* 393, 396.

[58] AL Smith, 'Other People's Property: Hip Hop's Inherent Clashes with Property Laws and Its Ascendance as Global Counter Culture' (2007) 7(1) *Virginia Sports and Entertainment Law Journal* 59, 62–64: arguing that graffiti is an element of hip hop culture despite, strictly speaking, predating it. Ferrell refers to 'hip hop graffiti': J Ferrell, 'Hip Hop Graffiti, Mexican Murals and the War on Terror' (2005) 1(1) *Crime, Media, Culture* 5.

felt strongly that graffiti was a part of hip hop and their motivations for writing included a sense of belonging to a wider cultural movement. This is relevant to the book because the attachments to the idea of respect in hip hop would explain, to some extent, the similar attachment to the concept in the graffiti subculture.[59] If graffiti writing is part of hip hop the creativity of the subculture itself may be placed in context of wider hip hop creativity and, specifically, its concern with originality as a means of gaining respect.[60] An engagement with hip hop may have been identified as a motivation for writing by participants but such an engagement is not determinative of adhering to the graffiti rules.

One writer who identified strongly with hip hop culture suggested graffiti's association with hip hop set it apart from street art:

> For me graffiti is part of hip hop culture, synonymous with it. It's more based on letters and like wording, typography, whereas street art is kind of probably birthed out of graff but is obviously more stencil art and more things that are pleasing to the eye, perhaps [with a] more modern feel to it. Whereas street art is a form of art, graffiti is a part of hip hop. That's basically the difference. (Anon27)

By contrast, another writer argued:

> I've spoken to older writers and they're like, back in the 70s hip hop didn't exist, we listened to disco and funk and heavy metal, we listened to Black Sabbath. … If you look at the best wholecars [pieces covering a whole train carriage] in the middle of [Subway Art] a lot of them are references to Black Sabbath. (Anon4)

Whether or not graffiti writing evolved with hip hop or was assimilated into hip hop, the association with hip hop played an important part in disseminating and developing the writing subculture from its origins in the 1960s.

Graffiti was brought to the attention of European art dealers in the late 1970s and early 1980s. According to *Spraycan Art*, published in 1987 when graffiti writing had already crossed the Atlantic, it was hip hop culture that brought it to a wider audience.[61] As hip hop culture expanded beyond American inner cities it brought graffiti writing to new audiences—graffiti writing was covered in videotapes, magazines and other media alongside rappers, DJs and breakdancers.[62] The best known example of this dissemination was the Rock Steady Crew: their concerts served to advertise graffiti by virtue of the fact that one of its members, Doze, was also a well-known New York writer.[63] This unconscious promotion also went the other way. The documentary *Style Wars* (1983)[64] is interspersed with

[59] On respect in hip hop, specifically rap lyrics see P Butler, 'Much Respect: Toward a Hip-Hop Theory of Punishment' (2010) 56(5) *Stanford Law Review* 983, 1002–05.

[60] A detail on a piece seen in Leake Street, London (Waterloo graffiti tunnel) during my doctoral studies read 'You gotta be original or else everyone's gonna dis you'.

[61] Chalfant and Prigoff (n 48) 8.

[62] ibid.

[63] ibid.

[64] Silver and Chalfant (n 44).

scenes of people breakdancing and rapping. The film *Wild Style*[65] also presents the connection between graffiti writing and hip hop. It shows, for example, people breakdancing. This suggests that while graffiti may not have originated within hip hop, its association with hip hop helped to spread it to Europe and beyond. For example, a Bristol writer cites watching *Wild Style* with a group of other young people in 1983 as a revelatory experience: 'The urge to emulate, to be involved, is instant, intoxicating and powerful.'[66] As Chalfant and Prigoff wrote in 1987:

> Through these media, the culture of graffiti was transplanted intact, embracing language, history, customs, and rules, bombing, 'racking,' [stealing] and the competitive spirit.[67]

Many participants suggested that the transplantation of graffiti culture meant that it was not only the style of letter writing that was disseminated but the very practice of writing too (as the empirical chapters indicate). As early as the 1980s, when the graffiti community was barely established in London, some writers argued that the transplant was effectively too perfect:

> Graffiti in this country has come like a model, an airplane model. It's come here already built. Graffiti in America has taken years to develop, all the styles like your wildstyle and bubble lettering. Over here we haven't added anything to it apart from brushing up on a few techniques.[68]

Of course many writers would disagree with this statement and argue that, to the contrary, as graffiti culture was transplanted, different styles evolved in different cities. London is known, for instance, for its hard, rough style whereas Paris graffiti is known for being 'pretty' (Anon10). Despite stylistic differences, the practice of graffiti was more readily accepted as a crystallisation of past cultural practices. Crucially, writers were aware of, and argued for abiding by, these rules even when in practice they may not have been relevant because, for example, there is more space on walls than there was on New York trains before the trains were buffed (cleaned) regularly. The rules went from being essentially pragmatic responses to a specific context to gaining an independent normative force.

The London/UK Scene

The arrival of graffiti writing and its subsequent uptake by Londoners and young people generally in the UK is usually traced back to a tour by The Clash (notably, not a hip hop group) in 1981.[69] Futura 2000, a writer with a highly distinctive style immortalised in *Subway Art* and a 'king' of the New York graffiti scene, toured with

[65] C Ahearn, *Wild Style*, Rhino, 1983.
[66] Braun (n 32) 11.
[67] Chalfant and Prigoff (n 48) 8.
[68] Fade2 quoted in ibid 60.
[69] See eg Chalfant and Prigoff (n 48) 58.

the band and so brought graffiti to a new audience.[70] As previously mentioned, the graffiti writer Doze was a member of Rock Steady Crew.[71] Doze created the artwork for their London tour.[72]

Initially, graffiti writers in London focused on walls[73] though writers also wrote on, and continue to write on, trains—despite long custodial sentences meted out to train writers for criminal damage.[74] As with the New York scene, a hierarchy exists between 'toys' and 'kings'[75] in London (though not everyone employs this language). It is maintained through a web of subcultural social relationships in which respect is won and lost based on the style and/or visibility of a writer's work. The community of writers has a shared history in the sense that they recognise their indebtedness to American graffiti but they also have an understanding of their own local history; they know and appear to respect the founding writers of the London scene. The continuing respect afforded to Robbo, a famous writer of the 1980s London scene, is a prominent example of this.[76]

This rich understanding of the history of graffiti has led to the self-identification, and the identification of other writers, as old school or new school. The 1970s and early 1980s graffiti writers mentioned by the key graffiti texts discussed above[77] are often referred to as exemplifying old school with many younger, present day writers belonging to the new school. However, this is not intended to insinuate that a rivalry exists or even a generational gap (since writers in their early twenties who had not even been born in the early 1980s may be old school) but rather there is an approach to the practice of graffiti that is distinguished in part by adherence to the rules (discussed in later chapters) emanating from subway writing in New York. As one participant pointed out, the schools are not merely about style but a state of mind or approach to the practice of graffiti:

> Old school is like the guys who were painting in the 80s, the guys who were … in it for a certain set of values and followed certain rules and their letters looked a certain way and they used certain colour combinations, and there was a specific style. And new school is the breaking down of all those rules, all those barriers. … The association with the hip hop mentality and like not wanting to do the wrong thing to people older, wiser and tougher than you because you'll be dealt with, whereas they're sort of like, I don't give a fuck. (Anon28)

Given these complexities, the scene is difficult to map. A beautiful re-working of a 'tube map' of the kings of the London scene from 1980 to 2000 by RareKind is one

[70] ibid 58.
[71] ibid 8.
[72] ibid 58.
[73] ibid.
[74] eg *R v Pease and Ors* [2008] EWCA Crim 2515.
[75] Novice or unskilled writers as opposed to writers generally accepted as masters of writing because of excellent style and/or their visibility.
[76] See chapter nine.
[77] Cooper and Chalfant (n 44); Chalfant and Prigoff (n 48); Silver and Chalfant (n 44); Castleman (n 49).

attempt.[78] These writers include Zomby, Fuel, Pic and Prime as well as Elk, Drax and Robbo all of whom made their name in the 1980s.[79] By contrast, now-famous writers active in the early 2000s are often referred to as new school writers (possibly, with respect to specific writers, a reference to age rather than any disregard for history and rules). They are distinguished by an extremely simple style of tag and their visibility on a variety of surfaces and, especially, placement on high-risk surfaces. Numerous other writers noted for their bombing and/or stylistic competence are profiled in London graffiti media or photographs. Their works are published (and many of their names will be familiar to the public because they are placed on tracksides and are thus easily visible to train passengers).[80] Various crews have been highly visible and influential within the subculture. DDS, for instance, are an example of a highly influential crew especially in the early days of the London scene,[81] and more recently, for example, ATG.[82] The tags of especially prolific writers and crews in particular remain visible in many parts of London. They form part of London's urban fabric which, intentionally or not, encourages us to ask questions about the meaning and use of public space.[83] The next chapter returns to this theme in discussing the existence of a graffiti-specific 'bounded commons' that encompasses both the physical commons of the street as well as the intellectual commons.

Elements of the Subculture

This section provides a brief overview of the graffiti subculture chief elements, its hierarchy and writers' preoccupation with style and visibility. It considers: the personal and community motivations for graffiti writing; the issues of respect and fame within a hierarchy from kings to toys; the importance of visibility ('getting up') versus the importance of style and the historical reasons for both; the difference between legal and illegal graffiti writing and between writing on trains versus writing on walls; and the type of property painted on (referred to in this book as *placement*). Finally, this part considers graffiti writers' attitudes to illegality and their reference to the existence of graffiti rules. The focus here is on graffiti writers as a community rather than street artists. There is undoubtedly an overlap between graffiti writing and street art, as the discussion above indicates, and so a number of the points made below, especially regarding personal fulfilment, will

[78] Reproduced in F Forsyth, *Crack & Shine* (London, FFF, 2009) 140–41.

[79] See generally ibid.

[80] eg in *Frontline Magazine*, Issue 1 (no date).

[81] See comments made in the trailer for *Underbelly*, an as yet unmade documentary about the crew: C Atkins and T Oswald, 'Underbelly: Graffiti Artists the DDS Crew Paint London Tube Trains—Video' *Guardian Online*, 1 May 2009, www.theguardian.com/artanddesign/video/2012/jul/09/underbelly-graffiti-dds-crew-london-video.

[82] Profiled, albeit obliquely via a collection of others' comments, in Forsyth (n 78) 188–89. The acronym was—due to the block writing—easily read during fieldwork in London.

[83] Schacter (n 24) 59.

also apply to street artists. In relation to whether certain actions were acceptable or not—for example going over another person's work—the justifications given for that stance were usually rooted in personal morality. By contrast graffiti writers were more likely to also cite the fact of belonging to a community with a shared history, language and aesthetic.

Motivations and Identity

Two motivations are crucial: writers write for fame[84] and for the pleasure of writing. Regarding the enjoyment of writing (fame is discussed in the next section) the graffiti writers interviewed stated that they were drawn to writing because it was fun and exhilarating. Participants received a form of 'personal fulfillment from painting' (Anon7).

Certain participants elaborated on the notion of personal fulfillment gained from engaging with the aesthetics of urban public space; specifically, to justify writing as an improvement.[85] Several writers (and also street artists) were critical of the commercialisation of public space and considered graffiti writing as a way of asserting themselves where they would otherwise be unwelcome.[86] It is worth emphasising, however, that many participants referred simply to the pleasure of writing or the adrenaline rush which was created by the risk of getting caught or injured and, in particular, the illegal nature of the activity. Historically, a writer who bought their paint would be less respected than a writer who racked (stole) it.[87]

The illegality of writing also heightened the adrenaline rush. Some writers compared it to an addiction[88] and certainly for most it is part of a 'career' that requires a high level of commitment.[89] As one writer stated:

> To paint a tube train you've got to cut fences, dodge CCTV cameras, laser trips and security guards. It's all part of the buzz and final achievement of your final product. … It's the mentality of a person what makes us different.[90]

The academic writing on the subject of graffiti and identity, especially youth identity, focuses on the sense of meaning and purpose graffiti provides to writers.[91]

[84] As *All City Writers* states, in 1967 'Cornbread and Cool Earl: two Philly writers [defined] the role of the modern day graffiti writer (the major objective is fame)': Caputo (n 17) 4.

[85] This point also made, based on their empirical research, in M Halsey and A Young, '"Our Desires are Ungovernable": Writing Graffiti in Urban Space' (2006) 10(3) *Theoretical Criminology* 275, 288.

[86] On the regulation of placement see chapter five.

[87] See eg quote from Zomby 'Racking paint in the days was part of being a writer, if you bought paint you were seen to be a toy' in book, perhaps more accurately a pamphlet, circulated within the graffiti subculture circa 2010: *London Handstyles* (no page numbers, no date).

[88] Drax has described 'days of full addiction where I ate, slept and lived for writing': Drax WD, 'Drax Interview from 1993' *Rocking the City* www.rockingthecity.com/storiesinterviews.htm.

[89] Macdonald (n 14) 63–93; for an account of graffiti as a career in the early days of New York graffiti see R Lachmann, 'Graffiti as Career and Ideology' (1988) 94 *The American Journal of Sociology* 2, 229–50, 234–36.

[90] Fume quoted in Forsyth (n 78) 102.

[91] See eg Macdonald (n 14) 179–227.

This includes the element of fun and making friends, pride in creating works and fame within the community.[92] Moreover, the act of writing may be seen as a 'genuine' form of creation that is distinct from the '[superficiality] and elitism'[93] of the art world. Instead, graffiti writing presents itself as a creative, sometime all-consuming, process that is removed from the superficiality of mainstream creative production. The motivation for writing graffiti is as much physical as it is psychological. The action or practice of writing is central to its appeal. One participant observed that 'the action and hard work are more important than style' (Anon7).

These motivations are very much tied up with identity because writing is all about making your name visible. It is the act of writing a name in an individual style (much like in skateboarding it might be the thrill of style, of moving through space differently)[94] that distinguishes graffiti writing from street art and other forms of creativity. Although much artistic production may be personal—in the sense that an author's personality is, arguably, poured into his/her creation[95]—graffiti writing makes the connection between the work and personal identity immediately apparent because writing a name is of critical importance. As *Subway Art* puts it: 'The name is the centre of all graffiti art.'[96] The name is thus closely related to visibility and fame as well as style (discussed below).

Writers write their name to be seen and acknowledged by their peers and, potentially, the public: this is the essence of 'getting up'.[97] The centrality of the name, and identity, as a motivation for writing graffiti also explains the historical and continued development of graffiti style. The desire to distinguish one's name led to development of new styles.[98] The graffiti rules, especially the rules against copying styles and names (biting), emerged to protect individual names and styles. The early history of graffiti contains examples of writers changing their names because they were too similar to the names of other writers in the scene, for example by including a number in the tag.[99]

Fame and Hierarchy

The motivations for writing, in particular personal and group validation or respect, may be referred to as a quest for 'fame' which is closely tied to respect.[100] Within the graffiti subculture this means gaining respect/fame within the graffiti

[92] Halsey and Young (n 85) 279.

[93] Bowen (n 9) 31. However, the regulation of graffiti creativity also operates to create an internal elite of creators.

[94] I Bordern, *Skateboarding, Space and the City: Architecture and the Body* (Oxford and New York, Berg, 2001).

[95] Adopting the language of copyright law—this point is discussed further in chapter two.

[96] Cooper and Chalfant (n 44) 45. This is not to say that graffiti writers never change their names. See eg Drax in Forsyth (n 78) 58; Castleman (n 49) 75.

[97] Castleman (n 49) 19.

[98] ibid 55.

[99] ibid 75.

[100] Macdonald (n 14) 65. Also: 'The currency of graffiti is fame' (Anon4).

community specifically, rather than the public at large. Two participants described this as follows:

> Graffiti is about fame end of story. I would never dream about robbing someone. It's about being a normal person, getting your name up. (Anon13)

> [B]ut kind of on the sly. 'Cause it's like your alter ego. (Anon14)

The acquisition of respect—some writers will have acquired more than others—produces a hierarchy within the subculture. Even when writing for him/herself, writers write in the context of a community.[101] The structure of the graffiti writing hierarchy depends on the relevant scene, which is dependent on geography (the London scene, the Berlin scene, etc) Nevertheless, writers everywhere will likely recognise the most prolific writers of the New York scene during the 1970s and 1980s. A writer gains fame by being prolific and/or having good style: 'The aim is to be up with more style than anyone else' (Anon21). Briefly, being prolific in this context means writing your tag on as many surfaces as possible, ideally in highly visible spots; having good style means demonstrating the skills to write in an original (in the sense originality is used within the subculture) individual style.

Common to each scene is the division of writers into categories[102] in which writers are either taggers or piecers. One category is not inherently superior to the other. Tagging and piecing are both means of gaining respect and therefore rising in the estimation of fellow graffiti writers. Taggers bomb (tag prolifically) and gain respect primarily for the visibility of their tags and throw-ups. Others may depend more on style. Some writers will be adept at both and, of course in any event, taggers will also have their own style of writing letters. The lines are blurred, as the sections below will show. A clear-cut trade off does not always exist between visibility and style. In either case writers will be aiming to gain, and keep, their fame. As already indicated, the writers with the most fame and respect may be referred to as kings[103] while less respected or inexperienced writers, especially those who have only begun writing, will be referred to as toys.[104] In the London scene a few writers, even if no longer writing, are the most respected, including those profiled in a book, *Crack & Shine*, looking back on the history of the London scene that was published in 2009. This includes names that were still visible on walls during the course of the fieldwork or mentioned in graffiti media such as 10 Foot and Cut.[105]

Crews (groups of writers working collectively), like individual writers, also compete for fame. Each scene will have crews (though not all writers in a scene will belong to a crew) whose members collectively work to enhance the name of

[101] This point was made eg in empirical research by Halsey and Young (n 85) 280.

[102] Referring to 'classes': DD Brewer and ML Miller, 'Bombing and Burning: The Social Organization and Values of Hip Hop Graffiti Writers and Implications for Policy' (1990) 11(4) *Deviant Behaviour* 345, 353.

[103] eg defined as '[t]he best with the most': Cooper and Chalfant (n 44) 27.

[104] eg defined as an '[i]nexperienced or incompetent writer': ibid. Calling someone a toy is a sign of disrespect: see chapter nine.

[105] Forsyth (n 78) 132, 204.

the crew. The name will usually be a three-letter acronym that writers may choose to add to the side of their own tags. Putting up the crew name is crucial. One writer alluded to the promotion of the crew name or acronym as being similar to brand promotion:

> Sometimes you do want to be seen as a brand because you're trying to get up as much as possible. (Anon27)

A crew will consist of around two to 12 writers and the writers will usually be friends.[106] The writers interviewed who belonged to crews pointed out that they were in crews with friends or crews where an existing crew member had recommended them to the group. A related feature of the subculture is that older, more experienced writers may act as mentors for younger writers starting out[107] though this 'apprenticeship' system is, according to participants, less common today.[108]

Three final points need to be made about fame and hierarchy. First, gossip—whether in person or via the internet—is crucial to the creation of a hierarchy. It can also be problematic and numerous participants alluded to the existence of 'politics' in the sense of not only knowing who is 'up' but understanding who gets on including which writers or crews have ongoing disagreements ('beef').[109] Gossip,[110] exclusion and other verbal forms of disrespect also function as sanctions for breaking the rule against going over other's work, though it can be difficult to tell whether a particular behaviour is being sanctioned and by whom or if there is merely personal animosity between two writers in situation where no rules had been broken. Knowing what is going on is especially important for out-of-town writers as one conversation demonstrated:

> M Are you in London to write?
>
> Anon Yes but I'm just doing legal walls. I don't want to get in trouble with the police when I've just got here.
>
> M Or the other graffiti writers.
>
> Anon [nodding] I don't know the scene. It's going to take some time to learn about it. (field notes 2010)

It is worth mentioning at this point that the interviews did not produce information about matters such as age, ethnicity, and personal history—to preserve anonymity such information was not sought from participants—and how these identifications feed into the subculture's politics.[111]

[106] Brewer and Miller (n 102) 354.

[107] ibid 356. On the graffiti subculture as a learning environment see I Valle and E Weiss, 'Participation in the Figured World of Graffiti' (2010) 26(1) *Teaching and Teacher Education* 128.

[108] eg Anon4 described a 'decline'.

[109] Chapter nine returns to the discussion of sanctions.

[110] 'We're all major gossips. Like before it was done through telephone and mail but now it's done through online chat and MSN' (Anon11).

[111] These are important issues and have been expertly covered elsewhere, eg on gender identity and graffiti in Macdonald (n 14). See also eg L Gauthier, 'Confessions of an Ethnographer: Reflections on Fieldwork with Graffiti Writers in Montreal' (2001) 43(2) *Anthropologica* 273.

Second, regardless of the extent to which the rise of hip hop culture aided its transplantation outside of the US, texts such as *Subway Art*[112] provided a means of disseminating the subculture worldwide. Today, the internet and the sharing of photographs through graffiti blogs, forums and sites such as flickr and facebook have made the sharing of graffiti culture even easier. This has not, as the chapters on originality and copying will elaborate, been without its challenges. The digital dissemination of graffiti culture has helped to embed graffiti writing in cities around the world. Yet it has also meant that works are more easily copied and that graffiti writers' experience of belonging to the subculture is different (since works may be viewed instantly on the internet instead of 'riding the lines' as the New York writers did).[113] Consequently, respect (and the threat of disrespect as a sanction) as a cornerstone of belonging to the graffiti writing community is devalued through writers gaining 'cheap fame' from internet exposure. One writer with a self-observed old school sensibility observed:

> [The internet] just waters down the scene. To be honest it just waters everything down, dilutes it, makes it easier for people to bite you. The internet's pretty bad for graffiti really. … People can look at your artwork, everything's a lot more accessible, takes a lot of time out of it and you're not respected. [In the early days of graffiti] people would say 'can I send you some work?' … or 'can I please see some of your stuff?' (Anon28)

Another writer wistfully recalled:

> Style is recycled so much now 'cause of the internet. Before I started I could tell the difference between North London and South London graffiti based on style. Now that's almost eradicated. People spend all day looking at flickr. … Half the part of graffiti used to be riding the lines [trains] going about the city, seeing what's going on. (Anon21)

In terms of gaining respect or fame, visibility on the internet was derided by numerous participants as cheap or 'fraudulent fame' (Anon29). It may be tempting for new writers but is counter-productive:

> Being on the internet is the opposite of being on the street. Some kids will fabricate their graffiti career but when they are found out their credibility will be shot. Respect is hard to get back. (Anon6)

Furthermore, one participant derided another writer for being interviewed in various magazines without producing anything new (Anon11). Another writer derided those who rely on this form of exposure as 'internet whores' (Anon13). At the same time, being prominent on a 'respected graffiti blog' (Anon27) was seen as less of a problem.

Third, street artists—with the exception of cross-over crews and individuals who are accepted as part of the graffiti subculture—are not part of the graffiti

[112] Cooper and Chalfant (n 44).

[113] This is closely related to 'the bench', ie gatherings of writers watching trains with graffiti on them go past. The bench at 149th in New York at which old school writers congregated is a good example. See S Powers, *The Art of Getting Over: Graffiti at the Millennium* (New York, St. Martin's Press, 1999) 136.

hierarchy. This also helps to account for why it is acceptable to go over a street artist's work (even if in practice most graffiti writers will not do so). Street artists, in contrast to graffiti writers, do not appear to identify directly with a community of creators the way that graffiti writers do. They are still concerned with reputation and fame but this concern is outwardly focused, towards the public rather than their peers (ie other artists). Nevertheless, the research participants identifying only as street artists raised a number of similar expectation with respect to originality and copying that closely track the graffiti norms discussed here. Of course writers may seek such public acclaim too, as well as seek to exploit their work commercially. Yet this form of public fame is entirely different to the fame needed to progress through the graffiti hierarchy.

Visibility, Placement and Style

This section discusses three linked concepts of visibility, placement and style all of which feed into the imperative to 'get up'. If the aim of a writer is to be 'up' in a recognisable style then the prominent placement of the work so that it is seen by others is critical. It might be placed on a commercial property wall, a legal wall set aside for graffiti (eg Leake Street under Waterloo Station, London), a rooftop or a train amongst many other surfaces. Style relates to the work itself including shape, colour and other artistic elements. Place also informs style to a certain extent. For example, if a writer wishes to place a work on a rooftop above a busy street (where visibility is high) the style of the work may need to be simplified. The writer may opt to place a throw-up (a two-colour tag, often in bubble letters) on the rooftop or use rollers to write his/her name in one-colour block letters.[114] The placement of a stylistically well-executed piece in a risky place (because of security, traffic or other factors that make it more likely the writer will be caught or injured) is therefore highly likely to gain the writer respect. The place will often dictate the medium of writing too. Tags are often written using markers with tips of varying thickness. Throw-ups and pieces will be made with spraycans.

The relationship between visibility and style is important because a graffiti writer with a very simple style may nonetheless gain fame by being prolific in putting up a tag on many surfaces, especially difficult to access surfaces all over the city (hence bombing and being 'all city'). The regulation of placement (the subject of chapter five)—not getting up 'indiscriminately'—ensures that writers know which places are safe for writing, for example because the place is unpatrolled[115] or because writing is permitted. Although fame and respect are key aspects of graffiti writing and enhanced through both the volume and visibility of a writer's work, placement is nonetheless informally regulated which effectively restricts the extent to which graffiti writers are visible. For example, certain surfaces are considered

[114] The technique was pioneered by the writers Cost and Revs (Anon2).
[115] Brighenti (n 24) 321.

unsuitable for the placement of graffiti because they are 'personal' private property such as cars or houses. Interestingly, the definition of 'personal' property has evolved. Julio 204 wrote on street signs because walls were 'personal property' and thus off-limits.[116] Today the identification of walls as 'personal property' extends to specific—individual rather than corporate—places such as churches and dwellings only.

At present, issues relating to placement and visibility have been thrown into sharp relief by the rising popularity of street art. This has resulted to some extent in contests over space, at least in relation to walls: trains and tracksides appear to be the domain of graffiti writers only—and created problems in situations where street artists go over a tag or other graffiti work without knowing the practices and rules (because they are outside the community and therefore not subject to the same normative constraints) and are liable to have their work gone over with another writer's work or lined (crossed out). One criticism of naïve street artists was as follows:

> You don't know anything about the evolution of art on the streets and you're going over stuff that you've got no idea what you're doing. (Anon5)

This may be because street artists, even if they are aware of the rules, would lack the knowledge of the subculture's 'politics', hierarchy and history to make an accurate assessment as to what is acceptable.

Visibility, style and the quest for fame are related and, as with much else in the graffiti subculture, the practice of graffiti and its associated norms for protecting and encouraging the writing of letters are the product of graffiti's history. Stylistic inventions contributed to a process of cultural production that resulted in the constitution of graffiti writers as a community as the different elements of style and techniques were passed on from writer to writer, from location to location.[117] When Taki183 began writing and others followed, the aim was specifically to get up (to be visible). Yet as more people began to write, style, not just visibility started to matter.[118] The graffiti rules then crystallised to protect writers' creativity. For example, the prohibition against biting seeks both to protect and encourage creativity: creativity in the choice of name as well as that in style. This in turn precipitated the evolution of graffiti-specific tools. Eventually, an industry sprung up producing aerosol cans specifically for graffiti writing which enabled graffiti writers to innovate and produce works that would have been more difficult to produce in the 1970s.[119] There is nevertheless some nostalgia for the old school:

> When I look at old school stuff, yes, I like it—the styles and skills—but … [e]veryone wants to see fresh stuff, still glimmering and drying.[120]

[116] Gastman and Neelon (n 2) 57. See chapter five.

[117] See Austin (n 39) 61.

[118] Ferrell, *Crimes of Style* (n 24) 7; Castleman (n 49) 55.

[119] J Rahn, *Painting Without Permission: Hip-Hop Graffiti Subculture* (Westport, CT, Bergin & Garvey, 2002) 10.

[120] Writer quoted in J Swami, *London Burners* (Munich, Prestel Verlag GmbH + Co, 2010) (no page number).

Old styles continue to matter. For example, while the original tags in 1970s New York were written in a very simple easy to read style, the writer Top Cat 126 began to distinguish himself by adopting a difficult to read style that was then taken up by others who called it 'Broadway Elegant'.[121] Brooklyn writers then began to use 'hearts arrows and swirls' while Bronx writers developed their own style again.[122] The stylistic innovations of this period have become common stylistic forms in present day graffiti writing in, for example, London amongst other scenes. Copying an arrow is not 'biting' (reproducing another's style) because anyone can add an arrow to a tag. However, it will often be done in a slightly different style by each individual writer. Crucially, the way in which fame is gained apart from visibility is the *originality* of a particular writer's style. This ties back to the requirement not to bite another writer's work. Copying (where such copying cannot, that is, be accepted as an homage) will diminish the writer's status in the community of writers.[123]

A good example of a stylistic form that is freely used is the halo above a tag. The first writer to use it, Stay High 149 in New York, took the idea from the stick figure in the television series *The Saint* and today writers everywhere use it over their tags in the same way[124] as they use exclamation marks, commas, arrows and other additions common to graffiti writing. Indeed, graffiti style as a whole is remarkably consistent.[125] Yet to graffiti writers, the distinctions between styles, how an old style is reinterpreted or built upon and how well a tag or piece is executed, mean that creativity flourishes within the stylistic confines imposed by graffiti history and culture.

Today, the graffiti subculture is well served with blogs (eg *Hurt You Bad*) and magazines (eg *Not Guilty*, *Keeping the Faith*, *Bomb Alert*) documenting the latest works by writers and therefore disseminating a wide range of styles. For the London scene in particular books such as *London Blackbook*,[126] *London Handstyles*[127] and *Crack & Shine*[128] document the evolution of London writers' styles as well as providing an account of the variety of writers' experiences. They also indicate that three main types of work continue to thrive, namely the tag, throw-up[129] and piece.[130] A stylistically good piece might also be described as having 'flow', referring to how 'letters overlap and touch, how a letter holds itself up against the one next to it'.[131] Furthermore, all works are created freehand (unlike street art which

[121] Castleman (n 49) 55.
[122] ibid
[123] See chapter seven.
[124] Creeper 167 copied Stay High 149 by using the figure (though his pieces had other stylistic innovations) in 1973 and the halo has been an element of style since that time: Stewart (n 29) 111.
[125] For one classification of graffiti styles see L Gottlieb, *Graffiti Art Styles: A Classification System and Theoretical Analysis* (Jefferson, NC, McFarland & Company, Inc, Publishers, 2008).
[126] *London Black Book* (no date).
[127] *London Handstyles* (no date).
[128] Forsyth (n 78).
[129] The 'dub' (a throw-up in more than two colours) may be considered as separate category rather or as a sub-category of the throw-up.
[130] This includes the abstract letterforms of the 'wildstyle' piece.
[131] Siege 52 quoted in Forsyth (n 78) 68.

includes stencils). Thus 'can control'—the ability to use a spraycan to create clean lines without dripping—is the mark of a technically proficient writer.[132]

As indicated above, a writer who has developed an original style and is 'up' (visible) is likely to be respected. The most respected writers will be up mostly illegally and are likely to have painted trains and tracksides[133] at some point: 'There's more props [respect] for a train than anything else' (Anon28). Indeed, a very simple tag that appears not to have any stylistic innovation associated with it will not hinder the respect granted to a writer who is truly 'all city'. The sheer amount of effort that goes into both choosing where to place work—locational creativity—and then undertaking the preparation and bearing the risk of doing so is also recognised and appreciated.[134]

Illegality and the Graffiti Rules

The aspects of the subculture discussed above—visibility, style, pleasure, respect, community—are encapsulated in the attitudes exhibited to the law as well as attitudes to the norms internal to the graffiti subculture. As with the other aspects of the graffiti subculture discussed in this chapter, the graffiti rules constitute, to some extent, a re-enactment of the graffiti practices of writers in late 1970s and early 1980s New York. This section summarises the participants' attitudes regarding the language used to describe the rules, how they are justified and followed (or not) and how disrespect serves as the basis of sanctions for rule-breaking.

Graffiti writers may paint walls with the permission of property owners. Yet when placed on a wall or train without permission, graffiti writing is likely to constitute criminal damage and/or anti-social behaviour.[135] While not disputing this, many writers expressed concern with the length of custodial sentences given for a non-violent crime: 'people go to jail for changing the colour of a train' (field notes 2010). At the same time, and as the preceding discussion has already begun to show, the graffiti subculture is distinguished by the existence of a normative framework to regulate behaviour. One of the few points on which unanimity of thought and feeling existed amongst participants (especially graffiti writers) was that graffiti should not be legalised. As one participant said: 'Graffiti isn't graffiti really unless it's illegal' (Anon21). This arose out of concerns both for the space ('what a mess it would be if it wasn't illegal!' Anon5) and for the motivation for doing graffiti (thrill-seeking: 'it'd take the fun out of it if it wasn't [illegal]', Anon13). One writer suggested that it would lead to a free-for-all in which 'we'd be painting everything

[132] See chapter seven.

[133] The terms 'tracksides' and 'trackside' are used interchangeably to refer to writing on walls alongside railway tracks.

[134] For an account of how writers choose spots to place their work as an activity that is both spatial and temporal see Ferrell and Weide (n 34) 50–51.

[135] Criminal Damage Act 1971, s 1; Anti-Social Behaviour Act 2003, s 43.

and there'd be no rules, there'd be no law' (Anon13). This appears to refer to both the graffiti norms and legal rules as relevant to the regulation of graffiti creativity.

The concept of a 'code' was often brought up unprompted. There is recognition that although unlawful, graffiti writing does have informal rules within the group which even if not necessary are at least desirable. The rules (variously referred to as 'rules', 'code', 'morals', 'etiquette') appear to exist at least in part as a response to the designation of the practice as illegal and serve to structure, even temper, illegal behaviour. The sanctions for rule-breaking as indicated earlier include going over (fully or partially destroying another's work), verbal disrespect and occasionally, violence. The threat of violence is also effective in preventing rule-breaking. The rules were justified on moral grounds (the right thing to do, notions of respect), pragmatic grounds (following the rules decreases the likelihood of getting caught or raises the profile of a writer), and/or grounds of history (following in the footsteps of 1970s and 1980s graffiti writers). These explanations for writing are explored in greater detail in the coming chapters especially where they overlap with the motivation for writing (such as the protection of personality).

Conclusion

The discussion of the historical development and elements of graffiti subculture in this chapter has endeavoured to explain why graffiti rules exist, to what extent they are followed and why. It has considered in particular not only the extent to which the graffiti rules present the crystallisation of certain historical practices but has also begun to explore individual motivations for graffiti and writers' reflections on creativity as part of a community. This is important because it suggests that the graffiti subculture as a community that is—in the terms presented here—an example of a 'bounded commons'. Graffiti, and the regulation of creativity within the subculture challenges the conception of both the physical and intellectual commons. Thus, alongside the nature of creativity as a process and the relevance of pleasure and space to the creative process, the creation of commons is discussed in the next chapter.

2

Copyright, Creativity and Commons

Introduction

Copyright regulates creativity. Though it may not be alone in doing so, copyright provides extensive economic rights over works to the owners of copyright and this sort of legal regulation is highly significant. Yet whether the grant of these rights is justified depends, at least in part, on what creativity is taken to mean in the first place and then, in turn, what sort of regulation is appropriate to the type of creativity and the desires of creators. Answering these questions means thinking, in particular, about the role of copyright law in the production of culture or, rather, cultures. This chapter focuses on two themes: on the relationship between creativity, the intellectual commons and the public domain; and on alternative (that is, non-legal) frameworks for regulating creativity.

As the first chapter suggested, the *process* of creation and the *place* of creation—whether with respect to a particular wall or train or a city—matter to graffiti writers. The process of creation and the significance of territory are not easily accommodated by copyright law which solely protects a *work*. It is thus informal norms, rather than copyright law, which provide a means of protecting and regulating creativity within certain groups and communities and which are more sensitive to the creative processes and needs of creators. Further, an examination of graffiti creativity provides the chance to study the intersection between the (socially unified) intellectual commons and the urban/physical commons by considering both the (im)materiality of graffiti writing and its territory through the concept of a 'bounded commons': the commons specific to the graffiti subculture, in which creativity is regulated by a distinct set of norms.

Justifications for Copyright

Various overlapping justifications are advanced in favour of copyright protection: these include utilitarian/incentive arguments, arguments based on labour, and those based on personhood. Before addressing the nature of the commons and the public domain, it is useful to consider (some of) these justifications, especially utilitarian arguments based on copyright's role in the production and development of culture.

A classic means of justifying copyright protection is to say that it provides an incentive for individuals to create and/or innovate.[1] Two strands of this argument are considered here: first, the strict utilitarian justification that, broadly speaking, the prospect of control over one's work will encourage creativity and, second, the centrality of potential economic reward from the exploitation of copyrighted works for the encouragement of creativity. An incentive structure lies at the heart of utilitarian theories which assume that the potential grant of property rights acts as an incentive because such a right will enable the owner to gather rewards in the marketplace and so it is in the public benefit to provide a property right as an incentive.[2] Yet this already assumes that resources are or should be allocated through market mechanisms. The literature tends to break down and emphasise different aspects of this argument, or rather, different aspects of modern political economy.

Although utilitarian justifications for copyright evolved at around the same time as the labour and personhood approaches, they became particularly important in the UK, by contrast to continental Europe, by the early nineteenth century.[3] One of the main arguments for the provision of intellectual property rights is that property rights provide an incentive to create, in a situation where intellectual goods can be freely copied, because the creator is granted the exclusive right to reproduce the work.[4] The incentive to create is provided because, according to the utilitarian argument, without copyright 'a socially optimal output of intellectual products would not exist'.[5] The social benefit, apart from economic reward for creators or economic growth generally, is that granting property rights will encourage creativity and thus promote cultural activities.[6] As Treiger-Bar-Am, for example, puts it: '[t]he purpose of copyright is to foster creativity'.[7] Thus the rationale can be ultimately framed in terms of creativity and the development of culture. That is how the World Intellectual Property Organization (WIPO) described the Berne Convention in 1978, drawing a link between copyright protection for literary and artistic works and 'the enrichment of national cultural heritage'.[8] Yet this position

[1] 'Innovation' is often used as a synonym for creativity though this is more likely in the context of patents.

[2] L Zemer, 'On the Value of Copyright Theory' (2006) 1 *Intellectual Property Quarterly* 55.

[3] M Borghi, 'Owning Form, Sharing Content: Natural-Right Copyright and Digital Environment' in F Macmillan (ed), *New Directions in Copyright Law, Volume 5* (Cheltenham, Edward Elgar, 2007) 212.

[4] On marginal cost pricing see SE Sterk, 'Intellectualizing Property: The Tenuous Connections between Land and Copyright' (2005) 83 *Washington University Law Quarterly* 417, 433–44, 435.

[5] EC Hettinger, 'Justifying Intellectual Property' (1989) 1 *Philosophy & Public Affairs* 31, 48.

[6] Zemer (n 2) 58.

[7] K Trieger-Bar-Am, 'Copyright, Creativity and Transformative Use' in H Porsdam (ed), *Copyrighting Creativity: Creative Values, Cultural Heritage Institutions and Systems of Intellectual Property* (Farnham, Ashgate, 2015) 169.

[8] Quoted in F Macmillan, 'Copyright and Corporate Power' in R Towse, *Copyright in the Cultural Industries* (Cheltenham, Edward Elgar, 2002) 99 (footnote omitted).

might also be framed in either fundamental or instrumental terms: the former variant suggests cultural development is paramount while the latter suggests the economic is.[9] In any event, the important feature of the utilitarian rationale is that it can be used to argue for the support of the development of creativity and culture apart from economic considerations even if, rhetorically, they might be assimilated through the assumption that economic growth is a social benefit. The chief problem with a utilitarian justification that twins the incentive to produce with social benefit is precisely this assimilation. While copyright protection *may* provide an incentive to create this does not mean that the creative outputs will be more readily available or capable of utilisation[10] for the benefit of society.

The law and economics approach is also based on incentive arguments (and might also therefore be considered a form of utilitarianism)[11] but the expected outcome is specifically the efficient allocation of resources through the market. The approach addresses what it identifies as the problem of the public good nature of intangible products. Infringement of a copyright work through reproduction, in economic terms, should be prevented because it is a form of free-riding.[12] The argument is that copyright is necessary to overcome the over-use of creative outputs by artificially creating scarcity.[13] Even the primary exponents of law and economics recognise, however, that providing an economic incentive to create may also have a social benefit.[14]

The 'law and economics' justification is usually associated in particular with the existence of incentives to innovate or engage in research and development.[15] Maurer for instance describes intellectual property as the 'only fundamentally new incentive scheme of the last 400 years.'[16] The law and economics theory is thus in turn a way of explaining the social contract between the creator and society, that is, the creator is granted a limited monopoly right. The difficulty for the theory lies in determining the optimal extent of copyright protection.[17] Nor is it easy to

[9] F Macmillan, 'Copyright, Culture and Private Power' (1998) 16(3) *Prometheus* 305, 307.

[10] Hettinger (n 5) 49. Hettinger comes to this conclusion by interrogating the assumption that the goal of private property rights is the '[maximisation of] the dissemination and use of information.'

[11] For a critique see eg A Rahmatian, *Copyright and Creativity: The Making of Copyright in Creative Works* (Cheltenham, Edward Elgar, 2011) 91–96.

[12] A Barron, 'Copyright Infringement, "Free-Riding" and the Lifeworld' in L Bently, J Davis and JC Ginsburg (eds), *Copyright and Piracy: An Interdisciplinary Critique* (Cambridge, Cambridge University Press, 2010) 97.

[13] WM Landes and RA Posner, *The Economic Structure of Intellectual Property Law* (Cambridge, MA, Harvard University Press, 2003) 21. The scarcity must be artificial because intellectual creations are non-rivalrous. But see also MA Lemley, 'Property, Intellectual Property, and Free Riding' (2005) 83 *Texas Law Review* 1031; Barron (n 12).

[14] Landes and Posner (n 13) 21. Landes and Posner note, however, that this is not always the case.

[15] On the economic function of copyright see eg L Davis, 'Globalisation, Digitisation and the Changing Role of Copyright' in F Macmillan (ed), *New Directions in Copyright Law, Volume 2* (Cheltenham, Edward Elgar, 2006) 81; J Aldred, 'Copyright and the Limits of Law-and-Economics Analysis' in L Bently, J Davis and JC Ginsburg (eds), *Copyright and Piracy: An Interdisciplinary Critique* (Cambridge, Cambridge University Press, 2010) 132.

[16] S Scotchmer and SM Maurer, 'Institutions: A Brief Excursion through History' in S Scotchmer (ed), *Innovation and Incentives* (Cambridge Mass., MIT Press, 2004) 2.

[17] Referring to intellectual property rights generally, see Lemley (n 13) 1065.

separate the optimal creation of intellectual goods (which copyright incentivises) from the optimal use of those works since the works have no value unless they are accessible to be used.[18] A noted flaw of the law and economics approach in justifying copyright is precisely its inability to explain *why* encouraging creativity is a social benefit in the first place.[19] Moreover, if copyright protection is calibrated so that protection is based only on what consumers desire this raises the problem of, for instance, the incentivisation of films rather than certain types of research.[20]

Unsurprisingly, law and economics arguments hold sway in democratic societies with market economies such as the UK. The argument that copyright (or intellectual property rights generally) provides an incentive to innovate is often closely tied to the pursuit of economic growth. The argument is that copyright will be an incentive to produce which in turn will create economic growth, to the benefit of society. Such thinking is at the core of, for example, the Hargreaves Report.[21] Economic growth is assumed to be inherently desirable. It is in part this assumption that copyright must serve an economic function that is at the core of criticism of the way in which copyright protects (or rather fails to protect) creativity. The entrenchment of corporate power is one example.[22]

Another common criticism of incentive theories generally is that they are less relevant to certain forms of creativity than others. It is indeed arguable that large media companies producing films or music are incentivised to create new works because of the potential economic rewards that might be brought about by copyright protection. However, artists, for example, produce works for a number of different reasons, many of which are not linked to expectations of a monetary reward.[23] By contrast, even when the economic incentive argument is made with respect to artists (that copyright enables them to have control over the exploitation of their work), it will still be market forces and the artists' relative economic power vis-a-vis other actors that will determine the financial reward they receive.[24] Economic power imbalances remain relevant in a way that is obscured by abstract discussion of economic incentives. Furthermore, grants and other forms of direct assistance to artists may provide an incentive to produce works quite apart from copyright.[25]

[18] Aldred (n 15) 133.

[19] Barron (n 12) 22.

[20] W Fisher, 'Theories of Intellectual Property' in SR Munzer (ed), *New Essays in the Legal and Political Theory of Property* (Cambridge, Cambridge University Press, 2001) 182.

[21] I Hargreaves, *Digital Opportunity: A Review of Intellectual Property and Growth*. UK Intellectual Property Office, May 2011. See also Gowers Review which also makes the link between intellectual property rights and growth: A Gowers, *Gowers Review of Intellectual Property*. HM Treasury, December 2006, 58.

[22] See Macmillan (n 8).

[23] There is not enough evidence of whether copyright acts as an incentive for creators: R Towse, C Handke and P Stepan, 'The Economics of Copyright Law: A Stocktake of the Literature' (2008) 5(1) *Review of Economic Research on Copyright Issues* 18.

[24] R Towse, 'Copyright, Risk and the Artist: An Economic Approach to Policy for Artists' (1999) 6 *International Journal of Cultural Policy* 1, 91–107; 96.

[25] ibid 100.

If the justifications above reflect Bentham's utilitarian arguments, a separate justification arises from the work of Locke. By contrast to the social contract justification such arguments are predicated on the existence of certain natural rights of the creator.[26] It is argued, broadly, that the creator has an intellectual property right because of the labour he/she has expended in the creation of the work. This is therefore an extension of Locke's reasoning with respect to tangible property,[27] though it is disputed whether or not Locke's reasoning can or ought to be extended to intangible property.[28] The notion of just desert or reward arising from this labouring is an integral part of Lockean justifications.[29] As such they seem to assume that private property rights are inherently just.[30] Yet, in common with social contract theories, Locke's justification from labour nevertheless assumes that the natural right of the creator is circumscribed by some kind of 'no-harm principle' which ensures that the granting of the right 'does not conflict with the common good'.[31] There is a tendency for Lockean arguments to mutate from notions of *property* (expending labour requires the granting of a property right) to *propriety* (expending labour makes the granting of that property right a natural or moral right).[32] However, it should not be supposed that the Lockean argument will always lead to the conclusion that copyright, as a property right, must be granted directly to creators. Notwithstanding the labour expended on the creation of a work, Lockean arguments can also be made in favour of common rather than private intellectual property ownership.[33]

Against the background of this discussion, it is easy to see how conflict over the best ways to regulate creativity through copyright is generated: how is the common good defined in democratic societies and what might a balanced system of copyright look like? One answer lies in a modified version of the Lockean justification. Zemer argues that a close reading of Locke's work on the relevance of experience, not merely innate ability in the acquisition of knowledge, suggests

[26] However, the Lockean argument may also be used to support a 'social value' (utilitarian) argument in the sense that a reward is provided as an incentive to perform labour which is assumed to be unpleasant and therefore requiring incentivisation: T Aplin, *Copyright Law in the Digital Society: The Challenges of Multimedia* (Oxford, Hart Publishing, 2005) 32.

[27] The point made in eg B Friedman, 'From Deontology to Dialogue: The Cultural Consequences of Copyright' (1994) 13 *Cardozo Arts & Entertainment Law Journal* 157, 157, 161.

[28] Doubting that Locke's reasoning can be extended to intellectual property: RV Bettig, *Copyrighting Culture: The Political Economy of Intellectual Property* (Boulder, Westview Press, 1996) 19–20.

[29] See generally T Aplin and J Davis, *Intellectual Property Law: Text, Cases and Materials* (Oxford, Oxford University Press, 2009) 8.

[30] Friedman (n 27) 161, arguing it cannot be assumed that Locke would take this view as opposed to a consequentialist view of property: 161–2.

[31] In Zemer's words: Zemer (n 2) 63.

[32] CJ Craig, 'Locke, Labour and Limiting the Author's Right: A Warning against a Lockean Approach to Copyright Law' (2002) 28 *Queen's Law Journal* 1, 15.

[33] SV Shiffrin, 'Lockean Arguments for Private Intellectual Property' in SR Munzer (ed), *New Essays in the Legal and Political Theory of Property* (Cambridge, Cambridge University Press, 2001) 156, 166–67.

that creation occurs in a collective cultural context.[34] The acknowledgment of the collective context of individual authorship raises questions over whether anyone can, as Locke argues, be considered to have property in their own person.[35] Furthermore, since the entitlement is to the fruits of one's labour it is unclear why the reward for labour must be its 'market value'; the product and its value are not the same thing.[36] However, even if arguments based on 'just deserts' are accepted, the question remains as to why copyright protection is the best form of reward for intellectual labour.[37] It is also worth noting that the labour justification is related to, but not the same as, the argument from unjust enrichment. This is a moral argument that the exploitation of another's work is 'reaping without sowing'.[38] It cannot, however, be considered an independent justification for copyright protection because it presupposes that the creator of the work ought to have a property right in it in the first place.[39] Even if a person ought to be rewarded in some way for creativity that reward might take a different form such as awards or financial compensation from the public purse.[40]

Perhaps the most important aspect of the labour justification to note here is the moral argument that labour ought to be rewarded even if creators are not motivated by reward, because their labour produces a social benefit.[41] Hughes summarises the position as follows:

> [I]t is possible also to treat the value-added theory as a normative proposition: people should be rewarded for how much value they add to other people's lives, regardless of whether they are motivated by such rewards.[42]

Yet this appears to suggest that the extent of the reward can or should be pegged to the extent of the perceived social benefit. Finding that copyright does not subsist or the refusal to enforce copyright on immorality or public policy grounds amongst others, suggests that this logic is already to some extent present in the copyright system.[43] Importantly for present purposes, the protection of graffiti writing, whose value as art is recognised by a relatively small group of people, may be more easily justified by reference to personhood arguments than to those focused upon economic incentives. The justifications identified by graffiti writers themselves—in discussing the different graffiti rules considered in this book's

[34] L Zemer, 'The Making of a New Copyright Lockean' (2005) 29 *Harvard Journal of Law & Public Policy* 891, 941–42, 945.
[35] J Waldron, 'From Authors to Copiers' (1993) 68 *Chicago-Kent Law Review* 841, 880.
[36] Hettinger (n 5) 39.
[37] M Spence, 'Justifying Copyright' in D McClean and K Schubert (eds), *Dear Images: Art, Copyright and Culture* (London, Ridinghouse, 2002) 399.
[38] ibid 395–96.
[39] ibid 396; Hettinger (n 5).
[40] Hettinger (n 5) 41.
[41] J Hughes, 'The Philosophy of Intellectual Property' (1988) 77 *Georgetown Law Journal* 287, 305–06.
[42] ibid 306.
[43] See chapter four.

empirical chapters—in fact encompass both positions, shifting from intuitive protectiveness of their work as the product of their labour and/or personality to an acknowledgment of the relational aspect of creativity. Moreover, as the discussion in chapter ten in particular will show, graffiti writers recognise, like Weinreb, that public expression restricts (or ought to restrict) their claims to control over their creativity.[44]

Moving on from that of Bentham and Locke, the work of Kant can be used to justify a form of copyright that recognises the links between a creator's rights and the public sphere, and the associated claim that only in this context is the development of culture possible.[45] This is a useful notion in light of the debates over creativity, copyright and culture. If speaking is a matter of speaking 'in one's own name'[46] then graffiti rules of the sort we will encounter, which inter alia restrict the use by one writer of another's name, might be conceptualised as an instance of protecting the freedom of writers to publicly express those names (tags). Unlike with many other forms of creativity, the tag is a name and the link between personality, autonomy and the name is therefore made apparent by the work itself: it is more than 'poured' into the work, it *is* the work. The tag is personality made manifest. Yet, the notion of personality that underpins the personhood justifications is 'thin'[47] in the sense that it is difficult to determine what copyright is trying to protect. Graffiti writers perhaps offer a way of tying personhood 'more tightly to a particular culture and time'[48] because their identity as writers is closely bound to graffiti culture. It is difficult, however, to find a specific, common notion of personality and culture in society at large which might apply beyond the graffiti context.

Focusing on the social benefits of the regulation of creativity—namely the development of culture—serves to highlight the communal aspects of creativity and its regulation, something which, as the discussion in this chapter will show, is particularly important to graffiti writers even though their pursuit of fame is often highly individualistic. Considered together with the discussion of creativity in the next part, a theme begins to emerge: creativity is a community as much as an individual endeavour and ought to be treated as such. As Rosenblatt argues, creativity might better be conceptualised as 'belonging' and include within it a concern with 'human flourishing'[49] that is absent from the treatment of creativity as

[44] See Weinreb (n 2) 65.

[45] See, regarding a reading of Kant regarding to communication and the conception of 'free culture': A Barron, 'Kant, Copyright and Communicative Freedom' (2012) 31 *Law and Philosophy* 1. See also Treiger-Bar-Am who argues that Kant's work may be used to bolster arguments relating to the 'autonomy of expression' of the creator: K Treiger-Bar-Am, 'Kant on Copyright: Rights of Transformative Authorship' (2008) 25 *Cardozo Arts & Entertainment Law Journal* 1059, 1062–63.

[46] M Borghi, 'Copyright and Truth' (2011) 12 *Theoretical Inquiries in Law* 1, 11.

[47] Fisher (n 20) 191–92.

[48] ibid 192.

[49] E Rosenblatt, 'Belonging as Intellectual Creation' (2014), on file, forthcoming at www.papers.ssrn.com/sol3/papers.cfm?abstract_id=2495970.

a thing as opposed to a process. Indeed, following Derclaye who combines a study of intellectual property law with happiness research, maybe the first question we should be asking is: what kind of regulation of creativity will increase happiness?[50] Though this may merely make explicit questions which are in fact already present within utilitarian justifications, in foregrounding happiness it offers the potential for subtly re-orienting the discussion towards a regulatory framework that reflects 'ethical values rather than the fallacious idea of progress'.[51]

Creativity and Commons

This part addresses the meaning of creativity and then looks at the regulation of creativity in the context of the literature on copyright and the intellectual commons and, within it, the public domain. It follows on from the discussion in the previous part by focusing in particular on arguments relating to the effect of copyright rules on the development of culture. This reflects to some extent—given the discussion of graffiti writers' motivations to create within a community that is building and safeguarding graffiti culture—the regulatory potential of both copyright law and the graffiti rules to impact upon the production of culture. Understanding how copyright regulates creativity within the intellectual commons may be contrasted with the regulation of creativity within the graffiti subculture. This is turn helps to reveal the contours of a different kind of commons, namely one that blurs the boundaries between the physical commons of the street and the intellectual (ie style) commons which is discussed in the next part.[52]

Creativity as Process, Pleasure and Space

Understanding the nature of creativity is important because it draws attention to the gulf between creators' conceptualisation of their creativity and a specific aspect of it—the *work*—that copyright law is in a position to protect.[53] This section is not intended, except in broad terms, to engage with the concept of creativity as it relates to specific copyright tests. It suffices to note that creativity is part of

[50] E Derclaye, 'Eudemonic Intellectual Property: Patents and Related Rights as Engines of Happiness, Peace, and Sustainability' (2012) 14(3) *Vanderbilt Journal of Entertainment and Technology Law* 495.

[51] ibid 543.

[52] See also the discussion of the 'style commons' in chapter five.

[53] Instead, as Ong argues in the context of 'recreative' works, 'when searching for evidence of authorial creativity, one ought not to confine oneself to looking just at the results of the recreative process but should also scrutinise the recreative process itself': B Ong, 'Originality from Copying: Fitting Recreative Works into the Copyright Universe' (2010) 2 *Intellectual Property Quarterly* 165, 183.

the originality test for determining which works qualify for protection.[54] What is more interesting perhaps is the way in which creativity was brought to the fore as an element of copyright law. Sherman and Bently show that pre-modern intellectual property law was concerned with creativity and the protection of 'the creative or human element embodied in the resulting product'.[55] The concept of creativity is implicit in references to personality or mental labour.[56]

It is unsurprising perhaps that the modern notion of creativity—as something human as opposed to divinely granted—became entrenched in the eighteenth century, at the time of the conception on the Romantic author.[57] The conception of 'Art' that arose at this time forms the foundation of the artistic work category in copyright law.[58] So even as modern intellectual property law is concerned with a 'detached, neutral and closed intangible property',[59] it reflects certain assumptions about creativity. Yet, in privileging the work, copyright law does not recognise other aspects of creativity that are also, perhaps equally, important—aspects such as the process of creating a work and the space in which this process occurs. It does not take into account past conceptions of authorship which included commentary and collective creation.[60]

The above is not to suggest that accounts of authorship and creativity have ignored the diverse ways in which people are creative, nor what creativity means in the context of the copyright work. A recent example of this is found in a collection entitled *The Work of Authorship*[61] in which van Gompel notes that scholarship in creativity studies differs from that of copyright law and goes on to address various theories of creativity.[62] One of the definitions canvassed by van Gompel is worth highlighting: that of creativity as a process that occurs within a certain set of constraints.[63] This usefully echoes graffiti creativity which, as discussed below, is conceptualised as a process by graffiti writers—encompassing both space and movement—but within a well-established set of constraints. The most obvious of these constraints is the requirement of writing letters while creativity is exemplified by writing letters in a way that is original. The spaces in which writers move

[54] B Sherman and L Bently, *The Making of Modern Intellectual Property Law* (Cambridge, Cambridge University Press, 1999) 200.

[55] ibid 47.

[56] ibid 202.

[57] PO Kristeller, '"Creativity" and "Tradition"' (1983) 44(1) *Journal of the History of Ideas* 105, 106.

[58] A Barron, 'Copyright Law and the Claims of Art' (2002) 4 *Intellectual Property Quarterly* 368, 375–76. However, Barron casts doubt on whether the work and originality requirements in copyright law can properly be said to reflect these Romantic conceptions arguing instead that it reflects Modernist values: 379–80, 398.

[59] Sherman and Bently (n 54) 200.

[60] M Woodmansee, 'On the Author Effect: Recovering Collectivity' in M Woodmansee and P Jaszi (eds), *The Construction of Authorship: Textual Appropriation in Law and Literature* (Durham, Duke University Press, 1994) 17.

[61] M Eechoud (ed), *The Work of Authorship* (Amsterdam, Amsterdam University Press, 2014).

[62] S van Gompel, 'Creativity, Autonomy and Personal Touch: A Critical Appraisal of the CJEU's Originality Test for Copyright' in Eechoud (n 61) 98–102.

[63] ibid 107.

may also be a constraint—both practical, relating to accessibility and chances of getting caught, and aesthetic, in terms of where the letters would get the best exposure. Finally, there are social constraints because the production of creativity is shaped by the creator's belonging to a particular community. In the same volume, Cooper provides an insight into creative practices, gained from five empirical case studies into different creative processes and different ways that creators understand authorship and the role of the audience.[64]

Moving away from the legal literature, there is further evidence of researchers taking into account the complex nature of creativity. Behavioural research into motivations for creativity belies the focus on incentives that underpins copyright law and instead highlights the desire for 'love, connectedness and esteem'.[65] This includes a focus on creativity as a product of 'love' rather than expectation of financial reward.[66] In her interviews with a wide range of creators, Silbey shows how creators and innovators began their work. Two of the elements highlighted to explain their creativity are luck and pleasure; there is a sense in which creativity is also *play*.[67] Graffiti writers, endorsing this notion of play, also emphasise pleasure as a motivation for their actions. Creativity is not therefore merely the expression of an idea that might be the basis of an artistic work in which copyright subsists. It is also 'the experience, the sensation'.[68] Pleasure is at the heart of the creative experience. As Tushnet argues, many experiences of creativity do not fit neatly into the 'incentive model' whether that model concerns money or reputation.[69] In Tushnet's words:

> [C]reativity routinely feels good. It brings the creator pleasure, and, if she's lucky, brings others pleasure as well. When we talk about pleasure (and agony) instead of utility, we get closer to the lived experience of creativity, and are in a better position to understand exactly how resistant or compliant creative practices are likely to be in response to the constraints and possibilities of copyright law.[70]

Closely identifying creativity with the 'work' and therefore with its 'author' is also problematic in that it de-emphasises the extent to which creativity builds on the

[64] E Cooper, 'Reassessing the Challenge of the Digital: An Empirical Perspective on Authorship and Copyright' in Eechoud (n 61).

[65] D Leenheer Zimmerman, 'Copyrights as Incentives: Did We Just Imagine That?' (2011) 12 *Theoretical Inquiries in Law* 29–58, 46 (referring to the work of Maslow).

[66] ibid 41. It is worth noting one of the difficulties with 'love' is the extent to which it leads to the expectation that creators without significant economic power will provide their creative labour for free because they love what they do. That is not the argument made here: the focus on pleasure is to highlight one of the key motivations for creativity—as graffiti writers themselves indicate (in chapter ten), commercial uses of their work ought generally to be compensated.

[67] J Silbey, *The Eureka Myth: Creators, Innovators and Everyday Intellectual Property* (Stanford, Stanford Law Books, 2015) 28.

[68] J Gibson, *Creating Selves: Intellectual Property and the Narration of Culture* (Aldershot, Ashgate, 2006) 140.

[69] R Tushnet, 'Economies of Desire: Fair Use and Marketplace Assumptions' (2009) 51(2) *William and Mary Law Review* 513, 522.

[70] ibid 526–27 (footnotes omitted—referring to the work of Debora Halbert and Michael Chabon).

work of others and occurs *with* others. This might serve to explain the attraction of creating within a 'bounded commons': the pleasure of creation can be experienced collectively and regulated in a way that is sensitive to the creator's place within a community. The conception of creativity as a communal or collaborative process is demonstrated in an empirical study of contemporary experimental music and dance composition, in which Waelde and Schlesinger show that while collaboration and improvisation amongst dancers and musicians is important, these elements cannot be fixed as a 'work'.[71] Instead, the creators interviewed revealed that creativity is better understood as a process that is both before and beyond copyright.[72] Dance, for example, is a collaborative process between the choreographer and the dancer or dancers and, as one of the participants in the study observed, a performance of even a choreographed dance will change depending on who is dancing.[73] Quite apart from what copyright can protect as a (dramatic) work or who it might protect as an author (the choreographer who has reduced the dramatic work to material form), it is clear that the composition of its dance and its performance, whether in preparation or on stage is, all of it, creative. Beyond simply a collaboration in a certain place and time, creativity is also a social practice. For example, creativity as it is understood in relation to the theatre encompasses more than the (dramatic) work written by the playwright; it depends on the interpretation of others.[74] None of this necessarily makes the meaning of 'creativity' easier to grasp except perhaps to note as the authors above do, that copyright recognises only one or more discrete elements of the creative process. Much else is excluded.

Creativity as a process in turn engages both with the experience of pleasure, belonging and an engagement of space. One writer interviewed neatly captured the relevance of emotion, process, time movement and space:

> For me it's like there are three pleasure steps, like the first one where you … find your style, the second is when you do it for real, taking risks etc., and the third part is when you see the thing you've made, when you see it in the daylight in the street. (Anon8)

The 'work', as the extract above suggests, is but one aspect of creativity here. The creative process implicates the body and the emotions of the writer and in doing so the bodies and emotions of others who see the trace left behind by this movement[75]—in the language of copyright, the 'work'—on the street. As the reference to 'steps' suggests, being creative means moving in, and transfiguring, space. As subsequent chapters will discuss, the norms within the graffiti community are

[71] C Waelde and P Schlesinger, 'Music and Dance: Beyond Copyright Text?' (2011) 8(3) *SCRIPTed* 257, 267–71.

[72] ibid 291.

[73] ibid 280–82.

[74] L McDonagh, 'Plays, Performances and Power Struggles—Examining Copyright's 'Integrity' in the Field of Theatre' (2014) 77(4) *Modern Law Review* 533, 538.

[75] Echoing the notion of writing *on* the city whereby graffiti writers use 'the cityscape as canvas': A Young, *Judging the Image: Art, Value, Law* (Abingdon, Routledge, 2005) 73.

not only directed towards the regulation of creativity but, inextricably, to the regulation of space by regulating *where* works are placed. These spatial/transformative aspects of creativity, and the norms that support them, are recognisable as mirroring those nicely set out in Brighenti's empirical study of a group of Italian graffiti writers.[76] Creativity in the graffiti subculture might then be viewed as an amalgam of works made freehand in blackbooks or on a wall (or a train) but also includes the movement preceding the work as 'spots' are chosen; the latter might usefully be designated *locational creativity*. It is from this perspective unsurprising that a set of norms would arise that is sensitive to the spatial impact of graffiti creativity.

Moreover, with respect to graffiti creativity, it is necessary to acknowledge that when it is practised without permission it may be classified at once as a criminal activity as well as a creative/artistic endeavour. The graffiti norms thus both regulate graffiti creativity and, at the same time, legitimate graffiti writing as a practice and graffiti writers as a community.[77] This legitimising function is something that copyright cannot, and is not necessarily expected to, provide. Understanding this goes some way to explaining why copyright presents an insufficient framework on which to build, and support, a (sub)culture. It also goes some way towards explaining why the regulation of creativity occurs within a subculture-specific graffiti commons that cannot be captured by formal regulation.

Copyright, Culture and the Public Domain

This section bridges the discussion of the meaning of creativity on the one hand and the meaning of the 'commons' on the other. Two points are considered: first, the nature of the intellectual commons and the public domain; second, the promotion and preservation of culture. This will help to draw out the approaches to creativity and the commons in the graffiti subculture which are reflected in the fieldwork data. Running through the account offered below is an implicit but strong concern with serving the public interest by ensuring that (some) creativity is accessible to all within the intellectual commons. It is important to note the limitations of such an approach at outset. As the first part of this chapter discussed 'social benefit' loosely, so does the public interest here become subsumed by a concern with delineating between the public and propertised domains. An assumption is made that publicly beneficial delineation might be found but without an account of what, precisely, that would be. As Alexander observes, the 'public interest' is 'as contingent and shifting as the notion of authorship'.[78]

[76] AM Brighenti, 'At the Wall: Graffiti Writers, Urban Territoriality, and the Public Domain' (2010) 13(3) *Space and Culture* 315.

[77] I am grateful to Kathy Bowrey and Debora Halbert for their comments on this point.

[78] I Alexander, *Copyright Law and the Public Interest in the Nineteenth Century* (Oxford, Hart Publishing, 2010) 11.

The conception adopted here of the intellectual commons is that of Deazley:

> [O]nce a work has been published it has ceased to exist within the private realm of the author and instead has entered a public cultural space (let us call this the *intellectual commons*) [Emphasis in the original].[79]

Deazley shows that both the public domain and the domain of copyright protected works are *carved out* of the intellectual commons.[80] Creative Commons licensing also complicates the picture by placing works that would otherwise fall within the propertised domain effectively into the public domain (with some restrictions): Deazley thus makes the distinction between the 'de facto' public domain and the 'private domain'.[81]

Settling on a definition of the public domain is not straightforward. In a survey of the public domain literature in 2006, Samuelson, for example, identifies 13 definitions of the public domain in the literature.[82] Dusollier in her comprehensive WIPO report provides five.[83] One of the key difficulties that arises is whether to include in the definition of the public domain both material that is no longer protected by copyright because the term of protection has expired as well as information that cannot be protected such as ideas.[84] In their survey of copyright law and the public domain Greenleaf and Bond identify 15 categories—their public domain categories are underpinned by a broad conception of 'public rights' while acknowledging that these might just as easily be termed, for example, 'liberties' or 'powers'.[85] The copyright public domain is defined as: '[t]he public's ability to use works without seeking permission and on equal terms.'[86]

Another study—on the value of the public domain—considered 'tolerated' uses more specifically by looking at certain creative communities (fan fiction is given as an example) to provide the following definitions of the public domain:

> In summary, the traditional legal definition of the public domain takes the copyright term as the starting point, and defines the public domain as 'out of copyright', i.e. all uses of a copyright work are possible. A second and third more fine-grained definition still relies on the statutory provisions of copyright law, and asks what activities are possible with respect to a copyright work without asking for permission (e.g. because works do

[79] R Deazley, 'Copyright's Public Domain' in C Waelde and H MacQueen (eds), *Intellectual Property: The Many Faces of the Public Domain* (Cheltenham, Edward Elgar, 2007) 23.

[80] ibid 28–29.

[81] ibid 23, note 6.

[82] P Samuelson, 'Enriching Discourses on Public Domain' (2006) 55 *Duke Law Journal* 783.

[83] These are: 'ontological', 'subject-matter', 'temporal', 'policy' and 'voluntary'. S Dusollier, 'Scoping Study on Copyright and Related Rights and the Public Domain' World Intellectual Property Organisation publication available at www.wipo.int/edocs/mdocs/mdocs/en/cdip_4/cdip_4_3_rev_study_inf_1.pdf, 35.

[84] See Samuelson (n 82) 791, note 31. This, of course, points towards the idea/expression dichotomy in copyright law.

[85] G Greenleaf and C Bond, '"Public Rights" in Copyright: What Makes up Australia's Public Domain?' (2013) 23 *Australian Intellectual Property Journal* 111–38, 114. The authors are interested specifically in defining the Australian public domain.

[86] ibid 122.

> not qualify for copyright protection, or use relates to 'underlying ideas' not appropriating substantial expressions, or because use is covered by specific copyright exceptions). A fourth definition includes as part of the public domain all uses that are possible under permissive private ordering schemes (such as creative commons licences). A fifth definition moves into a space that includes use that would formally be copyright infringement but is endorsed, or at least tolerated by certain communities of practice (e.g. 'machinima' cinematic production of computer games or fan fiction).[87]

The present study of the regulation of creativity within the graffiti subculture contributes to empirical studies of the public domain by engaging in particular with this last definition. It points to the possibility of a community-specific commons such as has been previously identified by Macmillan and which forms one of the foundations of this book (ie the graffiti-specific 'bounded commons').

Macmillan argues that '[t]he idea of the intellectual domain is heavily dependent on an analogy with physical space'.[88] Building on this claim, Macmillan shows how Roman law conceptions of the physical public domain might be relevant to the debate.[89] *Res universitatis* (allowing for the possibility of a community specific commons) and *res divini juris* (acknowledging that some things are too valuable to be capable of appropriation)[90] are both concepts which might be useful in describing aspects of the creative process within the graffiti subculture. The physical commons (eg the street) and the intellectual commons (ie the panoply of styles, letters, characters and other elements of graffiti creativity) fall within the first type. Within it, the sanctity of letters—that is, the freedom anyone has to use any of the letters in the alphabet, even if not in the particular combinations that have already been taken by someone else for their name—exemplifies the second.

Before turning to consider graffiti writers' subculture-specific commons in more detail, however, it is useful to explore the significance of the development of culture in the context of the regulation of creativity within the broader intellectual commons. One of the essential questions raised by the regulation of creativity through copyright is:

> Is copyright law about encouraging creativity and protecting the output of that creativity or is it about stimulating commercial exploitation of commercial/cultural output?[91]

The contours of the intellectual commons and the public domain are relevant to this question because the copyright regulation of individual works has an impact on the development of culture as a whole. Two points are of particular relevance for present purposes: first, community-specific bodies of norms for the regulation

[87] K Erickson, M Kretschmer, P Heald, D Mendis and F Homberg, *Copyright and the Value of the Public Domain* (2015) CREATe report available at www.create.ac.uk/publications/copyright-and-the-value-of-the-public-domain/, 27.

[88] F Macmillan, 'Many Analogies, Some Metaphors, Little Imagination: The Public Domain in Intellectual Space' (2010) 2 *Polemos* 25–44, 26.

[89] F Macmillan, 'Altering the Contours of the Public Domain' in Waelde and MacQueen (n 79).

[90] ibid 109.

[91] Macmillan (n 9) 307.

of creativity can be seen as a rational response to copyright's shortcomings; second, these normative frameworks outline an alternative 'copyright' that is sensitive to creativity as a process and as a community pursuit and which might influence the development or reform of legal norms so as to make them similarly sensitive.

A number of themes emerge from the literature on copyright, culture and the public domain/intellectual commons, some of which foreshadow concerns raised by graffiti writers and which are discussed at various points in subsequent chapters. These include resistance to private/corporate power, authorship and the communication of culture, and, the question of whether and to what extent copyright protection can be said to promote the development of culture. Of particular relevance here is what Fisher describes as the 'development of a just and attractive culture'.[92] The concept of such a culture includes accessing and sharing ideas and 'access to a variety of "constitutive groups"—in "real space" and in "virtual space"'.[93] The argument offered in this book is not that copyright ought to support a particular culture[94]—as the inability of intellectual property law to accommodate and protect collective forms of creativity suggests,[95] a certain form of culture is inevitably and inescapably privileged by the existing form of copyright rules, regardless of their particular substance. The rules within a 'bounded commons' can be thus understood however as being, at least in part, a reaction to this privileging. These rules support the production of non-privileged culture (or cultures), and do so in a way that is sensitive to individual creative processes *as part* of a group of creators[96] while also enriching the broader culture though access to a different form of creativity and a different kind of creative community. Thus, in discussing graffiti creativity and making claims about what copyright rules ought to be, the animating concern is the development not of a particular culture, but rather of a plural or diverse culture; that is, seeking the promotion of what Macmillan refers to as 'expressive diversity'.[97]

[92] Fisher (n 20) 192.

[93] ibid 192–93.

[94] One of the problems in the discussion of 'culture' in the humanities that has arisen is the 'privileging of Culture as a discrete canon of works of European art and literature': RJ Coombe, *The Cultural Life of Intellectual Properties: Authorship, Appropriation, and the Law* (Durham, Duke University Press, 1998) 12.

[95] See eg D Simone, 'Dreaming Authorship: Copyright Law and the Protection of Indigenous Cultural Expressions' (2015) 37(4) *European Intellectual Property Review* 240.

[96] See generally CJ Craig, *Copyright, Communication and Culture: Towards a Relational Theory of Copyright Law* (Cheltenham, Edward Elgar, 2011). Also described as 'process of working through culture alongside others': JE Cohen, 'Creativity and Culture in Copyright Theory' (2007) 40 *UC Davis Law Review* 1151, 1180.

[97] Regarding 'expressive diversity': Macmillan (n 89) 111. An insistence on plurality is particularly important given the 'cultural particularity of the public domain', specifically the racism of the Enlightenment ideas underpinning it: K Bowrey and J Anderson. "The Politics of Global Information Sharing: Whose Cultural Agendas Are Being Advanced?' (2009) 18(4) *Social & Legal Studies* 479, 481. This notion of diversity is married with Fisher's phrase introduced above, 'the development of a just and attractive culture' (Fisher (n 20) 192) in the remainder of the book in order to highlight the communal nature of creativity and its role in the promotion and development of culture generally.

Another aim is to avoid taking sides in the 'rights versus economics' debate: what creators have a right to expect ('individual agency') versus what economic efficiency or society requires ('social ordering').[98] As Cohen points out, such a dichotomy is unhelpful because it does not take into account existing literature on creation as an intersection between the self and society.[99] It is implied, however, by this work's focus on the protection or regulation of creativity through copyright that we must consider the protection and promotion of culture. The solution to the problem appears to be (at least in part) to consider the fact of creation, as this book endeavours to do, empirically,[100] and then to assess, on the basis of that empirical consideration, how copyright law might usefully be reformed.

Seeking to promote and develop culture raises—amongst many other issues—the question of how the balance should be struck between encouraging creativity and rewarding the creation of works with copyright protection.[101] While copyright is often viewed as the incentive for creation, it is not an absolute good, and 'over-protection can sabotage the equally constitutive dissemination-function of copyright law.'[102] In particular, the issue here is how to set the somewhat overlapping boundaries between the public and propertised domains within the intellectual commons in order to satisfy both individual recognition via the grant of a property right and the recognition of 'public rights' to access and build upon existing material. As Litman explains the point:

> The public domain should be understood not as the realm of material that is undeserving of protection, but as a device that permits the rest of the system to work by leaving the raw material of authorship available for authors to use.[103]

This assumes that such 'balancing' is an appropriate starting point. As Drassinower indicates, however, considering copyright as '[serving] the public interest in the production and dissemination of works of authorship'[104] is a hallmark of common law systems (by contrast to civil law conceptions that are underpinned by the recognition of the author's dignity as the creator of a work).[105] A better view, per Ginsburg, might be to eschew the notion of balance and instead to simply ask what is in the public interest, which 'comprises the goals and aspirations of authors and users, of publishers and educators, and so forth'.[106] The boundaries of the public domain are highly contested, as case law on the ambit of copyright exceptions

[98] Cohen (n 96) 1155.

[99] ibid 1155–56.

[100] ibid 1156.

[101] However, the balancing metaphor is flawed because it based on assumptions about what is valuable; Patry argues that the question instead ought to simply be 'what is the result we want?': W Patry, *How to Fix Copyright* (Oxford, Oxford University Press, 2011) 137.

[102] A Drassinower, 'A Note on Incentives, Rights, and the Public Domain in Copyright Law' (2011) 86 *Notre Dame Law Review* 5, 1869–84, 1872.

[103] J Litman, 'The Public Domain' (1990) 39(4) *Emory Law Journal* 965, 968.

[104] A Drassinower, 'Copyright Is Not about Copying' (2012) 3 *Harvard Law Review*, 108–19, 108.

[105] ibid.

[106] JC Ginsburg, 'Authors and Users in Copyright' (1997) 45 *Journal of the Copyright Society of the USA* 1, 4.

such as US fair use—a prime example of an attempt at reflecting in law the task of balancing—clearly shows.[107] If copyright is viewed as limiting creativity and the building of culture it is unsurprising that academic commentary seeks to 'defend' the public domain[108] and criticise the brakes placed on individual creativity by overzealous copyright protection. A specific concern here is the commodification of creativity, in particular the ways in which copyright law can be used in order to ensure and then entrench corporate control of the intellectual commons.[109]

Cultural imperatives often conflict with the economic. In cultural arenas, such as the entertainment industry, copyright law has enabled corporations to capture a large proportion of cultural output. This has occurred, for example, through the horizontal and vertical integration of entertainment companies and consequently limited the types of creative works that are made available to consumers.[110] The cultural landscape is thus privatised even where many people unreflectively consider the popular culture they consume to be part of the 'commons'[111] and treat it as such. In such an environment, for example, female fans' creation of Star Trek fanzines and slash fiction is a subcultural activity not merely because of its content and its circulation within a close-knit community of like-minded women but because they do not have permission to use and transform the relevant intellectual property.[112]

A related issue is the conceptualisation of creative production/intellectual property *as property* and the consequent potential for copyright law—in an attempt to protect creativity—to entrench particular forms of private, especially corporate, power.[113] The argument can also be made, however, that the 'language of property' does not necessarily favour the content industry but may be used in defence of the public domain.[114] The account offered here of the regulation of graffiti creativity within the subculture out of which it emerges calls into question the notion of copyright as property or, more specifically, the understanding of property which dominates in this context. It asks, for example, whether property is better understood under a stewardship model that recognises community

107 See eg comments on fair use and the courts: Litman (n 103) 1005–06.

108 eg J Boyle, *The Public Domain: Enclosing the Commons of the Mind* (New Haven, Yale University Press, 2008).

109 See especially Macmillan (n 8).

110 F Macmillan, 'Commodification and Cultural Ownership' in J Griffiths and U Suthersanen (eds), *Copyright and Free Speech: Comparative and International Analyses* (Oxford, Oxford University Press, 2005) 53. See also RV Bettig, *Copyrighting Culture: The Political Economy of Intellectual Property* (Boulder, Colorado, Westview Press, 1996): 'the law of intellectual property follows the expansionary logic of capital': 235.

111 Macmillan (n 110) 56.

112 For a discussion of the community and associated issues see Coombe (n 94) 111–23.

113 Macmillan (n 9); Macmillan (n 8).

114 H Dagan, 'Property and the Public Domain' (2006) 18 *Yale Journal of Law and the Humanities*, 84–93, 85. Dagan rejects the dichotomy that places the public domain at one end of the debate and property rights on the other arguing that 'property language' may also be used to make pro-public domain arguments based, for instance, on providing a proportional reward for labour: 90.

interests in the development of, for instance, the copyright exceptions.[115] The present study considers, in light of these factors, what happens when groups of people opt out of a system that ostensibly protects and encourages democratic participation[116] and asks whether a different set of creativity regulating rules might be better attuned to the needs of the creative community, the space in which creativity occurs, and the development of culture (here, the culture of graffiti writing within the subculture, but also the broader culture which subsists beyond the boundaries of that subculture).

Graffiti and the 'Bounded Commons'

This part takes up the themes of the preceding two parts by describing the existence of a graffiti writing commons that is at once a subculture specific *intellectual* commons and a physical space. It is a physical space in the sense that the creativity in question occurs in a specific territory (eg a city or neighbourhood) and it is an intellectual space in that it consists of the 'style' commons of the graffiti subculture (letters, colour combinations and other creative elements). The norms regulating creativity regulate within and across these two (overlapping) spaces. This section therefore combines insights relating to graffiti creativity and the literature on the intellectual commons and public domain in order to address two themes that will emerge out of, in particular, the chapters analysing the fieldwork data. It first considers the interface between the physical and intellectual commons in the existing literature as a precursor to discussing, second, the graffiti-specific 'bounded commons' and the nature of the challenge that bounded commons poses to both the physical commons (which it challenges by interrupting urban public spaces) and the intellectual commons (which it challenges by providing an alternative framework for the regulation of creativity).

Graffiti in the Physical and Intellectual Commons

In considering the form that the graffiti subculture's commons takes, two observations are relevant: that graffiti creativity and its regulation fits within the category of community-specific intellectual commons identified in the literature; and, that the study of graffiti creativity within this category enriches it by providing a more complex picture of the intellectual commons overall. It takes into account

[115] HR Howe, 'Copyright Limitations and the Stewardship Model of Property' (2011) *Intellectual Property Quarterly* 2, 183–214, 208–11.

[116] Copyright may be seen as essential to democratic participation insofar as it 'foster[s] the creation and public communication of original expression': NW Netanel, 'Copyright and a Democratic Civil Society' (1996) 106(2) *Yale Law Journal* 283, 347.

both intellectual *and* physical space in the process of creation and the production and consumption of works. In particular, the process of graffiti writing moves us beyond the concept of territory as jurisdiction (though this is also relevant to the regulation of graffiti creativity) to permit a consideration of the graffiti 'scene' as dependent on the regulation of both physical and intellectual space in order to legitimise graffiti writing as an artistic practice (because the material work placed on a wall or a train may constitute criminal damage).

The following aspects are considered ahead of a more detailed account of the graffiti-specific commons below: creativity within the graffiti subculture as an example of *res universitatis* commons and the interface between the physical and intellectual commons. The *res universitatis* commons may be defined as follows:

> [A] regime that is bounded by property rights but creates a type of limited public domain (or commons) within its boundaries.[117]

The definition suggests that the commons of a 'bounded community' (discussed here as the 'bounded commons') incentivises production within the group while seeking to enforce rights against those outside of the group. Indeed, graffiti writers have particular expectations about how non-writers use and share their work.[118] At the same time, creativity within the subculture is regulated in such a way as to effectively 'propertise' some elements of the commons and not others: for example, the letters of the alphabet are free for everyone to use, but a name will belong to a particular writer. The graffiti subculture therefore offers a more complex picture of the bounded commons because the graffiti rules regulate creativity within the subculture not to create a regulatory 'wall' to protect a graffiti-specific public domain but rather a 'walled' intellectual commons that has, within it, its own public domain. At the same time, this commons overlaps with the broader intellectual commons and public domain from which graffiti writers, like other creators, will also draw material and inspiration.

While the above—a commons and a public domain internal to a community—presents a broadly familiar picture, the 'bounded commons' of the graffiti subculture also offers a contrast to this conceptualisation. The literature on the intellectual commons/public domain pays relatively little attention to physical space. It is described here as the 'physical commons' since it encompasses both publicly and privately owned properties that are accessible to the public.[119] The aim is not to consider physical space as territory and therefore copyright law only in relation to jurisdiction nor to highlight the harmonisation of intellectual property across

[117] Macmillan (n 89) 106.

[118] See chapter ten.

[119] On the interplay between public and private property see K Gray and S Francis Gray, 'Private Property and Public Propriety' in J McLean (ed), *Property and the Constitution* (Oxford, Hart Publishing, 1999). This point touches upon a great literature on space, including regulation of urban space. See eg A Philippopoulos-Mihalopoulos (ed), *Law and the City* (Abingdon, Routledge-Cavendish, 2007).

national borders but to consider the regulation *of* creativity and how it impacts in turn the regulation of space and its potential territories (for graffiti writers, this may mean a neighbourhood, or a train line, or another city). As Cohen argues, it is unhelpful to consider the public domain in isolation from its 'spatial realities'—and the attendant distribution of resources that this implies—that impact upon cultural processes.[120] Taking into account space is also important because it shapes individual identities.[121] This latter point is of particular relevance to graffiti writers given the link between creativity and visibility: the acquisition of fame in the graffiti subculture depends on the creativity having a material presence.

To ignore the importance of urban public space—the physical commons—to graffiti creativity would be to misunderstand the nature of that creativity as a process that is inherently concerned with the production of a different type of urban commons.[122] The regulation of graffiti creativity is a means of both shaping the contours of the bounded (intellectual) commons that affects the production of graffiti within the subculture but also of shaping the experience of the physical commons for those within and outside of the graffiti subculture outside of it. This is not to say, however, that it is only graffiti normativity—or other such normative frameworks—that has the potential to shape the experience of space. Intellectual property law already exhibits this tendency. Trade mark law including the registration of scents—like planning or other more obvious forms of legal regulation of space—is a form of 'sensory control'.[123] The control is exerted at a remove, it '[dissimulates] itself as desire, that is as personal preference that "demands" Kodak, Coke, Apple, or beer-scented darts.'[124] These trade marks are both within the intellectual commons (though not in the public domain) as well as having an existence in the physical commons.

Similarly, Bartow identifies a link between the physical and intellectual commons through a discussion of the impact of trade mark law on the 'physical public domain'.[125] In particular, she argues that the re-naming of buildings such as sports stadiums or high schools with the names of individuals or brands has the effect of associating the place with certain values that in turn 'permeate the collective public conscience'[126] and, in particular, to entrench social privilege.[127] It is in this context of the commercialisation of public space—on which there is a longstanding

[120] Cohen (n 96) 1176–77.

[121] Drawing on critical geography: RJ Coombe, 'Authorial Cartographies: Mapping Proprietary Borders in a Less-Than-Brave New World' (1996) 48(5) *Stanford Law Review* 1357, 1358.

[122] See generally on creativity, social movements and commons: I Susser and S Tonnelat, 'Transformative Cities: The Three Urban Commons' (2013) 66 *Focaal* 105.

[123] A Philippopoulos-Mihalopoulos, 'Atmospheres of Law: Senses, Affects, Lawscapes' (2013) 7 *Emotion, Space and Society* 35, 42.

[124] ibid 42.

[125] A Bartow, 'Trademarks of Privilege: Naming Rights and the Physical Public Domain' (2007) 40 *UC Davis Law Review*, 919–70.

[126] ibid 932.

[127] Namely the 'wealthy, male and white': ibid 934.

literature[128]—that graffiti creativity and the act of putting up one's name[129] may be viewed specifically as a response to the privatisation of the physical commons rather than merely as a method of regulating creativity within an intellectual commons. In that sense, graffiti creativity reflects concerns analogous to those raised above with respect to the propertisation of the intellectual commons.

The Graffiti-Specific Commons

The discussion now turns to a more detailed discussion of the characteristic of the 'bounded commons' introduced above. When conceptualised as a commons that encompasses both physical and intellectual spaces, the concept of the 'bounded commons' overlaps with the concept of the graffiti 'scene' which encompasses both a territorial (physical) dimension and the various hierarchies and social relations present within the community of writers in that territory. In a more obviously copyright-like way, the 'bounded commons' is also distinguished by the intangible creative elements it encompasses from which graffiti writers may draw. The commons is not simply where creators draw on for their works but is both concretely (with respect to physical space) and intellectually, where graffiti culture is simultaneously created and legitimised. The graffiti-specific commons is also a space in which—whether or not writers express this in explicit terms—the process of producing works is a form of political resistance to private power.

In the most obvious sense the 'scene' can be viewed as a particular territory and those working in it; that is, the graffiti writers producing graffiti and competing for fame within a given city. The 'scene' in this sense is also normative, acting as a marker of something akin to jurisdiction. While graffiti rules might be broadly the same in London and Berlin, as chapter seven will suggest, to ensure that they are followed requires one to be familiar with the identity of writers who are active, or prominent, in that specific 'scene'. In other words, the graffiti rules are constitutive of the community; they are not just regulating creativity but also legitimating graffiti creativity and legitimating its creators as part of a community.

Although the graffiti rules may serve to legitimate graffiti writing as a creative practice this does not make it a closed circuit of influences; as indicated above, graffiti writers are not immune from broader cultural influences. The bounded commons has porous borders. For example, as identified in chapter one, graffiti writers in New York, as the subculture was evolving, incorporated numerous cultural references into their work, some of which became essential aspects of graffiti creativity in different 'scenes' as the influence of New York writers radiated outwards towards cities including London.

[128] eg M Sorkin (ed), *Variations on a Theme Park: The New American City and the End of Public Space* (New York, Hill and Wang, 1992).

[129] Or, more specifically, an 'authornym': LA Heymann, 'The Birth of the Authornym: Authorship, Pseudonymity, and Trademark Law' (2005) 80(4) *Notre Dame Law Review* 1377.

The issue raised is then how the use of these external elements, along with graffiti-specific elements, are regulated. For that reason, an examination of graffiti norms raises some of the same questions about the appropriate 'balancing' of interests between the individual creator and the broader public (or within the bounded commons, in relation to graffiti, others within the subculture) or in identifying the public interest. The 'bounded commons' contains its own, internal 'graffiti public domain' where certain creative elements are free for any writer to use; it is the combination of these elements that is potentially protected by the graffiti rules. There is also a related concern about the taking of another writer's name—specifically the meaning invested in a name in a particular 'scene'—and this is dealt with within the subculture via the rule that a graffiti writer ought not to adopt a name that is the same of very similar to the name of a fellow writer.[130] One criticism of copyright law is that the owner of copyright has 'expropriate[d] meanings and values generated by the creative activities of others'.[131] Of course those writers whose names are protected may have expropriated the graffiti commons to come up with that name but, crucially, this level of protection (ie that no one else can use the name) would not treated as an expropriation but rather as necessary to clearly mark the identities of individual writers within a subculture where writers and crews compete for fame. In other respects, graffiti writers grapple with some of the same concerns such as the delineation between freely available elements and those that are not.

Apart from using the conception of the 'bounded commons' to explore the regulation of creativity within the graffiti subculture, the value in this conception of the intellectual commons is, building on Macmillan's work, in creating places within 'intellectual space' that challenge corporate power.[132] Concerns with corporate power are reflected within the graffiti subculture, especially as these concerns focus specifically on the privatisation of urban public space.[133] This privatisation has implications not only for the creative expression of individual creators but also the development of culture. We must be conscious, then, that the relationship between copyright and the graffiti norms which subsist within the subculture is not only one of reinforcement (where parallels exist between the two regimes) but also at times one of challenge (where the graffiti norms call into question both the form of, and justifications for, the operation of copyright rules). One of the surprising elements arising out of the empirical data was how conservative some of the graffiti rules are in the sense that certain underlying assumptions—such as the need to respect individual authors and not copy their works—do not challenge fundamental assumptions within copyright law. By contrast, however, some of the most fundamental instantiations of graffiti creativity—writing on walls or trains without permission, for example—presents a direct challenge to criminal and real

[130] See chapter seven.
[131] Coombe (n 121) 1360.
[132] Macmillan (n 89) 108.
[133] See chapter five.

property laws of a sort which share (at least some of) the values and assumptions reflected by copyright law.

So, if copyright law is a '*politically* rather than *intellectually* contested terrain' (emphasis in the original)[134] the graffiti rules present a political alternative to the regulation of creativity. Yet, as has been noted, what is interesting is not just the functioning of the graffiti rules as an alternative 'copyright' but also that these rules evidence the possibility of an alternative regulation of space. This is due in large part to graffiti creativity being a self-consciously spatial practice which, when reflected in a series of subcultural rules, results in an explicitly spatialised normativity.[135] Ferrell and Weide make a similar point in arguing that graffiti writers need to find ways of being in the city that grants them visibility while evading the detection of the authorities which requires them to 'develop a keen sort of alternative spatial epistemology, collectively remaking the meaning of the everyday urban environment'.[136] The interface between the physical and intellectual commons again raises the issue of the political significance of graffiti writing and, in particular, the extent to which the regulation of creativity within the graffiti subculture should be understood as being simultaneously a counter-regulation of the physical commons.

Although some of the graffiti writers interviewed were clear that graffiti writing was not intended to be a political statement, their discussion of placement revealed a deep unease with the commercialisation of physical public space. Brighenti, for example, argues that walls are 'governmental objects'[137] on which graffiti writing represents a 'tactical intervention'.[138] A writer is however constrained in making such an intervention by the graffiti rules that require the placement of tags, throw-ups and pieces to be appropriate. This aspect of the graffiti norms indicates that the regulation of creativity is also a regulation of space. Indeed the graffiti work—a specific tag or piece for example—is both the material manifestation of the creative process as well as the production of a particular (kind of) territory.[139] Indeed it is this combination of the material work and the movement to produce it that places graffiti writing *beyond copyright* insofar as copyright law can protect neither the creative process which results in the material work, nor the space in which that process occurs.

It is in regulating *the where*[140] of creativity that the graffiti rules function somewhat differently from the alternative intellectual property frameworks

[134] A Julius, 'Art Crimes' in D McClean and K Schubert (eds), *Dear Images: Art, Copyright and Culture* (London, Ridinghouse, 2002) 487.

[135] Adopting the term from J Ploger, 'Foucault's Dispositif and the City' (2008) 7(1) *Planning Theory* 51.

[136] J Ferrell and R Weide, 'Spot Theory' (2010) 14(1) *City* 48, 60.

[137] Brighenti (n 76) 317, 322.

[138] ibid.

[139] On territory as an act: 'Each enacted territorialisation is the sociotechnical result of an act of inscription, an act of drawing or tracing, a movement.' In AM Brighenti, 'Lines, Barred Lines. Movement, Territory and the Law' (2010) 6(3) *International Journal of Law in Context* 217, 225.

[140] Note Cresswell's analysis of the law's regulation of graffiti as dependent on the 'crucial "where" of graffiti': T Cresswell, *In Place/Out of Place: Geography, Ideology, and Transgression* (Minnesota, University of Minnesota Press, 1996) 31.

discussed below. The rules are not merely alternatives to copyright or suggestions for how copyright law might be different but also a means of challenging the commodification of both creativity and urban space. In asserting their identity in urban spaces—the tag itself is the announcement, quoting Lady Pink, 'I'm here …'[141]—graffiti writers are also resisting authority and, Ferrell argues, in doing so are reclaiming public spaces that are regulated in such a way as to exclude young people.[142] As one writer put it:

> I feel like if I don't make an effort to do something to change my surroundings then I don't control it, it has control over me. (Anon12)

Graffiti writing thus becomes, even if not intended as such, a kind of symbol of resistance to those without resources to place their names or message in public space unlike others who can afford to pay for billboards.[143] As Austin suggests, writing graffiti encourages the formation of new kinds of urban space:

> Graffiti art provided (and still provides) a way of seeing something new: an-other visual order is possible, and so an-other city is possible, and so an-other life is possible as well.[144]

Perhaps, therefore, it is useful to think about the graffiti rules by considering the graffiti rules as a 'social practice of *commoning*' (emphasis in the original);[145] a practice with the capacity to re-imagine the city. As Young notes, graffiti writers and street artists are 'inhabitants of the uncommissioned city, occupying the same space as the legislated city, embody the possibility of both another life and another mode of legality.'[146] The graffiti rules, in offering the possibility of a different city, also constitute a counter-regulation[147] of real property as well as copyright. That is, graffiti normativity is about alternative rules—evident in other creative communities operating within a bounded commons—rather than the wholesale rejection of rules and rule-making. The existence of a graffiti commons, as described here, to which these alternative rules apply, points to a multitude of overlapping cultural spaces commensurate with the existence of numerous publics. Indeed, numerous alternative frameworks for the regulation of creativity exist.

[141] J Ferrell, 'Urban Graffiti: Crime, Control, and Resistance' (1995) 27 *Youth and Society* 73, 81.

[142] See ibid.

[143] This concern was identified in the empirical data and has also been noted elsewhere. See eg J Sharp, V Pollock and R Paddison, 'Just Art for a Just City: Public Art and Social Inclusion in Urban Regeneration' (2005) 52(5) *Urban Studies* 1001, 1015.

[144] J Austin, 'More to see than a canvas in a white cube: For an art in the streets' (2010) 14(1) *City* 33, 44. Sentence structure and spelling in original.

[145] Defined as 'collective and non-commodified': D Harvey, *Rebel Cities: From the Right to the City to the Urban Revolution* (New York, Verso, 2012) 73. Harvey discusses 'urban commons' in the context of protest.

[146] A Young, 'Cities in the City: Street Art, Enchantment, and the Urban Commons' (2014) 26(2) *Law & Literature* 145, 160.

[147] The practice of graffiti might be described as a 'counter-hegemonic nomospheric [project]': D Delaney, *The Spatial, the Legal and the Pragmatics of World-Making: Nomospheric Investigations* (Oxford, Routledge, 2010) 149.

Alternative Frameworks

The preceding discussion has focused primarily on the conceptualisation of creativity, the intellectual commons and the public domain and, in particular, the regulation of creativity in the graffiti subculture so as to constitute a 'bounded commons'. This part asks how and why certain forms of creativity flourish in the absence or forbearance of copyright protection and how creativity is regulated in these alternative commons. Before considering existing empirical studies of the non-legal regulation of creativity, this part addresses the way in which this book uses the terms 'norm' and 'rule' by placing it in the context of broader questions about the role of custom and practice in the production of alternative frameworks for regulating creativity.

Norms and Rules, Customs and Practice

Broadly speaking a norm might be defined as 'what people do out of a sense of obligation'[148] or a 'coordination focal point of what everyone is expected to do.'[149] When creators within a community (are forced to) forbear intellectual property protection, or it is not available to them, one outcome is that that activity becomes regulated by a set of internal norms. The graffiti rules described here are one such set of rules. What is significant about the graffiti rules is the extent to which, as chapter one indicated, they might be viewed as the crystallisation of customs or practices from the early days of graffiti writing to produce a set of norms that are, nevertheless, not law.

Custom, as Postema indicates,[150] has a normative dimension in which practice, rather than theory, produces and supports a set of norms that might be described as 'rules in action' rather than abstract rules.[151] Although Postema discusses custom in relation to customary international law, the following observation is salient here:

> It is *deeds* that create customary norms, but deeds also sustain them, refine them, and replace them with other customs. Although a robust notion of violation is a necessary condition of a customary regularity functioning as a norm—it must be possible to say with Hamlet, "it is a custom more honoured in the breach than the observance".[152]

[148] AK Rai, 'Regulating Scientific Research: Intellectual Property Rights and the Norms of Science' (1999) 94(1) *Northwestern University Law Review* 77, 81.

[149] Y Benkler, 'Designing Cooperative Systems for Knowledge Production: An Initial Synthesis from Experimental Economics' in M Biagioli, Martha Woodmansee and Peter Jaszi (eds), *Making and Unmaking Intellectual Property: Creative Production in Legal and Cultural Perspective* (Chicago, University of Chicago Press, 2011) 154.

[150] G Postema, 'Custom in International Law: A Normative Practice' in A Perreau-Saussine and JB Murphy (eds), *The Nature of Customary Law: Legal, Historical and Philosophical Perspectives* (Cambridge, Cambridge University Press, 2007) 287.

[151] ibid 291.

[152] ibid.

Indeed, psychological literature based on empirical research suggests that norms are a set of shared feelings and practices communicated within and outside the group through behaviour as well as speech.[153] Thus, where rules in subcultural groups are both recognised by group members and constituted and re-constituted through practice even their breach confirms the rule.

The graffiti norms discussed here are an example of custom or practice evolving into a normative framework but to whatever extent it is recognised and adhered to by the writers themselves, these rules are not 'law'. The rules are not law because, amongst other things, the sanctions associated with their breach—rather than being applied centrally and backed by the coercive power of the state—are applied in a more diffuse fashion within the subculture. While recognising the necessity of some form of sanction to enforce or at least encourage compliance, rules growing out of and supported by custom are therefore relatively weak yet nonetheless relevant. The key point is that in a situation of intellectual property forbearance, the collective practice of a close community might easily be transformed into—or reconceived as—a normative order which is no less real because it is not legal. In particular, the sanctions associated with the breach of the graffiti rules, even though not legal, will have significant consequences for a graffiti writer *as a writer* within a community. A shared history and culture allows informal sanctions such as disrespect and ostracism to be effective curbs to rule-breaking behaviour.

Further, the way in which writers themselves discuss—and thereby demonstrate themselves to accept the existence of—the graffiti rules is also relevant. Notwithstanding variations in terms of reasoning and explanation for the rules, the data shows a stable core of widely recognised rules related to, inter alia, originality, copying and destruction of works. These rules may be described simply as a 'normative order'[154] or a normative framework, one whose reach (the boundary of the graffiti commons) is determined by participation in graffiti culture. Moreover, the framework in many ways transcends national boundaries, in that the same basic rules apply in a variety of different territories (ie the 'scenes' in various cities) in which the same activity takes place. Again, the rules might not be 'law' but have an immediacy and relevance to graffiti writers' experience that simply does not exist in relation to, say, copyright law.

The present study is thus not concerned with demonstrating that the graffiti norms are law but no objection is raised to potentially viewing the graffiti rules and copyright law co-existing as legal orders in a legal pluralist sense. Certainly, there is some overlap between the two, especially in the appeal to morality for example with respect to subsistence in both copyright law and graffiti rules on what type of creativity is protected (see chapters four and five). This is evident also in claims relating to the 'propriety' of generating and using works. The relevant

[153] See MA Hogg and SA Reid, 'Social Identity, Self-Categorization, and the Communication of Group Norms' (2006) 16(1) *Communication Theory* 7, 7–8.

[154] BZ Tamanaha, *A General Jurisprudence of Law and Society* (Oxford, Oxford University Press, 2001) 173.

point here is that the graffiti rules are an example of regulation within a bounded commons that is itself embedded with the broader intellectual commons that is regulated by copyright law. Much of the existing literature on alternative frameworks draws on American law and social norms scholarship, especially the work of Ellickson in *Order Without Law*,[155] rather than the more extensive literature associated with legal pluralism of the kind identified with de Sousa Santos[156] and others.[157] The chapter now turns to a discussion of some of these studies.

Regulating Creativity Without Copyright Law

Creativity has flourished apart from, or in spite of, intellectual property law for as long as attempts have existed to regulate it and it is trite to note that creativity did not come into existence with the creation of intellectual property law.[158] An analysis of the graffiti norms both reflects and, insofar as it considers a form of creativity that involves often illegal activity, expands upon the existing literature on the regulation of creativity without intellectual property law. The focus here is the limited but vibrant recent scholarship on alternative normative frameworks and 'everyday' intellectual property.[159] As Tushnet notes, 'ordinary people have theories of creativity, fair use, and fair attribution, even if they do not have an elaborate theoretical apparatus'.[160] The existence of what has been termed 'IP without IP (Intellectual Production without Intellectual Property)' provides a basis for arguing how intellectual property laws might be changed so as to take into account forms of production to which these alternative frameworks apply.[161] On the other

[155] An empirical study of Shasta County ranchers: RC Ellickson, *Order Without Law: How Neighbors Settle Disputes* (Cambridge, MA, Harvard University Press, 1994).

[156] eg B de Sousa Santos, 'The Law of the Oppressed: The Construction and Reproduction of Legality in Pasargada' (1977) 12(1) *Law & Society Review* 5.

[157] See generally eg S Engle Merry, 'Legal Pluralism' (1988) 22(5) *Law and Society Review* 869; B Benda-Beckman, 'Who's Afraid of Legal Pluralism?' (2002) 47 *Journal of Legal Pluralism and Unofficial Law* 37.

[158] Music provides a useful illustration of this phenomenon. See eg P Tschmuck, 'Creativity Without Copyright: Music Production in Vienna in the Late Eighteenth Century' in R Towse (ed), *Copyright in the Cultural Industries* (Cheltenham, Edward Elgar, 2002); J Toynbee, 'Reggae Open Source: How the Absence of Copyright Enabled the Emergence of Popular Music in Jamaica' in L Bently, J Davis and JC Ginsburg (eds), *Copyright and Piracy: An Interdisciplinary Critique* (Cambridge, Cambridge University Press, 2010); J Opkaluba, '"Free-riding on the Riddim"? Open Source, Copyright Law and Reggae Music in Jamaica' in L Bently, J Davis and JC Ginsburg (eds), *Copyright and Piracy: An Interdisciplinary Critique* (Cambridge, Cambridge University Press, 2010).

[159] See eg LJ Murray, ST Piper and K Robertson, *Putting Intellectual Property in its Place: Rights Discourses, Creative Labor and the Everyday* (New York, Oxford University Press, 2014).

[160] R Tushnet, 'Payment in Credit: Copyright Law and Subcultural Creativity' (2007) 70 *Law & Contemporary Problems*, 135, 137 at note 5.

[161] R Cooper Dreyfuss, 'Does IP Need IP? Accommodating Intellectual Production Outside the Intellectual Property Paradigm' (2010) 31(5) *Cardozo Law Review* 1437, 1439.

hand the literature at times suggests that such alterations are not needed because creativity will continue with or without copyright protection. Thus, the attempt to protect 'difficult' types of creativity such as experimental dance or music might damage these creative practices.[162] The chief difference of this book as compared to existing accounts is the emphasis on illegal subcultural creativity, which is under-explored by contrast to more mainstream forms of creativity such as fashion.

The term 'negative space' was coined by Oliar and Sprigman as part of an attempt to explain why fashion design appeared to thrive both creatively (in the sense that new designs were constantly produced) as well as economically despite weak intellectual property protection.[163] The concept applies even more clearly where the protection of intellectual property is not just weak but largely absent. Crucially for current purposes, the 'negative space' of intellectual property often results in the emergence of an alternate set of norms to regulate creativity. Such free-standing norms must be distinguished from the use of custom to interpret existing copyright law.[164] This book is concerned specifically with alternative norms that parallel *copyright* notwithstanding that much of the literature refers to intellectual property more broadly. Furthermore, the literature tends use the language of 'norms' to describe the rules of conduct which exist so as to regulate creativity where intellectual property does not reach. That term is indeed used here, but it is used interchangeably with the term 'rules' because the former term was employed by some participants.

A welcome overview of the ways in which the concept of intellectual property's 'negative space' has been used in the recent literature is provided by Rosenblatt whose 'taxonomy' of 'negative spaces' is as follows:

> (1) doctrinal no man's land, where creations fall through the cracks of IP [intellectual property] protection; (2) areas of IP forbearance, in which creators could receive protection, but elect either not to seek protection or not to pursue infringers; and (3) use-based carve outs, in which lawmakers have exempted certain types of intellectual property use from liability.[165]

The creative production of graffiti writers as a form of subcultural creativity would likely fall within the second category since at least arguably graffiti works (especially throw-ups and pieces and possibly tags) could be protected as artistic works given the individual style of each.[166] Rosenblatt continues by setting out

[162] Waelde and Schlesinger (n 71) 291.

[163] K Raustiala and C Sprigman, 'The Piracy Paradox: Innovation and Intellectual Property in Fashion Design' (2006) 92(8) *Virginia Law Review* 1687. Compare SC Hemphill and J Suk, 'Law, Culture, and Economics of Fashion' (2009) 61(5) *Stanford Law Review* 1147.

[164] See JE Rothman, 'The Questionable Use of Custom in Intellectual Property' (2007) 93(8) *Virginia Law Review* 1899.

[165] EL Rosenblatt, 'A Theory of IP's Negative Space' (2011) 34(3) *Columbia Journal of Law and the Arts* 317, 322. See also, for a different approach, the empirical studies in BM Frischmann, MJ Madison and KJ Strandburg (eds), *Governing Knowledge Commons* (New York, Oxford University Press, 2014).

[166] For a rare examination of the intellectual property law as it might apply to graffiti works see T Rychlicki, 'Legal Questions About Illegal Art' (2008) 3(6) *Journal of Intellectual Property Law and Practice* 393.

four overlapping situations in which a 'negative space' might be produced including where the motivation for creativity is 'something other than exclusivity-based financial gain.'[167] The desire for recognition and the building of a community are identified as alternative motivations.[168] As Smith similarly argues in relation to street art, for example, creators do not require economic incentives in order to continue producing works.[169] Similarly, some graffiti writers may also seek to commercialise their work and may wish to enforce copyright in a commercial context but this is not usually the primary motivation for producing the work in the first place.

A variety of empirical studies of alternative normative frameworks show how groups produce norms that, to some extent, mirror copyright. This book fits specifically within the literature on the regulation of different types of creativity, which includes studies of stand-up comedy,[170] cooking,[171] magic,[172] typefaces[173] and Irish traditional music (ITM).[174] The graffiti rules are one example of an alternative framework for regulating creativity. What the graffiti rules have in common, amongst other things is a concern with reputation and attribution, and community belonging. Thus, a feature of empirical studies into these alternative normative frameworks is that the rules are highly attuned to the needs of the particular community in question. For example, the attention paid to style, used in a way that more closely mirrors the preoccupation with style in the graffiti subculture, occurs in ITM.[175] ITM would appear to be an example of intellectual property forbearance.[176] Empirical research shows that the style of music is important insofar as it determines which songs may be described as ITM and consequently which songs are likely to become part of the ITM canon.[177] The norms governing the production of ITM are centred on notions of originality and authorship.[178]

[167] Rosenblatt (n 165) 322.

[168] ibid 321.

[169] CYN Smith, 'Street Art: An Analysis under US Intellectual Property Law and Intellectual Property's "Negative Space" Theory' (2014) 24 *DePaul Journal of Art, Technology & Intellectual Property Law* 259.

[170] D Oliar and C Sprigman, 'There's No Free Laugh (Anymore): The Emergence of Intellectual Property Norms and the Transformation of Stand-Up Comedy' (2009) 94(8) *Virginia Law Review* 1787.

[171] E Fauchart and E von Hippel, 'Norms-Based Intellectual Property Systems: The Case of French Chefs' (2008) 19(2) *Organization Science* 187.

[172] J Loshin, 'Secrets Revealed: How Magicians Protect Intellectual Property Without Law' (2007) www.papers.ssrn.com/sol3/papers.cfm?abstract_id=1005564.

[173] B Fry, 'Why Typefaces Proliferate Without Copyright Protection' (August 2009) www.works.bepress.com/blake_fry/1/, 69. Note that in the UK typefaces are protected by design law: Registered Designs Act 1949, s 1(3).

[174] LT McDonagh, *Does the Law of Copyright in the UK and Ireland Conflict with the Creative Practices of Irish Traditional Musicians? A Study of the Impact of Law on a Traditional Music Network* PhD Thesis, School of Law, Queen Mary, University of London, 2011.

[175] ibid 137.

[176] See ibid 233 (based on empirical research).

[177] ibid 241–42.

[178] ibid 225.

Attribution of the originator of a particular composition (which is then arranged by others) is also expected though is not always followed in practice.[179]

The important difference between the forms of creativity mentioned above and graffiti (which is both a subcultural and potentially illegal activity) is that graffiti writers are effectively compelled to forbear copyright protection. The extent to which the graffiti rules parallel copyright rules is discussed in more detail over the course of the empirical chapters. At this point, however, it is useful to consider some of the aspects of subcultural creativity that inform the creation of parallel copyright norms by reference to existing studies of non-mainstream creativity. With respect to subcultural norm creation, existing works on, for instance, the anime fansubbing community are instructive. Anime fansubbing refers to the copying, translation and subtitling of Japanese cartoons.[180] The copies of anime films are made and placed on the internet without permission but anime fansubbers, being motivated by a desire to promote anime, therefore recognise a chief rule—'stop when the anime is licensed'—amongst other rules.[181] These rules of engagement with copyright law offer a nuanced approach to infringement that is based on the fansubbers love of anime: the licences of US publishers are respected because this allows the local anime industry to grow.[182] However, adherence to the rules has fractured such that fansubbing groups of different anime series and in different places will negotiate their own stance on what actions are and are not appropriate.[183] This is problematic where the efficacy of rules regulating creativity depends on a shared sense of culture and values (belonging to a community) for enforcement; where the sense of community weakens, the set of norms which regulate it cease to have an effect. As such, a number of the issues raised in this book regarding the, in practice limited, protection offered to graffiti creativity are not unique to the graffiti subculture.[184]

Conclusion

This chapter has identified a number of themes that are relevant to the exploration of UK copyright law as it relates to graffiti writing as well as the alternative normative framework of the graffiti subculture, in particular the nature of creativity and the constitution of the commons. The creation of an alternative framework by a creative community is unsurprising when financial reward is not the

[179] ibid 276.

[180] HK Lee, 'Cultural Consumer and Copyright: A Case Study of Anime Fansubbing' (2014) 3(3) *Creative Industries Journal* 237, 238.

[181] ibid 238, 247.

[182] ibid 249.

[183] ibid 19–20.

[184] See eg E Sarid, 'Don't Be a Drag, Just Be a Queen—How Drag Queens Protect their Intellectual Property Without Law' (2014) 10 *FIU Law Review* 133 discussing A Roundtree, 'Graffiti Artists 'Get Up' in Intellectual Property's Negative Space' (2013) 31 *Cardozo Arts & Entertainment Law Journal* 959.

primary motivator for creativity.[185] As chapter one indicated, in the graffiti subculture the currency is fame not money. The centrality of identity in subcultural and other communities that create outside the market paradigm re-affirms justifications stemming from personhood, as evidenced for example by concerns over the norm of attribution or, put another way, favouring credit over payment.[186] Labour, when used as a justification, is not coupled with an expectation of a monetary reward. The graffiti rules described here are closely attuned to the needs of creators because they are based, amongst other things, on shared experiences and cultural foundations. Alternative copyright norm creation is a way of formalising these relationships by setting the boundaries of the graffiti-specific commons. Moreover, the graffiti rules expand upon this literature because the empirical findings relate to the production of illegal subcultural creativity (unlike the creative activities considered in existing studies).

The examination of the regulation of creativity within the graffiti subculture also suggests a way of re-imagining copyright so as to appropriately serve individual interests within communities of creators. Moreover, insofar as 'intellectual property inadequately provides a means for the defence of the public domain',[187] a study of alternative normative frameworks which might conceive of the public domain in a more robust and compelling way helps to bolster some of the existing argument for copyright reform. Amongst other things it suggests a setting of boundaries between the propertised and public domains within the intellectual commons that are based on a 'situated, relational'[188] understanding of the author, or put another way, a communitarian approach to copyright in which creativity is protected and regulated in a manner that, sensitive to its spatial realities, serves to promote a just, attractive and plural culture. The alternating discussions of copyright and graffiti norms for regulating creativity discussed in subsequent chapters will reveal two different approaches to sustaining the intellectual commons and, moreover, how the regulation of the intellectual commons is bound up in the regulation of space.

[185] See eg D Fagundes, 'Talk Derby to Me: Intellectual Property Norms Governing Roller Derby Pseudonyms' (2012) 90 *Texas Law Review* 1093, 1141.

[186] On plagiarism amongst fan fiction writers see Tushnet (n 160) 155, 153.

[187] Macmillan (n 89) 109.

[188] Craig (n 96) 4. See also D Halbert, 'Feminist Interpretations of Intellectual Property' (2006) 14 *American University Journal of Gender, Social Policy & the Law* 431.

3

Methodology: Reflections on Fieldwork

I don't know how you're going to do this, everyone's got different opinions on all of it.
(Anon28)

Introduction

Curiosity and a rigorous and appropriate methodology for satisfying curiosity are essential aspects of legal scholarship.[1] My curiosity about the graffiti subculture was piqued by a casual conversation (well before I began my doctoral research) with someone who knew a graffiti writer. He said something like 'they wouldn't tag a church or a car'. When I inquired why not he explained that such tagging was considered unacceptable and I found myself re-evaluating what I thought I knew about graffiti. It was clear that the best way to understand if, and why, the graffiti writers I had heard about did abide by their own set of norms would be to undertake empirical research to find out if this was indeed the case. This chapter examines the fieldwork undertaken between April 2010 and September 2011.

Cooper Dreyfuss muses that:

> The discovery of IP without IP is an exciting development. The proliferation of case studies is testament to the fun involved in tracking these projects—in thinking about cooking, clowning, mountain biking, and windsurfing.[2]

This chapter builds on the discussion of alternative intellectual property frameworks in chapter two to address some of the pleasures and difficulties associated with undertaking such a project. Unlike the culinary arts or stand-up comedy, empirical research into the graffiti writing and street art subculture(s) presented numerous challenges—not least gaining access to potential participants. It is these challenges, and the challenges of analysing my fieldwork data, that this chapter explores. It begins by providing an overview of existing empirical research on graffiti before discussing data gathering (setting, participants, interviews, supplementary sources,

[1] D Feldman, 'The Nature of Legal Scholarship' (1989) 52(4) *Modern Law Review* 498, 502–03.

[2] R Cooper Dreyfuss, 'Does IP Need IP? Accommodating Intellectual Production Outside the Intellectual Property Paradigm' (2010) 31(5) *Cardozo Law Review* 1437, 1473.

and reflections on undertaking fieldwork) and data analysis (coding themes and coding categories).

Empirical Research on Graffiti

This section provides an overview of existing empirical research into graffiti writing and graffiti writers and in doing so focuses on the methodology as opposed to findings (considered in chapter one) in existing studies of the graffiti subculture. Whether investigating graffiti from the perspective of space[3] or identity,[4] the researchers' experiences suggest some common themes and problems in undertaking research into the graffiti subculture. These issues include gaining participants' trust, triangulation through the use of secondary sources,[5] immersion and the personal experience of fieldwork.

This book is distinguished from most of the existing empirical studies by the setting and timing of the research as well as the focus on attitudes to creativity. I began my empirical research in the aftermath of Banksy's rise in popularity and the subsequent public interest in street art. As suggested in chapter one, this has created a 'split' in subcultural creativity between graffiti writers and street artists, though the borders between those categories are porous. Nevertheless, the challenges inherent in studying the graffiti subculture discussed here are a common thread in empirical research including my own. As Ferrell wrote of graffiti research in the 1990s:

> [N]o matter how many studies are done they are not enough, since the study of deviant or criminal subcultures must emerge as the subcultures themselves evolve.[6]

My empirical research is thus documenting a community and a set of informal rules in flux due to the relatively recent emergence of street art, demographic change within the graffiti community, different stylistic schools of graffiti (old school and new school) and the rise of the internet as a tool of communication and a means of disseminating graffiti works. It builds on a number of wonderful, existing empirical works on graffiti (and also street art) beginning with Jeff Ferrell's *Crime of Style* (1996)[7] and ending, most recently, with Alison Young's *Street Art, Public City* (2014).[8]

[3] eg R Schacter, 'An Ethnography of Iconoclash: An Investigation into the Production, Consumption and Destruction of Street-art in London' (2008) 13 *Journal of Material Culture* 1, 35–61; AM Brighenti, 'At the Wall: Graffiti Writers, Urban Territoriality, and the Public Domain' (2010) 13(3) *Space and Culture* 315.

[4] eg N Macdonald, *The Graffiti Subculture: Youth, Masculinity and Identity in London and New York* (Basingstoke, Palgrave Macmillan, 2001).

[5] This is particularly relevant during coding: T Cresswell, *Research Design: Qualitative, Quantitative and Mixed Methods Approaches* (Los Angeles, SAGE, 2009) 191.

[6] J Ferrell, *Crimes of Style: Urban Graffiti and the Politics of Criminality* (Boston, Northeastern University Press, 1996).

[7] ibid.

[8] A Young, *Street Art, Public City: Law, Crime and the Urban Imagination* (Abingdon, Routledge, 2014).

An excellent study of graffiti and masculinity published in 2001, *The Graffiti Subculture*[9] by Nancy Macdonald, which included interviews with London graffiti writers, is notable for its insight into the workings of the subculture. Secondary sources, such as graffiti-specific magazines, also played an important part, as with my own research, in both supplementing the interviews and acting as a window into the subculture to make the interviews more effective and, at the beginning, to lay the groundwork for finding people to interview.[10] Macdonald's observations of the difficulties in undertaking fieldwork, particularly gaining access and trust, are useful and make the participant observation, including train yard painting, undertaken a remarkable feat.[11] This approach has much to recommend it in the graffiti context. In immersing herself in the subculture Macdonald recognised, as I also came to do, that 'graffiti was not just a pastime, their lives literally revolved around it'.[12] The idea that immersion or sympathy is to some extent required to understand subcultural creativity is exemplified by Jeff Ferrell's masterful study of a crew of graffiti writers in Denver in the 1990s in *Crimes of Style*.[13] Ferrell engaged in extensive participant observation. He argued that to truly understand groups engaged in criminal behaviour the daily lives of those individuals had to be studied.[14]

Brighenti, too, has addressed normativity amongst graffiti writers through empirical research.[15] However, unlike the research underpinning this book, Brighenti's ethnography focused on a crew of writers in Italy. Nonetheless, like the other studies discussed above, this work provides numerous insights into the methodological issues associated with empirical research into graffiti writing. Perhaps the most important insight to be gained from existing studies is that they seek to understand the subculture from within. Similarly, recent books by Young[16] and Schacter[17] respectively offer exciting new accounts of the lives and work of graffiti writers and street artists. Young, in her expansive study of graffiti and street art interviewed creators in a number of cities including London, New York and Berlin to show how street art produces the 'public city'.[18] Schacter, for instance, approaches the same set of rules identified on the blog *Hurt You Bad* that I found as part of my own fieldwork:

> Some things that were/will be asked of you: Have style. Learn history. Be respectful. Paint subway trains. Bomb. Rack. Travel. Don't snitch. Handle beef. Write for 10+ years.[19]

[9] Macdonald (n 4).
[10] ibid 51.
[11] ibid.
[12] ibid 52.
[13] Ferrell (n 6).
[14] ibid.
[15] Brighenti (n 3).
[16] Young (n 8).
[17] R Schacter, *Ornament and Order: Graffiti, Street Art and Parergon* (Farnham, Ashgate, 2014).
[18] Young (n 8).
[19] *Hurt You Bad* blog quoted in Schacter, *Ornament and Order* (n 17) 159, note 16. Available at www.hurtyoubad.com/2013/05/11/graffiti-3/ (no author, no date).

The difference is that where Schacter focuses on graffiti as a ritual, the present book builds upon the existing empirical studies discussed here by considering graffiti writing from a different, and I hope complementary, perspective in considering how writers regulate their creativity within a 'bounded commons'.

The primary difference between my work and that of existing empirical research on graffiti then is its focus. In creating a sociologically coherent picture of a subculture, its personalities and politics are best understood through immersion in that subculture as Ferrell, for example, demonstrates. Rather than engaging in participant observation my focus was on attitudes to creativity and perceptions of rules to regulate that creativity. This was most easily explored through interviews where questions could be asked and further details sought. For example, if I was to see a writer 'lining' (crossing out) someone's work that would not be enough for me to understand why they thought that action was appropriate. This is not to say that I did not attempt other means of immersion, as this chapter will go on to show, especially through the simple act of moving through the city and looking at spaces 'like a graffiti writer'[20] and observing graffiti writing in spots where it is allowed and at graffiti exhibitions and events. From time to time, I experienced feelings of paranoia similar to those described by Macdonald that the process of fieldwork would place participants in danger by somehow bringing them to the attention of the authorities.[21] This was perhaps more a reflection of the internalisation of the subculture's concerns. At the same time, in a similar experience to Gauthier, I felt safe during fieldwork.[22] That such a point ought to be made perhaps owes more to the public perception of graffiti writers as 'destructive',[23] as Gauthier puts it, than any realistic assessment of danger.

Choice of Research Methodology

The empirical research methodology that underpins the exploration of the graffiti subculture in this book is a qualitative research methodology. This methodology, and specifically the use of semi-structured interviews was chosen because it provided the best opportunity to let graffiti writers speak in their own words (and therefore share things I would not know to ask about) but also to direct attention to areas of graffiti creativity that are unexplored in existing studies and other sources on graffiti. This is why, for instance, a content analysis of texts and documents, perhaps also the graffiti writing itself on walls,[24] while useful, would not allow me

[20] This included cycling and walking around London, especially East London, throughout the fieldwork and a field trip to Berlin in May 2010.

[21] Macdonald (n 4) 54–55.

[22] L Gauthier, 'Confessions of an Ethnographer: Reflections on Fieldwork with Graffiti Writers in Montreal' (2001) 43(2) *Anthropologica* 273, 274.

[23] ibid.

[24] For an example of a content analysis including walls, albeit in relation to stencil art, see A Philipps and R Richter, 'Visual Content Analysis of Stencil Graffiti: Employing Street Reading for the Study of Stenciling' (2012) 1 *Visual Methodologies* 1.

directly to address issues regarding attitudes to copying in the subculture. While the supplementary sources, such as interviews with writers in magazines, indicate that biting (copying) is a concern and may provide information about reasons for the prohibition of biting it does not have the dynamism of a semi-structured interview that allows for follow-up questions to probe these issues in depth.

Data Gathering

I began setting the foundations for my fieldwork in November 2009 by beginning to immerse myself in the graffiti culture immediately available to me, specifically that of East London by, for example, attending exhibitions of street art and/or graffiti-related art in Shoreditch. I sought and received ethical approval for my research from King's College London in April 2010. Reading about fieldwork methodology was useful to an extent in preparing for fieldwork but I quickly found that the 'just do it' model[25] presents the most realistic approximation of what it is like to be in the field. The suggestion is not to enter the field in some way recklessly but rather to be open to the possibilities it offers when engaging in 'observation, interviewing and documentary analysis'.[26] This is not to suggest that the literature on undertaking fieldwork was not helpful. Fieldwork, especially where access is sought into an illegal subculture, is necessarily a little fraught[27] and the ethnographic literature, which places the researcher's experience at the centre of the fieldwork, was particularly useful because it encouraged a reflective approach to the research.[28] I found myself re-working my semi-structured interview questions, my modes of seeking interviews, discussing my findings in conversation with participants and further refining what to look out for. In my approach to fieldwork overall, I was interested in hearing about graffiti writers' and street artists' approach to their creativity but not to encourage engagement in street art and graffiti writing.

My fieldwork, as the ensuing discussion shows, relied on interviews and the gathering of documentary sources in particular. The interviews (either recorded and transcribed or recorded via notes taken during the interview) were complemented by experiences during the fieldwork. The latter include informal conversations, attendance at events, the process of gathering graffiti sources, and observations of where and what kind of graffiti and street art was to be found on the street or on tracksides, especially in the course of commuting by bike, going for a run, etc. The data discussed in the subsequent empirical chapters—specifically the quotations from research participants in the form 'Anon1', 'Anon2', etc—was

[25] M Punch, 'Politics and Ethics of Qualitative Research' in NK Denzin and YS Lincoln (eds), *Handbook of Qualitative Research* (Thousand Oaks, Sage, 1994) 83.

[26] ibid 84.

[27] Ferrell (n 6) 159.

[28] 'Just do it by all means, but think about it first': Punch (n 25) 95.

sourced from the recorded and transcribed semi-structured interviews. Where this is not the case a note indicates that the quotation has come from my field notes. It specifies the nature of the data for example, an informal conversation or from some other source, such as a comment made at a public lecture by an audience member.

This part reflects on the setting, participants, interviews and secondary sources. The process of doing fieldwork was a mixture of disappointment (not getting an interview) and elation (after an interview). I also learned very quickly that I was not going to fit in and there was little point in trying to be other than an engaged, sympathetic outsider. Indeed, I took Becker's argument that researchers ought to pick a side to heart.[29] This was not difficult—my sympathies were already engaged with graffiti writers—but in any case a commitment to graffiti writing as a valid urban practice throughout my fieldwork made the fieldwork easier and more enjoyable. As a corollary, if I was going to study an alternative normative framework for regulating creativity, it was imperative to take the creators of these works seriously.

Becker also argues, in the context of studying deviance, that since 'balance' is not possible, researchers ought to pick a side in accordance with their political commitments; they must also use their 'theoretical and technical resources to avoid the distortions'[30] that might occur because of this. The conscious decision to 'take sides' in a sense is merely the formal acknowledgment that values are embedded in all stages of the research process.[31] Choosing to explore graffiti writing from the graffiti writers' point of view does not mean that this engagement was undertaken uncritically and without an awareness of the particular strengths and weaknesses of using a qualitative research methodology, as the remainder of this chapter shows.

Setting

The setting for the fieldwork was, for the most part, London in terms of preparation and the continued observation of graffiti in public space, including halls of fame. Some fieldwork was undertaken in other places (including a field trip to Berlin in May 2010)[32] and some of the potential participants were from abroad or other UK cities. The setting is best understood not only as a physical space but rather, as graffiti writers themselves understand it, as the 'scene'. Certainly, this is related to geography since, as later chapters will show, different behaviour is

[29] HS Becker, 'Whose Side Are We On?' (1967) 14 *Social Problems* 239.

[30] ibid 247.

[31] T May, *Social Research: Issues, Methods and Process* (Maidenhead, Open University Press, 2001) 56.

[32] This included mapping of graffiti and street art in a Kreuzberg street. It was a rudimentary form of 'taking a walk' as described in: A Philippopoulos-Mihalopoulos, 'Mapping the Lawscape: Spatial Law and the Body' (2012) University of Westminster Working Paper No 12-06, www.papers.ssrn.com/sol3/papers.cfm?abstract_id=2041210.

expected or tolerated depending on where it takes place. The scene is the 'where' of my fieldwork. Finding graffiti writers to interview required me to understand the scene in order to find a way to access a community that is at once spectacularly visible (through tags and other works) and yet hidden from view.

The growing interest in graffiti, and especially street art, at the time of my fieldwork meant that I was lucky in being able to attend street art exhibitions, take graffiti and street art tours in London and spend an inordinate amount of time looking at graffiti and street art on flickr[33] and dedicated blogs. Following certain blogs in turn meant that I found out about yet more events, especially those advertising 'live painting'.[34] The relatively recent rise in the popularity of street art also presented a problem, however: the data I gathered had to be split according to whether I spoke to a graffiti writer or a street artist (noting, again, that the boundaries between graffiti writing and street art are blurred). It was not until I was several interviews into my fieldwork that I realised how wide the gulf was, and the ways in which participants managed to variously ignore, intensify or bridge that gap.

Although this was not true of all writers and certainly not of all participants interviewed, there was a sense that the scene is and ought to be all-consuming. Indeed, knowledge of and commitment to the scene is one of the fundamental differences between graffiti writers and street artists. It is street artists' lack of knowledge and a sense that street artists—who do not appear to belong to a 'scene' in the same way—are both trespassing on the physical setting for graffiti as well as on the 'scene' (eg by failing to show due respect to prominent graffiti writers) that forms one of the obstacles to the functioning of the graffiti rules.

The experience of observing writers at, for example, the graffiti competition 'Battle of Waterloo' in Leake Street (the Waterloo graffiti tunnel) in London in August 2011, helped me to understand not just the scene but to appreciate the physical aspects of writing in a particular space. As my early experience of observing (legal) graffiti writing showed:

> [The writer] spotted me and beckoned from a cafe on the street and I waited until he finished eating then we went over to the wall. Another writer was rolling a cigarette since he had arrived first and sprayed the bottom left corner of the wall. The third writer was busy up a ladder making a character and another was working on his section—as he later put it—of free style letters. At the end of the day he said he didn't like the style and would come back to fix it tomorrow. [He] told him that he was very particular.
>
> …
>
> Aerosol spray paint hurt my eyes even as I admired the way wisps of yellow paint flew from the wall as the other writer made outlines. My head hurts a bit but I don't know whether I can blame that on the spray paint.

[33] The photo-sharing site found at www.flickr.com.

[34] 'Live painting' usually referred to street artists painting legally during an art or music event but I also attended live graffiti writing events eg 'Meeting of Styles' in London in October 2011.

> It started raining fairly heavily towards the end and the paint started to drip.
>
> There is a lot to be said for observation. Yes, it helps a researcher understand the research subject as more than a subject of study but rather an equal—or more correctly perhaps—the researcher's teacher. All of which is to say that using a spraycan is much harder than it looks. (field notes 2010)

Attempts to tag along were gently rebuffed (my favourite reason being 'I don't take civilians'). Sometimes, when I was able to observe legal writing these excursions would lead to writers and artists agreeing to be interviewed, though as the next section shows, this was only part of the challenge.

Participants

Although I came into contact and spoke informally to a number potential participants (mostly graffiti writers) without taking notes, I interviewed 29 graffiti writers and/or street artists all of whom were adults. This section considers some of the difficulties faced in finding people to interview and provides commentary on the profile of participants formally interviewed. Based on self-identification, 21 writers, six street artists (identifications sometimes overlapped) and three others (unaligned) were interviewed. As discussed in chapter one, these categories are, however, less clear-cut than they appear. Within the graffiti subculture writers sometimes also divided themselves along creative lines as either new school or old school. A disproportionate number of potential participants appeared to be in their mid- to late twenties or thirties and therefore my sample was not necessarily representative of the 'younger generation' to which some writers referred to in interviews in exasperation at their perceived lack of respect. Another issue raised by the fieldwork was that, having interviewed only men, I did not account for gender, ethnicity, sexuality or class[35] in the data gathering and analysis which would have produced potentially different insights into the regulation of creativity.[36]

Attempts to speak to writers and street artists occurred on the street, at graffiti events, gallery openings and some social gatherings. For example, I attended a gathering of graffiti writers a contact had told me about. I arrived wearing jeans and an oversized hoodie. I would have worn this anyway (I was on my way home from the gym) but I thought it would help me to fit in. It did not. The second or third person I spoke to asked, I think partly in jest, 'Are you wearing a wire?' Explaining my project in terms that made it clear that I was interested in graffiti writing and what graffiti writers think, however, helped.[37] For example I would

[35] For helpful reflections on these points see Macdonald (n 4) 45–47.

[36] Macdonald interviewed men and women engaged in graffiti writing. One of the insights gained from this was the characterisation of graffiti writing as 'men's work': ibid 98–101.

[37] Similarly, in an attempt to put research participants at ease during the semi-structured interviews I was happy to share my own (usually positive) responses to graffiti writing.

explain that I was not interested in writing about graffiti in the way it is so often portrayed in the media as simply 'mindless vandalism'. More often than not it helped to have a conversation at the end of which I would suggest sitting down for a longer chat but this was not a guarantee that we would end up speaking. The rare occasions when I simply sidled up to a writer on the street who was taking a break from piecing and started a conversation were similarly hit and miss. On occasion, the fact that I was from King's was an asset since it was an institution that people had heard of and this seemed to make me trustworthy.

I recall attending a graffiti book launch attended almost exclusively by young men with blackbooks, writing tags and making stylistic comparisons. My field observations, including attending events, provided valuable background and context to graffiti writing. Interestingly, Snyder carried a blackbook with him when undertaking fieldwork and encouraged writers he met to write in it.[38] They were not asked to write their tags but rather to reproduce words (such as 'style', 'bomb', 'respect') in their own style.[39] This helped Snyder to start conversations with writers. My experience was different. Although some writers would quickly and expertly execute a tag before me I never asked them to do so especially after I began noticing that some writers would deliberately use their left hand to write normally (ie not in graffiti style). This, I guessed, appeared to arise out of a concern that their unique name and style would be traced back to them.

Finding people to interview was challenging though not nearly as difficult as asking people to take the time to sit down and talk once I had found them. Even so, after re-reading Macdonald's[40] account on undertaking fieldwork in the same scene (London) 10 years earlier, I understood the extent to which I was privileged in gaining any access to the subculture. It helped that, like Macdonald, I was a woman and an outsider though I undertook the fieldwork in my late as opposed to early twenties. Being a woman helped insofar as it made me an outsider[41] and allowed me truthfully to present myself as the person I was: a researcher hoping to understand a different world to mine. Like Macdonald I relied on successive access[42] and occasionally this placed me in contact with people I would not otherwise have been able to speak to. Face to face contact with a potential participant, whether or not mediated by someone else, was on the whole the best strategy for gaining an interview because I was able to speak to the person and explain who I was and why I would like to interview them. The selection of participants in this way poses particular problems that are indicative of a more general difficulty in undertaking systematic research.[43] As one writer I interviewed put it, 'The

[38] GJ Snyder, *Graffiti Lives: Beyond the Tag in New York's Urban Underground* (New York and London, New York University Press, 2009) 13–16.

[39] ibid 14.

[40] Macdonald (n 4).

[41] Noting that being a woman made her an 'outsider [who] represented a safe audience': ibid 61.

[42] ibid 55.

[43] See JC Johnson, *Selecting Ethnographic Informants* (Newbury Park, SAGE, 1990) 11.

more graffiti writers you talk to the less street artists you'll come into contact with [chuckles]' (Anon5). This was exactly right.

Moreover, I tried harder to find writers because I was so interested in what I was hearing. As my fieldwork progressed I found my focus shifted from attempting to interview anyone writing or painting on the street to a more focused attempt to pierce the layers of the subculture. My aim was to meet the graffiti writers who were constantly 'up' by writing in highly visible, dangerous places: train writers and the key figures whose tags I saw everywhere and whose names kept coming up in conversation. My enthusiasm for meeting purist graffiti writers[44] is evident in this extract from my field notes (2010):

> I don't ask who the top writer is but I bet he means [tag]. I am continually amazed by his audacity. He gets up, gets white washed, gets up again. And not just walls. Railway bridges. Underpasses. Impossible places.

Of course, speaking to purist graffiti writers, train writers and kings was largely impossible. As much as graffiti writers may be motivated by fame and respect this did not extend to talking to a doctoral student. This was in itself interesting. A core of purist writers exist within the community who do not seek publicity of any kind but merely let their tags speak for them. Indeed, several writers told me that the purists would not be interested in speaking to me. The participants I did speak to were clearly passionate about writing and/or street art, sometimes seeking to justify the practice but more often explaining things to an outsider (me) that would be obvious to those in the scene. As one writer put it, echoing a number of others: 'most graffiti writers love to talk about graffiti' (Anon11).

Taking advantage of any opportunities that arise but also adjusting to disappointment are hallmarks of fieldwork.[45] Undertaking interviews was more often than not an exhilarating experience. A good interview resulted in feelings of elation. The periods in between made fieldwork difficult. It was hard to plan, and even when plans were made there was no guarantee that an interview would actually take place. Many interviews were arranged but repeatedly postponed so that they were de facto cancelled. Although I met many more graffiti writers and street artists than agreed to be interviewed they were for the most part willing to speak about their passion for their writing/art. In fact, those I interviewed were broadly supportive of my aims summed up neatly in my explanation that I wanted 'to show that graffiti isn't mindless vandalism'. Such statements were made in the context of being clear that I was interested in how graffiti writers experienced graffiti creativity rather than having views about their creativity imposed upon them, but

[44] A 'purist' graffiti writer is defined here—based on my impressions during fieldwork and from the secondary sources gathered—as someone who exclusively writes letters, prizes train writing and is not inclined to seek publicity beyond the writing of their name. In the context of this chapter, the label 'purist' also refers to the deeply committed writer who is not interested in discussing graffiti writing with outsiders.

[45] P Schmidt and S Halliday, 'Introduction: Beyond Methods—Law and Society in Action' in S Halliday and P Schmidt (eds), *Conducting Law and Society Research: Reflections on Methods and Practices* (Cambridge, Cambridge University Press, 2009) 2.

also that I was not concerned with the specifics of what they did or would do. This also allowed me to demonstrate my knowledge of graffiti writing (this point is discussed further in the next section) and so demonstrate my seriousness in approaching the topic. Nonetheless, a couple of writers, prior to agreeing to an interview wished to see a summary of my doctoral thesis which I duly provided. Indeed, this broad summary came into being as I began to speak to more graffiti writers and began to hypothesise that the regulation of creativity within the graffiti subculture was an example of regulation within copyright's 'negative space'.[46]

Interviews

Choosing 'sides' does not mean that the fieldwork was biased. Legal scholarship in general demands a 'reflective open mindedness'[47] and this is a good principle for fieldwork generally. The ability to be open-minded and reflective was thus one of the reasons for choosing a qualitative approach and semi-structured interviews during which participants could tell me that my assumptions or conclusions were wrong. Feldman gives the example of Rawls' adoption of 'reflective equilibrium' which means thinking about a subject, in this instance graffiti, while 'constantly re-assessing the assumptions from which the train of thought began'.[48] The process of reflection carries on then from the fieldwork itself to the analysis of the subsequent data as the next part of this chapter examines. The analysis in the subsequent empirical chapters of the regulation of creativity through the graffiti rules thus highlights both general findings and the nuances and contradictions of participants' responses.

I conducted interviews between half an hour to two hours in length (four of the interviews had two participants). Given the difficulties relating to both self-identification and the subcultural nature of the practice, it is unclear what the size of the London graffiti scene is[49] and therefore to gauge the appropriateness of my sample. While this is a relatively small sample compared to some empirical studies[50] it is typical for studies of graffiti writing and street art given the difficulties of access already described: the empirical study by Macdonald, for example was based on 29 interviews, including 13 with graffiti writers from London.[51] Unsurprisingly, the difficulties of access made the supplementary material

[46] See chapter two.

[47] Feldman (n 1) 503.

[48] ibid.

[49] The picture is further complicated—and indeed this is also relevant to the fieldwork under discussion here—because graffiti writers visit other cities to write. The numbers of 'active' graffiti writers are thus likely to be in flux and I have been unable to locate useful figures in official and unofficial sources alike. *London Handstyles* (no date) says it is 'rumoured' to be over 1,000 (no page number).

[50] eg an empirical study of the miners' strike was based on 101 interviews including 51 picketing strikers: P Green, *The Enemy Without: Policing and Class Consciousness in the Miner's Strike* (Milton Keynes, Open University Press, 1990) 205.

[51] Macdonald (n 4) 50–51.

collected highly valuable not only in the sense of providing additional material on which to base the ensuing analysis but also to account for any bias arising from the selection of research participants. Furthermore, as the discussion in chapter one indicated, it is difficult to draw a clear boundary between graffiti writing and street art and research participants identified as either writers or street artists but sometimes a combination of both, or, were not necessarily interested in being classified as either street artists or graffiti writers. Nonetheless, the empirical data discussed here focuses largely on those self-identifying as writers and focuses on practices that are constitutive of the subculture such as writing letters, recognising the graffiti rules, or adopting a graffiti writing sensibility.

In undertaking the interviews I was alert to the need for anonymity. Van Maanen writing on ethnography, though the observation also applies here, argues that ethnography 'carries serious moral and intellectual responsibilities'.[52] Consent was sought in accordance with direction from the King's research ethics committee and most of the interviews were conducted anonymously or semi-anonymously through pseudonyms or fake tags rather than real names. This avoided the concern that a potential disclosure might be damaging because I was careful not to ask for identifying details such as tags, particular places or times at which writing occurred, nor did I enquire whether writing would be engaged with in the future. I thus avoided the 'ethical danger'[53] inherent in undertaking work that might potentially be of interest to the authorities. The majority of interviews were recorded on a voice recorder while I took notes of others depending on what a participant was comfortable with. The original recordings were destroyed after transcription and the transcripts themselves were further anonymised via the appellations in the manner of 'Anon[number]' and to remove potentially identifying details and also subsequently destroyed. This approach was taken to avoid the danger identified in existing studies of illegal activities with respect to the potential disclosure of field notes and transcripts to the authorities if required by court order.[54]

The interviews, in keeping with a qualitative methodology, were semi-structured. This was a useful approach because it allowed for flexibility in asking questions and openness to new data. It allowed for unexpected discoveries, for example of the importance of photographing the finished work on the wall which carries implications for how graffiti writers and street artists conceive of the nature of graffiti works overall. More often than not the questions were answered or insights gained without direct questions but instead evolved from the interviews themselves. The interviews often flowed more like conversations rather than following a strict researcher/participant script.

[52] J Van Maanen, *Tales of the Field: On Writing Ethnography* (Chicago, The University of Chicago Press, 1988) 1.

[53] G Lee-Treweek and S Linkogle, 'Putting Danger in the Frame' in G Lee-Treweek and S Linkogle (eds), *Danger in the Field: Risk and Ethics in Social Research* (London, Routledge, 2000) 18–19.

[54] On the legal and ethical implications of observing illegal behaviour and/or the disclosure of illegal behaviour by participants see D Feenan, 'Legal Issues in Acquiring Information about Illegal Behaviour Through Criminological Research' (2002) 42(4) *British Journal of Criminology* 762.

A recurring and enriching aspect of the interview process (though this also applies to informal conversations) was its reflexivity and inclusivity. Conducting an inclusionary form of fieldwork meant that participants were involved in arguments over whether graffiti rules existed or not and I encouraged participants to reflect on practices they took for granted. Indeed, the reflexive nature of the fieldwork often blurred the boundaries between data gathering and analysis as participants discussed not only their own experience but engaged with questions over what their experience might mean in the context of the scene as a whole and for my thesis. These 'metamoments' in which participants wondered and commented on the aims of my research[55] made them active participants in the research.

Trust played a crucial role in the fieldwork[56] in terms of explaining who I was, what work I was doing and why. I also showed my knowledge of graffiti in the later interviews to help build rapport and break down the barrier between researcher and participant. For instance, I became enthusiastic about the stylistic qualities of tags. At the beginning of my research I was appreciative though not particularly enthusiastic about them. That my position changed was illustrated by the following exchange:

Anon27	You're the only person [non-writer] I've ever met who likes tags.
M	Really, they make me feel better when I walk down the street actually.
Anon27	Wow, most people say I feel scared, I feel like I'm going to be raped, I feel like I'm going to be mugged, it doesn't feel safe, it brings houses prices down. The broken windows theory.
M	Yeah I know, which I think is a bit of a load, it's the exact opposite feeling for me because it's almost like I can imagine someone standing there.

Although sincere, this approach did not necessarily impress. As one writer challenged me: 'but would you want to meet them?'

I usually began with the same question 'How would you identify yourself, as a graffiti writer, a street artist …?' After that, graffiti writers in particular would often answer my questions before I asked them. Rules and codes, particularly the prohibition against copying, would come up in conversation naturally and so I was in a position to ask follow-up questions. Data-wise this was extremely useful. Yet it was also a problem when data analysis suggested questions I ought to have asked but had not. A particular problem occurred around asking questions about crews and how they collaborate to create pieces. By focusing on the process of creating the work I sometimes neglected important follow-up questions during the interview, for example about the significance of one person directing the process

[55] On metamoments and the impact on ethics and data analysis see SM Carter, CFC Jordens, C McGrath and M Little, 'You Have to Make Something of All that Rubbish, Do You? An Empirical Investigation of the Social Process of Qualitative Research' (2008) 18 *Qualitative Health Research* 9, 1264–76.

[56] As in eg Gauthier (n 22).

of creating the work, the ownership of the finished work and what it meant when writers put up the tags of writers who did not help to create the piece.

None of this is to say I became anti-street art in my attempts to court graffiti writers. Rather my early interviews with graffiti writes fostered a deep fascination with graffiti writing. This meant that I emphasised certain questions over others. For the most part participants were very open about their love of graffiti and their opinions about what mattered to them such as style, respect and the way the internet was changing the practice of writing. At the same time many of the participants were careful to preface their view with statements such as 'this is just my opinion'. As one writer put it, 'I don't know how you're going to do this, everyone's got different opinions on all of it' (Anon28). My response in the interview as with my approach to analysing the interview data (discussed in more detail below) was to acknowledge that while many participants were careful not to speak for other writers or street artists that I was being told 'roughly the same thing' by everyone. Common themes and concerns emerged from the interviews.

More importantly, perhaps, the process of interviewing had a positive impact on some of the participants because it gave them an opportunity to reflect on rules and practices. As one participant said:

> Sometimes, it's weird talking about graffiti because it's … I've thought about it a lot intellectually but it's quite hard to talk about it intellectually because it's quite simple really. (Anon12)[57]

By contrast, in response to an explanation of how crews work:

M	That's really interesting. I'm getting the sense that what at first glance is quite simple is actually incredibly complex and I want to know what these bits and pieces are.
Anon5	I don't even get it.
Anon6	[I]t's quite interesting talking to you about it because quite often a lot of the things you don't necessarily think about why they are. You['re] just kind of: 'it is'.
Anon5	The more you think about it, the more you talk about it the more confusing they are.

Others commented on the usefulness of my work and the need to 'theorise' graffiti (eg Anon13, Anon14) when I explained that I would not be publishing the interviews themselves but rather using them in my analysis.

The point made in the quotation at the start of this chapter that 'everyone's got different opinions' (Anon28), was reiterated by many participants. All of the participants grappled to some extent with how their creativity was regulated, to look behind the fun and danger to see why writers acted in particular way. For

[57] A similar response was given by Anon27.

instance, statements questioning the importance of the graffiti rules were made in the context of reflection over what it means to be a writer. Participants often recognised the contradictions in their answers or thought critically about their practices. In response to a question about what places are unsuitable for writing one participant responded:

> [Y]ou've asked me if there's anything I wouldn't paint but off the cuff I can't think… Like but I've blatantly hundreds of thousands of times, I've looked at something and thought 'no, you can't paint that'. (Anon12)

Such engagement with the questions was made possible by the semi-structured nature of the interviews which presented opportunities to find unsought but pertinent information. It also offered challenges by requiring interesting information to be sifted out because it was only marginally relevant to the question of how graffiti writers regulate their creativity. In order to allow participants to speak freely and give their own opinions I avoided commenting on the politics within the subculture. This showed participants that their opinions mattered and were not being coloured by the opinions of others. A common question I received was who else I was talking to and my standard response was 'not as many people as I'd like'.

It is difficult to state with any precision when saturation was reached since the recurring themes, such as the concern with copying, style and respect emerged as a pattern a third of the way through conducting the interviews. By the final interview I had begun to anticipate many of the answers and observations made. Yet the differences in emphasis and detail suggest that a wide-ranging study that took into account both graffiti writing and its factions vis-a-vis street art would require further interviews to account for differences between the groups.[58] Such a study of the sociological factors accounting for the differences in opinion is a potential avenue for future research. In this book, however, the focus is specifically on the parallels between the copyright rules and graffiti rules in regulating creativity. This came to be the focus of my research around the time of saturation as a certain consistency in the responses started to emerge that pointed to the existence of rules within the subculture that regulated creativity. In particular, I had expected to acquire data about the regulation of space—and I did, with respect to placement—but as I discovered, placement was only part of the picture; there was the rule against biting for starters.

Supplementary Sources

I gathered data from a variety of sources on graffiti both at the start of, and during, my fieldwork to provide necessary background and context. Documents may

[58] An example of a wide-ranging study of street art across numerous cities is to be found in Young (n 8).

on their own be an important source of data and include any written text.[59] The supplementary sources referred to here are those used to enrich and validate the data gathered through interviews. The supplementary sources were also valuable in helping to correct for any bias arising out of my making my sympathies and interest in graffiti writing clear to research participants and also to account for any bias arising out of the selection of research participants. However, any data gathered on graffiti writing, will only ever present a snapshot of an evolving subculture (notwithstanding evident continuity of concerns over time, and across national boundaries, about copying and style for example as indicated by the discussion of graffiti history and the transplant of graffiti culture in chapter one).

As indicated above, the number of interviews, while representing a good sample of graffiti writers and street artists given the difficulties of access described, was relatively low by social science research standards. Thus secondary sources were used to access accounts of graffiti writing from the kinds of participants who were otherwise inaccessible (eg because they are purists, very famous or live abroad) but also, crucially, to confirm my findings through interviews. Indeed I have often found almost exactly the same language being used to describe similar concerns especially with respect to style. Yet what I also frequently found was that I was asking questions that simply were not being asked in blog or graffiti magazine interviews especially those related to copyright law. Since many participants interviewed assumed that copyright law did not apply to works in public/works painted illegally,[60] it is not surprising that views on copyright are not evidenced in the supplementary sources.

The secondary sources used as additional data and for validation were of three types. The first type, as indicated in the first chapter, consisted of historical accounts of graffiti especially those sources that were referred to by graffiti writers themselves as influential. *Subway Art*,[61] which several participants referred to as 'the bible' of graffiti (eg Anon28), is a case in point. The other crucial texts include *Spraycan Art*[62] as well as the documentary *Style Wars*.[63] These texts are important both as sources of the graffiti rules, especially given the reverence some writers expressed in interviews for this period in graffiti history. For example, when the New York trains were not cleaned there was not enough space for everyone meaning that adherence to a hierarchy of style[64] dictating what kind of work could go over another was important. Given there is no such constraint now, these texts were also used by writers to explain why some rules were less relevant today—such

[59] May (n 31) 178.

[60] But see chapter ten, suggesting the position is more complex.

[61] M Cooper and H Chalfant, *Subway Art* (London, Thames & Hudson, 1984).

[62] H Chalfant and J Prigoff, *Spraycan Art: Henry Chalfant & James Prigoff* (London, Thames & Hudson, 1987).

[63] T Silver and H Chalfant, *Style Wars*, Public Art Films, 2007 (released 1983).

[64] Loosely refers to the rule that a throw-up goes over a tag, a piece goes over a throw-up: see chapter nine.

as 'not going over'—because the practices in 1970s and' 80s New York that gave rise to the graffiti rules were specific to that time and place.

The second type consists primarily of books written about graffiti both of a scholarly nature (especially *Crimes of Style*,[65] *The Graffiti Subculture*)[66] as well as more popular accounts (eg *Beyond the Street*,[67] *Bomb the Suburbs*)[68] and books in-between (eg *Graffiti Lives*).[69] Books written by and/or about graffiti writers and street artists were also a significant source of information. For example, *All City-Writers*[70] proved to be a treasure trove of information on the worldwide evolution of graffiti writing. I also collected numerous coffee table books which chronicled the work of particular artists and the art in other cities through photographs.[71] Many of these books contained transcripts of interviews with writers and street artists—Rahn's *Painting Without Permission*[72] is a good example—which functioned akin to primary data. Data gained in this way has to be treated with caution especially since the questions asked in these interviews were different to my own and asked in a different context both in terms of place and time. Nevertheless, books were a valuable source of information.

The third source consisted of media directed at graffiti writers and to a lesser extent street artists. This material was gathered intensively for 19 months to February 2012 and intermittently after that time. It included magazines (including *Bomb Alert, Keeping the Faith, Not Guilty*), blogs (including UK graffiti blogs *Hurt You Bad, The London Vandal*), online forums such as *12oz prophet*, flickr[73] and the website artcrimes.org. Some content specific blogs such as *Original y Copya* (a blog posting examples of similar graffiti works next to each other and asking whether they are examples of biting) were also used. Most importantly, and apart from commentary by participants on their own practice, these additional sources gave me a window into the more self-referential aspects of graffiti writing. Graffiti DVDs made specifically with graffiti writers as an audience captured the excitement and danger associated with painting trains. The film *70 k*.[74] (about a crew of Melbourne train writers) is an example.

I gathered data from these secondary sources primarily by subscribing to the RSS feeds of approximately 15 graffiti and street art blogs (including those listed

[65] Ferrell (n 6).

[66] Macdonald (n 4).

[67] P Nguyen and S Mackenzie (eds), *Beyond the Street: The 100 Leading Figures in Urban Art* (Berlin, Gestalten, 2010).

[68] WU Wimsatt, *Bomb the Suburbs: Graffiti, Race, Freight-Hopping and the Search for Hip-Hop's Moral Centre* (Berkeley, CA, Soft Skull Press, 2008).

[69] Snyder (n 38).

[70] A Caputo (ed), *All City Writers* (Bagnolet, France, Kitchen93, 2009).

[71] eg A Grunhauser, *Smash137: Smash Proof* (Berlin, From Here to Fame Publishing, 2009).

[72] J Rahn, *Painting Without Permission: Hip-Hop Graffiti Subculture* (Westport CT, Bergin & Garvey, 2002).

[73] This site was used to search for photographs of works by specific writers I had become aware of on walls during the course of my fieldwork and to consider the comments left on particular pieces.

[74] tksom. *70k* (no date).

above). Posts referencing 'rules', biting and similar concepts, posts containing interviews with writers and posts containing photographs of the consequences of rule-breaking (eg going over) or photographs of different types of works and in different places (eg pieces on trains) were identified and stored electronically. Reading these texts for evidence of how creativity is regulated at the same time as undertaking fieldwork provided an important 'insider' perspective.[75] Sometimes the sentiments (eg on style or biting or motivations for writing) were expressed using exactly the same words. Of course the supplementary data often made very clear that my particular pursuit of the rules of subcultural creativity was, to an extent, esoteric. The overwhelming feeling pulsating through the sources was the pure commitment to the practice and joy of graffiti writing and/or street art rather than a concern with 'rules'.

I was warned about relying on certain blogs and forums by some graffiti writers as being less useful because they were generally concerned with the politics of the subculture rather than the substantial questions that I was asking about creativity. One graffiti writer cautioned me about using material found on the internet:

> I mean it's the internet so everybody's anonymous and you can't take anything as given … [O]pen internet chat on graffiti is often bogus and riddled with lies and people's own agenda. It's the personal chat that happens through MSN, facebook and flickr that's really important. (Anon11)

Thus the field observation—for example, attending public events, informal meetings and socialising—was essential in providing a fuller and more authentic insight into street art and graffiti writing culture(s).

Data Analysis

This book adopts a grounded theory approach[76] insofar as the qualitative data gathered is analysed in order to reveal the structure of how creativity is protected in the graffiti subculture. This is not to say that a theory is absent from the beginning of the process of fieldwork and analysis since the groundwork for the fieldwork suggested the existence of some rule-creation and adherence amongst graffiti writers. The theoretical framework is more than 'the container into which the data must be poured'.[77] That new norms or ways of thinking about creativity were revealed by the data gathered (eg the relevance of photographs) while confirming the existence of some expected norms (eg the prohibition against biting/copying) suggests that this approach worked well. It provides for the flexibility

[75] A similar point on 'insider media' is made by Macdonald (n 4) 54.

[76] See generally Cresswell (n 5) 64–65.

[77] Lather in ibid 65.

to discover new concepts while providing additional details for concepts whose discovery was expected.

The analysis of the data has allowed me to generalise that graffiti writers adopt a set of norms that serve to informally regulate the practice of writing. In undertaking qualitative research, the generalisations made about the regulation of creativity within the subculture are based on an implicit understanding that the project I undertook in analysing the data presented neither a rejection of the possibility of generalisation nor a desire to totalise the experience of graffiti writers.[78] The generalisations presented in this book are better understood as being akin to 'moderatum generalizations' that are specific to a certain time and culture and subject to change.[79] These generalisations

> resemble the modest, pragmatic generalizations drawn from personal experience which, by bringing a semblance of order and consistency to social interaction, make everyday life possible.[80]

The caveat made earlier in the chapter stands: the concepts and themes drawn out of the empirical data are bounded by the limitations of the data gathered. Any generalisations about how creativity is regulated through the adoption of informal rules remain tied to the time, setting, participants interviewed and supplementary material obtained.

In reading the interview data I identified numerous themes and, within them, categories that captured the participants concerns, attitudes, explanations and reflection on their creativity. One of the crucial themes to emerge from the data was the reference to rules or norms (coded R). This theme linked, to varying degrees, with other themes of which the nature and experience of the graffiti subculture (coded G), creativity (coded C), and, space (coded S) were especially prominent. The insights gained from the interplay of these themes and their individual categories produce a complex picture of the regulation of creativity within the graffiti subculture.

The data were coded according to a set of four categories based on the themes of subculture, creativity, space and rules that emerged from the data. A code may be defined as a term or concept, the collection of which becomes a category or theme. The process of coding data includes 'raising questions and giving provisional answers (hypotheses) about categories and their relations'.[81] An example from my data would be the way concepts related to both creativity and rules are transformed by their relationship to space. Indeed, the sum of the coding revealed the emergence of a number of themes identified in chapter two and discussed in subsequent chapters such as the privatisation of space, creativity, movement and

[78] On 'interpretive sociology' versus 'total or axiomatic generalizations': G Payne, 'Generalization in Qualitative Research' (2005) 39(2) *Sociology* 295, 296.

[79] ibid 297.

[80] ibid.

[81] Strauss in May (n 31) 138.

pleasure, and the relevance of the graffiti rules to belonging within the graffiti subculture.

A preliminary table of themes was created after reading but prior to the coding of the data and the table and coding was refined through the process. The interview data were also re-read for specific relationships between categories in order to place them into particular chapters. The initial process of analysis involved manually coding nearly 400 pages (approximately 210,000 words) of hard copy interview transcripts with underlining using coloured pencils to make the themes readily identifiable. The code for each category was noted in the right hand column of each page. The following is an indicative list of the categories identified under each theme:

History G-HIS
Internal structure G-STR
Fame/respect G-RES/R-RES

Creativity and style C-STY
Motivation and incentives C-MOT
Personality C-PER
Identification C-ID
Appropriation and borrowing C-APP
Exploitation and commercialisation C-EXP
Attitude to protection C-PR
Documentation C-DOC

Perceptions of property S-PR
Perceptions of the public/private distinction S-P/PR
Justifications for writing practice (placement) S-JUS
Territoriality S-TER

Rules and their perception R-PR
Originality R-ORG
Collaboration R-COL
Consequences of breaches R-CON
Destruction of work R-GO
Sources R-SO
Learning and ignorance R-LRN
Skill R-SK

Where the data indicated that there was an interaction between the categories the relationship of one code to another was also noted on the page. For example acceptability of copying in light of the distinction between public and private property: R-COP—S-P/PR. Another example was the recurrence of the relationship between the category motivation/incentives (C-MOT) and identification (C-ID) were often linked to concerns over originality (R-ORG). Quotations that were particularly clear in exemplifying a theme and/or category were also identified. Thus 'rules and their perception' (R-PER) was used as a code for analysing the interview data in ration to graffiti writers understanding of, if and how their creativity was regulated. Comments akin to 'The first rule of graffiti is that there are no rules' (Anon29) might appear to introduce a contradiction in the data, and certainly they serve as a warning not to overstate the efficacy of the graffiti rules.

Yet while there is a difficulty in making generalisations, semi-structured interviews also presented opportunities for the revelation of interesting, reflexive and unsought material such as that related to the importance of documentation and preservation of graffiti culture (eg reference to 'photo culture' discussed in chapter five). This viewpoint was shared by other participants. It produced a new point for analysis: the graffiti work is both the original train panel or wall and the photograph documenting it. This also suggests that the distinction between the original and the copy are blurred. The emphasis on documentation described above gave rise to numerous questions (discussed in the empirical chapters) including: what is a 'work' and how is it defined within the subculture and in copyright law; to what extent does the materiality of an artistic work matter? The significance of the specific code C-DOC lay in revealing that the 'photo culture' amongst graffiti writers not simply a passive archiving of graffiti creativity but rather an integral part of building graffiti culture. The relationships between themes such C-DOC, R-ORG and G-RES produced a grounded theory of how the rules worked which was in turn interpreted[82] as a parallel to copyright rules. Specifically, the final point of analysis of the data was its interpretation in relation to copyright rules.

Conclusion

In this chapter I have discussed the methodology used to gather empirical data in the context of existing empirical research into the graffiti subculture. I also identified the challenges presented in gathering data on a difficult to access group and reflected on the process of undertaking fieldwork. As Sayers states, 'no work of scholarship ever attains a static perfection'.[83] This is perhaps all the more true of graffiti writing and its seemingly simple rules, the reasoning for their adoption and the sanctions for breaking them.

Undertaking fieldwork in the graffiti subculture presented a range of challenges, especially those related to access. Although part of the fieldwork engaged with street art, its more mainstream nature meant that it presented fewer challenges in terms of access, at least in terms of finding out about and attending gallery

[82] See generally on the process of data analysis: Cresswell (n 5) 185.
[83] In Feldman (n 1) 504.

openings and certain events (eg live painting). The fundamental challenge was not, however, one of access but rather perception. The primary and secondary data gathered had to be analysed subject to the same caveat as with any empirical data: the resulting work does not represent an 'immaculate perception'.[84] Certainly my views are coloured to some extent by 'taking sides'. However, the responsibility I feel towards portraying the scene accurately does not necessarily mean portraying it positively. Rather it means letting graffiti writers speak for themselves. The book is thus intended to be empowering, albeit in a small way, by allowing the community to tell its story. This contrasts with dominant legal and political discourses of graffiti writing where graffiti is viewed as a deviant practice and graffiti works as a disease that must be eradicated from the city.[85] The voices of graffiti writers and street artists are largely absent and it is their voices regarding the operation of the graffiti rules as a form of 'copyright' beyond law to which I now turn, contrasting these with the application of copyright law to graffiti creativity.

[84] Van Maanen quoted in Macdonald (n 4) 49.

[85] A similar point is made with respect to 'aesthetic order' and the 'war on graffiti' in J Austin, *Taking the Train: How Graffiti Art Became an Urban Crisis in New York City* (New York, Columbia University Press, 2001) 146.

Panel II

Form

4

Copyright—Subject Matter

Introduction

Does copyright subsist in graffiti writing? This chapter identifies some of the key issues related to the protection of graffiti writing under UK/European Union (EU) copyright law. This is useful for two reasons: first, graffiti writing, due to its public placement, is highly visible and readily exploitable and commodified, and certain creators may be in a position to protect it;[1] and second, it serves to illustrate some of the difficulties and idiosyncrasies in applying subsistence rules to an impermanent form of subcultural creativity that is both art and writing. The analysis of subsistence also serves as the basis of comparisons and contrasts drawn between copyright and the graffiti rules in chapter five. Both this chapter and the next offer insights into the rules governing the identification of certain forms of creativity as objects of regulation whether within the graffiti subculture's 'bounded commons' or the intellectual commons more broadly.

This chapter briefly considers qualification for copyright protection before moving on to consider the artistic and the literary works categories[2] which best reflect how graffiti writing might be protected through copyright law. Whether graffiti writing is an artistic or a literary work it will mean that graffiti writers will have certain economic and moral rights in their work. The nature of the economic rights will also differ depending on whether copyright subsists in graffiti as a literary or an artistic work. The chapter then considers the particular issues raised by fixation (insofar as graffiti writing is a literary work) and permanence (in relation to graffiti as an artistic work). Finally, it addresses public policy as a bar to copyright subsistence. The originality requirement—discussed briefly in this chapter insofar as the EU standard challenges the closed list of UK subject matter—is discussed fully, together with infringement, in chapter six.

[1] On the non-subcultural reproduction of graffiti creativity see chapter ten.
[2] Copyright, Design and Patents Act 1988 (CDPA), s 1(1)(a).

Graffiti Writing as a 'Work'

In broad terms, a 'work' is 'an objectification, in a bounded expressive form of human creativity'.[12] The Berne Convention provides the foundation for the copyright definition of a 'work' stating that:

> The expression 'literary and artistic works' shall include every production in the literary, scientific and artistic domain, whatever may be the mode or form of its expression[13]

It further provides a non-exhaustive list including books and drawings.[14] In the UK, copyright subsists in an original *work* that fits within one of the subject matter categories in the Copyright, Design and Patents Act 1988 (CDPA).[15] The key question is how to determine whether there is a 'work'. A 'work', although not its underlying ideas, will be in the propertised domain of the socially unified intellectual commons. This is important because an overly expansive copyright law for the categorisation of works may, where such protection goes beyond the base level expected by the Berne Convention, make the public domain smaller[16] and so interfere with the ability of individual creators to build on the creativity of others. This in turn may interfere with the promotion of culture.

Unlike certain civil law jurisdictions in the EU, the UK operates a 'closed list' of subject matter which includes 'artistic' and 'literary' works.[17] Yet following *Infopaq*,[18] the CDPA definition of a 'work' does not seem to be consistent with the Infosoc Directive. The harmonised notion of the 'work', Handig suggests, is not exhaustive and includes works that fall outside the closed list in the UK suggesting that the UK definitions are not consistent with EU copyright law on this point.[19] Indeed, Rosati argues that closed lists altogether are not compatible with EU law.[20] At the very least, the EU 'intellectual creation' test means that the interpretation

[12] A Barron, 'Copyright, Art, and Objecthood' in D McClean and K Schubert (eds), *Dear Images: Art, Copyright and Culture* (London, Ridinghouse, 2002) 291.

[13] Berne Convention, Art 2(1).

[14] Berne Convention, Art 2(1).

[15] CDPA, s 1(1).

[16] G Greenleaf and C Bond, '"Public Rights" in Copyright: What Makes up Australia's Public Domain?' (2013) 23 *Australian Intellectual Property Journal* 111, 126.

[17] On the differences between closed and open list approaches see T Aplin, 'Subject Matter' in E Derclaye (ed), *Research Handbook on the Future of EU Copyright* (Cheltenham, Edward Elgar, 2009).

[18] Case C-5/08 *Infopaq International A/S v Danske Dagblades Forening* [2009] ECR I-6569. See also Case C-393/09 *Bezpečnostní softwarová asociace v Svaz softwarové ochrany v Ministerstvo kultury* [2011] ECDR 3.

[19] C Handig, 'Infopaq International A/S v Danske Dagblades Forening (C-5/08): Is the Term 'Work' of the CDPA 1988 in Line with the European Directives?' (2010) 32(2) *European Intellectual Property Review* 53, 55–56.

[20] E Rosati, 'Closed Subject-Matter Systems Are No Longer Compatible with EU Copyright' (2014) 12 *GRUR Int* 1112–18.

of existing UK subject matter categories should be more generous.[21] Support for this view may be found in *SAS Institute v World Programming*[22] in which Arnold J states:

> In the light of a number of recent judgments of the CJEU, it may be arguable that it is not a fatal objection to a claim that copyright subsists in a particular work that the work is not one of the kinds of work listed in s.1(1)(a) of the Copyright, Designs and Patents 1988 and defined elsewhere in that Act. Nevertheless, it remains clear that the putative copyright work must be a literary or artistic work within the meaning of art.2(1) of the Berne Convention[23]

As Aplin argues, a closed list may be interpreted in 'an open-ended manner'[24] even if in practice, it has been interpreted so as to limit the kinds of creative expression that attract copyright protection. An example is found in *Creation Records*[25] in which a collection of objects arranged in and around an empty swimming pool was found not to be an artistic work in the form of a sculpture, a collage or a work of artistic craftsmanship.[26] The arrangement could be described as an installation. The present list of works in the CDPA, however, echoes formalist art theory according to which art is 'an aesthetic object that exists and is perceived in virtue of its form'.[27] This might explain the lack of protection of an installation—the aesthetic is bypassed in favour of a consideration of whether or not it has the formal characteristics of a sculpture, a collage or another type of artistic work listed in the CDPA. Creativity as a process is even more difficult to recognise.

Part of the problem with a closed list of subject matter is that artistic expression like the work in *Creation Records* may be unprotected, even though it may bring social benefits with respect to promoting culture. Instead, the closed list means that copyright law effectively ignores many different types of creativity that are part of contemporary art practice.[28] Restricting copyright to certain forms of creative endeavour may not regulate creativity in a manner that produces an attractive and diverse culture. In any event, due to EU harmonisation, *Creation Records* may well be decided differently today.[29] Derclaye argues that 'the term "work" is an autonomous concept in EU law, even if the Court has not had to say it explicitly as it has never been asked the question'.[30] In any event, the EU

[21] Arguing that subject matter categories need to be 'revisited' in light of the 'intellectual creation' requirement: Bently and Sherman (n 6) 61.

[22] *SAS Institute Inc v World Programming Ltd* [2013] EWHC 69 (Ch).

[23] ibid [27].

[24] Aplin (n 17) 71.

[25] *Creation Records Limited and Others v News Group Newspapers Limited* [1997] EMLR 444, 449–50. The case was decided on the basis of breach of confidence.

[26] Arguments that the arrangement was a dramatic work also failed: ibid [448].

[27] J Pila, 'Copyright and Its Categories of Original Works' (2010) 30(2) *Oxford Journal of Legal Studies* 229, 231.

[28] See A Barron, 'Copyright Law and the Claims of Art' (2002) 4 *Intellectual Property Quarterly* 368.

[29] Bently and Sherman (n 6) 61–62.

[30] E Derclaye, 'Assessing the Impact and Reception of the Court of Justice of the European Union Case Law on UK Copyright Law: What Does the Future Hold?' (2014) 240 *Revue Internationale Du*

conception of the work is consistent with the open list approach to works found in the Berne Convention[31] which seeks to protect 'every production in the literary, scientific and artistic domain'[32] and provides an indicative, but not prescriptive, list of works that might be offered copyright protection.

The above discussion is relevant to graffiti writing because it is a candidate for categorisation into both the artistic and literary works categories. The (potential) illegality of its creation is irrelevant to a determination of whether a 'work' does or does not exist in the first place. Unlike some forms of contemporary art, graffiti writing does not appear to escape categorisation but only when looking at the final work; the creative process remains very much beyond the scope of copyright protection.[33] The remainder of this part considers the subject matter classification of graffiti writing in copyright law and, briefly, trade mark law. This approach will be contrasted to the analogous concern with the requirement to write letters in chapter five.

Graffiti Writing as an Artistic Work

Tags, throw-ups and pieces (especially a piece containing cartoon-style characters or other figurative elements) are likely to be classified as artistic works, specifically 'graphic works'. A 'graphic work' includes, according to section 4(2)(a) CDPA 'any painting, drawing, diagram, map, chart or plan'. Graffiti writing created on walls using spray paint would be likely to constitute a painting while preliminary sketches in blackbooks (writers' sketchbooks) created using markers would be likely to constitute drawings. This section is concerned with graffiti writing on walls, that is paintings made freehand and using spray paint. Two issues are discussed below: the first relates to the intention to create art and the second, discussed in the next part, relates to the (im)permanence of graffiti writing. Although a 'painting' is protected 'irrespective of artistic quality'[34] the association of graffiti style with crime makes it easier than it ought to be to call its categorisation into question.[35]

In deciding whether a 'new' form of artistic endeavour such as graffiti writing is an artistic work it is helpful to consider whether it is intended as art, whether

Droit D'Auteur 5–117, paper available at www.eprints.nottingham.ac.uk/3613/2/RIDA_article_derclaye_April_2014_eprints.pdf, 18 (citations refer to e-print paper).

[31] ibid 8.

[32] Berne Convention, Art 2(1).

[33] See chapter two.

[34] CDPA, s 4(1)(a).

[35] See J Ferrell, *Crimes of Style: Urban Graffiti and the Politics of Criminality* (Boston, Northeastern University Press, 1996). Copyright protection has been denied for a 'meaningless' work created while drunk: *Fournet v Pearson Ltd* (1897) 14 TLR 82. The analogy cannot be drawn with graffiti writing which does provide meaning: see chapter one.

or not it is well-accomplished art.[36] In *Merchandising Corporation of America v Harpbond*[37] the Court of Appeal indicated that a 'painting' must be given its ordinary meaning:

> [I]t is a question of fact in any particular case whether that which is under discussion is or is not a painting. … A painting is not an idea: it is an object; and paint without a surface is not a painting.[38]

This appears to point in a particularly blunt fashion to a concern with the *materiality* of the artistic work as indivisible from its intangible 'essence'[39] and the related issue of permanence (discussed below). The CDPA makes no mention of the need for a material form of the artistic work because such a work 'necessarily takes material form'.[40] This assumption appears to be made in the extract from *Harpbond* above. This is in contrast to literary, dramatic and musical works.[41]

The above is not to say that the distinction between the tangible and intangible aspects of the artistic work is illusory. The materiality of the artistic work as 'an object' has been addressed, albeit indirectly in the context of the adaptation right and the exhaustion of copyright, by the Court of Justice of the European Union (CJEU) in *Art & Allposters International BV v Stichting Pictoright*.[42] That case concerned the transposition of an image by lifting the ink from a poster and transferring it to canvas.[43] The preliminary ruling concerned, effectively, the question of whether the copyright in the works had been exhausted upon the first sale of the posters or whether, once the alteration had been made, the further sale of the canvass would constitute an infringement of the distribution right.[44] The CJEU answered in the affirmative[45] observing:

> [T]he EU legislature, by using the terms 'tangible article' and 'that object', wished to give authors control over the initial marketing in the European Union of each tangible object incorporating their intellectual creation.[46]

[36] A similar point is made by reference to a (hypothetical) painting on a wall in a house—it 'must at least have been intended to be a work of art to be enjoyed as a visual thing': K Garnett, G Davies and G Harbottle, *Copinger and Skone James on Copyright Volume One*, 16th edn (London, Thomson Reuters, 2011) [3-57].

[37] *Merchandising Corporation of America v Harpbond* [1983] FSR 32.

[38] ibid.

[39] ie the work as the combination of material support and its *corpus mysticum*: Spoor in J Griffiths, 'Dematerialization, Pragmatism and the European Copyright Revolution' (2013) 33(4) *Oxford Journal of Legal Studies* 767, 770, note 16.

[40] J Griffiths, 'Copyright's Imperfect Republic and the Artistic Commonwealth' in L Bently, J Davis and JC Ginsburg (eds), *Copyright and Piracy: An Interdisciplinary Critique* (Cambridge, Cambridge University Press, 2010) 345.

[41] Which must be 'recorded, in writing or otherwise': CDPA, s 3(2).

[42] Case C-419/13 *Art & Allposters International BV v Stichting Pictoright* [2015] ECDR 8.

[43] ibid [15].

[44] The questions are stated in full at ibid [21]. See summary at [23].

[45] ibid [40].

[46] ibid [37].

This suggests that while the artistic work might be a separate intangible expression, that expression is incorporated: the artistic work is not *the* object, contrary to *Harpbond*, but is fixed *in* an object while maintaining an independent existence as an intangible creation.[47] A wall—the typical surface on which graffiti writing is found—would be a 'surface' in the *Harpbond* sense (assuming this is still necessary for copyright to subsist) as would a train carriage.

Furthermore, given the conservatism of the courts in defining 'artistic works'[48] whether graffiti writing would qualify ought not to be considered as entirely settled notwithstanding that it is prima facie a 'painting'. This is especially the case if the *context* of the work matters. Context as an indicator of whether there is an artistic work or not is identified in *Lucasfilm Ltd v Ainsworth*[49] as a relevant factor but in relation to display in traditional art spaces such as galleries. That case considered, amongst other issues, whether costumes (namely, 'storm trooper' helmets) in the *Star Wars* films were sculptures. The Court of Appeal quoted the trial judge:

> A pile of bricks, temporarily on display at the Tate Modern for two weeks, is plainly capable of being a sculpture. The identical pile of bricks dumped at the end of my driveway for two weeks preparatory to a building project is equally plainly not. One asks why there is that difference, and the answer lies, in my view, in having regard to its purpose. One is created by the hand of an artist, for artistic purposes, and the other is created by a builder, for building purposes.[50]

The Court of Appeal's approach in *Lucasfilm* may be described as a 'common sense' approach[51] to determining whether a work exists. This approach, however, hides the difficulties inherent in determining what a work is.[52] Graffiti writing could potentially fall foul of 'common sense'; a court would need to make a call that 'reflects a concerning (if not popular) view'.[53] On the other hand, the context of a work would only be one relevant factor, suggesting that the approach approved in *Lucasfilm* is flexible enough to accommodate graffiti writing as an artistic work.

The Supreme Court disagreed with the more expansive suggestion of an 'elephant test' or 'knowing one when you see it' test but adopted the 'multifactorial approach' of the Court of Appeal.[54] A relevant factor with respect to

[47] Akin to 'surface decoration' in UK unregistered design law. See *Flashing Badge Co Ltd v Groves* [2007] EWHC 1372 (Ch) [22].

[48] T Aplin and J Davis, *Intellectual Property Law: Text, Cases and Materials* (Oxford, Oxford University Press, 2009) 63.

[49] *Lucasfilm Ltd and Others v Ainsworth and Another* [2012] 1 AC 208 (*Lucasfilm*, SC).

[50] *Lucasfilm Ltd and Others v Ainsworth and Another* [2009] EWCA Civ 1328 [54] (Jacob LJ) (*Lucasfilm*, CA).

[51] Pila (n 27) 240.

[52] ibid.

[53] ibid 240.

[54] *Lucasfilm*, SC (n 49) [47]. The Court was referring to *Lucasfilm*, CA (n 50) [77].

graffiti writing might then be whether it is *intended* to be art (as opposed to a functional object); the creator's intention being one of several factors relevant to determining whether a creation qualifies as an artistic work.[55] Moreover, if a 'graphic work… can comprise a painting which (however bad it might be in artistic terms) is unlikely to be anything but decorative'[56] then the fact that graffiti writing is *not* exclusively decorative—graffiti writing is more than simply a painting, it is a means of creating social meaning within the subculture—might matter. The privileging of visual enjoyment echoes the need to provide 'information and instruction or pleasure'[57] in relation to literary works. However, in the same paragraph of *Hollinrake v Trusswell* the Court of Appeal suggests that a work such as a diagram or plan may also be an artistic work even if it is also functional.[58] Therefore, it is important not to overstate the importance of a work being purely 'decorative'.

Even taking into account the complex set of motivations for graffiti writing (eg writing as a demonstration of personal autonomy, the quest for fame, friendship with other writers, seeing your name, the thrill of being 'up') it would appear that, even if it is not intended to be art, graffiti writing is meant to be enjoyed as a 'visual thing' and is thus an artistic work.[59] Visual enjoyment seems closely allied to the *Lucasfilm* notion of artistic purpose because there is a common concern with the creation's impact on a viewer. It also echoes the concept endorsed by Lord Oliver in *Interlego v Tyco*[60] that an artistic work needs to be 'visually significant'.[61] Taking a graffiti writing piece with letters, characters and background using several colours and a background on a surface (wall) as an example, this appears to meet the criteria of a visually significant painting. In any event, a persuasive argument can be made that in light of recent CJEU jurisprudence that it is originality only—and not subject matter *and* originality—that is determinative for granting copyright protection.[62] As Derclaye argues in light of *Flos SpA v Semeraro*:[63]

> All that is required is that the author has made free and creative choices so as to imprint the work with his personal stamp. This formula does not require that the author of an artistic derivative work must add something visually significant.[64]

Of course as with other creative practices that serve to create social meaning, graffiti creativity is more than the final work that might attract copyright protection. The tag, or throw-up or piece is simply one aspect—but the only aspect that

55 ibid [54] (quoting the judge at first instance).
56 ibid [43].
57 *Hollinrake v Truswell* [1894] 3 Ch. 420, 427–28. See discussion below.
58 ibid.
59 Garnett et al (n 36) [3-57].
60 *Interlego AG v Tyco Industries Inc* [1989] AC 217.
61 ibid 266. See also Pila (n 27) 234.
62 E Rosati, *Originality in EU Copyright: Full Harmonization through Case Law* (Cheltenham, Edward Elgar, 2013) 206.
63 Case C-168/09 *Flos SpA v Semeraro* [2011] ECDR 8.
64 Derclaye (n 30) 15.

may be copyright protected—of this creativity. The purpose of a piece is to demonstrate a superior *style* for other writers to look at and appreciate. Yet these different elements of creativity—pleasure, process, space—place graffiti creativity 'beyond copyright'[65] regardless of whether an open or closed list of subject matter is adhered to.

Graffiti Writing as a Literary Work

Copyright may also subsist in graffiti writing as a literary work. The reason this distinction matters is that the economic rights associated with artistic and literary works differ with the primary difference being that the owners of copyright in a literary work can exercise public performance and adaptation rights.[66] By contrast there is no public exhibition right with respect to artistic works.

A 'literary work' is defined in section 3(1) CDPA as 'any work, other than a dramatic or musical work, which is written, spoken or sung'. Graffiti creations will primarily consist of words, specifically names. A tag is a signature written in one colour, usually black, with a spraycan or marker. Because of the angles and/or intricate shapes of the letters it is often not legible to non-writers. A literary work is meant to afford 'information and instruction or pleasure of a literary kind'[67] but there is no requirement of literary quality.[68] That the letters of a tag may be generally unreadable is irrelevant to the question of whether a tag is 'writing' as defined in section 178 CDPA. Insofar as graffiti alphabets contort the existing alphabet to the point of unreadability for the non-writer, the tag would nevertheless be in 'writing' as a 'form of notation or code'.[69] Three issues then arise: whether copyright can subsist in a single word such as a name, the relationship between copyright and trademarks with respect to names, and, assuming that graffiti writing might be covered by both, the overlap between the literary and artistic work categories.

The case law, as exemplified by *Exxon v Exxon Insurance*,[70] suggests that copyright cannot subsist in a single word or short phrase even where the word is invented and in that sense original. Stephenson LJ stated that the word 'Exxon' was not a work as it gave neither information, instruction nor pleasure.[71] A tag is intended to convey information as to the identity of a particular writer and

[65] Using the phrase from C Waelde and P Schlesinger, 'Music and Dance: Beyond Copyright Text?' (2011) 8 *SCRIPTed* 3, 257–91.

[66] CDPA, ss 19 and 21.

[67] *Hollinrake v Truswell* (n 57) 427–28.

[68] By reference to *University of London Press Ltd v University Tutorial Press Ltd* [1916] 2 Ch 601. See Aplin (n 17) 56.

[69] CDPA, s 178. A tag is written 'by hand' on a wall.

[70] *Exxon v Exxon Insurance* [1982] Ch 119.

[71] ibid [143].

their coverage of a particular area (being 'up') in the same way that 'Exxon' is used merely to identify the company.[72] It might thus be argued that a tag is used merely to identify a particular writer; the tag itself is not information.[73] A tag might be said to grant pleasure through its style, and this goes more to its form as an artistic work rather than the name itself.

It appears difficult to argue that the name is to be enjoyed 'in the form of literary enjoyment'[74] and yet writers often choose names that 'sound good' or evoke particular emotions in themselves and, potentially, others.[75] This is especially the case where a tag is not 'invented' (eg Drax, Dreph)[76] but rather is an ordinary, descriptive word (eg Cut, Fuel, Fume, Teach, Prime).[77] As Cullabine argues, the reasoning in *Exxon* merits re-thinking because it is not clear why an invented word, as opposed to an ordinary word, should not be protected despite meeting the originality criteria.[78] An argument might be made that at least certain tags, such as those combining letters and numbers in unusual combinations do provide 'pleasure' broadly conceived. A better view is that any written word is a literary work and whether copyright subsists is a matter of meeting the requisite originality standard.

The objections relating to copyright protection for single words might also apply to crew name acronyms (eg DDS, ATG).[79] By contrast, in the aftermath of *NLA v Meltwater*[80] (holding that copyright could subsist in newspaper headlines) copyright might subsist in the full names of the crews (eg Diabolical Dub Stars, Ahead'a the Game).[81] In *Meltwater* the Court of Appeal referred to *Infopaq*, stating that the 'author's own intellectual creation' test had not modified the existing test that required a literary work to be both 'literary' (consisting of more than one word, likely a phrase) and 'original':

> A headline is plainly literary as it consists of words. The word 'original' does not connote novelty but that it originated with the author. … Although the Court refers to an 'intellectual creation' it does so in the context of para.35 which clearly relates such creation to the question of origin not novelty or merit. Accordingly, I do not understand the

[72] ibid [144] (Oliver LJ).

[73] Graffiti writers are likely to disagree. The tag, in conjunction with the space in which it is found, provides other members of the subculture with the necessary information to determine the respect owed to a writer and to understand their patterns of movement within the physical commons. Of course, copyright does not recognise placement as relevant.

[74] *Exxon* (n 70) [143] (Stephenson LJ).

[75] eg 'I chose Lord as my first tag. Looking at my real surname, which started with Von, it gave off a kind of 'noble' aura.' Dare in A Caputo (ed), *All City Writers* (Bagnolet, France, Kitchen93, 2009) 138.

[76] Examples from F Forsyth, *Crack & Shine* (London, FFF, 2009).

[77] ibid.

[78] JN Cullabine, 'Copyright in Short Phrases and Single Words English Law' (1992) 14 *European Intellectual Property Review* 6, 205–10, 208.

[79] These are examples of crew acronyms that were visible in London during the fieldwork; also profiled in Forsyth (n 76).

[80] *Newspaper Licensing Agency Ltd v Meltwater Holdings BV* [2012] RPC 1.

[81] Forsyth (n 76). The acronym is probably more important than the crew name since it is invariably the acronym that is placed on crew pieces, etc.

> decision of the European Court of Justice in *Infopaq* to have qualified the long standing test established by the authorities referred to in para.19 above.[82]

Meltwater is notable for finding copyright could subsist in phrases. If crew names are literary works their authors will need to show that they are original (ie their 'own intellectual creation'). It is possible that *Exxon* might be decided differently today[83] yet tags are likely to remain unprotected notwithstanding a harmonised conception of the work since copyright subsistence is likely to depend on whether a phrase meets the EU originality standard[84] which is likely to pose a bigger hurdle for graffiti writers' tags.[85]

Graffiti Writing as a Literary *and* an Artistic Work

Thus, if the difference between a literary and an artistic work is that between a word/writing and a picture,[86] graffiti writing therefore gives rise to the question: what happens when a word is also a picture? It is arguable that graffiti writing is *both* a literary work *and* an artistic work rather than one or the other. This issue arose in *Sandman v Panasonic*[87] where the High Court considered whether a circuit diagram was a literary and/or an artistic work. Similarly, *Anacon Corp v Environmental Research Technology*[88] concerned a circuit diagram as being potentially both an artistic and a literary work.[89]

Calligraphy offers a useful analogy to graffiti writing here. The observation made by Pumfrey J with relation to calligraphy is pertinent:

> A calligraphic work in which the calligraphy is part of the work (say an e e cummings poem about a cat in the shape of a cat, or a chinese calligraphic work) is, I would have thought, plainly both literary and artistic, and two copyrights must subsist.[90]

Chinese calligraphy is a form of creativity that is at once writing (a literary work) and a stylistic endeavour[91] that is difficult to master. Similarly, by analogy to

[82] *Meltwater*, Court of Appeal (n 80) [19], [21], referring to *University of London Press v University Tutorial Press* and *Ladbroke (Football) Ltd v William Hill (Football) Ltd* [1964] 1 WLR 273.

[83] Bently and Sherman (n 6) 111.

[84] ibid.

[85] See chapter six.

[86] D Booton, 'Framing Pictures: Defining Art in UK Copyright Law' (2003) 1 *Intellectual Property Quarterly*, 38–68, 40, 42.

[87] *Aubrey Max Sandman v Panasonic UK Limited and Another* [1998] FSR 651.

[88] *Anacon Corp Limited and Another v Environmental Research Technology Limited and Another* [1994] FSR 659. Diagrams, maps, charts and plans are 'graphic works': CDPA, s 4(2)(a).

[89] Contra Laddie J stating that although a work may be either literary or artistic in 'borderline' cases it must be one or the other: *Electronic Techniques (Anglia) Ltd v Critchley Components Ltd* [1997] FSR 401 [413].

[90] *Sandman v Panasonic* (n 87) [658].

[91] The classification of calligraphy styles is a field of academic study. See eg Y Zhuang, L Weiming and W Jiangqin, 'Latent Style Model: Discovering Writing Styles for Calligraphy Works' (2009) 20(2) *Journal of Visual Communication and Image Representation* 84.

calligraphy, graffiti writing may be considered as both a literary and an artistic work. Graffiti writing creativity is word-based but—as large scale, colourful pieces make evident—it is also meant to be enjoyed visually for the mastery of its writing style, a style that takes years to develop. Graffiti writing might therefore be described, like calligraphy, as 'visual words'[92] that makes it difficult to distinguish between the literary and artistic categories.

This brings us back again to the usefulness of adopting open categorisation of subject matter as a way of avoiding difficulties posed by works that straddle, or escape, existing (UK) categories. The High Court in *SAS v World Programming* offers the following observation of subject matter categorisation:

> In the light of a number of recent judgments of the CJEU, it may be arguable that it is not a fatal objection to a claim that copyright subsists in a particular work that the work is not one of the kinds of work listed in s.1(1)(a) of the Copyright, Designs and Patents 1988 and defined elsewhere in that Act. Nevertheless, it remains clear that the putative copyright work must be a literary or artistic work within the meaning of art.2(1) of the Berne Convention[93]

Perhaps such difficulties of categorisation may be sidestepped by adopting the EU 'intellectual creation' test to so that it does not matter which category a graffiti throw-up, for example, might fit but only that, having identified the literary and artistic work categories as relevant, it is its author's intellectual creation.[94]

Graffiti Writing as a 'Work' and a Trade Mark

Regardless of whether the tags and crew names are literary works, names and short phrases may simultaneously be protected as trade marks.[95] An argument might also be made that a graffiti tag is similarly a signature that is a sign capable of being registered as a trade mark. Trade mark law is concerned with whether the mark is distinctive in the sense of allowing one seller's mark to distinguish their goods and services from those of another.[96] A graffiti tag presents an easier case for trade mark protection than more straightforward signatures because it will usually be written in a 'particular graphic style'.[97] It is striking how the description of a signature in *Elvis Presley Trade Marks*[98] inadvertently leads Laddie J to capture

[92] ibid 84.

[93] *SAS Institute* (n 22) [27].

[94] Noting that the subject matter categories remain as the 'starting point' even if EU harmonisation necessitates that all intellectual creations are protected: Bently and Sherman (n 6) 62.

[95] Simultaneous protection has been subject to debate. See eg in the Australian context: D Lyons, 'Copyright in Trade Marks' (1994) 16(1) *European Intellectual Property Review* 21, 25.

[96] Trade Marks Act 1994, s 1(1); Directive 2008/95/EC, Art 2 to approximate the laws of the Member States relating to trade marks.

[97] *Elvis Presley Trade Marks* [1997] RPC 543, 558.

[98] ibid.

the graffiti writer's style of writing—specifically, wildstyle—and its significance to an individual writer:

> [Signatures are] a substantially unique and frequently highly distorted way of writing the author's name. They are in a sense a private graphic tied to one person.[99]

A tag might thus be considered a 'sign' that could be registered as a trade mark. Such distinctiveness in terms of style is not necessary, a simple signature will also be protected because it is 'a unique sign of authenticity'[100] or, the word (name) itself could be registered as a trade mark.[101] Tags or pieces and any characters associated with them—which may be protected as artistic works that are drawings under copyright law—may also be figurative marks akin to logos.[102] Unlike the names of authors generally, graffiti writers would appear to present a situation in which an author name is equivalent to a trade mark.[103] The problem is not so much that a name is the same or similar but that it will cause confusion within the 'scene' rather than within the market for a certain class of good.[104]

Fixation and Permanence

Aside from the requirements of a qualifying 'work', a literary work must also be fixed. There is also, arguably, an implicit requirement for permanence of artistic works. The questions considered here are whether graffiti writing is 'fixed' as a literary work and whether the ephemeral nature of graffiti writing matters in determining whether it is an artistic work. This part discusses fixation and permanence in relation to the relevant UK law but it is worth noting that if, as suggested above, it is accepted that the 'intellectual creation' test has harmonised the concept of the 'work' then fixation may no longer be a requirement for copyright protection.[105] The Berne Convention leaves to individual countries to determine whether works will be protected only when 'fixed in some material form'[106] and as it is, other EU Member States regulate copyright subsistence without a fixation requirement.[107]

[99] ibid 588.

[100] *In re Applications by the Estate of the Late Diana, Princess of Wales* (25 January 2001, TM Registry) [59].

[101] The other requirements for protection will also need to be met: Bently and Sherman (n 6) 942–44.

[102] See chapter six.

[103] On the difficulties with using names as trade marks: G Lastowka, 'The Trademark Function of Authorship' (2005) 85 *Boston University Law Review* 1171, 1194–95 (not referring to graffiti).

[104] Some graffiti-related businesses do register trade marks, eg Molotow, a German spray paint producer's registered Trade Mark No E2418424 (classes 02, 16, and 25) and, similarly, Montana, Trade Mark No. E5095021 (class 02).

[105] ie in order to provide a broad base of copyright protection, based on an interpretation of recital 9 of the Infosoc Directive. This aspect of subsistence is regulated at state level: Derclaye (n 30) 7–8.

[106] Berne Convention, Art 2(2).

[107] Griffiths (n 39) 790.

Fixation and permanence are discussed here in order to demonstrate, as with the difficulties associated with the categorisation of works, the limits of copyright law in protecting graffiti creativity.

Fixation of Literary Works

As mentioned above, literary works must be fixed 'in writing or otherwise'.[108] Literary works, as with musical and dramatic works, ought to be fixed but this need not mean that such works must be permanent.[109] Graffiti writing is fixed because the marker or spray paint (or, occasionally, a paint roller or paint-filled fire extinguisher) is applied directly to a wall or train carriage. It would appear irrelevant for the purpose of determining fixation that the writing was placed on property without the property owner's permission. Permission is addressed in the CDPA only in relation to making a record without the permission of, for example, a speaker.[110] This is not relevant to graffiti writing because it is predicated on the action of physically writing one's name on a surface.

Materiality of Artistic Works

While there is no explicit requirement of fixation for artistic works in the CDPA such a requirement would appear to be implicit in the types of artistic works[111] listed in section 4 CDPA. The *form* of an artistic work is a 'material object'.[112] For instance, a painting or drawing attracts copyright protection because the act of creation produces something in material form. This implicit requirement of fixation is closely allied to the more problematic requirement of permanence.[113] A number of related questions arise regarding graffiti: whether graffiti writing is, by its nature, too ephemeral to be protected as an artistic work; the relevance of destruction to the subsistence of copyright, and the relevance of the photography of graffiti writing as a record of the original work.

The issue here is whether the definition of an artistic work implies that it must be permanent. *Metix v Maughan*[114] suggests not: in that case Laddie J commented that the impermanence of an ice sculpture would not be a bar to its being considered an artistic work.[115] Permanence is not, this case suggests, intrinsic to the

[108] CDPA, s 3(2).

[109] E Derclaye, 'Debunking Some of UK Copyright Law's Longstanding Myths and Misunderstandings' (2013) 1 *Intellectual Property Quarterly* 1, 12.

[110] See CDPA, s 3(3). See generally Cornish et al (n 3) 463 [11-34].

[111] Garnett et al (n 36) [3-121].

[112] Pila (n 27) 237.

[113] See Cornish et al (n 3) [11-33].

[114] *Metix v Maughan* ([1997] FSR 718.

[115] ibid 721 (Laddie J).

artistic work. By contrast, a set of arranged objects in *Creation Records* was found to be ephemeral.[116] While this suggests a lack of clarity regarding the requirement (or lack thereof) of permanence for artistic works,[117] it would seem that in the case of graffiti creativity there are no questions of a missing element such as the lack of adhesive which meant the *Creation Records* objects did not constitute a collage.[118] A piece, even if quickly buffed (ie removed), is a painting fixed to a wall or train.

Copyright law's apparent concern with the materiality of artistic works is exemplified by the statement in *Harpbond* that a painting 'is not an idea: it is an object'.[119] The expectation that a painting will be on a 'surface'[120] would likely include walls. Furthermore, to say that 'If the marks are taken off the face there cannot be a painting'[121] is to suggest, by analogy, that because graffiti writing can be removed from walls or trains (by implication, leaving the walls and trains, like the face in *Harpbond*, intact) that there cannot be a painting. The better view is that so long as graffiti writing is fixed at some point, even if it was intended to last only a short period of time, it appears that it would attract copyright if the other requirements for copyright protection were met.[122] Underlying the issue of permanence is copyright law's deeper concern with the materiality of artistic works. The artistic work is fairly easy to identify as an object when the work, for example a sculpture, is indivisible from its material form.[123] Indeed, Derclaye argues that both *Harpbond* and *Komesaroff v Mickle*[124] have been incorrectly interpreted and rather that '[a]rtistic works need not be recorded and a fortiori need not be permanent either.'[125]

Graffiti writing is not inherently ephemeral but it is subject, in certain locations, to swift destruction, meaning it may only exist as a material object for a very short period of time, possibly hours. Where an artistic work is placed on a building wall the work requires a material support but the work itself may be destroyed without destroying this material support (ie the wall). Thus, if a work is distinct from the material on which it is made and copyright may nevertheless subsist in it, it is unclear why the potential impermanence of its support should prevent copyright from subsisting because the work is *expected* to be ephemeral rather than, as with any artistic work, merely being at risk of future destruction whether on purpose or by accident. For example, setting fire to a painting does not prevent

[116] *Creation Records* (n 25) [450] (Lloyd J).
[117] S Stokes, *Art and Copyright*, 2nd edn (Oxford, Hart Publishing, 2012) 54.
[118] *Creation Records* (n 25) [450] (Lloyd J).
[119] F Macmillan, 'Is Copyright Blind to the Visual?' (2008) 7(1) *Visual Communication* 97, 112 quoting *Harpbond* (n 37) [46].
[120] *Harpbond* (n 37) [46].
[121] ibid.
[122] Garnett et al (n 36) [3-110].
[123] See ibid [3-111].
[124] *Komesaroff v Mickle* [1988] RPC 204 (regarding a 'sand picture').
[125] Derclaye (n 109) 12.

copyright subsisting in the painting. Neither then would the imminent buffing of graffiti writing (an artistic work). An Australian case on the infringement of an artistic work in the form of a mould that had been destroyed, *Darwin Fiberglass Pty Ltd v Kruhse Enterprises*[126] indicates that destruction does not prevent a copyright infringement claim. The existence of a culture of documentation amongst graffiti writers—as one participant said: 'I write for the photographs' (Anon15)—would be relevant to evidencing the existence of a particular work after it had been buffed.

Even if there is an implied requirement of fixation it is met through the photography of graffiti. If artistic works must be fixed in order to qualify for protection, it seems logical that a record of the work in the form of a photograph should meet this requirement: graffiti creativity is recorded in a way that constitutes fixation for other forms of original works including literary and musical works. Thus even if a piece is buffed immediately after having been painted on a wall it can be considered fixed much as a lecture might be recorded to create a fixed literary work. In light of EU harmonisation it would seem that such a photograph would be sufficient to demonstrate the existence of a work (ie an 'intellectual creation') in which copyright subsists. As Griffiths argues in regard to the dematerialisation of works in EU copyright law:

> If the only relevant criterion for copyright entitlement is creativity, the maintenance of a recording requirement may increasingly come to be viewed as anomalous and potentially unlawful. Equally, there is a danger that the UK's statutory 'closed-list' system may also be regarded as incompatible with an exclusive focus on creativity.[127]

The EU standard would seem to be a more appropriate one as far as the protection of graffiti writing is concerned.

Public Policy and Illegality

On balance, the preceding discussion indicates that much graffiti writing may qualify for copyright protection as a literary and/or artistic work because it meets the relevant requirements for protection. The question addressed in this section is whether, when graffiti is placed on surfaces without permission, this prevents copyright subsisting in graffiti writing or, alternatively, if it would prevent the enforcement of copyright which did in fact subsist. Graffiti writing without permission could constitute criminal damage.[128] Some graffiti writers, especially those who specialise in bombing (extensively covering an area with tags), may be referred

[126] *Darwin Fiberglass Pty Ltd v Kruhse Enterprises* (1998) 8 NTLR 1.
[127] Griffiths (n 39) 785.
[128] Criminal Damage Act 1971, s 1.

to as vandals within the subculture.[129] The argument might be made that works resulting from criminal damage should not be protected on immorality or public policy grounds. The argument would be that the denial of copyright protection is necessary so that socially undesirable behaviour is not encouraged and rewarded. As such, the discussion of immorality and/or public policy is perhaps most clearly tied to the use of copyright to produce a certain type of culture. The denial of protection will act as a disincentive to create these (undesirable) works.[130] In practice, however, this may make the work more readily accessible because it has been placed in the public domain so allowing it to be reproduced more freely.[131]

Questions relating to graffiti writing in the context of immorality and public policy are part of a much broader concern with art and crime.[132] One of the main concerns of such discussions is how the law ought to regulate offensive art, for example through laws relating to obscenity.[133] Pornography or other obscene works are unlawful by virtue of their form and content, while graffiti writing is unlawful by virtue of its placement without permission on public and private property.[134] It is unlawful because it is the product of a 'clash of aesthetics'.[135] The difficulty with conceptualising graffiti writing as a 'crime of style'[136] is that the legal determination of its acceptability might be made *either* on the grounds that it is the product of a criminal act *or* on the grounds that—since once cannot tell from looking at it what the specific circumstances of creation were—that it looks as though it was created without permission and is therefore undesirable. However, focusing on aesthetic cues to identify 'immoral' works would hurt the legal graffiti and street art industry (such as the commissioning of creators to decorate exterior walls) and the type of economic growth copyright law might seek to foster. Indeed a normative claim might usefully be made here for the protection of graffiti writing (and also street art) in order to promote a diverse culture.

It would be logical to avoid the problem of determining the morality of copyright subsistence and consider enforcement instead. This would allow for an analysis of the *effects* of protection as immoral or against public policy rather than addressing the *content* or *form* of the work, the way one might consider pornography.[137] Still, this does give rise to the question of why copyright law

[129] eg Paul 107 (ed), *All City: The Book About Taking Space* (Toronto, ECW Press, 2003) 51.

[130] Bently and Sherman (n 6) 123.

[131] ibid.

[132] See A Julius, 'Art Crimes' in D McClean and K Schubert (eds), *Dear Images: Art, Copyright and Culture* (London, Ridinghouse, 2002).

[133] See generally J Phillips, 'Copyright in Obscene Works: Some British and American Problems' (1977) 6 *Anglo-American Law Review* 138.

[134] Referred to as the 'crucial 'where' of graffiti', see T Cresswell, *In Place/out of Place: Geography, Ideology, and Transgression* (Minnesota, University of Minnesota Press, 1996) 31.

[135] Discussing Ferrell's work: Julius, 'Art Crimes' (n 132) 495.

[136] Ferrell (n 35).

[137] Copyright does subsist in pornography unless it is of a particularly extreme nature such as child pornography. See A Sims, 'The Denial of Copyright Protection on Public Policy Grounds' (2008) 30(5) *European Intellectual Property Review* 189, 190.

as opposed to more suitable laws regulating expression generally should not be pressed into service. This is especially the case when a denial of copyright subsistence or a refusal to enforce copyright would make no difference to the production of graffiti given this type of creativity already flourishes without the prospect of copyright as a reward and, furthermore, produces its own set of norms to regulate creativity.

Immorality is a subset of a broader concern with affording copyright protection to works that are deemed to offend 'public sensibilities' or rewarding works where the exploitation of copyright would be contrary to the public interest.[138] To that extent, the concern with immorality reflects social benefit justifications for copyright. Copyright will not subsist in a work, or copyright will not be enforced, according to *Glyn v Weston Feature Film Co*[139] where the work is 'grossly immoral'.[140] In that case the author of a novel that contained scenes of adultery sued a filmmaker for copyright infringement. Younger J described the book as being of a 'cruelly destructive tendency'.[141] Perhaps the change in sexual mores since this case was decided suggests that a different result would be reached today[142] though it is not difficult to see how similar language might still be used to describe graffiti writing in a hypothetical copyright case. The refusal to enforce copyright could be a response to graffiti writers' apparent disrespect for real property.[143]

Yet this assumes that interference with, or the destruction of, property is in itself an immoral activity, which is by no means obvious. Another argument would be that (some) negative public reactions to graffiti writing, particularly its association with feelings of insecurity and harm,[144] militate against providing encouragement to authors of literary or artistic works of graffiti. The flaw in this argument, however, is that it would require the work under discussion to be viewed in the context of all the other works that share its style, that is, to argue that it is immoral because it is produced through the graffiti subculture rather than in a more traditional studio setting, for example. Yet even where the work was created illegally and such effects could be attributed to it—the tendency to deprave young people perhaps—illegality cannot automatically be equated to immorality.[145]

[138] H Laddie, P Prescott, M Vitoria, A Speck and L Lane, *The Modern Law of Copyright and Designs*, 3rd edn (London, Butterworths, 2000) [20.3].

[139] *Glyn v Weston Feature Film Co* [1916] 1 Ch 261.

[140] ibid [269]. According to *Copinger*, a determination of such gross immorality will lead to a refusal to enforce copyright; it is not a matter of subsistence: Garnett et al (n 36) [3-304] note 1527.

[141] *Glyn v Weston* [270].

[142] Laddie et al (n 138) [20.3].

[143] But see chapter five.

[144] eg L Rosewarne, 'Visual Terror: Graffiti and Outdoor Advertising as Street Harassment' Refereed paper, Australasian Political Science Association Conference, October 2004, www.adelaide.edu.au/apsa/docs_papers/Others/Rosewarne.pdf.

[145] The better option is that judges continue carefully to exercise their discretion: Sims (n 137) 197–98.

Dicta in the *Spycatcher*[146] case suggest that 'disgraceful circumstances'[147]—in that case the publication of a book in breach of the Official Secrets Act 1911—would prevent enforcement of copyright.[148] However, criminal damage does not seem to be on a par with the revelation of official secrets. The next point to consider is whether illegally produced works may be denied copyright protection on public policy grounds more broadly. The case law that has considered matters of public policy is not entirely clear on whether it can be an absolute bar to the enforcement of copyright, but the refusal to enforce copyright on public policy grounds is clearly possible.[149] At the same time public interest may be a defence to copyright infringement.[150] The public policy ground is related though not the same as the public interest defence which also relies on section 171(3) CDPA. That section provides:

> Nothing in this Part affects any rule of law preventing or restricting the enforcement of copyright, on grounds of public interest or otherwise.

While a refusal may be based on public interest it may also be based on the (broader) public policy grounds which are exercised through the court's inherent jurisdiction.[151] The precise basis for claiming that such matters can be determined via the exercise of a court's inherent jurisdiction is unclear but an explanation was attempted in *Hyde Park v Yelland*[152] as follows:

> The jurisdiction to refuse to enforce copyright, which I believe has been recognised, comes from the court's inherent jurisdiction. It is limited to cases where enforcement of the copyright would offend against the policy of the law. … The action [in *Lion Laboratories* [1985] QB 626] was based upon documents which in the circumstances reeked of turpitude. As Lord Mansfield CJ said in Holman v Johnson (1775) 1 Cowp 341, 343: 'No court will lend its aid to a man who founds his cause of action upon an immoral or an illegal act.'[153]

The question then is whether the court is to look specifically at the work or its creator.

Illegality may activate the public policy ground as well as the public interest ground. For example, in the first instance judgment in *Hyde Park v Yelland*[154]—though decided on the basis of the public interest defence and not the public

[146] *Attorney-General v Observer Ltd. and Others* [1990] 1 AC 109.
[147] ibid 275 (Lord Griffiths).
[148] Whether the operation of the immorality ground leads to a denial of subsistence or a denial of enforcement remains unclear: Bently and Sherman (n 6) 122.
[149] Citing *ZYX Music GmbH v King* [1995] FSR 566, 577: Sims (n 137) 189, see also 192.
[150] P Johnson, 'The Public Interest: Is It Still a Defence to Copyright Infringement?' (2005) 16(1) *Entertainment Law Review* 1, 2.
[151] Sims (n 137) 193.
[152] *Hyde Park Residence Ltd v Yelland* [2001] Ch 143 (CA).
[153] ibid 167–68 (Aldous LJ).
[154] *Hyde Park Residence Ltd v Yelland* [1999] RPC 655.

policy ground relating to the enforcement of copyright—Jacob J noted that 'public policy can prevent copyright enforcement completely'.[155] On appeal,[156] Mance LJ expressed the view, by reference to public interest in breach of confidence cases, that the circumstances in which copyright will not be enforced are where it is:

> (i) immoral, scandalous or contrary to family life; (ii) injurious to public life, public health and safety or the administration of justice; (iii) incites or encourages others to act in a way referred to in (ii).[157]

Some graffiti writing will be unlawful because it constitutes criminal damage but it is not immediately clear whether this places it within any of the categories identified above. Viewed narrowly, as criminal damage, it relates to an offence against a private property owner not the public at large, notwithstanding the arguments made that, for example, graffiti lowers the public's 'quality of life'.[158] On the other hand, if the 'circumstances in which public interest may override copyright are not capable of precise categorisation'[159] then such 'public life' concerns could arguably be taken into account. However, that graffiti writing is viewed by (some sections of) the public as aesthetically displeasing or associated with criminality seems a dubious basis on which to refuse to enforce copyright. This is especially the case given the recent rise in the popularity of street art and to a lesser extent graffiti writing. Similarly, graffiti writers will not be 'incited' to write because their copyright will be enforced; to suggest otherwise is to misunderstand graffiti writers' motivations.[160]

A court may, for example, refuse to award the graffiti writer damages[161] when finding in their favour rather than refusing to enforce copyright. However given that in a criminal damage case the Court of Appeal noted the creativity of graffiti writing,[162] it would seem odd to doubly punish graffiti writers—first by (potentially) sentencing them to imprisonment and second, by refusing to enforce copyright in the creativity (artistic works in the form of graffiti) of the kind that is encouraged because, if commercialised, it would provide economic benefits to the graffiti writer upon release as well as contribute to the production of culture.

[155] The obiter discussion at first instance by Jacob J in ibid 665 is provided as evidence of the ground's continuing existence: Sims (n 137) 192.

[156] *Hyde Park v Yelland* (CA) (n 152).

[157] ibid 168 (Aldous LJ). By contrast, Mance LJ treats breach of confidence cases as distinct from copyright, noting that if fair dealing was not made out neither would there be a public interest in overriding copyright: [75], [79].

[158] See eg J Austin, *Taking the Train: How Graffiti Art Became an Urban Crisis in New York City* (New York, Columbia University Press, 2001) 151.

[159] Approving of the view put forward by Mance LJ in *Hyde Park*: *Ashdown v Telegraph Group Ltd* [2002] Ch 149 [58] (Lord Phillips).

[160] See chapter one.

[161] See A Stirling, *World Copyright Law: Protection of Authors' Works, Performances, Phonograms, Films, Video, Broadcasts, and Published Editions in National, International and Regional Law* (London, Sweet & Maxwell, 2008) [6.33].

[162] Quoting the trial judge as to the writer's 'considerable artistic talent': *R v Pease and Others* [2008] EWCA Crim 2515 [14] (Judge CJ).

An alternative means of addressing the above issues would be to apply the rule against illegality[163] to prevent a finding that copyright subsists in graffiti or, if it does, that copyright ought not to be enforced. By analogy to *Bakewell*[164] (a land law case) since a property owner could have granted permission for the graffiti to be placed on the wall, the illegality of the act of creation is no bar to a finding that copyright subsists in the graffiti.

Although there are no reported UK cases on graffiti and copyright, two cases from other jurisdictions are instructive. In the German case *Re Pictures on the Berlin Wall*,[165] the Court explained that:

> It is not in principle relevant to the possibility of copyright protection by statute for the creation of a work that the way in which it was produced is evidently unlawful—in this case by virtue of an act of damage to property subject to civil and criminal sanctions … The property rights in objects embodying a work subject to copyright protection may only be exercised without prejudice to the copyright (section 903 of the Civil Code). The owner's power to dispose of a material object therefore in principle meets its limits where it amounts to an infringement of copyright.[166]

Private property rights take precedence over the author's rights but with an important limitation: the property owner does have rights over his/her property but not the right to then sell the work.[167] This point seems to be in line with the distinction between a chattel (eg the canvas) and the right to exploit the copyright in the work it embodies. A similar distinction perhaps also ought to be made between the circumstances of the work's creation and the exploitation of copyright. This argument is difficult to make, however, in the context of the principle that a person should not profit from a criminal activity.[168]

Similarly, the French case *Aichouba v Lecole*[169] concerned a mosaic made without permission on the side of a building. The creators were granted two months to remove the mosaic after which the owner was allowed to remove it at the creators' expense because the creators were not the owners of the building when the mosaic was made.[170] Certainly the approach in *Aichouba* appears to provide a useful way to determine whether to enforce copyright in graffiti, that is, by attempting to accommodate two sets of private rights rather than attempting to determine what is publicly acceptable. Usefully added to this would be an acknowledgement of broader public interests in the enforcement of copyright in graffiti, not in the sense above in terms of determining public 'acceptability' or 'unacceptability' of

163 The law on illegality remains unsettled. See *Tinsley v Milligan* [1994] 1 AC 340; *Jetivia v Bilta* [2015] UKSC 23.

164 *Bakewell v Brandwood* [2004] UKHL 14 holding that illegality was no bar to the right arising by prescription because by its nature the owner of the common could have granted the right of way.

165 *Re Pictures on the Berlin Wall* [1997] ECC 553.

166 ibid [8], [10].

167 Stirling (n 161) [6.33].

168 ibid. See *Attorney-General v Blake* [1997] TLR 687.

169 *Benjamin Aichouba et autres c Francis Lecole* TGI Paris, 13 October 2000 (2003) 195 RIDA 378.

170 Summary provided in Stirling (n 161) [6.33].

the content of the work but, perhaps, to consider its placement within the physical commons in order to produce a more nuanced understanding of how the public interest might be taken into account.[171]

Conclusion

This chapter has considered how graffiti creativity might be protected by copyright as a literary or artistic work by focusing on subject matter and fixation requirements. The public policy/immorality ground, and to a lesser extent public interest, was also considered as a separate means by which copyright might be found not to subsist in copyright works (or provide a basis for refusing to enforce copyright). On the whole, while tags appear to be too insubstantial to be considered literary works, tags, throw-ups and pieces would qualify for protection as artistic works. However, where graffiti creativity is placed on property without permission, this presents a potential bar to protection.

The discussion above indicates that graffiti blurs the cultural distinction between literary and artistic works as well as the distinction between the process of creating a work and the work itself. The tag is not merely a product (work) but also a practice with all the emotional impact and awareness of space that this entails. The requirement that there is a 'work' excludes the recognition of creative activities that are antecedent to, and an integral part of, the work's production. Unsurprisingly then, the alternative normative framework within the graffiti subculture is better placed to embrace the very features—overlapping categorisation, the relevance of process and space—that challenge copyright law. The next chapter turns to the question of how writers seek to protect their creativity within the graffiti subculture's 'bounded commons'.

[171] See chapter ten.

5

Graffiti Rules—Write Letters, Choose Spots

> [W]hen you are on the train you're looking out for spots, you're always watching. 'Oh that's a good spot' and then you go back. … I love letters. I love style, styling a letter to make it. (Anon10)

Introduction

Chapter four considered whether copyright subsisted in graffiti writing as literary and/or artistic works and, if so, whether copyright might be denied on public policy grounds. The present chapter addresses the same issue—how certain creative expressions are protected, and whether and why any protection offered might be circumscribed on grounds of morality—by looking at how graffiti writing is regulated within the subculture's 'bounded commons'. Notwithstanding that they position themselves against copyright law, the empirical research suggests graffiti writers adhere to a set of norms that parallel the subject matter and morality/public policy rules in copyright. The difference is that these rules, unlike copyright law, are more highly attuned to the process of creating graffiti and the space in which it occurs.

The purpose of this chapter is to discuss three aspects of the regulation of creativity within the graffiti subculture: first, that the creativity regulated is the writing of *letters*; second, that graffiti writing must be placed on an *appropriate* surface; and third, that graffiti writing is *(im)material.* These aspects yield two preconditions for the production of graffiti writing: 'write letters' and 'choose spots'. Each norm is contrasted with the relevant copyright law rules discussed in chapter four with a view to considering what copyright law would need to look like in order to be more sensitive to the needs of creators and, in so doing, to help encourage the development of a just, attractive and diverse culture. (Originality, the other key element of copyright subsistence, as well as infringement is discussed in the next chapter, while the equivalent rules on originality and copying within the graffiti subculture are discussed in chapter seven.)

Writing Letters

As the overview of graffiti in chapter one indicated, graffiti writers primarily write letters as opposed to concentrating on more figurative content. The regulation of creativity within the graffiti subculture is therefore oriented towards the regulation of the writing of letters namely to the originality of a writer's chosen name and the originality of the style in which that name is written. Writing letters is therefore not a rule so much as a constraint to which writers willingly adhere and, in doing so, enter the commons of the graffiti subculture in which their creativity is regulated. This part of the chapter builds upon the discussion in chapter one on the practice of graffiti writing by examining the requirement of writing letters, the different types of writing (tag, throw-up and piece) and how to write (spraycans, freehand) in more detail.

Writing and Writers

The rule in the graffiti subculture to 'be original' (see chapter seven) is based upon the assumption that what will be original is the graffiti writer's *writing* of letters, numbers and certain other associated elements (eg haloes,[1] and sometimes 'copyright signs').[2] These creative elements are within the graffiti-specific public domain and available for any graffiti writer to use. The use of letters and other elements is also important because it identifies a creator as a participant in graffiti culture and as someone who is cognisant of its history.

Letters, as the potential object of protection within the graffiti subculture, are not considered to be merely capable of conveying information in literary form. A writer illustrated the breakdown between creative categories by referring to words as 'visual thing[s]':

> For me it's not because of the risks, it's more because of a need to express something thanks to the letters and words, not necessarily the meaning of the words but the meaning of the shape that your word is going to take like the dynamics of letters and words and the visual thing a word can make ... (Anon8)

Similarly, in the late 1990s, another writer referred to writing as 'the marriage of name and picture'.[3] Writing is inextricably linked to the style of writing.

Indeed, writing letters has its roots in the historical definition of a 'writer' found, for example, in *Subway Art*: 'the practitioner of the art of graffiti'.[4] Historically, the

[1] eg writing letters has been described as one of the 'formal aspects of graffiti': J Rahn, *Painting Without Permission: Hip-Hop Graffiti Subculture* (Westport, CT, Bergin & Garvey, 2002) 9.

[2] M Cooper, *Tag Town* (Arsta, Dokument Forlag, 2008) 53.

[3] S Powers, *The Art of Getting Over: Graffiti at the Millennium* (New York, St. Martin's Press, 1999) 10.

[4] M Cooper and H Chalfant, *Subway Art* (London, Thames & Hudson, 1984) 27. The same definition is provided in H Chalfant and J Prigoff, *Spraycan Art* (London, Thames & Hudson, 1987) 12.

simple act of writing a name was enough to distinguish one writer from another. As graffiti writing grew in popularity, stylistic innovations enabled writers to make their 'signatures' stand out.[5] Thus, today, the writing of letterforms in a discernible style is an essential component of graffiti writing. Very simple tags are the exception but then it is their very simplicity that makes them memorable—that such a strategy is successful is only because of well-established stylistic conventions.

The importance of writing is evident in writers' own self-identification even where some profess not to mind whether they are called graffiti writers or graffiti artists as such. Of the 21 participants who were identified as graffiti writers or graffiti artists, the majority explicitly or implicitly confirmed the importance of writing to being a graffiti writer and/or belonging to the subculture. For example, in response to the question of identification one participant observed:

> Got into hip hop and rap music and then found out that they did graffiti as well, wrote words like 'scene' and 'break' on the wall but that was like … you didn't think then 'I'm a street artist', you just said 'graffiti'. 'What do you do?' 'Graffiti.' … This is what it's all about. Doing words. … But that was 25 years ago so now it's progressing, now it's like … the whole street art scene. (Anon2)

As described by Anon8 above, the distinction between literature and art is broken down so that graffiti creativity is both art—insofar as the graffiti writing is enjoyed visually—and literature—insofar as graffiti writing is meant to be read for meaning—broadly conceived. This creativity tends to fall within certain recognised categories.

Types of Writing

As explained in chapter one, graffiti writing takes a number of forms. The original and basic form is the tag. The original tags were hand written, the way anyone would write a word;[6] the various stylistic developments came later. A key criterion is the use of writing:

> A tag is a logo in the form of an alias. It consists of letters and/or numbers and refers to one individual or a crew.[7]

All tags are written but not all writing is a tag. Another criterion is the placement of tags in public space without permission[8] (discussed below) but the exact meaning of a 'tag' is unsettled.

Beyond the tag are 'throw-ups' and 'pieces' but also writing in between such as 'dubs' (between throw-ups and pieces) and productions (pieces with characters

[5] J Stewart, *Graffiti Kings: New York City Mass Transit Art of the 1970s* (Abrams, NY, Melcher Media/Abrams, 2009) 46.
[6] Cooper (n 2) 53.
[7] ibid.
[8] ibid.

and a background). These categories were described in conversation with a writer, pointing at examples in a blackbook, as follows:

Anon27	So you've got your tag then your throw-up's your quick filled in, and the dub's your silver ... the dub is your piece with like silver.
M	So like a chrome and black?
Anon27	Yeah or a chrome and red.
M	So a throw-up's bubble letters with no fill?
Anon27	Yeah, like a quick thing.
M	And a piece would be above that.
Anon27	Yeah, the piece is above the dub so that your piece is like your main, your top level and then you've got your dub underneath that and your throw-up is like bubble letters or like a quick thing.

Not all creativity that uses letters can be classed as graffiti creativity. This distinction between letter style and the other elements in a piece or production highlights two important points with respect to letterforms: both the way of writing (discussed below) and the audience matter. When a writer calls a graffiti word a 'visual thing' (Anon8) it is clear that, within the subculture, the creativity that is informally regulated through the graffiti rules is the combination of highly stylised letters. As one participant explained:

> I like the letterforms. It's a lot about the letterforms and how they look together you know, because a lot of people, they have their favourite letters and yeah, I think that's part of it too. You don't want to be writing something all the time that you don't enjoy writing or locking things together you know. And for me and my style it's a lot about symmetry, you know, so I like balancing letters out. I like having the middle one as an anchor and the two on the end kind of pull it together. (Anon18)

Pieces, too, though they consist of words are not merely literary expressions. The letterforms and numbers are often embellished with figurative elements. The 'abstracted, insider art form'[9] of the 1970s developed to introduce, for instance, cartoon characters.[10] However, the letters remained the focal point of a graffiti piece and graffiti writers' raison d'etre. Similarly, some stickers are examples of graffiti creativity, the most obvious one being the 'Hello my name is…' with a tag written in the space. Stencils by contrast are the domain of street artists rather than graffiti writers.[11] As chapter one suggested, the graffiti rules are the product

[9] R Gastman and C Neelon, *The History of American Graffiti* (New York, Harper Design, 2010) 91.

[10] ibid.

[11] eg 'Stickers have always been part of graffiti as its another means of putting your name out there. Stencils isn't graffiti'. Robbo interviewed in *Frontline Magazine*, Issue 1 (no date).

or crystallisation of a set of historical cultural practices centering on train writing in 1970s and 80s New York:

> Everyone sort of looks at New York where graffiti started: biters, gangs, tags, throw-ups, buffing. All the terminology, it's all come from there but it filters down to [other] countries. (Anon15)

Thus, although some participants professed not to mind what they were called they were acutely aware of the differences between street artists and graffiti writers. For example:

> [G]raffiti writers, we talk to ourselves, we talk to our peers and our own people. So I'd write my name but not for you to care whereas street artists do it for the public and they want [you] to care. (Anon19)

The 'you' in this extract appears to refer to members of the public who are not writers. Moreover, in writing for other writers, the process of creating graffiti also matters, not just the name.

Ways of Writing

Graffiti writing is created freehand with spraycans or marker pens.[12] As one participant said:

> [I]t depends on what style, how you apply what you're doing. If you're using masking tape and scalpels and stencils and, you know, all that sort of stuff then you're definitely a street artists or stencillist or whatever, you know. Graffiti tends to be done just with cans. (Anon27)

The importance placed on freehand creation is relevant; it has the benefit of allowing the names to be executed quickly, helped by the adoption of a short name.[13] It is important for the writing to originate with the writer. Writing freehand has an obvious immediacy in providing a connection between the graffiti writing and its creator via a wall or train surface: the creativity is an extension of the writer.

The points made with respect to graffiti writers' motivations in chapter one—that graffiti creativity makes an explicit connection between writing and identity—is also relevant here. Graffiti writing is inextricably linked to the writer. As one participant said:

> [Graffiti writers] make forms on a wall in expression of themselves, that's the way it should be. It's like you can look at a piece and you can get a feel for you, the person. (Anon18)

This is interesting because it implies that personality, specifically the notion of pouring one's personality into a work that is at least arguably common to all

[12] An exception is the use of rollers. Revs and Cost were early proponents of the technique: E Seno (ed), *Trespass: A History of Uncommissioned Urban Art* (Koln, Taschen, 2010) 57.

[13] See Cooper (n 2) 15.

artistic endeavours, is made explicit in graffiti creativity. This attitude explains, for instance, why the destruction of, or other interference with, a writer's creativity is experienced as a personal affront.[14]

As chapter two suggested, creativity in the graffiti subculture is expressed in the artworks made freehand but also movement through the city as 'spots' are chosen (locational creativity) and the practice and improvisation within blackbooks that leads to the piece on the wall or train. This combination of both material artwork and the prior movement to produce the work is part of what places creativity within the graffiti subculture beyond copyright and, therefore, the graffiti rules beyond copyright law.

Copyright *Beyond* Copyright—Subject Matter

Unlike copyright law, which must contend with a range of potentially protectable creative expressions, the graffiti rules regulate the creativity of self-selecting creators who already identify with graffiti culture. Yet even if writing letters is not a graffiti rule as such, it has a parallel in the subject matter requirement in copyright law because it is writing that triggers the operation of the graffiti rules. A number of points of contrast arise in relation to subject matter categorisation: the role of community in the categorisation of creative expressions, its impact on the intellectual commons, and the way in which subject matter categories can embrace 'new' forms of creativity.

The categorisation of works, whether through the subject matter requirement in copyright law or the requirement of writing as a prerequisite (which may be met in other ways) for belonging in the graffiti subculture and therefore abiding (or being expected to abide) by the graffiti rules, cannot be determined independently of the community in which the creativity takes place. Although it appears to be treated as such in copyright law, a work is not 'autonomous' but rather the product of interaction with its audience.[15] This condition—that creativity is the product of social mediation—is something that graffiti writers implicitly recognise.

Unlike UK copyright—and in fact closer to the EU conception of the work as the author's own intellectual creation—creativity within the subculture is treated as emanating from a creator. It remains unconcerned with classifying the resulting creativity as a literary or artistic creation so long as the initial requirement of writing is met. In contrast, this is not the only relevant criterion: a determination as to its originality entails a judgment by the community of writers in terms of how they look.[16] Beyond the broad requirement of writing, graffiti creativity is also

[14] See chapter nine.

[15] RH Rotstein, 'Beyond Metaphor: Copyright Infringement and the Fiction of the Work' (1993) 68 *Chicago-Kent Law Review* 725, 804.

[16] See chapter seven.

divided into various forms. Much as artistic works are categorised as paintings, drawings or sculptures for example, a similar impulse can be detected in categorising works as tags, throw-ups or pieces. Yet it is the use of letters that is crucial here regardless of the type of graffiti they form. For example, with a wildstyle piece (where the letters may be stretched or otherwise reformed to the point of unreadability)[17] it is the letters that form the foundation of a judgment as to their stylistic impact. The originality of a writer's style of writing cannot be considered if there is no writing in the first place.

The community's requirement of writing also has an impact on the delineation of the boundary between the public and propertised spaces in the subculture's 'bounded commons'. When creating within the graffiti subculture, graffiti writers, to adopt Elster's more general point about creativity and constraints,[18] make a '*choice of constraints* followed by *choice within constraints*' (emphasis in the original).[19] Creators might choose to work in a particular genre for example[20] and those works are then potentially copyright protected. The creative choices are regulated by the creative community. The choice to limit expression to a certain form—writing letters—are regulated by the graffiti norms. Producing creativity within the subculture means participating in a common artistic endeavour from which the more specific constraints, such as writing letters, arise.

Within the 'bounded commons' of the graffiti subculture, the boundary of the graffiti 'public domain' in the graffiti-specific intellectual commons—which of course exists within the intellectual commons more broadly in supplying writers with creative inspiration—is determined in such a way as to make letters, numbers and certain symbols (such as haloes and arrows) free for all writers to use. Keeping letters free within the graffiti public domain while simultaneously requiring the *use* of letters as the predominant form of creative expression provides a creative constraint that encourages the development of graffiti culture. Specifically, it encourages the development of new styles within these constraints. Copyright, by contrast, does not function to constrain creativity at its inception in this manner even if subsequently categorises works in order to determine whether copyright subsists.

Notwithstanding these different approaches, the reasons offered by writers for the protection of their creativity are not that different to historical justifications for protecting artworks as the embodiment of the creator's genius.[21] Within the

[17] The wildstyle is 'the subculture's most complex letter form, characterized by its angular interlocking letters, distorted letter boundaries, accompanying arrows and extensive use of colour': N Macdonald, *The Graffiti Subculture: Youth, Masculinity and Identity in London and New York* (Hampshire, Palgrave Macmillan, 2001) 159.

[18] See S van Gompel, 'Creativity, Autonomy and Personal Touch: A Critical Appraisal of the CJEU's Originality Test for Copyright' in M Eechoud (ed), *The Work of Authorship* (Amsterdam, Amsterdam University Press, 2014) 107–08.

[19] ibid 108.

[20] Summarising Elster: ibid 108.

[21] For an historical perspective see eg B Sherman, 'Appropriating the Postmodern: Copyright and the Challenge of the New' in D McClean and K Schubert (eds), *Dear Images: Art, Copyright and Culture* (London, Ridinghouse, 2002) 333.

subculture's commons, certain stylistic innovations become associated with a particular writer and are protected on the basis of that writer's output as a whole whether or not a single work embodying that style continues to exist on a wall somewhere. One participant described the link between personality and style as follows:

> I don't think you instantaneously have your own style or maybe you do but you develop it over time and yeah that becomes very signature and very personal and if you see someone copying your style you might get irritated. (Anon4)

The relevance of the close personal link between a graffiti writer and their writing makes the reservations such as those expressed by judges with respect to gaining 'a monopoly of part of the English language'[22] in recognising words or short phrases as literary works (which presumably would have a negative social impact in terms of discouraging further creativity and hampering economic and cultural development) are less relevant. Tags are intended to set writers apart—the name indicates that a certain individual is the source of the graffiti work—and to that extent function akin to trade marks. As one participant implied, these limitations are accepted:

> I was trying to find a name that seemed sort of memorable and that hadn't been taken, one that not everybody, that hadn't been taken in the graffiti world which is the hardest thing to find because there's literally thousands and thousands. (Anon3)

As the above quotation suggests, graffiti writers are concerned with carving out a niche to distinguish themselves from other writers by effectively capturing interesting letter and number combinations to the exclusion of others. This point is discussed in more detail with respect to territorial exceptions to the biting (copying) of tags in chapter seven.

While both the requirement of writing in the graffiti subculture and the subject matter rules in copyright law are implicitly concerned with the regulation of creativity in the intellectual commons, there are some crucial differences. The regulation of writing is similar to the policing of subject matter boundaries in UK copyright law insofar as it privileges the writing of names, however, it is important to qualify the parallel drawn by noting that the importance of writing in the graffiti subculture is that it is a prerequisite for *belonging* in the graffiti subculture. This being the case, the necessity of writing letters is at the expense of other types of creativity (such as street art), much as the closed list approach in UK copyright law serves to exclude 'new' or non-traditional forms of creativity that do not fit within the subject matter categories even as it seeks to incentivise creativity generally through the copyright regime.

A further difference between the two types of regulation of creativity is that one (copyright law) obscures the cultural and historical roots that produced the categorisation of works while the other (graffiti rules) does not, but in fact both

[22] *Rose v Information Services Ltd* [1987] FSR 254 [255] (Hoffman J).

forms of regulation are undoubtedly shaped by these developments. The debt owed to history is more explicit within the graffiti subculture to the extent that the boundaries between culture and customary/cultural practice are effectively broken down and merged. The customary practice (ie writers have written letters since the subculture's origins in the US) becomes the condition that triggers the operation of the graffiti rules (ie only letter writing is protected).[23] Graffiti writers, specifically 'purist' or 'old school' writers make no apologies for this exclusive approach: it is understood that to be a writer within the subculture it is necessary to *tag* and to do so prolifically.

Yet, as 'new school' and more outward-looking writers suggest, just as copyright law struggles to accommodate new forms of art within the closed list of subject matter, even graffiti writers must evaluate what is and is not graffiti writing. There is an acknowledgment that the lines between writing and street art are blurred. This means that writing is defined not only by its content (ie whether it is made up of letters) but its context. This makes it a slightly different requirement to the subject matter requirement in copyright law because—although intention and placement may be considered when determining whether a work is a sculpture, for example[24]—in the graffiti subculture these concerns are highlighted. Some creativity may belong to the graffiti subculture even without meeting its most fundamental requirement in terms of form (ie being categorised as writing). As one participant stated:

> If you've got like a character or something that you want to get up graff style … like traditionally getting up, putting the work in, going out at 3am in the morning, scaling stuff in order to get it done, which is how it started. If you're applying that you're still kind of, it's really graff … (Anon27)

To complicate matters, letters are obviously the foundation of graffiti creativity but determining which forms of creativity will attract protection still leaves the question of *who* and *whose creativity* is judged to be inside or outside of the graffiti subculture. The perhaps uneasy rapprochement between graffiti writers and street artists is an example of the way in which graffiti creativity and culture are built not only through the individual creative processes or the recognition of certain rules but in the process of communicating and actively reinforcing the boundaries of the culture: the exclusion of street artists serves to reinforce the boundaries of the graffiti-specific commons. Recognition is the product of a dialogue—graffiti creativity and graffiti culture is built through the informal interactions between creators.

The expectation that graffiti creativity comprises *writing* still leaves open how the style of the letters is written. A fluid approach to style means that writers can push the boundaries of what it means to write letters and enter into a dialogue with others about whether their work constitutes graffiti writing. For example

[23] Echoing the notion of practice as a source of tribal law eg E Rosser, 'Customary Law: The Way Things Were, Codified' (2008) 8 *Tribal Law Journal*, 18–33, 20.

[24] *Lucasfilm Ltd v Ainsworth* [2009] EWCA Civ 1328.

one participant stated that he 'deliberately didn't want work to look like graffiti' (Anon5). Nonetheless he identified, and was identified, as a writer. The graffiti rules, despite the constraints, adopt a more flexible means of judging creativity by not distinguishing between literary and artistic categories. Graffiti writers face clear creative constraints and, given this, and in common with copyright law, the graffiti rules are underpinned by a concern with the exercise of 'creative choices'.[25] In terms of producing a copyright law that is sensitive to the needs of creators—in this book, graffiti writers—the explicit harmonisation of subject matter standards in the UK via the removal of subject matter categories altogether appears to be both appropriate and necessary.

Appropriate Placement

Apart from the aesthetic constraints described above, graffiti writers' creativity is also constrained spatially[26] in limiting how a writer may use a wall or a train surface. The graffiti rules relating to *which* surfaces are appropriate for placing tags, throw-ups and pieces are based on distinctions made by graffiti writers between private and public property. These considerations must be balanced, however, against a writer's desire for visibility. The rules regulating appropriate placement (or, the set of moral constraints identified by participants that writers are expected to abide by) is broadly analogous to copyright's public policy grounds on copyright subsistence and/or enforcement. The difference is, however, that questions of morality relate not to the work itself but instead to where it is situated. As such, the regulation of graffiti creativity is, indirectly, also the regulation of urban public space.

Two points are relevant here. First, while this part focuses on appropriate placement, the space of graffiti creativity has a significance beyond the regulation of appropriate surfaces on which to write. In particular, breaches of the graffiti rules may activate spatially relevant sanctions, such as the destruction of works within a certain scene.[27] Second, to 'get up' is not a rule as such—there is no penalty for not being visible, though a writer who wishes to secure fame will have to be 'up'. But the norms relating to appropriate placement limit the potential of all out 'bombing'. Before considering the public/private continuum with respect to appropriate placement this section examines graffiti as a spatial practice in which concerns with visibility and the hierarchy of placement (trains versus walls as surfaces) are tempered by pragmatic concerns (especially, the need to choose places where a writer is less likely to get caught and/or to preserve a place from over-exposure). These issues

[25] DJ Gervais, 'Feist Goes Global: A Comparative Analysis of the Notion of Originality in Copyright Law' (2002) 49 *Journal of the Copyright Society of the USA*, 949–81.

[26] See generally Moeran in van Gompel (n 18) 110.

[27] See chapter nine.

will be placed into a broader context as we turn to a discussion of the political justifications for writing.

Visibility and the Hierarchy of Placement

Graffiti writers, as Ferrell and Weide[28] explain in their theory of how graffiti writers place their work, must be adept in terms of both technique and style as well as choosing appropriate spots. This in turn requires an extensive knowledge of urban space.[29] It includes being aware of the flow of motor vehicle and pedestrian traffic, the visibility of the spot and the extent of policing in the area.[30] The ability to place graffiti writing appropriately is an important skill and writers develop an 'eye' for good places to write. Three aspects of placement are discussed below: visibility and the choice of places to write; the quality of the surface including how often it is buffed; and, most importantly, the hierarchy of placement (ie the respect afforded to writing on trains compared to walls, and walls compared to legal walls).

Fundamentally, in terms of 'getting up', a good place is a place where a tag or throw-up, for instance, will be visible. As one participant explained:

> [T]here's so many different ways of choosing spots actually but there's like, say, one thing is obviously if a lot of people are going to see it, yeah, that's important. If... a lot of people are going to see it, everyone's going to see it and it's dangerous. (Anon2)

Certainly, visibility and risk are closely entwined. Another participant echoed the point above:

> [W]hen you're bombing and getting your name up, tagging and stuff, the more difficult a place it is to tag the better. ... If you're bombing it's more about ... how on top it is. The more difficult or the more busy it is to tag, if you get your tags up you get a lot more respect. It's like 'fucking hell'. ... It's no good doing down the back of somebody's house and writing on the garage 'cause no one's going to see it. (Anon14)

An analogy might be drawn to the 'skater's eye'[31] because graffiti writers, like skateboarders, see and thus perform space differently.[32] In particular writers find new, dangerous ways to *be* in urban space and new ways to exploit spaces not merely 'as things but as a set of affordances, as process of production, as experience and event'.[33] Creativity and the rules regulating it cannot be separated from the

[28] J Ferrell and RD Weide, 'Spot Theory' (2010) 14(1) *City* 48.

[29] ibid 49.

[30] ibid.

[31] I Bordern, *Skateboarding, Space and the City: Architecture and the Body* (Oxford and New York, Berg, 2001) 218.

[32] Fieldwork provided an insight into how this graffiti sight develops. As my fieldwork progressed, I found myself walking and cycling through London constantly on the lookout for graffiti especially on bridges, canal-sides and rooftops.

[33] AM Brighenti, 'At the Wall: Graffiti Writers, Urban Territoriality, and the Public Domain' (2010) 13(3) *Space and Culture* 315, 317.

space in which the creativity occurs. Graffiti writing, unlike creativity embodied in certain chattels, is not portable; it is part of the fabric of urban space.[34] (Although, given the more recent trend for freight train graffiti documented by Ferrell it may be, if not portable, then in a sense moveable.)[35]

It is not only visibility that matters. Alongside the visibility point, which was mostly agreed upon as important, some participants indicated that the quality—the feel and look—of the surface also matters:

> I like to write on spaces that are dirty and worn in. I like the aesthetic of an old building or rusty metal gates. Graffiti for me sits really well in like a dirty kind of run down environment, high profile spots that get a lot of human traffic walking by. It feels nice to have something that's out on display for a lot of people to see and it makes the act a lot more interesting if the place is busy. (Anon11)

The underlying justification is that graffiti improves urban space by providing a new visual point of interest. Graffiti creativity is thus implicitly justified because it provides a certain social benefit. However, these considerations, as with the others under discussion here, condition the primary motivation of the writer, which is to be visible or to 'get up':

> [I]t's visual. The graff actually looks good around there, you know, the abandoned buildings. It actually looks good on there, it helps, helps it look good so I think that's, that's part of it and it's more obviously where people are going to see it. (Anon27)

A point related to visibility—and pertinent to the discussion of permanence below—is the likelihood of a particular place being 'buffed'. As one participant explained:

> [Y]ou try and find places that are going to be seen a lot … But also places that aren't … the hardest thing is find[ing] places that aren't going to get painted over 'cause so many places will get painted within a week or within a few days. And then you've also got to find places where I mean … lots of people take really risky places. I'm not much of a climber, I'm not much of an athlete so I tend to, most of mine tend to be street level … (Anon3)

At the same time, just because a place is easy to paint does not mean that writers will bomb it. Graffiti writers need to negotiate both the politics of the city (that seeks cleanliness through, eg, periodic crackdowns on graffiti writing)[36] and the politics of the subculture. This second point relates to problems caused when writers from a different territory (usually a different city) or writers who are toys (young or inexperienced writers) are unaware that a place such as a particular train

[34] See A Young, 'Written on the Skin of the City': A Young, *Judging the Image: Art, Value, Law* (London, Routledge, 2005) 50.

[35] J Ferrell, 'Freight Train Graffiti: Subculture, Crime, Dislocation' (1998) 15(4) *Justice Quarterly* 587.

[36] eg on the 'war on graffiti' and the 'authorized aesthetic': J Austin, 'More to See than a Canvas in a White Cube: For an Art in the Streets' (2010) 14(1) *City* 33.

yard is 'hit' only intermittently in order not to draw the attention of the authorities via over-exposure. This point comes across in the interview notes below:

> In a foreign country, have to have respect for that landscape. The same rules apply therefore need local knowledge i.e. need to respect the local writers. E.g. backlash in London over two Australian writers painting tube who drew police attention to one particular line. Also true of toys 'ruining a place'. Train writers are careful about where/how often they paint so they can keep painting. (Anon5 and Anon6)

The necessity of careful placement is particularly evident with respect to trains not merely because of the inherent danger in train writing (including electrocution by the third rail) but also because of the seriousness of the punishment (a possible custodial sentence).

Nevertheless, train writing remains the pinnacle of achievement for writers. The importance of train writing, as chapter one suggested, is due in part to history and the enduring influence of 1970s and' 80s New York train writing. As discussed with respect to the trade-off between visibility and style, writing on a train remains a great achievement:

> Well, you know, there's tags, there's throw-ups which is simple one colour fill ins. There's pieces which can be done on walls or anywhere but to do a really well-executed, colourful, technically proficient colour piece on a train is perhaps, arguably, the most difficult thing to do, especially in today's climate, you know. ... the movement's been around for a while. I guess people know how to protect their trains better. Yeah, in London, the security here is just insane ... (Anon4)

Train writing has its own language to describe the extent of train coverage such as window-down (writing below the windows on a train carriage) or wholecar (covering the entirety of a train carriage usually with a piece). While it is common for the very front of a train to be tagged[37] it is the graffiti writing on the train carriages that draws attention. As numerous graffiti DVDs[38] show, a crew will enter a yard and usually each writer will pick a carriage on which to place a piece. Writers create their pieces in a highly charged atmosphere and, unsurprisingly, graffiti writing on trains attracts a large amount of respect within the subculture. One writer went so far as to describe it as 'two cultures, train and wall' (Anon5). Another participant described it as follows:

> I think the rush of it ... it's more of the rush and also the whole atmosphere of it too. You've got varying climates and varying changes of the situation or where you have to paint, who you have to look out for, where there are dogs. You've got a lot of different situations, you have to know exactly where you're going to go. ... You get a lot more respect for, definitely, for your output but I think you get a lot more respect too for the quality of panel that you do in the time allotment. I think a lot of it comes down to the time allotment and how long you have to do it. I think you gain respect for that. ... I was always looking at graff on the trains. It always ... the thing that got me into graff was riding trains and looking at graff. (Anon18)

[37] As photographs in graffiti magazines demonstrate: eg *Bomb Alert*, Issue no 3, Winter 2005, 15.
[38] eg *London Tonight*, Vision Films UK (no date).

The experience of writing, as the quotation above emphasises, is very important and the pleasure and adrenaline rush, as another writer emphasised:

> Yeah huge, adrenaline. Brain pumping in your head, throbbing, heart pumping out of your chest. (Anon11)

Unsurprisingly, writing on legal walls does not carry the same cachet as train writing or illegal wall writing. This is not to diminish the importance of halls of fame (legal or tolerated graffiti spots) but the complex combination of spatial and personal negotiations required to write illegally, especially on trains, explains why a particular set of practices and rules have arisen to support this type of creativity.

Adherence, or at least acknowledgement, of the graffiti rules enables writers to prosper, and perhaps it would be appropriate to infer from the terms in which writing is discussed that it also encourages self-actualisation. Apart from the egotistical value of seeing one's name up,[39] writing was described as a positive force for some: if you can paint a train 'it shows you can do whatever you want in life' (Anon19). Even so, as the next section shows, limitations on appropriate placement based largely on notions of what is public or private/personal, commercial or non-commercial further restrict graffiti creativity.

Public versus Private Property Placement

If abiding by moral conventions and, more importantly, *being seen* to abide by moral conventions is fundamentally a display of respect for others[40] then for graffiti writers, being able to distinguish between appropriate and inappropriate locations is a display of respect, primarily, towards 'individual' and sacred property. Moreover, if following that convention is an expression of an individual's morality as well as, perhaps more importantly, the morality of a particular group,[41] then abiding by this norm also indicates that one belongs within the graffiti subculture. Within the subculture, appropriate behaviour means protecting 'personal' private property (such as cars or houses) but not public or corporate property (with some exceptions made for culturally significant public art and buildings, and also places of worship). Unlike the graffiti rules against copying ('don't bite' in chapter seven) or destroying someone's work ('don't go over' in chapter nine), the regulation of placement is described in explicitly moral terms.

A recurring explanation for the appropriateness of placing graffiti writing in urban space in the first place is that, unlike advertising and other commercial uses of urban space, graffiti writing is non-commercial (these points are discussed in

[39] 'Graff's about personality as well … if you're up everywhere or go into spots that other people can't … that makes you different' (Anon27).

[40] R Harrison, 'The Moral Role of Conventions' in A Perreau-Saussine and JB Murphy (eds), *The Nature of Customary Law: Legal, Historical and Philosophical Perspectives* (Cambridge, Cambridge University Press, 2007) 49.

[41] ibid.

more detail below). Apart from that, other themes emerged from the discussion of how to 'get up' without straying from graffiti's 'moral code'.[42] First, following the rules of appropriate placement distinguishes graffiti writing from other creative pursuits.[43] One writer observed with respect to learning the rules limiting 'getting up' as follows:

> I'm sure we worked it out for ourselves. At 13 I might've tagged a church. But if you're an actual graffiti writer then [you] wouldn't. (Anon21)[44]

Second, just as appropriate placement appears to be something that writers will grasp intuitively, it does not appear to attract the same range of sanctions as breaking other rules. In particular, no writer suggested that someone would go over another's work over this kind of infraction whereas, sanctions would be employed where a writer had been copied or gone over. Yet, loss of respect also functions as a sanction within a community and one participant observed that 'if someone was tagging a church I would have less respect for them' (Anon11).[45]

The reasoning provided by participants was largely consistent in principle if not always in practice. Being drunk or a toy were cited as examples of when the appropriate placement norms were not followed.[46] The adherence to notions of appropriate placement will thus depend on the stage of a writer's career with older, more experienced writers noting that it is 'kids' who break the rule. One writer explained why he would not tag a school or house even if it were in a highly visible spot:

> There's definitely ethics involved. And there are kids who'll do it but it's very frowned upon. The people who do that shit are normally 14 year olds with absolutely no idea and bad attitudes. There's not many experienced graffiti writers who would do that kind of stuff. (Anon4)

A number of reasons were provided as to why 'that kind of stuff' would not be done.

Interview extracts are provided below in order to illustrate the mode of reasoning employed, namely appeals to morality, respect for the feelings of others, concerns with the aesthetics of urban space, an implicit concern with community, and respect for 'personal' private property, amongst others. Broadly speaking, the

[42] References to morality were made by several participants. The expression 'moral code' is also adopted by Ferrell and Weide both of whom were graffiti writers for five years and 20 years respectively: Ferrell and Weide (n 28) 61, note 1.

[43] However, the moral reasoning provided was also largely consistent with the view of street artists interviewed.

[44] A spirited discussion in the comments of a now-defunct blog included the following: 'Graffiti writers choose their targets carefully and have ethics. If you think otherwise then show me the pictures of where any respected graffiti writer has ever vandalised a historic church.' Dr Funky, 'In No Ones Pocket' *Street Art is Dead*, 23 February 2011.

[45] The same concern with churches as 'off-limits' was expressed by street artists eg 'There's certain places you don't [paint]. It's that, you know, churches and whatnot and all that, you don't go near it.' (Anon16).

[46] See also Ferrell and Weide (n 28) 54–55.

justifications for classifying some surfaces as appropriate and other property as inappropriate for graffiti writing related to respect for individual or 'personal' property. For some writers this was generalised into a critique of the commercialisation of space and their own political alienation.

'Personal' Property and Respect/Morals

With respect to 'personal' property, in its more basic form the requirement of appropriate placement means that writers will refrain from writing on cars, houses and churches. For example:

Anon11	People's houses, unless on busy main roads in metropolitan areas, are pretty much no go. You respect someone's space. In the city they've chosen to live there and they understand the environment that things will be painted on and they should be part of that. Like, suburban houses and private properties, [not cool]. Commercial vehicles, vans, trains is all fair game for the most part most people would think.
M	Why not people's houses though?
Anon11	Out of respect for people's personal space I guess, yeah.
M	But commercial buildings would be ok or public buildings?
Anon11	Yeah.
M	Why's that? Why is that different to a person's house for you?
Anon11	Just out of respect. Not wanting to upset someone unnecessarily without, like, great reason to. … Might feel a bit guilty.

Another writer put it more succinctly: 'just because we do graffiti doesn't mean we're not respectful people' (Anon13). This justification forms part of a broader justification for painting graffiti for at least one writer who credited graffiti with '[building] manners and courage to a great extent' (Anon19).

One writer elaborated upon this empathetic approach—the effect of writing on people—to exclude culturally significant buildings as well:

> [A] museum, sculpture or something that has lots of history on it or which is in any way precious … Sometimes you can feel that you hurt not the building but a board or a van or something when it's too clean, too new … sometimes it's a little bit disturbing, for me it depends totally on people. … [F]or me that's a question of respect … for me there are some rules, some things that you cannot do, it's too bad. (Anon8)

The moral argument is accompanied by the pragmatic concerns identified with respect to surface choice and visibility above. Respectful placement makes it easier to continue writing. One writer explained that writing on property

> can upset people and I can fully understand that, really I can. The thing you learn in graffiti, and it's a shame 'cause it's dying but we had rules back in the day and we wouldn't write on churches or houses or public buildings. It was kept to tracksides, alleyways,

car parks. Alright, main roads because you wanted to get up but you'd be careful about where you write your name 'cause [you] don't want, the point is to go through all of this world and live the graffiti writer's lifestyle: try not to affect anyone so you can keep going. (Anon19)

Interestingly, the same (old school) writer continued by lamenting that, specifically the very prolific, new school writers were getting up without regard to the placement rules: 'they're just wild. They want fame … [They] will just write on anything' (Anon19).

The view that old school writers were more likely to adhere to norms of appropriate placement was rejected to an extent by a new school writer:

Never tagged a car, I'd always prefer to [tag a large retailer] than a private van, that has double the meaning. [Nor a] [h]ouse. But only because [the] council come and clean it for free so not a problem whatsoever. (Anon29)[47]

Although the notion of respect is less evident in the attitude to writing on a house, the implication is nevertheless there. Such placement is considered fine by the writer because the owner is not left worse off.

Furthermore, while some writers expressed uneasiness at writing on doorways, for instance, even when these spots where highly visible[48] there was a sense that notions of appropriate placement are determined by the nature of the relevant space but also by time. As one writer explained:

[I]t's very aggressive, [a] very aggressive statement to put a big fat cap tag all over a door, the door frame and the doorway but for hundreds of little tags that have just kind of been snuck in over a long time is more acceptable and I don't know why, I can't explain that I think … (Anon5)

'Personal' Property, Commercial Property and Urban Aesthetics

Another writer, speaking of a similar respect for private property and private choices, echoed the empathetic reasoning above but with a distinctly aesthetic twist by which the appropriateness of the place is related to its owner's own respect for their property:

[Y]ou know, like churches. We spoke about it, like, I'm kind of … I've got no problem with painting on another person's property but also I've got a basic respect for people like that … you know, I respect that someone's made, thought about the way their house looks or you know, or thought about the way their shop looks and I'm not going to go out of my way to damage that but at the same time I feel that [if] someone's not even thought about it, doesn't take any pride in their space then, you know, or thought about, doesn't take any pride in their space then.… At the end of the day they're part of the city, they've got a responsibility so if they're not, if they're ignoring that I've got no problem painting on their property. (Anon12)

[47] From interview notes.

[48] This contrasts with the proliferation of tags and throw-ups on apartment blocks in Berlin especially in Kreuzberg (field notes, 2010).

The explicit appeal to the aesthetic of urban space was a minority position though participants did appeal to beauty in terms of surfaces as indicated above for example, not writing on a surface that was 'already beautiful' but writing on a surface that was 'old and decayed' (Anon9). More interesting is the way in which discussions over placement are related to an appreciation of history and the personal aspect of creativity:

> Look back at the Bronx, it's on fire, buildings and shit everywhere. You're creating your name, art, something beautiful, obviously has a bit of you, materials you've nicked. Essentially that's wrong but you've created something nice that no one can ever take away from you. You've put in a bit of yourself for free. (Anon27)

A position shared by many more writers was the above writer's reasoning with respect to public versus private space that moved beyond notions of respect for 'personal' property to encompass, not necessarily consciously, political statements about the commercialisation of public spaces.

Extending the moral reasoning relating to respect, 'small' commercial properties like 'small' company vans presented a grey area with respect to the appropriateness of placement. In addressing concerns over the commercialisation of public space (and implicit concerns with corporate power), the tension was resolved by distinguishing between small business and large corporations. This led to nuanced consideration of the qualitative differences between big and small commercial properties, for example:

> And other surfaces where it's definitely dangerous and you feel like it's not a crime against a small business or an individual, it's a crime against a big company that makes big profits and it's something that I can overlook morally. (Anon9)

This appeal to the difference between individuals and 'faceless' corporations was a recurring theme in the interviews.

The uncertainty over painting vans or small businesses, unlike the unanimous agreement that writing on churches is inappropriate, is also circumvented to an extent by painting roller shutters since this only affects the night-time urban space:

> [T]he shop keepers will normally not paint over them. They normally last and they're visible at night so, yeah. … I guess it's [for] people who are out after dark. It's not the average 9–5er, or it is the average 9–5er who has a nightlife and is part of the city or town that they're in. It's not the average 9–5er who [goes] home and [goes] to bed, it's someone who's enjoying the town and the space they live in. (Anon7)

There is a sense that writing serves to create a different city and that this acts as both a motivation for writing and its justification. This echoes arguments made earlier about the spatial aspect of graffiti writing meaning that 'an-other city is possible'.[49]

What the above discussion suggests is that placement is less about hard and fast rules relating to appropriateness than a constant act of negotiating what the

[49] Austin (n 36) 44.

rules of appropriate placement are, or should be, for an individual writer. Thus, for example, one writer spoke of graffiti creativity in terms of claiming forgotten parts of urban space. The writer considered painting on shutters as a part of 'this idea of limbo and I think that's the place that graffiti occupies' (Anon12). Yet another writer outright rejected the implication that appropriate placement is geared towards an intentional re-ordering of urban public space, as these interview notes show:

> When in full bombing mode you don't have [a] concept of public space, [you] have an absolute conception of you. To read into graffiti that way would be wrong. (Anon29)

Nevertheless, writers did tend to make choices related to appropriate placement which often included distinguishing between appropriate and inappropriate public buildings and other properties that suggested some recognition of the political implications of designating certain types of spaces as effectively off-limits.

Trains and Tracksides as Public/Private Property

In contrast to houses and churches, trains and tracksides—unsurprisingly given the history of graffiti writing—present appropriate surfaces for writing. For example:

> I'm not sure if any of these railways ... are really public property. The railways have been privatized. ... It's all up for debate, I think, whether it's public or private space. ... A train station or train yard doesn't feel very public to me anytime even when I've bought a ticket ... it still feels like a private, cornered off, fortified space that is not public and free and open. I mean in other countries you get railway systems that are really open. You can move across the train tracks and feels more like public space than the railway system in Lond[on], greater London. (Anon9)

For another writer, the lack of harm or moral acceptability of painting trains or tracksides flows from the nature of the location itself as 'dead space' (Anon5).[50] Its emptiness is enlivened with graffiti writing; it 'induces a performance from otherwise "lifeless spaces"'.[51] A similar argument but coming at the issue from a different angle is to assume that train yards are public space and therefore appropriate for painting. The argument at the fore here is not a moral one about respect for people and their property but instead emphasises the public nature of the train. Continuing to discuss 'dead space' Anon5 said:

> I'm sure the train companies would argue that their side of the train isn't dead space [*chuckles*] but I see that as public.

The placement of tags on tracksides where the surface is not on an ordinary wall or fence but rather the wall of a house or apartment block brings into conflict the expectation that 'personal' property is off-limits while train-related property

[50] See also reference to 'blank' space and 'negative space' in M Halsey and A Young, '"Our Desires Are Ungovernable": Writing Graffiti in Urban Space' (2006) 10(3) *Theoretical Criminology* 275, 286–89.
[51] ibid 288.

is not. The broader issue here is the attempt to regulate appropriate placement where it conflicts with the motivation to 'get up' in a place that is both highly visible and culturally significant (because of the historical importance of trains and tracksides). The 'private' quality of houses will also be dependent on their position in urban space, which in the case of a busy public thoroughfare makes the exterior of the house public. When asked about this, one writer responded:

> [If] it's the side of someone's house and it's on the tracks like that [it's] fair game to paint even though I've just said it's not. … But if it was obviously on the side of someone's house that you couldn't see from the track that would just be out of order. (Anon27)

Although visibility appears to trump respect for 'personal' property in the justification provided, it is perhaps better to think of tracksides as an exception to the rule relating to 'personal' property: the walls of houses are inappropriate surfaces on which to write unless the wall itself is on a trackside. Another writer explained the exception in a different way in noting that trackside writing on a house would not matter because it was not visible to the occupiers. The reasoning was thus consistent with concerns about respecting 'personal' property:

> If it's somebody's house it's too personal, you're going to really piss' em off and they're going to clean it. If it's the back of the house where they can't see it or where the railway tracks are coming past then yeah … (Anon2)

Placement, Commons and Political Justifications

As the discussion of norms regulating placement suggests, graffiti writers regulate their creativity within a graffiti-specific commons in which the intellectual and physical commons coalesce to produce the space where creativity occurs. As such, the regulation of creativity within the subculture is simultaneously the regulation of space and, therefore, raises a number of political questions about who and what public space is for. This section thus builds on the preceding discussion to consider the more overtly political explanations offered for graffiti writing by the writers interviewed. These explanations begin to form a picture of the *kind* of commons that the graffiti rules create. They might be contrasted with copyright law's focus on the regulation of creativity within the intellectual commons, while neglecting its broader spatial effects.[52] What the graffiti rules show is that in regulating creativity within a 'bounded commons' the graffiti writers' experience of space—as they watch to see who is 'up'—is affected. Yet so is the experience of the general public as embodied in the passerby on the street or a passenger on a train who will experience graffiti writing in some locations but not others.

For some writers, placement moved beyond appropriateness—that is the prohibition against writing on particular surfaces, to a re-ordering of urban public

[52] Which is not to say that such spatial effects have remained unnoticed: eg A Philippopoulos-Mihalopoulos, 'Atmospheres of Law: Senses, Affects, Lawscapes' (2013) 7 *Emotion, Space and Society* 35.

space, as the notes for one interview showed: 'Rules of graffiti in public space [are] different to people who can just pay' (Anon21). This observation seems to suggest that in making themselves visible, graffiti writers are able to challenge the economic inequalities preventing their equal participation in the visual vistas offered in public spaces. The comparison was often drawn between graffiti and advertising with graffiti writing described as 'less sinister than adverts trying to sell something' (Anon21). For other writers this reasoning broadened out to describe writing as a 'fuck you to the government' (Anon19) as well as commercial or corporate interests. A rare writer who considered writing explicitly as a political action seemed to lament the lack of political reflection on the part of some fellow writers:

> [A] lot of people [writers] don't realize that they've entered an anarchic way of life, stealing everything, breaking law number of times a day but without being politicized. (Anon29)

By contrast, another participant was more pensive in describing a plan to encourage graffiti writing in places that 'need lifting':

> I wish there were more things that were government related that would push certain parts of graffiti out there. There's so much allocation to corporate billboards but whereas if they did a bit more community orientated commission projects a lot of grey spaces would look really colourful and people ... I've had elderly people, I've had, you know, old grandmas and things like that coming [up] to me and watching me do pieces because they like it, they like it. If they could just get a consensus on people that like graffiti and find areas that might need lifting through nice commissioned murals ... (Anon18)[53]

Talking about placement in terms of politics muddies the distinction between the regulation of creativity for the benefit of writers in order to safeguard the writing within their subculture and the broader arguments employed to justify graffiti writing in urban space. Yet even without making such a link explicit, the norms of appropriate placement allow the assumptions of property protection, and the commercialisation of urban space, to be questioned. The regulation of creativity within the subculture implicitly serves as a critique of corporate power. One graffiti writer/street artist explained why he preferred the outdoors to being inside a gallery:

> I suspect that it has a sort of political ring to being outdoors, it's more challenging and the space needs to be challenged. ... If you don't get up for what you want and believe in you're just going to get bulldozed over because we don't have financial might. (Anon23)

After further discussion, the participant continued:

> Take a bus around central London on a Sunday and you don't really see independent business and it sort of, it does sort of concern me. And the financial crisis we're going through at the moment but the answers are right there. Capitalism, the monster it is, is having such a detrimental effect on normal people ... I really want to smash that but you

[53] The participant added this at the end of the interview prefacing these comments with 'If there was one thing you could add to your interview it's the fact that ...'. It seems relevant to acknowledge the way in which here, as elsewhere, 'metamoments' (see chapter three) arose in the fieldwork.

> could just be jumped on before you pulled a can out because it's so paranoid and [*inaudible*] about terrorism and protecting its corporate interests, when all the students and anti-capitalists go out and riot the police should be protecting the people because that is their job but they are protecting big business. (Anon23)

Another writer made a rare, explicit link between graffiti and political economy: 'Graffiti writers are exempt from capitalism' (Anon29). This point of view is echoed in certain graffiti sources which carry quotations from graffiti writers, for example:

> Which represents more negativity … adverts or tags? Tags lead us to artistic development, creativity or just more tags, oh and maybe a cleaning bill. Advertising leads us to greed, want, envy, jealousy, capitalism, corruption, recession, robberies and muggings. …[54]

A consistent set of justifications based on the political impact of graffiti was not evident across the interviews. Nevertheless, there was an implicit understanding—demonstrated in the reference to the aesthetic experience of space in the foregoing quotations—of the power of graffiti. The regulation and protection of graffiti writing serves to re-order urban space; it is more than a means of regulating, for example, the originality of letter styles.

For some writers then, appropriate placement is not merely a restriction on writing but an opportunity to make a political statement. Such a statement may be made without explicitly having the public in mind as the audience for that political statement, as one writer demonstrated:

> There's a graffiti writer called Tox who is ridiculously everywhere, all over the city. He kind of talks to the public about freedom. The message he portrays is freedom: 'I'll write my name anywhere in this city' and that's true freedom. But that's the closest you'll get to graffiti writers talking to the public or doing their work for the public. (Anon19)[55]

The notion of graffiti writing as resistance (which is the implication of the argument in this section and of the quotation above) is highlighted in the academic literature on the subject.[56] As that discussion indicated, graffiti writers' creativity is regulated within, and ensures the preservation of, a graffiti-specific commons. Although the concern with morality maps neatly onto the morality/public policy exclusions in copyright law, in regulating physical placement, the graffiti rules move beyond copyright.

Copyright *Beyond* Copyright—Morality and Space

Considerations of morality are common to the graffiti rules and copyright law. As Young explains, graffiti normativity is not so far removed from formal legal rules:

[54] Attributed to Steas DTB: *London Handstyles* (no date).

[55] Visibility will increase a writer's stature: Ferrell and Weide (n 28) 51. However, this does not mean the work is created *for* the public.

[56] See especially J Ferrell, 'Urban Graffiti: Crime, Control, and Resistance' (1995) 27 *Youth and Society* 73, 83–87.

> Norms and conventions regarding surfaces that should or should not be written on flow through graffiti and street art cultures; they may or may not be followed, as with all norms and conventions, but their existence points to the fact that the citizens of the uncommissioned city are not immune to the powers and pleasures of legalities based on exclusion and ownership.[57]

Yet, quite unlike copyright law, underpinning the graffiti rules is a concern with the moral implications of placing creativity in certain locations and not others. The above discussion of appropriate placement serves a similar function to public policy in determining whether copyright subsists, or will be enforced, in a particular work. Both the graffiti writers' concerns with the acceptability of surfaces and copyright law's concerns with morality and/or public policy are, at heart, about the propriety of the generation and use of creative expressions and adopt 'legalities' to match.

In the respect for 'personal' property the graffiti writers' placement norms find a, perhaps unexpected, kinship with both real and intellectual property law in recognising and respecting an individual property owner's ability to exclude others. The placement norms differ in not generalising this to encompass all property adopting instead a quasi-Marxist conception of 'personal property': property is respected only insofar as it is clearly and directly linked to an individual in contrast to property owned at a remove (and in a potentially exploitative fashion) by, for example, a corporation. The exception for places of worship does not fit neatly into the category of 'personal property'; it is an autochthonous norm for the regulation of placement that demonstrates particularly well how the regulation of creativity in the graffiti subculture has responded to the moral implications of producing creativity in urban space.

At a more general level, both notions of appropriate placement in the graffiti rules and public policy in copyright law enable a turn outwards away from the work and its creator to situate the work in society: the underlying concern in relation to both is with how (and where) the work was created. As such, concerns over immorality/public policy (in copyright law) and appropriate placement (in the graffiti rules) suggest a concern with social benefit. Restrictions based on moral considerations may not sit easily with the attempt to incentivise creativity generally; they do, however, serve to incentivise creativity of a particular, socially useful kind.

This is not to say that the modes of reasoning are equivalent but simply that in both spheres it is necessary to decide what is offensive and what is in keeping with prevalent social or subcultural mores respectively. The difference perhaps is one of emphasis: for graffiti writers, although they may put themselves in the shoes of a 'personal' property owner, they reason 'personally' (from empathy) without attempting to determine whether a particular spot is off-limits because it is *generally* against

[57] A Young, 'Cities in the City: Street Art, Enchantment, and the Urban Commons' (2014) 26(2) *Law & Literature* 145, 160, note 35.

'principles of public order and morality'.[58] The effect is, however, the same. Thus one participant, in disagreeing that vans were off limits, described the distinction between appropriate and inappropriate placement as follows:

> [I] own a vehicle, I don't really have a problem with that but I wouldn't write on someone's window. ... That just seems a bit too aggressive. ... [I]t's a bit like using the cunt word or something. It's like ooh, there's a line. And maybe I wouldn't necessarily do that because for me the window is like the thing you look through and it's kind of like if it was on my wall it wouldn't affect me but if it was on my glass I'd have to do something about it. (Anon23)

Brighenti argues, drawing on Foucault, that graffiti writing is a 'tactical intervention'.[59] That such an intervention is also meant to be *appropriate* indicates that the graffiti rules are, even if indirectly, regulating space at the same time as regulating creativity. Thus in regulating locations as appropriate or inappropriate surfaces on which to write, whether these are 'dead space' (Anon5) or otherwise, the graffiti rules produce a *spatialised normativity*.[60] An argument might be made that not only can graffiti writing be interpreted as a form of political resistance to, amongst other things, economic injustice, but also to imagine a different, *just* city.[61] Art, may, at the very least 'offer urbanites a new way to perceive their environment'[62] or, put another way, offer the possibility of experiencing the city differently, to be enchanted.[63]

The justifications for, and consequently the form copyright rules take, are the product of, and have an effect on, political, social and cultural development. Of course, within the graffiti subculture, part of the requirement to place works appropriately is pragmatic because it allows writers to keep writing without making a particular space 'hot'. But writers also recognise the broader social effects of their creativity and so suggest a direction in which copyright could usefully develop. The spatialised normativity within the graffiti subculture's commons presents the outline of an alternative form of copyright rules by asking, for instance, what copyright law might offer in encouraging documentation of this form of

[58] *Hyde Park Residence Ltd v Yelland* [2001] Ch 143 (CA) [161] (Aldous LJ) discussed in A Sims, 'The Denial of Copyright Protection on Public Policy Grounds' (2008) 30(5) *European Intellectual Property Review* 189, 192.

[59] Brighenti (n 33) 322.

[60] Ploger uses 'spatialized normativity' to describe the legal regulation of space: J Ploger, 'Foucault's Dispositif and the City' (2008) 7(1) *Planning Theory* 51, 67. Arguing that writers 'develop a keen sort of alternative spatial epistemology, collectively remaking the meaning of the everyday urban environment': Ferrell and Weide (n 28) 60.

[61] See P Bengtsen and M Arvindsson, 'Spatial Justice and Street Art' (2014) 5 *Navein Reet: Nordic Journal of Law and Social Research* 117, 120 in light of the work of Andreas Philippopoulos-Mihalopoulos on spatial justice.

[62] I Susser and S Tonnelat, 'Transformative Cities: The Three Urban Commons' (2013) 66 *Focaal* 105, 114.

[63] Young (n 57) 149. Noting also that 'Street artists have spoken to me of their desire to represent things otherwise, to change the way citizens experience their cities, to point towards the existence of multiplicities within the singular of the city': 155. This point—in light of the 'right to the city'—is revisited in the Conclusion.

enchantment. What copyright law—as opposed to planning or cultural heritage law—could offer in this regard is to consider the placement of works in public spaces as a relevant factor in determining whether the reproduction and dissemination of such works is a 'fair' dealing or use (a point returned to in chapter ten) on the basis that allowing certain uses of publicly placed works would be beneficial to the promotion and development of culture.

The focus within subcultural communities on identity (ie identification as a member of a group) and its close relationship to respect within the territory of a particular scene appears to call into question the usefulness of existing copyright rules in protecting subcultural creativity. In contrast, the identification with a community is a particularly important aspect of subcultural creativity and this is reflected in the graffiti rules. Where the scene—understood as both a geographical location and a, self-selecting, group of writers—is the whole of the community to whom the rules apply these insights cannot be easily 'scaled up' to, for example, suggest that copyright law ought definitively to protect short names as literary works. What can be usefully reconsidered is the role of space in copyright, including in relation to the (im)materiality and permanence of works.

Placement, Permanence and (Im)materiality

Participants generally did not expect their works to last since they were usually placed on properties without permission. This section builds upon the discussion of placement to consider the question of permanence in relation to graffiti works. It considers: writers' acceptance of their work's (potential) ephemerality; attitudes to the protection of the original, material work on a wall; and the preservation of photographs of such work.

The expectation that graffiti writing on a wall or train surface will be transient is deeply ingrained. Writing is accepted as being transient even when placed on legal walls since these walls may have an especially high turnover of pieces. One participant referred to graffiti writing as 'totally temporary' (Anon29). In light of this expected ephemerality, one of the questions in the semi-structured interviews asked whether the participants thought their work should be protected in some way. This invariably resulted in a request for clarification of what that might mean and led to a discussion of either copyright protection or the Perspex covering Banksy works –'I hate this whole thing with Perspex' (Anon16)—or a dismissal of the notion that graffiti writing would be protected in any way. The physical element of writing is crucial rather than the protection of the creative output itself:

> It's [a] physical thing. You want to see your name up, you want other people to see … once it's out there it's out there. (Anon27)

The physicality of the creativity is linked not to the production of a work that maintains a material presence in a city street for example but rather in the movement that forms part of the creative process and crucially, the record of the work that becomes a stand-in for, perhaps more accurately *becomes*, the (now buffed) work.

As one writer stated, 'unless you get good photos you don't get anything from it' (Anon18). Graffiti writing is vulnerable to buffing and so writers both accept the transient nature of graffiti but are also inclined to document it.[64] This impulse to document is significant because effectively the copies of the graffiti work, including those placed on the internet by members of the public, are considered to be equivalent to the original work. Participants were aware that taking photographs was crucial to preserving their work (though not all writers are concerned with preservation, preferring instead the pure action of creating the work). This instinct to preserve is a product of graffiti writers' sense of a shared cultural history that includes, pre-internet, the sharing of photographs of graffiti.

Writers are acutely aware that a photograph is the only evidence they will have of their work. It is irrelevant whether they or someone else takes the photograph so long as it is preserved. One writer explained:

> There are cases where a piece is just of some great stylistic magnitude and technical innovation that it's seen as a landmark piece within graffiti and people will give it particular respect. But I also think it is this acceptance that graffiti is ephemeral that has led to the photo culture in graffiti because you know that you might not ever see your train again once you leave the yard and your piece might be buffed the next day so you really should get a photo of it straightaway, and documentation is really important to graffiti writers. (Anon4)

The above quotation also points to an important aspect of the transience of graffiti creativity: some pieces will survive and by virtue of their survival (because of the writer who created it and/or because of its stylistic qualities) attract protection under the 'don't go over' rule discussed in chapter nine.

The emphasis on fame amongst graffiti writers means that 'getting up' matters more than the preservation of a physical piece. Visibility in urban space is crucial but the impermanence of tags, throw-ups and pieces means that documentation can aid a writer's quest for fame. This, as the writer above explained, is not a new concern:

> All [Seen's] stuff is documented so widely you can't avoid his name…whereas there are other people who are bigger pioneers than him in New York who aren't documented enough like someone like, a very important name in graffiti is Phase2. (Anon4)

The concern with fame points to a different issue as well: graffiti writers are concerned with writing having a material presence on a wall or a train[65] at a certain point in time but the name (tag) is also understood to have a separate, immaterial

[64] There are exceptions—in particular, 'purist' writers (described in chapter three) do not appear concerned with documentation. Others, including street art and graffiti bloggers, will document the tags.

[65] To pretend to have tagged somewhere by faking photographs of tags is deeply problematic and respect will be difficult to earn again once this is discovered.

existence. Graffiti writers may treat writing in the form of a tag, throw-up or piece as a discrete, intangible 'thing' that attaches to the writer in particular circumstances. Associating a graffiti writer with a certain name within a certain territory is a good example of this. Graffiti writers, to an extent, disaggregate the physical creative output such as the tag on the wall from the tag itself. A name belongs to a writer whether or not it has a material presence in public space.

Copyright *Beyond* Copyright—Materiality and Permanence

Two points arise from the above discussion of placement and permanence. The first relates to whether the apparent interchangeability between the 'original' work on a wall and its photograph challenges the conception of the 'artistic work' in copyright law. The second point relates to graffiti writing as a practice in which the eventual creation of a tag, throw-up or piece is only part of the creative process of making works in urban space. As such this approach to permanence suggests the outline of a more expansive approach to subject matter in UK copyright law by de-emphasising both fixation and permanence. This approach is perhaps more closely echoed in the open list approach of other EU Member States and indeed in an expansive reading of the meaning of 'intellectual creation'. This would allow for copyright protection to be both decoupled from subject matter categorisation—which in any event has been challenged to the point that it may not be compatible with EU law anymore—and from any implicit retirements of fixation and permanence to focus simply on the exercise of creative choice.[66]

With respect to graffiti's ephemeral nature, the implied expectation of permanence is a symptom of copyright's law focus on the materiality of the work rather than the process of creating it[67] (ie graffiti writing as a creative object versus graffiti writing as a creative practice). Also, to reiterate an earlier point, the closed list of works means that creativity that might broadly be described as artistic will not necessarily qualify for protection as an artistic work. The closed list and the fixation and permanence requirements suggest that copyright law cannot take into account the dynamism inherent in the production of works.[68] This is demonstrated by an empirical study of contemporary dance and music by Waelde and Schlesinger.[69] As discussed in chapter two, the authors argue that experimental

[66] See chapter four.

[67] F Macmillan, 'Is Copyright Blind to the Visual?' (2008) 7(1) *Visual Communication* 97, 105, 107. Similarly, in the Australian case *Komesaroff v Mickle* [1987] VR 703, 'sand pictures' were found not to be artistic works or works of artistic craftsmanship because 'no sand landscape is a static feature for any length of time': 710.

[68] The fixation requirement has been singled out for criticism for excluding certain forms of creativity such as land art and performance art, eg SK Katyal, 'Semiotic Disobedience' (2006) 84(2) *Washington University Law Review* 489, 537 (drawing on the work of Peter Jaszi and Marta Woodmansee and Anne Barron).

[69] C Waelde and P Schlesinger, 'Music and Dance: Beyond Copyright Text?' (2011) 8(3) *SCRIPTed* 257.

dance and music creativity are *before* and *beyond* copyright law because copyright law cannot capture the unfixed creativity that forms the preparation and some of the performance of these 'works'.[70] As one writer stated, making a similar point, 'it's something you do. It's not a spectator sport' (Anon27).

Graffiti writers' understanding of (im)permanence might usefully speak to issues within copyright law, specifically whether implied fixation and permanence requirements—insofar as the discussion in chapter four suggested such requirements exist—may be satisfied by taking a photograph of the creative expression on the wall rather than expecting the material manifestation of it (the spray paint making the tag, throw-up or piece) to last *on* the wall. The 'photo culture' amongst graffiti writers raises a separate issue about the regulation of photographs of graffiti writing especially amongst non-writers which will be discussed in chapter ten. At this point it suffices to contrast the position of graffiti writing on the wall or train and the photograph preserving the graffiti writing, on a graffiti blog for example, long after the original has been removed. The former (material work) is not expected to last and part of the apparent insouciance with which destruction of the original is met by graffiti writers is explained by their attitude to the latter (the immaterial copy of the material work).

The regulation of creativity within the graffiti subculture echoes a strict interpretation of the wording in section 4 of the Copyright, Design and Patents Act 1988 (CDPA), that is, that there is no fixation requirement for artistic works, nor a permanence requirement. Yet even if such requirements have been implied into the artistic works category in the case law[71] the preservation of intangible artistic expression in a photograph—as the regulation of creativity within the subculture shows—ought to be sufficient to ensure that copyright subsists in graffiti writing as an artistic work (or indeed as a literary work that has been 'recorded') regardless of how long the work had lasted on the wall.[72] In that sense, the graffiti writers' understanding of how works ought to be regulated in situations where the work is not likely to have a long material existence lends credence to the observation in *Metix v Maughan* that creativity ought to be protected regardless of its ephemeral nature.[73] The graffiti rules thus present a means of both critiquing (a certain, narrow view of) UK subject matter rules and presenting an alternative that is respectful of creators' understanding of their own creativity.

This attitude also points to a deeper question about the materiality of artistic works, and a point of difference between the graffiti rules and copyright law.

[70] ibid 291.

[71] See S Stokes, *Art and Copyright*, 2nd edn (Oxford, Hart Publishing, 2012) 53–54.

[72] This also presents difficulties with respect to the (potential) dual copyright protection offered to the graffiti writer who has created the work and the person who has taken the photograph. Whether exact reproductions of the underlying work may be copyright protected is a matter of controversy. See K Garnett, 'Copyright in Photographs' (2000) 22(5) *European Intellectual Property Review* 229; R Deazley, 'Photographing Paintings in the Public Domain: A Response to Garnett' (2001) 23(4) *European Intellectual Property Review* 179.

[73] *Metix (UK) Limited and Another v G.H. Maughan (Plastics) Limited and Another* [1997] FSR 718, 721 (Laddie J).

Teilmann, for instance, has identified the value of the material, original artistic work as holding a value above that of its copies.[74] This argument is relevant to graffiti writers given the importance of the material work on a wall or train but it applies slightly differently. The first, material original matters but not because it is first or unique but rather because it has been made, as part of a creative *process*. This process includes movement through the city, the choice of location and surface, creating with a view to belonging, and then using spray paint or a marker to write a name. The copy, for example a photograph of a throw-up, is not inferior so much as it is different. Neither the material work nor its copy encapsulate the creativity but rather both offer a record of a point in a creative process. The problem with any implicit requirement that an artistic work takes material form is not that such a requirement cannot be met by a graffiti writer—it plainly can—but rather that this will only ever be part of the story.

Macmillan suggests that copyright law ought to distinguish between material and immaterial works then the attendant rights might also need to be 'different depending upon whether or not they are creating works intended to be unique one-off pieces or… works that are purely for the purposes of reproduction.'[75] Graffiti writing occupies a ground between this insofar as the works are one-offs—in being displayed on a particular wall at a particular time—but also expected to be reproduced in order to be documented without having been created specifically for that purpose. The useful forms of protection here are both protection against destruction (discussed regarding the integrity right in chapter eight) as well as limitations on copying by allowing reproductions for non-commercial purposes only (discussed in chapters six and ten).[76]

Examining the regulation of creativity within the graffiti subculture where the norms are attuned to creativity as a process in a particular territory and within a particular community (the scene) is also useful in highlighting what copyright cannot do. In particular, this chapter suggests that a major point of departure between the formal and informal regulation discussed here is that the graffiti rules directly recognise—via the rules relating to appropriate placement and the photographing of works in the physical commons—the relationship between creativity and space, specifically the intertwining of the physical and intellectual commons. Copyright law is ostensibly concerned with creativity but it is not necessarily well adapted to protecting creativity that is resistant to commodification. The regulation of creativity within a 'bounded commons' is thus an attractive alternative means for safeguarding and promoting graffiti culture.

[74] In the moral rights context: S Teilmann, 'Framing the Law: The Right of Integrity in Britain' (2005) 27(1) EIPR 19, 23.

[75] Macmillan (n 67) 112.

[76] Macmillan makes a similar point: 'It might be argued that as a right against copying, copyright is irrelevant to works of visual art in which the value resides in the original one-off work. On the other hand, it is also arguable that the creators of such works are entitled to protection from unauthorized commercialization of such works in the form of, for example, photographs': ibid 113.

Conclusion

This chapter has provided an overview of the graffiti rules relating to the requirements of writing letters and placing graffiti on appropriate surfaces. The most noteworthy finding was the concern with morality, an example perhaps of a universal tendency to produce rules that are sensitive to social context. The discussion of parallels between the graffiti rules and copyright rules that are both *without* and *beyond* copyright suggests some similarities but also serves to highlight differences in the protection of creativity with the graffiti rules, indicating the need for a more fluid approach to creativity that is adapted to the personal motivations and group dynamics of graffiti writers as well as the space in which they write. The alternative norms, however, are a product of a close-knit community and the experience of writers cannot necessarily be generalised with respect to suggesting alternative copyright law rules except to note that the regulation of creativity by copyright law would benefit from recognising the intangible essence of artistic works. To that end, the EU harmonisation of the originality standard—discussed in chapter six—is to be welcomed.

Panel III

Copying

6

Copyright—Originality and Infringement

Introduction

This chapter examines copyright rules relating to originality and infringement. For copyright to subsist in graffiti writing an *original* literary or artistic work needs to be identified. The second element of copyright subsistence—originality—is discussed here for two reasons. First, in light of EU copyright harmonisation[1] the presence of originality (ie the existence of an author's 'own intellectual creation') is determinative of copyright subsistence. Potentially this makes the discrete identification of a subject matter category into which an expression should fit unnecessary. Second, post-*Infopaq* and other EU cases (discussed below) it is the taking of an original part that determines whether or not an infringement has occurred making the identification of an *original* work critical to the vindication of an author's economic rights.

Notwithstanding the challenge posed to subject matter categorisation by EU harmonisation, the first part of this chapter looks at graffiti writing as an original literary and/or artistic work in order to consider whether copyright subsists in graffiti writers' style of writing and/or their names. The second part considers the issue of authorship and joint authorship—relevant to the production of works by graffiti crews—given that the author will be the first owner of copyright[2] and thus enjoy certain economic rights. The third part considers infringement through reproduction and communication to the public but also distribution. The fourth part provides an overview of (some) relevant defences to infringement. As with chapter four, this chapter applies copyright law rules to the production, and also sharing, of graffiti creativity within the graffiti subculture—and so identifies copyright's limitations when applied to subcultural creativity—but the issues raised are also relevant to reproduction and sharing by non-writers. It shows both why graffiti writers would seek to regulate their creativity in a manner that moves

[1] For a summary see eg L Bently and B Sherman, *Intellectual Property Law*, 4th edn (Oxford, Oxford University Press, 2014) 205. For a strong statement on harmonisation see E Rosati, *Originality in EU Copyright: Full Harmonization through Case Law* (Cheltenham, Edward Elgar, 2013).

[2] CDPA, s 11(1).

beyond copyright law but also, the difficulties posed more generally by copyright rules in promoting culture.

Originality

Originality is central to graffiti writers' understanding of creativity, as it is to the understanding of creativity more broadly. It has been described as 'a central theme in the efforts to understand human evolution, thinking, innovation, and creativity'.[3] What it means for a work to be 'original' as a matter of copyright subsistence is not straightforward. Gervais argues that a commonality might be found across jurisdictions in the requirement that an author make 'creative choices',[4] though it is contestable whether and to what extent this holds true for the UK. This requirement 'provides a way to measure creativity by measuring the quality and quantity of creative choices'.[5] In turn, measuring the level of creativity that makes a work original it is necessary to first consider the 'values we are protecting and why'.[6] In the UK, the question has been asked via a consideration of the meaning of 'skill, labour and judgment'. At the EU level the central issue is the meaning of 'author's own intellectual creation'.[7] Of course, in light of EU copyright harmonisation it is the latter rather than the former that is the relevant test for the originality of authorial works in the UK.[8]

As with other copyright rules, applying the originality test to graffiti writing presents a number of challenges (discussed below) and calls into question the assumptions made by copyright law about the forms creativity takes. Sherman argues in relation to Australian Indigenous creativity that determining whether a type of work, rather than any one individual work, is original is influenced by 'the crucial role that cultural prejudices play in shaping decisions as to a work's originality.'[9] This is pertinent to graffiti creativity because, arguably, a similar

[3] EF Judge and D Gervais, 'Of Silos and Constellations: Comparing Notions of Originality in Copyright Law' (2009) 27 *Cardozo Arts and Entertainment* 375–408, 376.

[4] See ibid 388; D Gervais, 'Feist Goes Global: A Comparative Analysis of the Notion of Originality in Copyright Law' (2002) 49 *Journal of the Copyright Society of the USA* 949, 969 (concerning France); 974 (concerning Canada, the UK and Australia).

[5] ibid 974 (footnotes omitted).

[6] D Leenheer Zimmerman, 'In Pursuit of Copyright's Elusive Essence' (2005) 28(2) *Columbia Journal of Law and the Arts* 187, 189.

[7] The phrase is found in Directive 2006/116/EC, Art 6 on the term of protection of copyright and certain related rights. It has been adopted in, inter alia, Case C-5/08 *Infopaq International A/S v Danske Dagblades Forening* [2009] ECR I-6569 in relation to Directive 2001/29/EC on the harmonization of certain aspects of copyright and related rights in the information society (Infosoc Directive).

[8] eg E Derclaye, 'The Court of Justice Copyright Case Law: Quo Vadis?' (2014) 36(11) *European Intellectual Property Review* 716, 716; Bently and Sherman (n 1) 99.

[9] B Sherman, 'From the Non-Original to the Ab-Original: A History' in B Sherman and A Strowel (eds), *Of Authors and Origins: Essays on Copyright Law* (Oxford, Clarendon Press, 1994) 127.

(if perhaps lesser) difficulty is faced by graffiti writers in that attitudes to graffiti generally may affect the determination that a specific work, such as a tag, is original.

Graffiti Writing as an Original Literary Work

This section considers how graffiti writing—as literary creativity—might be treated under UK copyright law, as harmonised. Although names (tags) and crew names are unlikely to attract copyright protection because they are not 'literary works', the originality point is discussed because it provides a useful contrast with the rule on name originality in the graffiti subculture which is explored in the subsequent chapter. In copyright law, unlike the law relating to trade marks, the length of a phrase matters because it bears upon whether an original literary *work* exists.[10] As previously suggested, the issue in terms of infringement is whether—assuming the 'skill, labour and judgment'[11] or 'intellectual creation' test is met (to the extent that intellectual creation is equivalent to the UK test)[12] someone should be free to copy 'an invented word which is original'.[13] The difficulty is that the application of the EU standard has not been consistent in the 15 cases decided after *Infopaq* dealing with originality and infringement.[14]

The UK case law indicates that short phrases, such as the book title 'Splendid Misery' in *Dick v Yates*,[15] lack the requisite originality. In that case the combination of two ordinary words was insufficient for the work to be original. The phrase itself was considered to lack 'intellectual effort … [because it] had long been in public use'.[16] Yet the same cannot be said of a fanciful name such as the crew name Burning Candy,[17] which is an unlikely combination of words, not already in public use. This suggests that the name is potentially original because of the creative choices made in combining the two words in a way that, at least arguably, demonstrates a 'personal touch'.[18] By contrast 'Ahead'a the Game'[19] is the appropriation

[10] J Davis and A Durant, 'To Protect or Not to Protect? The Eligibility of Commercially Used Short Verbal Texts for Copyright and Trade Mark Protection' (2011) 4 *Intellectual Property Quarterly* 345–70, 347.

[11] Also sometimes referred to as 'labour, skill or judgment'.

[12] As it is assumed to be in eg *Temple Island Collections v New English Teas* [2012] EWPCC 1.

[13] JN Cullabine, 'Copyright in Short Phrases and Single Words in English Law' (1992) 14 *European Intellectual Property Review* 6, 205–10, 209.

[14] E Derclaye, 'Assessing the Impact and Reception of the Court of Justice of the European Union Case Law on UK Copyright Law: What Does the Future Hold?' (2014) 240 *Revue Internationale Du Droit D'Auteur* 5–117, paper available at www.eprints.nottingham.ac.uk/3613/2/RIDA_article_derclaye_April_2014_eprints.pdf, 18 (citations refer to e-print paper).

[15] *Dick v Yates* (1881–81) LR 18 Ch D 76.

[16] ibid 92. See also *Francis Day and Hunter Ltd v Twentieth Century Fox Corp Ltd* [1940] AC 112.

[17] See chapter one.

[18] As in Case C-145/10 *Painer v Standard Verlags GmbH* [2012] ECDR 6.

[19] See also chapter six.

of a fairly common turn of phrase (albeit expressed in a distinctive manner when written) and would thus be less likely to meet the originality requirement. Indeed, the 'intellectual creation' test in *Infopaq* suggests that words by themselves cannot be original but that creativity might be expressed through 'choice, sequence and combination'[20] where this consists of putting two incongruous words such as 'burning' and 'candy' together. There may be an additional problem here which is that the composition of the words in any graffiti crew name might be found to be 'too slight'[21] to be considered original. It is also an open question whether this would constitute an 'intellectual creation' in the terms set out in recent CJEU copyright jurisprudence. Indeed, the originality of single words may also need to be considered as a possibility post-*Infopaq*.[22]

There is case law to suggest that short phrases, as opposed perhaps to single words, at least may attract copyright protection.[23] Some support for this argument may be found in the reasoning regarding 'intellectual creation' in *Newspaper Licensing Agency v Meltwater*.[24] In the High Court Proudman J held that certain headlines were an 'independent literary work'.[25] The Court of Appeal described this position as 'unassailable'.[26] It held that copyright could subsist in newspaper headlines as original literary works noting:

> A headline is plainly literary as it consists of words. The word 'original' does not connote novelty but that it originated with the author. This test was clearly established in the domestic law of England by the decision of Peterson J. in University of London Press Ltd v University Tutorial Press Ltd [1916] 2 Ch 601 approved by the House of Lords in Ladbroke (Football) Ltd v William Hill (Football) Ltd [1964] 1 WLR 273.[27]

The Court of Appeal emphasised that the post-*Infopaq* originality test, in focusing on origination rather than novelty, did not change the existing UK originality test.[28] Notwithstanding the Court's argument that the originality test remains unchanged, in light of past judicial resistance, the extension of protection to newspaper headlines suggests a change. There is now support for the proposition that copyright might subsist in single words and short phrases. However, *Meltwater* did not clarify the position on copyright subsistence in single words focusing instead on the *Infopaq* emphasis on the combination of words.[29] In light of this lack of clarity on the protection of single words, for words in the form of

[20] *Infopaq* (n 7) [45].

[21] Regarding the phrase 'The Lawyer's Diary', *Rose v Information Service Ltd.* [1987] FSR 254, 255. For an overview discussion see Bently and Sherman (n 1) 97.

[22] C Waelde and P Schlesinger, 'Music and Dance: Beyond Copyright Text?' (2011) 8 *SCRIPTed* 3, 272, note 75.

[23] Davis and Durant (n 10) 349.

[24] *Newspaper Licensing Agency Ltd v Meltwater Holdings BV* [2012] RPC 1 (*Meltwater* (CA)).

[25] *Newspaper Licensing Agency v Meltwater Holding* [2010] EWHC 3099 (Ch) [72].

[26] *Meltwater* (CA) (n 24) [22] (Morritt LJ).

[27] ibid [19].

[28] ibid [20].

[29] Davis and Durant (n 10) 354.

tags to be considered original the extension to the argument would need to be made that it is the combination of *letters* that constitutes the author's own intellectual creation.

Particular tags clearly originate with an author and are not common words. They are instead 'invented' in the manner of 'Exxon'.[30] Thus, it is difficult to argue that tags are not the author's own intellectual creation without simply invoking a *de minimis* requirement[31] that a literary work must be of a particular length. It appears strange that the creativity (or labour) inherent in combining words would be rewarded with copyright protection while the creativity inherent in the creation of a new word via a certain combination of letters would not.[32] There is also a more general difficulty here and that is the underlying assumption that only literary *texts* convey meaning[33] and even then only in being made intelligible through the meaning of the word combinations. The aesthetic and aural aspects of the text—how the combination of a set of letters looks and sounds, both matters relevant to graffiti writers—fit uneasily with a determination of originality limited to the form of textual creativity that is produced only through the stringing together of words.

A further difficulty in finding graffiti names to be original lies in the more recent rejection of keywords which were part of a computer program as intellectual creations in *SAS Institute v World Programming*.[34] The Court of Appeal quoted the lower court in saying:

> [K]eywords, syntax, commands and combination of commands ... considered in isolation, are not, as such, an intellectual creation of the author of the computer program.[35]

The requisite creativity would be demonstrated through 'choice, sequence and combination'.[36] In relation to the meaning of 'intellectual creation' more generally the court observed that '[t]he essence of the term is that the person in question has exercised expressive and creative choices in producing the work.'[37] Tags could be distinguished here from a computer program keyword which serves a particular function within a program and cannot, unlike a name, be said to be 'expressive' of the author. It is also worth considering the use of tags in conjunction with crew

30 See *Exxon v Exxon Insurance* [1982] Ch 119.

31 Describing *Exxon* as 'a limiting instance of textual minimalism': Davis and Durant (n 10) 366.

32 Pointing to this as one of the distinctions that separates invented words from the potential acknowledgement that copyright subsists in short phrases: ibid 366.

33 I am grateful to Fiona Macmillan for this point. For a more expansive reading of the meaning of a 'text' to include both the visual and the written, and also aural see eg, referring to the work of Barthes, P Jaszi, 'Toward a Theory of Copyright: The Metamorphoses of 'Authorship" (1991) *Duke Law Journal* 455, 458, note 9.

34 *SAS Institute v World Programming* [2014] RPC 8 (*SAS Institute* (CA)).

35 ibid [58] (quoting lower court at [66]). See also Bently and Sherman (n 1) 112.

36 *SAS Institute* (CA) (n 34) [58].

37 The court continued: 'The more restricted the choices, the less likely it is that the product will be the intellectual creation (or the expression of the intellectual creation) of the person who produced it.' ibid [31].

names. For instance, pieces might be signed with a tag and crew acronym (eg Elk PFB)[38] or, less commonly, the crew name. Such a combination, akin to the combination of words that form a newspaper headline, may potentially be original in the sense that it is the 'author's own intellectual creation'. On the other hand, it may be considered purely algorithmic, serving a purpose similar to keywords in a computer program to identify the origin of a work as belonging to a writer from a particular crew—the potential combinations are limited to the names of crew members.

Yet meaning is also produced by the pure combination of letters themselves independent of style (style is discussed below). The combination of letters may be chosen for their social or aesthetic significance *apart* from the style in which they are drawn. For example the use of the same letters or similar letter shapes to provide symmetry.[39] The combination of letters also matters in producing certain associations with the writer[40] especially because it will seek to capture something of the writer's individuality or personality. In that sense the name is original precisely because it provides social meaning within the subculture; it takes skill then to make the necessary creative choices to choose a name which is 'clever', in that it both bears some socially significant meaning and provides a good 'set' of letters for the expression of individual style. What is interesting here is that the significance that graffiti writers attach to their name is theoretically (even if not practically) better recognized in the German definition of originality meaning that:

> Not only must the work originate from the author, it must also have been shaped by the author's individual distinct personality; it must not just be commonplace, a work that could be attributed to anyone.[41]

While with certain graffiti tags, for example Cut,[42] it might be more difficult to argue that the requisite individuality is present others such as Dondi[43] seem to possess that elusive quality of individuality or personality that is at the core of the 'intellectual creation' test.

But to look at a tag as a word in isolation is perhaps to miss the point. A tag also gains meaning from 'context and juxtaposition',[44] that is through its visibility in the 'bounded commons' of the graffiti subculture: on the street (the physical commons) and in being spoken of, of being well-respected and having the name associated with one particular writer in the scene (the graffiti-specific intellectual commons). In the graffiti context—though it is unlikely that this is what the court

[38] An example from F Forsyth, *Crack & Shine* (London, FFF, 2009) 21.

[39] eg the interlocking/anchoring letters Anon18 described in relation to letterforms in chapter five.

[40] eg 'names that sounded cool': M Cooper, *Tag Town* (Arsta, Dokument Forlag, 2008) 15.

[41] A Rahmatian, 'Originality in UK Copyright Law: The Old 'Skill and Labour' Doctrine under Pressure' (2013) 44(1) *IIC International Review of Intellectual Property and Competition Law* 4, 17.

[42] An example of a name noticed on walls during fieldwork.

[43] A New York writer whose work is documented in eg M Cooper and H Chalfant, *Subway Art* (London, Thames & Hudson, 1984) 65.

[44] *Exxon* (n 30) [130].

had in mind in *Exxon*—is also gained from its spatial context. It is the navigation of space and, in particular, having to write words quickly in particular spaces, that would seem to suggest that letters are carefully chosen and combined to form words. It seems odd that a name—where the name is 'made up'—might be refused protection for being short when its very brevity is the product of careful creative choices. Bently and Sherman cite a French case to exemplify the more generous approach to intellectual creation in France in which copyright was found to subsist in a single-word title.[45] The UK approach, assuming it has not been altered by EU harmonisation, however, remains far less generous when it comes to assessing the originality of names. But even adopting the apparently more open approach to originality of the 'intellectual creation' test would still pose difficulties where a name is simply a 'common' word unless, and this is beyond the scope of copyright law as we now understand it, its context—as a name recognised as belonging to an individual within the subculture—was recognised and protected.

Graffiti Writing as an Original Artistic Work

If EU copyright harmonisation has had the effect of making subject matter categorisation irrelevant so that the only thing to look for in relation to the subsistence of copyright in graffiti writing as original works is that it meets the 'intellectual creation' standard, it is still nevertheless easier to consider graffiti as an original artistic work. The highly individualised style—demonstrating skill, labour or judgment or 'personal touch'[46]—in which names are written more readily suggests that graffiti writing in the form of a tag, throw-up, or piece is likely to be protected as an original artistic work. The relevant issues discussed in this section are: the status of preparatory sketches in a blackbook and successive versions of graffiti works; whether the simplicity of a tag or throw-up (either as a drawing in a blackbook[47] or as a painting using spray paint on a wall or train) is a bar to originality; and, whether the stylistic similarities in the form of tags, throw-ups and pieces means graffiti writing lacks originality. A further issue discussed is whether copyright subsists in faithful reproductions of historically significant pieces by present-day writers.

Before considering the issue of simplicity of tags and throw-ups, and leaving aside for the moment the issue of stylistic similarities of graffiti writing generally, pieces would undoubtedly qualify for copyright protection as original artistic works (as paintings). The combination of intricate letter style and colour in

[45] 'Clochemerle': Bently and Sherman (n 1) 111 note 134.

[46] eg *Painer* (n 18) [92]. Described also in Case C-604/10 *Football Dataco Ltd v Yahoo! UK Ltd* [2012] 2 CMLR 24 as 'making free and creative choices' [38].

[47] A blackbook is a graffiti writer's sketchbook used to practice style, including tags and colour schemes. A piece is usually sketched in a blackbook before a writer goes to produce it on a wall or train.

graffiti writing is indicative of 'the creative and individual character of those works'[48] and such a contention appears to apply to pieces in particular. The 'skill, labour and judgment' test could be made out with respect to pieces because of the difficulty in executing them (freehand, requiring excellent can control) and the choices made in determining letter angles, shapes, background colours, fills, the addition of characters and other elements. The importance of choice in putting together the various elements of an artistic work is closely tied to the conception of the work itself: subject matter and originality are inseparable.[49] In an infringement case which considered the originality of paintings, *Krisarts v Briarfine*,[50] Whitford J stated:

> [T]he features in which copyright is going to subsist are very often the choice of viewpoint, the exact balance of foreground features or features in the middle ground and features in the far ground, the figures which are introduced, possibly in the case of a river scene the craft may be on the river and so forth. It is in choices of this character that the person producing the artistic work makes his original contribution.[51]

This case concerned the infringement of paintings of Westminster Bridge and its surrounds.[52] The court considered whether such a well-known London scene could be original and concluded, as the above extract indicates, that it could.

Whether or not 'skill, labour and judgment' is effectively the same test as the 'author's own intellectual creation', a typical graffiti piece—a product of numerous creative choices—would appear to be original regardless of which test is applied. The creative choice element was also highlighted in *Temple Island Collections v New English Teas*,[53] relating to the infringement of a photograph of a similar London scene (a red bus in an otherwise black and white photograph of Westminster Bridge with the Houses of Parliament in the background) where the Patents County Court[54] applied the 'author's own intellectual creation' test on the basis that it was equivalent to 'skill and labour'.[55] The Court in *Temple Island* referred to the extract from *Krisarts v Briarfine*[56] above and noted that:

> Plainly the claimant's work is original and I so find. It is the result of Mr Fielder's *own intellectual creation both in terms of his choices* relating to the basic photograph itself: the

[48] T Rychlicki, 'Legal Questions About Illegal Art' (2008) 3(6) *Journal of Intellectual Property Law and Practice* 393, 398. On the applicability of US copyright law see S Sandifer, 'Unauthorized and Unsolicited: Is Graffiti Copyrightable Visual Communication?' (2009) 12 *John F Kennedy University Law Review* 141–50.

[49] J Pila, 'Copyright and Its Categories of Original Works' (2010) 30 *Oxford Journal of Legal Studies* 2, 229–54, 245.

[50] *Krisarts v Briarfine* [1977] FSR 557.

[51] ibid 562. The case it referred to and quoted from to illustrate this point in Pila (n 49) 245.

[52] The plaintiff was seeking an injunction to prevent infringement by the two defendants: *Krisarts v Briarfine* (n 50) 557–58.

[53] *Temple Island* (n 12).

[54] Intellectual property cases are now heard in the Intellectual Property and Enterprise Court.

[55] eg *Temple Island* (n 12) [21], [53].

[56] ibid [25].

precise motif, angle of shot, light and shade, illumination, and exposure *and also in terms of his work after the photograph was taken to manipulate the image to satisfy his own visual aesthetic sense.* The fact that it is a picture combining some iconic symbols of London does not mean the work is not an original work in which copyright subsists. The fact that, to some observers, icons such as Big Ben and a London bus are visual clichés also does not mean no copyright subsists. It plainly does. [Emphasis added.][57]

In discussing whether the work was infringed the court emphasised that the 'visual contrast features'[58] of the work were copied, including the red bus on the black and white background.[59] Limited weight can be attached to this decision, given that it is only a first instance decision, but it is nevertheless instructive in terms of what it suggests about the application of the 'intellectual creation' test to graffiti pieces as artistic works. The creation of a piece is very much a matter of exercising aesthetic choice in determining minute details relating to angles and shading. It also emanates from the writer as the author of the artistic work suggesting that, at the very least, such an example of graffiti writing would be original.

Before a writer creates a piece on a wall he/she will likely have created a drawing in a blackbook with black and/or coloured markers[60] that is effectively the piece in miniature. This might be considered akin to a preparatory sketch. It is likely that a separate copyright will subsist in these drawings as original artistic works. The painted piece on a wall cannot be described as a 'mere copy' of the blackbook drawing. Writers are not creating different versions of effectively the same work as was the case in *Interlego v Tyco.*[61] The transformation of the drawing into the painting is clearly a material alteration of it[62] since a different tool (a spraycan) is used. In any case, *LA Gear v Hi-Tec*[63] indicated that copyright would subsist in early versions of a work regardless of the originality of successive versions.[64]

A question remains, however, as to whether successive versions of the same tag in a blackbook are original. Tags are commonly practised repeatedly in a blackbook by writers.[65] Smaller scale tags may also be placed on walls, doorframes, street furniture and the like that are the same as the tags in a blackbook. Writers will usually use markers to create both. The question is whether copyright can subsist separately in these successive versions on walls given they are (and within the subculture, are understood to be) reproductions of the initial tags practised in a blackbook. The case law suggests that they would not be separate, original

[57] ibid [51].
[58] ibid [63].
[59] ibid [59].
[60] See eg *London Black Book* (no date).
[61] *Interlego AG v Tyco Industries Inc.* [1989] AC 217.
[62] See K Garnett, G Davies and G Harbottle, *Copinger and Skone James on Copyright Volume One*, 16th edn (London, Thomson Reuters, 2011) [3-133].
[63] *LA Gear Inc v Hi-Tec Sport Sports Plc* [1992] FSR 121, CA.
[64] Garnett et al (n 62) [3-136].
[65] Writers may write their tags in others' blackbooks as well as copy others' tags in their own: see chapter seven.

works merely due to a change of scale, because such a change would not be visually significant.[66] The relentless copying of one's own tag may then be understood in terms of a writer exercising their right to reproduce their own artistic work. The same tag transformed and enlarged into a throw-up or piece would, of course, attract separate protection as an original artistic work assuming it meets the relevant originality standard.

A more pertinent question is whether the simplicity of tags and throw-ups (some of which may consist of only a few stylised letters eg a name seen on London tracksides during fieldwork, Tox, occasionally written as Toxic) indicates that they are not original artistic works. Some tags are elaborate to the point of being illegible to the non-writer: are such tags original while tags written in neat, straight letters are not? (This issue does not apply to throw-ups which may be created using two colours; the choice of colour combinations is likely to ensure that copyright subsists in them as artistic works.)[67] Simplicity in and of itself is not a bar to the finding of originality.[68] A tag originates with its author and, certainly in the case of the more evidently 'calligraphic' tags, the choice of angles and the shapes of the letter created with a marker or spraycan suggest that they are the writer's 'intellectual creation'. Considered in terms of 'skill, labour and judgment', a set of stylised letters forming a tag would also meet these criteria. A tag, especially a good tag in graffiti writing terms—that is, a tag meeting the subculture's own aesthetic criteria[69]—created with an individual style that is also skilfully executed, is very difficult to master. Such mastery will often be the result of years of practice.[70]

Tags that are 'neat' or more easily read may, on the face of it, not qualify for protection as artistic works as a result of being too simple and therefore lacking in evidence of 'skill, labour and judgment' or of free, creative choices. Yet, given the skill required to create a 'new' (in terms of graffiti writing as a subculture rather than copyright law) style for a seemingly simple tag, it is difficult to predict which tags would be protected as original artistic works and which would not be. So long as the tag is 'visually significant'[71] it is difficult to determine that it is too simple to be protected.[72] Perhaps the best argument for the originality of tags notwithstanding their apparent simplicity lies in an analogy with the logo in question in *R Griggs Group v Evans*.[73]

[66] Garnett et al (n 62) [3-133].

[67] ibid [3-131].

[68] ibid [3-130]. See also eg the court's comment that the 'simple' drawing of a cape was original: *Merlet v Mothercare Plc* [1986] RPC 115 [118].

[69] On style, see chapter seven. Note, by contrast, that under CDPA, s 4(1)(a) artistic works are to be protected 'irrespective of artistic quality'.

[70] See eg video series of writer's creating tags in blackbooks writersblock187. *Kanal von writers-block187*, www.youtube.com/user/writersblock187?feature=watch.

[71] *Interlego v Tyco* (n 61) 258 (Lord Oliver).

[72] See in the context of a subject matter discussion on simple artistic works: Garnett et al (n 62) [3-56].

[73] *R Griggs Group v Evans* [2003] EWHC 2914 (Ch). The two appeals did not consider the original work point and the originality point was not further discussed in the first instance decision except to note that copying would amount to an appropriation of the author's 'skill and labour': [27].

This raises the question of how to distinguish between the taking of an idea (ie a particular stylistic innovation such as a way of interlocking letters, or the adding of additional elements such as a halo or arrow) versus its expression (ie the angles or colours used to write a name). Again, the above reasoning also implies that it is the appropriation of another's labour that is problematic. For example, where one writer writes his/her own name using a different set of letters and letter combinations but reproduces the angles and colours of another writer's piece, is this an infringement? The same question applies to the reproduction of letter angles in a tag but using a different set of letters. The picture might be complicated further where some, but not all, of the same letters are used in the potentially infringing artistic work in the form of a tag or piece. This issue arises with respect to the copying of non-graffiti artistic styles as well.[143]

Protecting style in graffiti writing appears to fall foul of the distinction made between an idea and its expression. The UK cases, *Baigent v Random House*[144] and *Temple Island v New English Teas*[145] provide some insight into how graffiti style might be treated in relation to copyright infringement. In *Baigent v Random House* the Court of Appeal considered whether taking the themes in a literary work could amount to a reproduction, holding that the 'central theme' in the claimants' work was 'not of a sufficiently developed character'[146] so as to form a substantial part of their work. The case raises the possibility that 'architectural similarities' in the 'detailed treatment' of characters, themes and the like could constitute infringement by reproduction.[147] The notion of thematic copying is, arguably, analogous to the copying of style in the sense that the overall structure—for example, copying a certain *kind* of lettering—makes the *flow* of the piece is the same. Applying the *Baigent* reasoning to artistic works requires an assessment of whether the copying of another writer's style would be infringing where the copying is more than, say the idea of a chrome and red throw-up that is taken but rather the entire visual 'architecture or structure'[148] of a piece. Thus, even if different letters are used, the details in terms of the type of angle, the type of shading and the type of colour contrasts used could amount to the appropriation of the first writer's skill, labour and judgment (or rather, 'intellectual creation').

The difficulty in determining what constitutes 'substantial part' gives credence to the view that the idea/expression dichotomy is unhelpful and that what courts must actually determine is whether an expression is 'protectable' or not, since there

[143] Albeit regarding a film, Nourse LJ indicated that using an artistic style to produce 'entirely different subject matter' would not be infringing: *Norowzian v Arks Limited (No 2)* [2000] EMLR 67 [74].

[144] *Baigent v Random House* [2007] FSR 24.

[145] *Temple Island* (n 12) [25].

[146] *Baigent v Random House* (n 144) [154] (Mummery LJ).

[147] ibid.

[148] Architecture and structure are referred to interchangeably as 'the product of the skill and labour involved in the creation of a literary work': ibid [85] (Lloyd LJ).

can be no idea without an expression.[149] Unsurprisingly, the line here is very fine, as *Temple Island v New English Teas* demonstrates. Styles of art are not protected by copyright while the expression in a particular style of art would be.[150] Yet, in that case, taking into account the 'visual contrast features'[151] of the red bus against a black and white background does seem perilously close to protecting an idea rather than its expression. The defendant had not photocopied the photograph but taken his own photograph with the same features, colours, etc. However, the visual contrast was one of the elements identified by the judge as being the plaintiff author's 'own intellectual creation'.[152] Having addressed both composition and the 'visual contrast' features Judge Birss QC (as he then was) held:

> In the end the issue turns on a qualitative assessment of the reproduced elements. The elements which have been reproduced are a substantial part of the claimant's work because, despite the absence of some important compositional elements, they still *include the key combination* of what I have called the visual contrast features with the basic composition of the scene itself. [Emphasis added.][153]

Similarly, in the hypothetical example of copying the angles and colour schemes that form part of a writer's style, it would seem that such copying, though indirect, could constitute infringement once we carry out a qualitative assessment of the combination of features or the reliance on the structure or architecture of the first (ie allegedly copied) artistic work. It is worth noting that proving that the apparent simplicity of letter angles is in fact more complicated and fully an example of skill, labour and judgment or of 'intellectual creation' would likely require expert evidence to be called.[154] The experts in this hypothetical would likely be graffiti writers working legally. However, a judge would still be required to interpret the taking of these apparently simple elements to be qualitatively significant.

With respect to copyright infringement, however, a strict interpretation of the 'substantial part' provision as relating to expression is perhaps preferable to the more nebulous concept of style, overall 'look' or the reproduction of structure. Making a distinction between ideas and expression ostensibly avoids attempts to use copyright rules to stifle creativity because ideas can be freely used. One argument, in the US context, is that the 'underlying style' should not be a factor in determining infringement:

> Copying style and appropriating evocative power are not copyright infringements unless the resulting work is substantially similar to the inspirational one. Allowing comparisons of style rather than complete works to underpin a substantial similarity analysis is what

[149] RH Jones, 'The Myth of the Idea/Expression Dichotomy in Copyright Law' (1990) 10(3) *Pace Law Review* 551, 552.
[150] Stokes (n 83) 6. Pointillism is provided as an example of a style.
[151] *Temple Island* (n 12) [52]–[53].
[152] ibid [53].
[153] ibid [63].
[154] On the use of expert evidence regarding a musical work, see eg *Redwood Music Ltd v Chappell & Co Ltd* [1982] RPC 5.

> enables, for example, the heirs of Alexander Calder to bully and intimidate artists making kinetic metal mobiles, ... Any use of copyright power that impedes the creation and distribution of new works inherently undermines the very goals of copyright law and needs to be challenged.[155]

The problem posed by graffiti creativity—in fact a problem inherent in the application of copyright rules to creativity generally—is that the distinction between the appropriation of 'evocative power' and its more concrete expressive form can be difficult to draw. When a graffiti writer resurrects a 1970s style of letterforms and colours it would not necessarily be difficult to pin point a piece where these exact same forms are used.[156] Yet an overzealous guarding of graffiti styles would have a detrimental effect on the safeguarding of graffiti culture, given the choice of an 'old' style may have been motivated by a desire to acknowledge and build upon the work of early graffiti writers and so demonstrate belonging within the subculture.

A greater difficulty may lie in showing how the pieces differ as a matter of fact when, to the lay or untrained eye, they may appear to be essentially identical. By contrast, to graffiti writers minute changes may be significant enough to show that a 'substantial part' has *not* been taken. *Designers Guild v Russell Williams* is again useful here. Notwithstanding the different ways the issue of copying was approached in that case, the majority considered the appropriation of skill and labour to be crucial.[157] This is because while the original writer's labour and skill in developing a new aspect of style may have been appropriated, the injection of the new writer's contribution makes the copying insubstantial. The problem remains, however, in determining the extent of skill and labour taken when the original work is itself part of a strong tradition of graffiti creativity building upon the work of others. The reproduction rules are ill-equipped to deal with subcultural creativity where the approach to copying, as chapter seven will show, is highly nuanced. Graffiti writers show an intolerance for the copying of apparently minor stylistic parts of a work but, at the same time, accept the copying of certain styles as necessary for the development of graffiti culture. By contrast, outside the workings of the subculture, copyright law would have no trouble in finding that an exact reproduction, by way of a photograph, of a whole graffiti piece taken by a member of the public would be an infringement.

This section now turns to the reproduction of a discrete element from a piece as opposed to its style more broadly. Apart from the application of the copyright rules on reproduction it is, again, difficult to escape from the contention that the outcome would depend in large part on how evidence is treated. In other words, it would seem to matter who the audience is here. The audience for a work may

[155] A Bartow, 'Copyrights and Creative Copying' (2004) 1 *University of Ottawa Law & Technology Journal* 75, 96.

[156] Subconscious copying might also be at issue given the familiarity many writers have with early, important pieces in the subculture.

[157] Stokes (n 83) 65.

be concerned with aspects of the work that are irrelevant to an assessment of the part of the work taken.[158] In *Billhofer*, discussed above in relation to originality, the court observed:

> To whom, one asks, would the flow-line have been the salient feature and the dimensions 'crucial'? Not to a visitor observing the exhaust pipe mounted on a plinth at the Tate Gallery but to the engineer wanting to make an exhaust which would fit under a Marina. In my judgment, therefore, the question in this case is whether the particular dimensions and spatial arrangements taken by Mr. Hardcastle from the Billhöfer design would to an engineer have been of sufficient importance to constitute a substantial part of the overall drawing. This is a question of fact and degree.[159]

Graffiti writers will be in a position to judge an allegedly infringing work not only in a way that might appear more sensitive to its content—and thus a more sensitive consideration of whether a substantial part had been taken from an earlier discrete work—but also to its context, so that the assessment of the reproduction takes into account any number of works that form part of the graffiti-specific intellectual commons. In relation to this latter point, it makes little sense to assess any two works without also assessing their position in the subculture more broadly especially since the allegedly infringed work would also be constituted by numerous influences such as to make any similarities between them explicable by reference to the wider culture.[160]

Two further points can be made here. First, the assumption that the 'correct' audience to determine whether a substantial part of graffiti writing as an artistic work had been taken is necessarily an audience of graffiti writers is problematic. It suggests that graffiti writing is not also art in which case the public generally might be an appropriate audience (as it is in fact when the works are placed in the street). The difficulty of course is that the latter audience may miss tiny but significant parts of a copied work while the former would not. Additional complexity is introduced by the reference in *Billhofer* above to an audience in a certain *space*. In particular, it is interesting to note the invocation of the Tate, echoing the Court of Appeal in *Lucasfilm*,[161] as potentially emblematic of how spatial context might change the assessment of subject matter and/or infringement. But when it comes to graffiti writing the street is the relevant space for both audiences. This in any event does not offer assistance in determining the taking of a substantial part. The exercise of locational creativity necessary for choosing appropriate surfaces would be a relevant aspect of a work but not one that can be accommodated by copyright law. Second, the perspective of a graffiti audience would be especially relevant to gauging the significance of the incorporation of creative expressions drawn from

[158] Bently and Sherman (n 1) 201; suggesting instead a focus on substantial part by reference to the work *Designers Guild* (n 127) per Lord Hoffmann.

[159] *Billhofer* (n 85) 122.

[160] See in context of the public domain discussion in chapter two.

[161] *Lucasfilm Ltd and Others v Ainsworth and Another* [2009] EWCA Civ 1328 [54] (Jacob LJ).

graffiti culture. Yet while the copyright rules relating to infringement may be useful in determining whether a 'substantial part' had been taken, existing copyright law provides little or no protection from the more generalised use of graffiti style, for example, using such a style in advertising that might be considered exploitative of graffiti culture as a whole.

The difficulties that arise in applying copyright law to graffiti creativity are exemplified by a copying controversy within the graffiti subculture. The controversy related to alleged copying by Fab Five Freddie of elements of works from writers Sever, Aroe and others.[162] This is an example of an allegation that several aspects of the work of different authors had been appropriated rather than a complaint based on the copying of the overall style of another's work. Without reproducing all of the works in question, if the extracts below from the complaint by Revok (the writer who made the allegation of copying on his own website) were to be decided on the basis of copyright rules on infringement as opposed to the graffiti rules, it is not entirely clear what the result would be.

When it is a matter of taking an element, the allegations related to a series of canvas works consisting of interlocking letters painted on to a background made up of a collage of train carriages.[163] The specific allegations of copying regarding a number of works were:

> SEVER's S upside down as well as a E from a SEVER piece. The top letter is a Y, flipped upside down and stolen from YES2 out of the Bronx. …
>
> … SEVER's R is the central focus here, turned 45 degrees counter-clockwise surrounded by more elements from SEVER's pieces.
>
> SEVER's E is at the center here, rotated 180 degrees counterclockwise. Looks like a M belonging to TOTEM is also centre.
>
> Another of SEVER's E's as well as another of his V's…[164]

Furthermore, the allegation was made that these elements were 'photoshopped' (presumably as opposed to have been inserted freehand) onto the canvas.[165] The difficulties in determining whether infringements have occurred here are broadly similar to those faced by the Court in *Designers Guild v Russell Williams* in determining whether a fabric design called 'Marguerite' infringed the 'Ixia' fabric. Both included stripes overlaid with flowers, the 'same brushstroke technique' and the same leaf colour.[166]

[162] Revok. '"Yo" Fab 5 Freddie, you're a corny wannabe, where's Sever's check?' *Revok1* (webpage no longer available). The controversy related to the alleged copying of works placed on walls in paintings on canvas rather than copies that were also placed on a wall.

[163] For the relevant photographs see piece by Sever from the book, Rime and A Grunhauser, *The Exchange* (Berlin, From Here to Fame Publishing, 2012) 12.

[164] Revok (n 162).

[165] ibid.

[166] Summary of findings of fact of the trial judge: *Designers Guild* (n 127) [10] (Lord Hoffman).

One issue that springs out of Revok's allegations is that only one element (a letter in Sever's style) was taken from a larger piece and turned. Although infringement is a matter of quality rather than quantity it is unclear whether taking one letter out of five from Sever's original work would constitute a 'substantial part' of Sever's work for the purposes of copyright law. The idea/expression dichotomy is not relevant here as it was not the idea of an 'S' for instance that was taken but the 'S' itself in the relevant style. It is, unlike with the fabrics, a 'discrete part'.[167] Yet, as *Designers Guild v Russell Williams* indicates, a finding of infringement cannot be avoided by arguing that the letter itself is not original.[168] It would not therefore matter if it transpired that this element was typical within graffiti culture. Instead, the court would look to the importance (quality) of the 'S' in Sever's work.[169] The reasoning with respect to the fabrics is equally applicable here: determining whether it is a substantial part 'depends on the importance to the copyright work'.[170]

Quite apart from the cultural significance of letterforms to graffiti creativity, taking one letter from a complex piece would appear to amount to a substantial part of the artistic work because every single letter is integral to it. Taken in the context of the *whole* piece consisting of letters in that style, taking one letter from a piece is an appropriation of the author's skill, labour and judgment (or, intellectual creation) because of the time, effort and technical proficiency required to execute the letter in an individual style. It is not relevant that the letter by itself may not have attracted copyright protection.[171] The *Designers Guild* approach to reproduction discussed above appears to offer some flexibility in determining what 'substantial part' might mean with respect to graffiti creativity but this would depend on a highly sensitive application of the test that took into account the perspective of graffiti writers themselves.

Intellectual Creation, Reproduction and the Adaptation of Graffiti Style

To the extent that reproduction potentially interferes with the personality of the author and, given the difficulty of categorising graffiti work because it can be categorised for the purpose of determining copyright subject matter as literary or artistic, the intellectual creation approach which simply asks whether an original part has been taken, presents, post-*Infopaq*, a successor to the qualitative

[167] ibid.

[168] ibid [60] (Lord Foscote).

[169] On the importance of the quality not the quantity of the taking see *Ladbroke v William Hill* (n 129) [276] (Lord Reid).

[170] *Designers Guild* (n 127) [41] (Lord Millett).

[171] See *Baigent v Random House* (n 155) [131]–[132] (Mummery LJ).

assessment demanded by *Designers Guild*.[172] Whether the outcome of an assessment of reproduction under the harmonised test will produce a distinguishably different outcome to the application of the UK 'substantial part' test is, however, an open question.[173]

Returning to the example above regarding the alleged reproduction of letters from a graffiti piece, the question a court would ask would be whether the letter was a part, as stated in *Infopaq*, 'contain[ing] elements which are the expression of the intellectual creation of the author of the work'.[174] The meaning of reproduction is, the CJEU continued, to be 'construed broadly'[175] in line with certain Infosoc Directive recitals:

> [T]o introduce a high level of protection, in particular for authors to enable them to receive an appropriate reward for the use of their works, including at the time of reproduction of those works, in order to be able to pursue their creative and artistic work.[176]

This is notable, apart from the appeal to labour and desert justifications for copyright protection, because it would appear to make it relatively straightforward for the graffiti writer to isolate the letter in question and demonstrate that—through the choice of angles, colours, shading, etc—that this 'part' is original and has been reproduced. The reproduction of a part of a tag might pose more difficulty in the sense that the (creative) choices exercised in relation to the execution of a single letter are—or at least appear to the non-writer—to be highly constrained.[177]

Moving away from a concern with the reproduction of a discrete part of a graffiti piece leads to a question of whether taking the general design of a graffiti piece would be an infringement.[178] This might mean, for example, copying the precise style of another writer with a similar means of interlocking the letters in a piece without using any of the same letters. Another example might be the re-contextualisation of graffiti from one surface, or one space, to another.[179] It is not clear at present how the reproduction of an artistic work's layout might be protected post-*Infopaq*.[180] Notwithstanding that the Infosoc Directive has only harmonised the reproduction right and not the adaptation right it seems

[172] At least with respect to the reproduction of authorial works and also communication to the public and distribution; adaptation seems to remain under the old test: Bently and Sherman (n 1) 196.

[173] ibid.

[174] *Infopaq* (n 7) [39].

[175] ibid [41].

[176] ibid [40].

[177] Both *Infopaq* (n 7) and *Meltwater* (n 24) considered originality of phrases rather than single words, however, the issue that presents itself here is not that a single word or letter cannot be an intellectual creation but simply whether the single letter contains the relevant kind of creativity. On the relevance of 'creativity *per se*' see Griffiths (n 123) 784.

[178] This is the difference between 'partial' and 'altered' copying identified in *Designers Guild*: Griffiths (n 123) 784.

[179] See, on the adaptation of authorial works, including artistic, K Treiger-Bar-Am, 'Kant on Copyright: Rights of Transformative Authorship' (2008) 25(3) *Cardozo Arts and Entertainment Law Journal* 1059, 1079–80.

[180] Bently and Sherman (n 1) 215.

possible that the CJEU will expand the *Infopaq* reasoning to cover rights other than reproduction.[181] The UK adaptation right covers literary, musical and dramatic works only[182] but it may be that reproduction will be interpreted in such a way as to cover the adaptation of artistic works too by bringing it within the ambit of the reproduction right post-*Infopaq*.[183]

In the recent *Allposters* decision the CJEU was careful not to interpret 'adaptation' as it appears in the Berne Convention[184] but, as Rosati argues, adaptation was neither ruled out nor explicitly said to be covered by the Infosoc Directive.[185] The CJEU instead proceeded to find that a change in an artistic work's material support—from paper poster to canvas—and its sale implicated the distribution right.[186] This interpretation of the distribution right, combined with the expansive reading of reproduction in *Infopaq*, suggests that for Member States 'the room left for independent definitions of the right of adaptation and related exceptions... is considerably tight.'[187] In any event, in terms of graffiti creativity, an expansion of the right of adaptation to cover artistic works would fit more easily with the copying of style—chip lettering, Bronx style, for example—that is otherwise difficult to cover by the reproduction right because it is an example of *altered* (or, 'colourable imitation')[188] rather than *partial* copying.[189]

Communication to the Public of Literary and Artistic Works

Under section 20(1)(a) CDPA the 'communication to the public of the work' is an act restricted to the owners of copyright in authorial works. Communication to the public includes electronic transmissions such as broadcasts.[190] This in turn includes placing the works on the internet:[191] the Infosoc Directive refers to 'wire and wireless means'.[192] The communication to the public of graffiti creativity as literary and/or artistic works occurs, for example, in the context of publishing photographs of the works in subculture blogs. Photographs, especially recent photographs of pieces or throw-ups on trains ('runners'), are submitted anonymously to magazines and blogs which are read by writers and those interested in the graffiti subculture.

[181] See Griffiths (n 123) 784.

[182] CDPA, s 21(1). The line between reproduction and adaptation has been recognised as 'unclear': *Hodgson v Isaac* [2010] EWPCC 37, [21].

[183] Griffiths (n 123) 784.

[184] Case C-419/13 *Art & Allposters International BV v Stichting Pictoright* [2015] ECDR 8, [27].

[185] E Rosati, 'CJEU Says that Copyright Exhaustion Only Applies to the Tangible Support of a Work' (2015) 10(5) *Journal of Intellectual Property Law & Practice* 327, 329.

[186] Infosoc Directive, Art 4.

[187] Rosati (n 185) 330.

[188] *Designers Guild* (n 127) [38] (Lord Millett).

[189] On which see Griffiths (n 123) 784.

[190] CDPA, s 20(2).

[191] See generally W Cornish, D Llewelyn and T Aplin, *Intellectual Property: Patents, Copyright, Trade Marks and Allied Rights*, 7th edn (London, Sweet & Maxwell, 2010) [12-37].

[192] Infosoc Directive, Art 3(1).

As indicated in chapter one, the sharing of photographs is an integral part of the graffiti culture. Historically, writers traded photographs and when technology enabled it, published them in graffiti magazines.[193] The photographs in key graffiti texts such as *Spraycan Art*[194] played an important part in disseminating graffiti culture. At present the dissemination of photographs of graffiti on the internet, some argue, has had a corrosive effect on the graffiti subculture by providing the opportunity to garner fame without effort (ie fame based on internet visibility rather than visibility in urban space).[195] On the other hand, this also makes different styles, new and historical, available to other writers for inspiration.

The reproduction of graffiti in the form of photographs on blogs and linking to graffiti material including photographs and reproductions of sketches would appear to be a communication in the sense of 'making available to the public'.[196] Therefore, the digital dissemination of graffiti culture, notwithstanding that such sharing is crucial to the maintenance and promotion of graffiti writing within the graffiti subculture's commons, is likely to constitute copyright infringement. (The same point will apply to reproduction and communication by non-writers sharing images on social media for example.) A trickier issue is presented by hyperlinking. In *Svensson v Retriever Sverige AB*[197] the CJEU reasoned that providing a link to a work was making that work available but that the provision of the link will not necessarily be an infringement of the communication right. The crucial issue, according to the CJEU was that the material was not being communicated to a 'new public'.[198] What this appears to mean is that, in relation to graffiti writing, for a link not to be infringing the works needed to have been made available initially by the writer or someone else who was granted permission to post the work. Yet, such a scenario is unlikely: such permission would either not be granted, or in any sense be obvious. This is another example of a gap between the creative process within the graffiti subculture and the regulation of creativity through copyright law.

In short, in applying the communication right to the production and dissemination of graffiti creativity within the subculture it becomes clear that much of what is taken for granted as acceptable by graffiti writers—such as the dissemination of photographs of graffiti on social media—would likely constitute an infringement of the right to communicate the work to the public. Copyright notions of authorisation make very little sense in the graffiti context for this reason. Further difficulties also arise with respect to the meaning of distribution, in particular with respect to the exhibition of artistic works.

[193] GJ Snyder, *Graffiti Lives: Beyond the Tag in New York's Urban Underground* (New York, New York University Press, 2009) 171.

[194] H Chalfant and J Prigoff, *Spraycan Art* (London, Thames & Hudson, 1987).

[195] On 'cheap fame' see chapter one.

[196] CDPA, s 20(2)(b).

[197] Case C-466/12 *Svensson and Others v Retriever Sverige AB* [2014] 3 CMLR 4.

[198] ibid [24]–[30].

Distribution of Artistic Works

Applying the distribution right to graffiti creativity raises further issues: the distribution of graffiti creativity via small circulation specialist magazines and the distribution of graffiti creativity via books[199] is also relevant to the sharing of graffiti culture by non-writers. Were the distribution right to be raised in the case of specialist magazines available in online stores and in shops specialising in the sale of graffiti-related materials, a question might arise as to whether it would constitute distribution to the *public*. Bently and Sherman suggest that the distribution right would not catch sharing within 'a small personal network, such as a family network or within a firm'.[200] The graffiti subculture potentially falls through the cracks of copyright regulation here. The graffiti 'scene' is not perhaps so small to count as a family network but it does not seem fitting to consider publications with graffiti writers as the expected audience a general public distribution either. On the other hand, certain magazines could be bought by any member of the public online—including a PhD student researching graffiti writing—which suggests public distribution, albeit limited.

Another issue is the display of graffiti works in exhibitions and art fairs directed at least in part to graffiti writers and street artists. The 'showing' or 'performing' of a work in public is restricted, in section 19 CDPA to literary, musical and dramatic works[201] and sound recordings, films and broadcasts.[202] Artistic works are not included at all under this heading—there is no separate right to exhibit or display artistic works—and so graffiti writing could only be protected if the work was first shown to be a literary work, which (as chapter four showed) is a difficult task. The display of (a photograph depicting) graffiti writing will not therefore infringe under this section. Moreover the distribution right has not been harmonised at the EU level so as to include display or exhibition of artistic works.[203] Some sharing of graffiti creativity would thus appear to fall between the protection offered by the right to communicate to the public and the distribution right.

Defences to Infringement

The preceding discussion indicates that copyright is likely to subsist in graffiti writing, most likely as an artistic work, and so graffiti writers will hold certain economic rights that will be infringed when, for example, one writer copies part

[199] eg R Schacter, *The World Atlas of Street Art and Graffiti* (London, Aurum Press, 2013).

[200] Bently and Sherman (n 1) 150–1.

[201] CDPA, s 19(1) regarding 'performance'.

[202] CDPA, s 19(3) regarding 'showing'.

[203] Bently and Sherman (n 1) 150 discussing Case C-456/06 *Peek & Cloppenburg SA v Cassina SpA* [2008] ECR I-2731.

of another writer's style. This part provides an overview of those defences to copyright infringement that would be most relevant to graffiti creativity if it were not regulated by the graffiti rules within the 'bounded commons' of the graffiti subculture, but the discussion is also relevant to interaction with graffiti of those not within the subculture, especially members of the general public. It considers first the applicability of fair dealing for the purposes of private research and study and briefly, second, fair dealing for the purpose of reporting news and current events. Other relevant exceptions, the section 62 CDPA public placement exception, quotation and the more recent (and even more recently quashed) personal use exception are considered in chapters seven and ten.

Fair Dealing for Research or Private Study

Under section 29(1) CDPA copyright in a literary or artistic work[204] is not infringed where there is fair dealing for the purposes of research or private study with the proviso that a 'sufficient acknowledgment' is provided. The acknowledgement is normally in the form of a name though in the case of graffiti writing an argument might be made that, since the work is the name (albeit an alias), acknowledgment is provided automatically, since it is the tag that is significant to graffiti writers as an audience.[205] On the other hand, a 'sufficient acknowledgment' cannot be provided because, while the author's pseudonym is obvious, their actual name may not, and could not, be 'ascertain[ed] ... by reasonable inquiry'.[206] In any event, it is clear that the CDPA is not calibrated to account for subcultural creativity of this kind.

A further requirement for an individual seeking to take advantage of this defence is to demonstrate that the dealing is 'fair'. This raises questions about the ways in which graffiti creativity is accessed and whether works placed in public places would constitute works that have been made 'readily available'.[207] If so, this might make it more likely that a dealing will be 'fair'. While taking the whole work will likely not constitute a fair dealing, perhaps, by analogy to the copying of a (publicly accessible) short, literary work on a tombstone,[208] the copying of graffiti as an artistic or literary work might also be covered because a work on a public street is similarly accessible. If so, the research and private study defence would be available with respect to graffiti writing in this context.

This exception to copyright infringement is particularly relevant to graffiti writers because of the practice of copying other writer's tags, throw-ups and pieces

[204] Subsection (1) also refers to dramatic and musical works.

[205] By reference to *Pro Sieben Media AG v Carlton UK Television Ltd* [1999] 1 WLR 605; Garnett et al (n 62) [9-34].

[206] CDPA, s 178.

[207] Bently and Sherman (n 1) 237.

[208] *Hubbard v Vosper* [1972] 2 QB 84, 98. Dicta did not turn on the question of public availability here.

in a blackbook. For new graffiti writers especially, copying others is a crucial aspect of working out their own style. Others' work is copied into the blackbook as a way of 'researching style' and to practice the skill of writing letters. For section 29(1) CDPA to apply, the use of the work must be non-commercial which would likely be the case when it comes to graffiti writers' reproductions of others' work in blackbooks.[209] The exception would likely not, however, cover graffiti writers who copy another's work and place it on a wall because this would be difficult to construe as *private* study.

In terms of copying on walls and trains, that is, when graffiti writers are competing for fame rather than practising in blackbooks (though the line between practice and fame-seeking is blurry when wall practice is needed too, to improve style) they would not be able to take advantage of the private study exception. This does the raise the question of whether a fair use defence as it exists in the US would be useful here.[210] Its application could mean that certain reproductions of graffiti works by writers, for example in adopting certain stylistic innovations, would be transformative.[211] Such an argument would be relevant to the Fab Five Freddy controversy described above insofar as the various elements allegedly taken were 'turned' at a different angle and incorporated as part of a larger work referencing the graffiti subculture's roots (as evidenced by the background which consisted of train carriages).

A minor but interesting point is also raised in the application of the argument in *Express Newspapers*[212] with respect to tit for tat copying. A writer may argue that copying (but transforming) parts of other writers' work was a common practice than was integral to the development of style in the subculture as a whole. In that sense, a writer might conceptualise it as a defence not for private study but rather for the promotion of culture, a view that only makes sense within a 'bounded commons' in which a community has a common conception of culture. Finally, there is unlikely to be a 'sufficient acknowledgment'[213] of the other writer unless perhaps the writer whose style is copied happens to be acknowledged in a 'shout out'[214] for example, by writing that writer's tag (though not in their style) on the fringes of a piece to acknowledge the use of the work.

[209] Private study is defined as being study that is otherwise than directly or indirectly commercial: CDPA, s 178.

[210] 17 USC § 107 (2000). See chapter ten.

[211] J Litman, 'Lawful Personal Use' (2007) 85 *Texas Law Review* 1871, 1899, note 161: 'Although … transformative use is not absolutely necessary for a finding of fair use … the goal of copyright, to promote science and the arts, is generally furthered by the creation of transformative works.' See *Campbell v Acuff-Rose Music, Inc.*, 510 US 569, 578–79 (1994).

[212] *Express Newspapers plc v News (UK) Ltd* [1990] FSR 359.

[213] CDPA, s 30(1).

[214] See chapter seven.

Fair Dealing for Reporting Current Events

Other exceptions appear to be potentially relevant but are, on closer inspection, revealed to be of little use where subcultural creativity is at issue. One such exception relates to fair dealing for reporting current events. The question here is whether the creator of a graffiti specific magazine or graffiti blog may take advantage of the news reporting exception to the extent that graffiti creativity has been made available to the public, specifically via 'exhibition'.[215] In particular, fair dealing for the purpose of reporting current events[216] might be applied to the hypothetical scenario—since such reproduction increases the exposure of the writer's work and would likely not be opposed—of a graffiti writer seeking to prevent the reproduction of their work in a graffiti magazine. The producer of the magazine could seek to take advantage of this defence, except that—even accounting for the broad construction in the case *Newspaper Licensing Agency v Marks & Spencer*[217]—it is not clear that the reproduction of graffiti writing would constitute either 'events' or reporting given the types of cases where such an argument has been successful focus on mainstream, as opposed to subcultural, occurrences such as large-scale sporting events. That graffiti magazine use would not appear to be covered by the exception is problematic because this is the kind of exception that would be needed for the development of graffiti culture and, in the context of the discussion in chapter two, the promotion of an attractive and plural culture more broadly.

Conclusion

In conjunction with the discussion of subject matter in chapter four, this chapter suggests that, when potential public policy difficulties are set aside, graffiti creativity, especially in the form of a piece, can be an original artistic work in which copyright subsists. In providing an overview of the copyright rules relating to originality and infringement by reproduction and communication to the public, this chapter serves as a precursor to the discussion in chapter seven of the analogous rules within the graffiti subculture regulating originality and biting (copying). As the discussion above indicates, graffiti creativity presents an uneasy object of regulation by copyright law both because of the manner of its production and the form that sharing takes within the subculture. In particular, the notion that sharing ought to be prevented makes little sense when the dissemination of copies

215 CDPA, s 30(1A)(d).

216 CDPA, s 30(2). But note that photographs are excluded.

217 *Newspaper Licensing Agency v Marks & Spencer* [1999] EMLR 369 [17].

of graffiti works is important to the promotion of graffiti culture so that originality and copying mean something different within the subculture's own intellectual commons. We can see once more the difficulties faced by a body of legal rules—here the copyright rules on originality and infringement—which apply at the level of the polity as a whole and so must be (at least superficially) neutral as to the form which creativity takes when faced by a subculture which is constituted by a commitment to the value of one type of creative process and specific types of creative work. In forbearing copyright protection graffiti writers actively produce an alternative set of norms in the graffiti subculture's 'bounded commons' that reflects the richness of their experience as writers within the subculture and seeks to protect their works from unacceptable exploitation while allowing the subculture to flourish.

7

Graffiti Rules—Be Original, Don't Bite

> [I]t doesn't have to be beautiful for people to like [it], it has to be, you know, you have to just do your thing: [it's] consistency and originality. But that's all part of the rules which people know, which is a part of, which is an important part of the scene … You can be inspired or, you know, maybe reference something but you've got to have your own twist on it, you've got to be different, you've got to have your own take, you know, which is what makes us all different. (Anon27)

Introduction

The graffiti rules and practices described in this chapter can be summarised in the simple exhortation: 'be original'. Graffiti writers' understanding of originality is closely bound up with their preoccupation with the concept of style and more specifically, the need to *have* style. As chapters one and five indicated, 'getting up' is one of the key motivations for engaging in graffiti writing. This chapter is therefore concerned with what it means to be 'original' while getting up. A writer will gain respect for being 'up' but lose respect if it transpires that his/her style was illegitimately copied from another writer. This chapter considers what has broadly been termed the rule against biting (copying) but actually covers two closely related concerns. The first is to have an original style of writing, which includes having 'can control' (ability in using a spraycan). The second is the prohibition against biting the name or style of other writers. The first part of the chapter thus examines style as originality (ie the meaning of originality in the graffiti subculture's 'bounded commons') while the second part of the chapter examines name originality. The third part of the chapter examines norms that function as exceptions to the 'don't bite' rule.

Style and Originality

An original style of graffiti writing is one that is neither a copy (ie it has not been bitten from another writer) nor is it so far from graffiti's 'aesthetic dialect'

(Anon5)[1] that it can no longer be considered graffiti writing. Creating an original style recognises the indebtedness writers have to the creativity of others but requires seemingly minute additions or twists to pre-existing styles to distinguish their tags, pieces or throw-ups as 'new'. The graffiti rules then are directed towards regulating the creativity of a self-selecting group of creators willingly engaging in a creative process that restricts their output to that recognised as 'graffiti' within the subculture.

As participants in the process of graffiti writing, graffiti writers are expected to write their name (tag) in their own style. Having an original (in the graffiti rather than copyright sense) style is an implicit requirement of graffiti creativity. In broad terms it means writing the letters of your tag in a way that is both creative and intelligible in terms of graffiti culture. One writer explained:

> [I]f you imagine a word with like an arrow underneath and commas, [it] will look better than just a word on its own so that's all what goes into style you know. And other graffers know that. … A piece might look good to someone walking … but as graffiti artists we're looking at style and everything else and originality you know, and whether it's kind of been used before. (Anon27)

The writer indicates here that other writers are recognised for their style, specifically whether the style is original in the sense of being new. While 'to the person who doesn't know anything it probably all looks kind of similar' (Anon19) graffiti writing is in fact the product of delicate stylistic negotiation. Style is perhaps as important as 'getting up': a very simple style will garner respect for a writer who is exceptionally prolific (ie 'so simple that *is* his style', Anon21). The references to originality by Anon27 above and to simplicity by Anon21 therefore identify the two axes of achievement within the graffiti subculture: visibility and style. Of course the latter will also be accompanied by visibility since the style will need to be seen if it is to be respected as 'original'. The discussion below considers this second aspect in examining the style of letterforms and attendant creative aspects such as use of colours, figurative features[2] and other elements such as commas or exclamation marks.

Pieces and productions may have (cartoon-type) characters and other figurative elements. However, these elements are additional and do not replace the key purpose of the piece or production: writing a word or words. The use of characters and other additions may be appreciated by other writers but these additions will not make up for the lack of an original *writing* style. In an interview on the *Art Crimes* website a writer explained the difference between these decorative elements as 'not having style in terms of writing, that's ability to apply artistic technique'.[3] While proficiency in executing characters and shading undoubtedly

[1] Describing the superficial uniformity of graffiti writing or adherence to a graffiti aesthetic.

[2] One writer eg explained that the form of graffiti—the tag, throw-up and piece—refers to words but 'a character is separate' (Anon3).

[3] S Farrell, 'Atomeone email interview (Part 4) 1997', transcript at *Art Crimes* www.graffiti.org/atome/atome_4.html.

makes for the production of 'good art', the writer also asks 'who is that person's audience'?[4] The implication is that if the audience is other graffiti writers then the writer will concentrate on the style of the *letters* rather than any other elements: either the writer focuses on letterforms, with other graffiti writers as the audience, or that the writer is doing it for purely commercial gain.[5] In any event, the norms relating to the originality of style refer specifically to the originality of letters.

Style, in the context of the graffiti subculture, is a difficult concept to define. It is both an aesthetic aspect of the finished tag, throw-up or piece as well as a process that is integral to a writer's creative development:

> [S]tyle isn't a crutch or a shtick. It is understanding why that connection you bit flows, or why that colour scheme bumps. Style is the process to an appealing end. Once you got it down to a science, you can reinvent letterforms to suit yourself.[6]

One writer's recollection moves beyond process to focus on the aesthetics of writing by emphasising the importance of 'flow' to style.[7] The writer calls it one of the 'rules and regulations about graffiti letters' and goes on to describe style as follows:

> Each graffiti outline is for me a series of dozens of different decisions, at every corner, every upright, every curve and every connection, every intersection. The first letter is a good place to start. It's the first two letters that sets the blueprint for the style of the piece. The outline should have a rhythm. That rhythm can be a complete 4-bar loop or it can be a drum fill, but it's got to bang. The way the third letter works with the other two, sets the rhythm of the flow.[8]

Because graffiti creativity—in order to be the kind of creativity recognised by participants as belonging to the graffiti subculture—is constrained by the need to write letters, the significance of letter style cannot be exaggerated. The musical metaphors employed above suggest that graffiti originality may be described as consisting, amongst other things, in the movement through the string of letters.

Similarly, the following explanation of style is offered in *Subway Art*:

> [Style] is form, the shapes of the letters, and how they connect. There are various categories of style, ranging from the old simple bubble letters or peppermint-stick letters to the highly evolved and complex wildstyle, an energetic interlocking construction of letters with arrows and other forms that signify movement and direction.[9]

Style is the aspect of writing that distinguishes one writer from another making originality highly prized. The determination of originality is made by reference to other works by writers.[10]

[4] ibid.
[5] This is implied through the use of multiple dollar symbols in the interview transcript: ibid.
[6] S Powers, *The Art of Getting Over: Graffiti at the Millennium* (New York, St. Martin's Press, 1999) 155.
[7] F Forsyth, *Crack & Shine* (London, FFF, 2009) 68.
[8] Attributed to Siege 52 in ibid 68.
[9] M Cooper and H Chalfant, *Subway Art* (London, Thames & Hudson, 1984) 66.
[10] In that sense it plays a similar role to genre: see S van Gompel, 'Creativity, Autonomy and Personal Touch: A Critical Appraisal of the CJEU's Originality Test for Copyright' in M Eechoud (ed), *The Work of Authorship* (Amsterdam, Amsterdam University Press, 2014) 102.

The word 'style', apart from referring to how letters are written and connected (angles, shading, etc) by an individual writer, is also used as a descriptor in categorising *forms* of graffiti writing as well as to group together stylistic commonalities in the overall aesthetic of writing. These styles (forms) of graffiti writing are themselves expected to *have style* (ideally, to be original in the sense of indicating a particular writer's individual style). For example, 'wildstyle' pieces are a form of graffiti writing (in the same camp as tags, throw-ups and pieces). But 'wildstyle' may also refer to the *manner* in which letters are executed, for instance, creating pieces in a 'wildstyle' style. This understanding of style is closer to the conception of style found in fine art (though to complicate matters, in graffiti creativity certain styles are only associated with certain forms ie styles associated only with tags or only with pieces).[11] Moreover, what might be described as 'iconic graffiti art styles'[12] exist from which writers draw inspiration. A historical example is 'Broadway Elegant'[13] as well as styles that built on existing styles such as '"soft crash" (overlapping bubble letters) and "shadow-3D"'.[14]

To illustrate the use of 'style' in the sense of identifying aesthetic commonalities, one participant described London style, and his own preferences, as follows:

> [L]ondon style is quite old school traditional graffiti, in that it's now even wildstyle as in you know America for example, where it started. Now there's a lot of wildstyle, there's a lot of arrows and everything just twists together and here it's not much like that, it's about reading. … Something quite blocky, making the letters be the same thicknesses and you know, you think about those things. So I think [the] simple piece or the traditional graffiti piece is something like that: a very simple, stylish, readable letter. (Anon10)

As the extract above indicates, a concern with having an original style is not limited to letters, nor to the overall look of the graffiti writing but also applies to component parts, for example, the style of an arrow. Finally, style is the product of individual or group creativity as well as location.[15] The graffiti writer above, for instance, associates a particular, 'simple' style with a territory (London).

The remainder of this part considers style as originality in the sense of novelty and its relationship to stylistic heritage in more detail; the difference between biting (copying) and inspiration by way of examples from the interviews with participants; the importance of execution (including can control); and the particular challenges posed by the internet, which has made biting much easier than it once was. Finally, this part considers what parallels might be drawn between the prohibition against biting in the graffiti subculture's 'bounded commons' and the form

[11] By contrast Pop Art style eg may be associated with painting, sculpture, etc: L Gottlieb, *Graffiti Art Styles: A Classification System and Theoretical Analysis* (Jefferson, North Carolina, McFarland & Company, Inc., Publishers, 2008) 78.

[12] ibid 3.

[13] C Castleman, *Getting Up: Subway Graffiti in New York* (Cambridge, Massachusetts, The MIT Press, 1982) 55.

[14] ibid 64.

[15] 'Styles vary from writer to writer, from crew to crew, and from line to line': Cooper and Chalfant (n 9) 67.

of, and justifications for, copyright rules on both originality and infringement by reproduction.

Novelty and Stylistic Heritage

Originality in graffiti writing is the product of graffiti writers' constant re-working of letterforms. This section considers the nature and justifications for the 'don't bite'/'be original' rule identified by participants. It focuses on the participants' concerns with remaining within the historical and cultural parameters of what constitutes graffiti style—that is, how to be 'original' when to be writing graffiti at all means creativity needs to take certain forms. The writers interviewed indicated that graffiti creativity builds on the expressions of other graffiti writers. The themes that arose in the fieldwork data were: the history of graffiti writing as inspiration for becoming a writer, a demonstration of respect for stylistic heritage while nevertheless being original by 'adding something new', and moving beyond the 'rules' of style to challenge stylistic conventions rather than creating within them.

Regarding inspiration—from within the subculture—one participant put it succinctly in saying: 'There's always the piece that made you start writing' (Anon28). Often this piece will have been found in *Subway Art*[16] or another key piece of documentation. Even in *Spraycan Art*,[17] now one of the books famous for documenting the early graffiti scene, the writers quoted in its pages noted the historical evolution of style and their indebtedness to it.[18] Similarly, a participant recounted statements in an unnamed documentary on graffiti with approval:

> [T]hey're like 'when we first saw *Style Wars* and read *Spraycan Art* and whatever when it came out in 82', all that stuff in the videos came out between 1980 and 83 so everyone's like 'when I saw that I was inspired' and then 20 years on they're doing their thing. So it's all been inspired from there … (Anon27)

Individual creativity within the subculture is tied to subcultural stylistic constraints. Although writers are concerned with having an original style, for some the style of a piece *as a whole* will usually not be considered to 'belong' to the writer because graffiti creativity is a process of being inspired by and building on the creativity of others. As one participant explained:

> And I think especially for kind of graffiti writers to come along and be like 'that's my piece, I did that', it's a bit rich sometimes. It's like claiming you own the aesthetic of graffiti. It all depends on the content of your piece. I mean if you did genuinely invent chip letters and 3D block style and things like that then perhaps you have a right … (Anon5)

Specifically, letters do not belong to anyone, and neither do colours. Writers are distinguished by the *style* of letters and, less so, by the use of colour: 'no one's got

[16] ibid.

[17] H Chalfant and J Prigoff, *Spraycan Art* (London, Thames & Hudson, 1987).

[18] eg Phase2: ibid 9.

the patent on colours ... but you can tell if someone's doing a style' (Anon27). As Bowen states: 'the lettering forms the basis of artists' style and their use of colour and skilful use of spray paint becomes the essence of the work.'[19] Skill or can control is considered below.

There were at least 22 instances of explicit references to the relationship between stylistic heritage and the rules of style in the interview data.[20] Writers understand that in looking back at graffiti culture and demonstrating a respect for it in their writing they are also allowing graffiti writing culture to flourish. The adherence to stylistic convention and the valuing of heritage is a dynamic process. Graffiti writers study style and attempt to create original works within these constraints. Writers' individual creativity contributes to a collective 'library of style'. As one writer stated:

> Like the style's really important to me because style's this cultural thing that is there and if you contribute to that sort of library of style then you've made a difference, like I was saying, a feeling that you've changed something, that you've kind of contributed to some sort of library of the culture ... (Anon12)

The writer further explained that creating within this cultural framework is inherent to the development of graffiti:

> [Y]ou're part of the development and in a way you're responsible for...but I think it's interesting to play with that, see how far you can take it. (Anon12)

Writers' reverence for graffiti history and culture makes it is easier to understand why the graffiti rule on originality operates within relatively strict parameters. One writer described it as an 'aesthetic dialect' (Anon5). It is within this 'aesthetic dialect' that writers produce something that both 'fits' but is at the same time 'new'. Originality was viewed by other participants as something to be exceeded by moving beyond subcultural constraints while still recognising the existence of an aesthetic dialect on top of the expectation that being part of the graffiti subculture means writing letters (as discussed in chapter five). Individual style is informed by 'a memory bank of different styles in your head' (Anon18).While not referred to as a novelty requirement as such, most participants demonstrated a concern with adding something new in the sense that it was the writer's *own* contribution to graffiti creativity as a whole. The writer must develop an individual style while '[understanding] the shared codes and conventions of ... shared style'.[21]

Still, a graffiti writer might create letterforms that are *too* new. One participant noted this by reference to the use of 'abstract shapes' based on 'traditional

[19] TE Bowen, 'Graffiti Art: A Contemporary Study of Toronto Artists Graffiti Art : A Contemporary Study of Toronto Artists' (1999) 41(1) *Studies in Art Education* 22, 25.

[20] This included both graffiti writers' and street artists' responses. It suggests that, in some respects, the approach to originality between these creators is not dissimilar notwithstanding their operation within separate, if overlapping, creative spheres.

[21] J Ferrell, *Crimes of Style: Urban Graffiti and the Politics of Criminality* (Boston, Northeastern University Press, 1996) 86–87.

New York lettering' (Anon6). Another writer concurred, stating that something may be original but, problematically for some purist writers, this might mean that it is not graffiti writing at all:

> Yeah, no, those shapes are based on the serifs and the angles and the space that comes from traditional New York graffiti but like I've been in so many weird discussions and rows with people and they're the purists who call it 'style writing' and it has to have this and it has to have outline, it has to have skinny [spraycan cap] ... and you're a toy if you're not doing that ... (Anon5)

As the above extract shows, what constitutes originality—including the extent to which a writer's style should be tethered to stylistic heritage—in the graffiti subculture is contested. Certainly there appears to be a tension between being 'original' and being so creative that it is no longer graffiti writing as it is understood within the subculture's 'bounded commons'. Most importantly, along with the letter writing requirement discussed in chapter five, the expectation that writers will heed the stylistic heritage of graffiti blurs the distinction between norms regulating the production of graffiti creativity (ie how and when it might be acceptable to copy) and the stylistic conventions that constrain the aesthetic content of those works. Ferrell argues that the prohibition against biting and the corresponding emphasis on style operates in the same way as the prohibition against forgery or copyright infringement.[22] One way of considering this point is to imagine that copyright law required works to be, not only original, but to be original within the parameters of an Impressionist style (ie imposed an explicit, substantive constraint on being recognised as part of the culture, as a subculture must by definition do) in order for copyright to subsist. This is very much beyond the copyright that lawyers would recognise.

The respect shown to stylistic heritage, which on the one hand makes it difficult to create something 'new', also makes copying more acceptable out of necessity. One writer's reasoning for this was as follows:

> I think the older the art form gets the more those lines [between biting and homage] blur because there's a lot of people, there's so many different subgenres within the movement where a lot of people go 'you know what, my favourite thing when I was growing up was Bronx graffiti in the 80s so I'm going to paint like that'. ... You know and people will look at the piece and go 'that's really Bronxy, man'. That's one of the most overused things overheard about graffiti. ... well yeah it is but you're kind of just doing what people did back in the 80s but also, I like that too so that's alright. So then it becomes a bit different and I think possibly when a movement gets that old it's alright to do homages (Anon4)

Interestingly, the writer does not then claim that the recycling of creativity only occurs within the subculture. Writers do not merely cannibalise existing styles but copy from other cultural quarters too. Pointing to a picture the same writer observed, 'well look at this, it's Dondi. He's ripped off Michaelangelo', continuing,

[22] ibid 87.

'there's a lot of that re-sampling in graffiti' (Anon4).[23] This indicates that writers' understanding of creativity as building on the creativity of others extends beyond the recognition of the subculture's stylistic heritage to embrace material from the intellectual commons more broadly. It is not simply a question of recognising the 'don't bite' rule in the sense of not copying at all but rather recognising how to copy, including what to borrow from popular culture for example, in a way that is sensitive to graffiti culture and the specific needs of the art form.

Even so, novelty remains an indicator of an original style within the subculture. However, there are different understandings amongst graffiti writers of what, specifically, originality means. For some new school writers this means bending the 'visual rules' (Anon27) which define graffiti as a result of its historical development. This might mean, for example, inverting typical colour schemes in throw-ups through the use of a light border for the letters' outlines, with a dark fill. One writer's style was described as being 'just a step away [from graffiti style]' but he nonetheless received respect because he was 'instantly recognisable' (Anon6). This suggests that style is not enough to gain a writer respect. Visibility and distinctiveness matter too.

Finally, the writers' approach to originality—producing something new while recognising stylistic heritage—is tied back to one of the motivations for graffiti writing (asserting one's individuality in a quest for fame/respect). The rules relating to an original style are important because, as one writer put it:

> It's flow, finesse, style, how you've used the paint, how you've done it, whether it's all nice and looks like a sticker or quick and you've kind of been scared or you know someone's coming and you've run half way or the pen's dried up and it looks like someone's done it when they're drunk. … [S]tyle is what sets us all aside basically, little flicks, little things. Style is like one of the most important things in graff because it sets you aside from another person. (Anon27)

Style and the skills necessary to execute a tag, etc are integral to a writer's personality but also to belonging to a community of writers. In attempting to differentiate themselves some writers will break stylistic boundaries, that is, the conventions set down by 1970s and 80s writers. One participant offered the following explanation:

> [Y]ou wouldn't do a white piece with a yellow outline because you wouldn't see it very well, things like that. But now a lot of the new school guys do things like that because it's different … and then they also go over other rules. (Anon27)

The problem here, however, for one participant was that breaking stylistic convention would lead to 'other rules' being broken such as the prohibition against going over (discussed in chapter nine) and potentially challenging group cohesion.

[23] There is overlap here with sampling as an integral part of hip hop music production. See OB Arewa, 'From JC Bach to Hip Hop: Musical Borrowing, Copyright and Cultural Context' (2006) 84 *North Carolina Law Review* 547, 627–28.

Identifying Biting and Justifying Sanctions

Building on the above discussion of individual style and stylistic heritage and the dynamics between writers in determining whether a style is 'new', this section considers the day-to-day approach to biting within the subculture; in particular how writers determine whether someone has been legitimately inspired by material in the subculture's 'bounded commons' or has unjustifiably copied another writer: how it is, in short, that biting might be identified. As such it serves as a prelude to the discussion of exceptions—the conditions under which biting might be legitimate—in the chapter's third part. The final section of the current part contrasts graffiti originality to the position under copyright law in an effort to explain the fundamental importance of the 'don't bite' rule in more detail.

If a piece, for instance, is a 'map of inspirations' (Anon12) how much inspiration is acceptable? Acceptable copying, that is, copying while still producing something new, might be described as it was by one participant quoting an older, respected writer as follows:

> Certainly like I think I'm going to do something like this guy on… like a little flavor, put a little flavor on it. I'm not going to copy someone's stuff or idea. I actually avoid… anything that people have done in terms of ideas. I have such a hard time with myself because I don't feel comfortable doing something that's similar to someone else … but if someone's better than me and they do one of my ideas then it's flattering … (Anon12)

There are no bright lines to determine whether a work is original. Yet even if biting may be considered flattering if done well, it would not be flattering if it is the whole of a writer's style that is taken.[24] The above writer suggests that it is important to distinguish between a nibble (using a small, acceptable amount of someone's style) and a bite. The reference to an 'idea' echoes the references to novelty in the previous section: a writer's contribution—the idea—is the novel twist on graffiti style. The distinction is not made, however, between the copying of an idea and the copying of expression; the idea/expression dichotomy familiar from copyright law is, it seems, not employed in order to determine the boundary of acceptable behaviour. The extent to which copying is justifiable is not based on such distinctions but instead it is a matter of negotiation or rather, as the allegation of copying in the controversy discussed in chapter six indicates, a matter for conversation and debate that may not satisfactorily resolve the matter.[25] Certainly, the acceptability of the copying depends on its social context. For the writer above, for example, this meant evaluating the acceptability of biting by looking not just at what stylistic innovation has been taken but also *who* has taken it and the skill with which that person has employed it in their own work.

[24] This point was made by both Anon13 and Anon14.

[25] This is evident in the comments section of blog posts, eg the discussion forum containing arguments between American and European writers over copying on the graffiti website *12oz Prophet* (webpage no longer available).

Nevertheless, participants did explain how biting might be both avoided and identified, drawing again on the notion of being aware of graffiti's stylistic heritage while producing something a little bit different. For instance, while any writer may use an arrow as an element the way the arrow is written will differ:

> That's the same with painting, it's like ok, I know how to do his style, now I'm going to add a few connections there and an arrow there but I've got my own, my own arrow, 'cause I don't know if you've noticed but there's all the arrows in graffiti. … So everyone's got their own arrow but there's a lot of different ways to draw an arrow. And you might formulate your, a new kind of … a new variant on the arrow and that, and people will go, that's [tag's] arrow and they'll go 'why are you biting [tag's] arrow?' you know. (Anon4)

Another writer explained that it is not merely a matter of copying elements but also angles:

> If there's only a bit, people can't identify where it came from but once there's a curve and a few straights, you know, a few different angles, people pick up on it and go 'I know where that came from'. (Anon28)

The implication appears to be that the biter is appropriating the new element that the writer has gone to the trouble of creating. Thus, taking elements from someone else has to be 'really subtle. If it's at all obvious people will give you shit about it' (Anon28). These extracts underline too the attention to minute detail which exists among members of the subculture and without which a meaningful assessment of (subculturally recognised) originality is almost impossible.

Furthermore, in terms of identifying whether an element has been taken, there is a clear concern with whether the writer copying has access to another writer's work or whether it was created independently. One participant explained that:

> [I]f you start doing something really individual that you don't see anywhere else and then suddenly someone you know who has looked at your photos or was there when you were painting or whatever when you did it and then they start doing that technique they they're biting, you know. (Anon28)

Despite the understanding that graffiti writers will be inspired and create within a particular culture and set of broad stylistic constraints, individual copying is still frowned upon unless it is so famous everyone will know it is a copy. The same writer continued:

> But when you're at a stage when like some of the guys from America like the MSK crew, everyone in the world bites them, what are they going to do about it? They're at the top of … you get to a point where you're so good that everyone will bite you … (Anon28)

This seems to introduce a different element into the assessment of whether biting has occurred or not: the possibility that some styles, although original, may nevertheless be used because they have become ubiquitous (making this a closer parallel to trade mark than copyright law).[26] Alternatively, it might suggest that in

[26] Regarding the revocation of marks that have become 'common': Trade Marks Act 1994, s 46(1)(c).

the absence of an effective 'remedy' for biting that the rule against it breaks down and is incapable of regulating behaviour effectively.

Similarly, for example, one writer distinguished between taking someone's 'form' as opposed to their colours. This was a response to a question about the difference between biting and inspiration in which the writer described how to avoid biting in practice:

> [T]here's colours that go with each other and colours that don't ... [Y]ou're always going to see repetition in that. I think it's not even style. I think you would have to, it would have to be the actual form. If you take someone's form, someone's actual shape, the little bits they've added in, if you do something along them lines but progress, add your own flair, don't think about it while you're doing it, don't look at it don't—look—at it while you're doing it. ... You can always say that looks like him who looks like him who looks like him ... it's like a heritage, like a bloodline but you can't say he looks exactly like him cause that's a bite. (Anon15)

The writer continued, however, by explaining that unless one writer knows another writer personally it is difficult to say that there has been biting (a point that may relate back to the question of identifying the biting on the basis that the writer had access and was familiar with the style). In fact, some participants, while acknowledging the concept of biting, rejected the notion that the prohibition against copying was relevant within the subculture. One writer stated boldly that 'people don't really care about copying, it happens, everything's sampled' (Anon11). This attitude again reflects an awareness that creativity does not occur in a vacuum but is instead dependent on building on existing creativity in the intellectual commons.

Regardless of this, the field data suggested a strong personal identification between a writer and his/her style. Graffiti writers' justifications for the importance of having an original style are based on the time and skill invested in creating an individual style as well as the personality of the writer. Unsurprisingly, taking someone's style is partly viewed as an appropriation of this labour and therefore the fame of the original writer. The originality of a style is important because a good style will become inextricably linked with the writer's name and therefore with the writer him/herself. The requirement of originality is thus also important in producing the hierarchy of the subculture: a good style will help a writer to gain respect and fame within the graffiti community.

Appropriating another writer's style under the wrong circumstances—for example, where biting cannot be justified as a mere nibble—is problematic precisely because graffiti writing is viewed as 'an expression of self' (Anon4). Another writer described it as follows: 'it's your personal identity ... so you don't do it [bite]' (Anon13). One writer commented at length on the 'don't bite' rule, with a dash of self-deprecation, drawing on both personality and labour justifications. That discussion is reproduced in full here:

M Why does it actually matter that people copy?

Anon4 Why does it matter? Because ultimately graffiti is an expression of self and when you're expressing yourself no one else is you and if someone else is claiming to be you through their style then that's not cool ... 'cause everyone's delicate snowflakes you know, everyone's completely fucking different and precious and whatever. But you know, if you've dedicated a big portion of your life to learning this craft, spent years and years developing your style and then someone else comes and says 'I'm going to take that' without putting any effort in, it's offensive. It's really offensive.

M How much would they have to take for it to bother you or a graffiti writer?

Anon4 Oh, it could be completely petty. If someone goes like 'the "e" in your tag is the same as my "e" you know 'cause I developed that "e" and now you're doing my "e". What?' You know what I mean. Doesn't even have to be in a piece, it could just be in a tag. [A] tag is a signature, an imprint, it's like someone's handprint ... it's kind of like ... here's an analogy. Maybe this is a bit extreme. Cave paintings were signed generally with people blowing stencils over their handprint. It's kind of like cutting off someone's hand and blowing a stencil print over your own piece and saying 'this is mine'.

M Which it isn't.

Anon4 No.

M That's interesting.

Anon4 But some people take it that seriously and I don't know if I would agree with it being that serious but you know it's definitely ... I don't agree with biting, no one agrees with it I think.

As this extract makes clear, the protection of a writer's style is closely linked to the protection of self. The prohibition against biting then serves to protect the identity (albeit pseudonymous) of the writer. The close link between writing and identity is not merely a question of creating a particular identity but also enjoying the experience of writing that is strongly linked to pleasure.[27] If graffiti writing is rightly described as 'affective'[28] then the prohibition against biting is also a means of protecting the experience of writing from the encroachment of others.

Notwithstanding that a prohibition of biting may protect the experience of writing, that the prohibition remains malleable is necessary for the protection and development of graffiti culture: the norm is defined not only, on one side, by the desire to protect individual labour and personality but also, on the other, by the fact that a strict rule against all copying would make it impossible for graffiti creativity to flourish. This notion of the benefit to be gained from appropriate

[27] M Halsey and A Young, '"Our Desires are Ungovernable": Writing Graffiti in Urban Space' (2006) 10(3) *Theoretical Criminology* 275, 278.

[28] Halsey and Young adopt the notion of 'affect' to describe the pleasures of writing, and specifically, the interaction between the potential of the graffiti writer's body and its interaction with space: ibid 279–88.

copying was captured by one writer who stated, with respect to the ubiquity of arrows in graffiti creativity:

> [I]t's part of graffiti and so the only way that graffiti develops is by people referencing other people you know, it's a cultural thing. It's like because it's so introspective, maybe you're communicating with people who know what you're talking about so … you're almost saying when you tag, yeah my tag's a bit of Futura,[29] a bit of you know, this guy. (Anon12)

The writer above seems to suggest that copying is in itself a form of communication or, at least, a means of signaling belonging to the community of writers.

Having identified the operation of the 'don't bite' norm in the context of stylistic heritage and the identification of biting, the next section focuses on the execution of graffiti writing: a writer may have an original style but he or she must also be skilful enough to produce it on a wall or train.

Style and Skill (Can Control)

Alongside producing an *original* style, the skill of a writer in producing that style is crucial.[30] It is not sufficient that a writer has expended considerable effort in producing a tag, throw-up or piece. Instead, it is a mastery of writing letterforms that enables a writer to consciously develop a new style. As one writer put it: 'I think that people who are acknowledged are the ones who've mastered letterforms and they can deconstruct it' (Anon4). Can control or skill more generally means practising style extensively in a blackbook as well as on walls in order to hone a style and execute it.

The importance of skill in graffiti writing is unsurprising given it played an important part in the history of the subculture. *Subway Art*, for instance, devotes a chapter to 'techniques' and the importance of practising in a blackbook.[31] Practice was especially important when writers were constrained to the use of skinny caps.[32] This was before the 1990s and the marketing of specific graffiti spraycans with different nozzles, pressures and opacities.[33] Fat caps (spray can tops which release more paint) make filling in easier, for example. The description of can control provided in *Subway Art* is useful here, demonstrating the link between skill and style:

> This step [the second outline], which defines the forms, is the most crucial and it requires a very steady hand. It is difficult to learn to control spray paint. The hand must move quickly and with certainty when outlining, to avoid dripping.[34]

[29] A New York writer profiled in *Subway Art*: Cooper and Chalfant (n 9).

[30] Style and skill are inseparable. Identifying graffiti writing as the combination of skill and style, along with the repetition of tag writing (a series) as a 'technique of the body': AM Brighenti, 'At the Wall: Graffiti Writers, Urban Territoriality, and the Public Domain' (2010) 13(3) *Space and Culture* 315, 327.

[31] Cooper and Chalfant (n 9) 32.

[32] See Castleman (n 13) 64–65.

[33] R Gastman and C Neelon, *The History of American Graffiti* (New York, Harper Design, 2010) 259.

[34] Cooper and Chalfant (n 9) 34.

Although 'can control' refers to the use of a spraycan, skilled use of markers is also important. It is also possible to execute a huge tag or one-colour piece on the side of a building using rollers rather than spraycans or markers. A distinctive block style that appears to be dependent on the use of rollers, is a good example of the variation which exists.[35] The aim of consistent practice, in graffiti writing as in other things, is to be skilled enough for the writing to seem effortless.[36] One writer described the way style just 'clicks into place' as follows:

> All of a sudden the style kind of flips over and it's a weird thing, I can't explain it ... it becomes an unconscious thing rather than a really contrived, you know like a hard job to do, it becomes natural. (Anon5)

In other words, the creation of an original style is not only a matter of having an idea as to what might be a new twist on a letter or arrow. It must be actually produced and reproduced—the style grows out of practising it. To get an original style, as one participant put it, 'you work, you work and sketch and sketch and paint and paint and paint and just keep working at it' (Anon28).

The idea of producing a style through repetition is not unique to graffiti writing. Noting that Picasso developed his own style through repetition one writer said:

> With graffiti you've just got one word, [letters]. ... I've written that word thousands and thousands and thousands of times. ... it's the exact same [thing] Picasso does. ... He painted the same picture 100 times and that's how he identified his style, by painting the same thing over and over again. ... if you were to just get an orange, something as simple and boring as an orange and draw the same object hundreds and hundreds and hundreds of times that's how you develop your style because you're no longer trying to make it look like the orange, you're trying to make it look like how you see the orange. (Anon3)

As the final sentence in the extract above suggests, practising is important because it enables the writer to create an individual style; the writing of the word comes to be imbued with the writer's personality.

The uniqueness of a writer's execution means that even if they change their tag, others will know from the style of their letters who they are. Both a name and a style are therefore forms of identification for writers. The close identification between skills and style again suggests why biting someone's style may be considered a personal affront. One writer referred to the ability of writers to recognise others by their style as a form of 'forensics':

> No it's true you can [tell if a well-known writer has a new tag]. Style, letters, the finesse, the way people do things. ... say you've got something with an 'e' in it so you do an 'e' in a certain way and you've got another tag with an 'e' in it, I'll be able to tell from your 'e' who you are. (Anon27)

[35] eg the word 'Type' could be seen during the fieldwork.

[36] This does not mean that all lines will be clean. Controlled drips on a tag using a marker are technically difficult to execute and will, contrary to a first glance, indicate a high level of skill.

'Can control', apart from enabling the creation of an original style, is also important because the result of having 'superior skills', for instance, will be that the writer gains respect within the subculture (Anon26). Although having can control is not a graffiti rule as such, as an aspect of having style, it can help the writer gain respect. More importantly, it underpins the rule 'don't go over' (discussed in chapter nine) insofar as the operation of that graffiti rule depends in part on the quality of the writing. As one participant put it 'if you can't beat it don't go over it' (Anon13). At the same time, being 'up' may compensate for a lack of skills: 'they don't have can control but they're up so much you kind of have to [respect them]' (Anon27); referring to a famous London crew, 'I have more can control but would never go over them' (Anon19). Finally, can control is relevant quite apart from the creation of an original style in that it is a necessary part of the practice of illegal writing because speed is essential: 'the longer it takes to execute the danger goes up' (Anon11).

Copyright *Beyond* Copyright—Originality and Copying

As the above discussion indicates, the graffiti rules combine the requirement that a style is original with the prohibition against copying. If '[o]riginality is a cardinal criterion of copyrightability',[37] the exploration of graffiti-commons originality, stylistic heritage and skill carried out above suggest that, on the face of it, the importance attached to the originality of a style is mirrored in the alternative normative framework in the graffiti subculture. Yet the requirement to 'be original' is more strict than copyright law because of the adoption of a novelty standard that compares the new work to existing works and because this is coupled with the expectation that the work will be produced with a certain level of skill. It is also less strict because the respect afforded to existing works within graffiti's 'bounded commons' makes copying of certain styles, and even whole works, acceptable in the case of homages. These differences might be accounted for by graffiti writers considering themselves to be individual creators within a community of creators.

There are affinities between the originality requirement in copyright law and the requirement to 'be original' (and also 'don't bite') in the graffiti rules. Specifically, much like the emphasis placed on 'visual significance' in the copyright case law,[38] graffiti writers seek to put a perceptible twist on existing styles or to create a new style. The difference is that, within the graffiti subculture, the significance of the visual changes made are evaluated in light of the specific stylistic requirements of the subculture (the writing of letters in graffiti style broadly conceived). Nevertheless, the premium placed on individual expression echoes the EU intellectual creation test and, in particular, the importance of protecting the author's 'personal

[37] A Drassinower, 'Capturing Ideas: Copyright and the Law of First Possession' (2006) 54 *Cleveland State Law Review*, 191, 191.

[38] See chapter five on, inter alia, *Interlego v Tyco* [1989] AC 217.

touch'. While the skill ('can control') requirement is superficially similar to the 'skill, labour and judgment' test under UK copyright law, it is the harmonised European test that most clearly resonates with the graffiti writers' concern with graffiti creativity emanating from a particular writer. Moreover, if the graffiti rule requiring originality can be described as the combination of novelty, acknowledgment of stylistic heritage and skill, it can be distilled into the requirement of creative choice which (arguably) underpins both the UK and EU originality tests (as discussed in chapter six).

Creativity—even if the threshold is very low—lies at the heart of the concept of originality as a requirement for copyright protection.[39] Copyright law is, at least arguably, intended to encourage creativity.[40] While UK copyright law has been more concerned with 'the sweat of the brow rather than the brain',[41] the element of judgment in the UK 'skill, labour and judgment'[42] test indicates that creativity is an implicit requirement of the originality test.[43] This suggests that it may not be too far removed from the post-*Infopaq*[44] test of 'author's own intellectual creation' which places creativity at the centre of the originality test.[45] Viewed in this way, the requirement of originality suggests an affinity with personhood theory.[46] Yet, as the more stringent—be original, don't bite—standard of the graffiti writers suggests, a concern with creativity may be more closely allied to the development of culture. Of course, a more stringent requirement makes sense where the range of acceptable creative outputs is narrow—that is, the requirement to write letters. Nevertheless, this points to something important about the nature of creativity; specifically, its experience as a community, rather than merely an individual, endeavour.

Some of the recitals to the Infosoc Directive[47] in fact echo to a certain degree the concerns of graffiti writers in referring to reward (recital 10) and the 'independence

[39] MJ Madison, 'Beyond Creativity: Copyright as Knowledge Law' (2010) 4 *Vanderbilt Journal of Entertainment and Technology Law* 817, 819. See also S Ricketson, 'The Concept of Originality in Anglo-Australian Copyright Law' (1991) 39 *Journal, Copyright Society of the USA* 265.

[40] JE Cohen, 'Creativity and Culture in Copyright Theory' (2007) 40 *UC Davis Law Review* 1151, 1151.

[41] L Bently and B Sherman, *Intellectual Property Law*, 4th edn (Oxford, Oxford University Press, 2014) 43, note 1. See also B Ong, 'Originality from Copying: Fitting Recreative Works into the Copyright Universe' (2010) 2 *Intellectual Property Quarterly* 165, 171. Originality is a requirement for copyright protection of literary, artistic and dramatic works: CDPA, s 1(1)(a).

[42] *(Football) Ltd v William Hill (Football) Ltd* [1964] 1 WLR 273, 278.

[43] See also Case C-5/08 *Infopaq International A/S v Danske Dagblades Forening* [2009] ECR I-6569 [45]: 'It is only through the *choice, sequence and combination* of those words that the author may express his creativity in an original manner' (emphasis added).

[44] ibid. A reproduction under Directive 2001/29/EC, Art 2(a) on the harmonisation of certain aspects of copyright and related rights in the information society occurs where it 'reflect[s] the originality of the work in question, with the result that they contain a number of elements which are such as to express the intellectual creation of the author of that work' [50]. See also chapter six.

[45] E Derclaye, 'Case Comment: Infopaq International A/S v Danske Dagblades Forening (C-5/08): Wonderful or Worrisome? The Impact of the ECJ Ruling in Infopaq on UK Copyright Law' (2010) 23(4) *European Intellectual Property Review* 247, 248.

[46] Referring to 'personal creation': EF Judge and D Gervais, 'Of Silos and Constellations: Comparing Notions of Originality in Copyright Law' (2009) 27 *Cardozo Arts and Entertainment* 375, 386.

[47] Directive 2001/29/EC on the harmonisation of certain aspects of copyright and related rights in the information society.

and dignity' of creators (recital 11). The encouragement of creativity as a driver of economic growth (recital 4) by contrast does not provide a relevant parallel with creativity within the graffiti subculture. The tensions that arise in attempting to protect individual creativity while promoting culture as a whole are evident in recital 9:

> Any harmonisation of copyright and related rights must take as a basis a high level of protection, since such rights are crucial to intellectual creation. Their protection helps to ensure the maintenance and development of creativity in the interests of authors, performers, producers, consumers, culture, industry and the public at large. Intellectual property has therefore been recognised as an integral part of property.[48]

The assumption that a high level of protection is necessary suggests a conflict with the aim of '[developing] creativity' for creators *and* the public. This is problematic especially in situations where the public are at once consumers and creators, building upon the work they consume.[49] The study of alternative copyright norms is thus useful in imagining a different copyright—one that provides protection to creators via a strong originality rule but only to the extent that it allows the maintenance and development of graffiti culture and the scene—that is nonetheless comfortingly familiar.

Insofar as the harmonisation of copyright in the EU raises a question regarding the values that are being protected by copyright, considering graffiti originality raises questions about the extent to which the protection offered to a single work[50] ought to be based on the place of the work within (graffiti) culture more broadly. To determine how different interests ought to be taken into account it is therefore necessary to rethink the principles on which copyright law is based, not merely to reconsider how different interests might be balanced against each other.[51] One of these principles relates to the understanding of creativity. The foundation on which the notion of creativity rests might be considered a combination of assumptions about both individualism and tradition: creativity results from individual effort while being part of a network. Authors create while they borrow.[52] If creativity may be defined as the act of transformation—history is

[48] This echoes recital 11 of Directive 2006/116/EC on the term of protection of copyright and certain related rights: 'The level of protection of copyright and related rights should be high, since those rights are fundamental to intellectual creation. Their protection ensures the maintenance and development of creativity in the interest of authors, cultural industries, consumers and society as a whole.'

[49] On the nature of creative consumption see generally J Banks and M Deuze, 'Co-creative Labour' (2009) 12 *International Journal of Cultural Studies* 5, 419–31. For a critique of the author/consumer binary see also PJ Liu, 'Copyright Law's Theory of the Consumer' (2003) 44 *Boston College Law Review*, 397–431.

[50] As the discussion in chapter two and elsewhere suggests in relation to graffiti creativity, the final piece on the wall is only part of the process of writing.

[51] E Rosati, 'Originality in US and UK Copyright Experiences as a Springboard for an EU-Wide Reform Debate' (2010) 41(5) *International Review of Intellectual Property and Competition Law* 526.

[52] P Drahos, *A Philosophy of Intellectual Property* (Aldershot, Ashgate, 1996) 62.

replete with examples of creators building upon the work of others[53]—then copyright is potentially an obstacle to creativity even as it protects the creative expression of the 'first' creator.[54] Even in rethinking what creativity means, the notion of 'balancing' remains problematic because it fails to challenge the notion of the creator as the 'value-originator'.[55]

Ginsburg identifies two fundamental problems that might be added to the difficulties raised above regarding understandings of creativity and the balancing of interests:

> First, if creativity now is so dispersed, then no one can claim to have originated a work of authorship, so perhaps no one can fairly own a copyright, either. Second, the communal culture undermines the incentive rationale for copyright.[56]

The reason why this link between the protection of creativity and culture is important is that it asks whether copyright protection in its present form, if at all, is best placed to safeguard cultural diversity. Certainly one of the insights gained from studying the graffiti originality norm is to see what an originality rule might look like that takes into account not only the creator but their context too, both in terms of community and space, and how this would serve the development of culture.

As indicated above, unlike in copyright law, the aesthetic value of a work (determined by the originality of a style, and including its execution) is openly discussed in the graffiti subculture. The aesthetic quality of the finished work is discussed and where it is judged to be 'good', prized. This means that the graffiti norms diverge from copyright law insofar as the Copyright, Designs and Patents Act 1988 (CDPA), on the face of it, protects works 'irrespective of artistic quality'.[57] Graffiti writers will disagree on what constitutes a good style and have preferences for the kinds of writing styles they like, but will nonetheless appreciate and give respect to a writer whose style is original. Indeed, it seems difficult to separate aesthetic judgment from the requirement of originality because style itself is so difficult to define; it is a matter of both the overall impression the work gives and its technical detail (eg angles, shading). A writer may not lose respect for merely 'not copying' or creating a homage but respect will be gained by following the originality rule strictly and managing to produce something 'new'.

In including a 'novelty' requirement the graffiti rules therefore arguably set a more stringent originality standard than does copyright law. Participants' attitudes to originality suggest that novelty is *evidence* of origination. The concern

[53] eg borrowing characters and/or themes: LA Heymann, 'The Birth of the Authornym: Authorship, Pseudonymity, and Trademark Law' (2005) 80(4) *Notre Dame Law Review* 1377, 1444.

[54] K Treiger-Bar-Am, 'Authors' Rights as a Limit to Copyright Control' in F Macmillan (ed), *New Directions in Copyright Law, Volume 6* (Cheltenham, Edward Elgar, 2007) 363–65.

[55] A Drassinower, 'A Note on Incentives, Rights, and the Public Domain in Copyright Law' (2011) 86(5) *Notre Dame Law Review* 1869, 1879.

[56] In a study of authorship that takes into account recent technological changes: JC Ginsburg, 'The Author's Place in the Future of Copyright' (2015), Working Paper No 512, Columbia Law School, 7. www.papers.ssrn.com/sol3/papers.cfm?abstract_id=2574496.

[57] CDPA, s 4(1)(a).

with adding something new suggests a form of protection reminiscent of design law protection for those registered designs that are 'new and [have] individual character'[58] rather than copyright. UK unregistered designs are offered protection where they are 'original' meaning that they are 'not commonplace in the design field in question'.[59] Moreover, graffiti writers are concerned with creating an individual style by reference to the existing 'library of style' (Anon12) within the subculture's intellectual commons. Common to all of the design frameworks is a concern with assessing the protection of creativity by reference to existing creativity, something that is also evident within the alternative normative framework in the graffiti subculture.

Indeed, a further parallel might be drawn here with the requirement of novelty (by reference to prior art) and inventive step in patent law.[60] There is a demonstration in the graffiti subculture of a more fundamental concern with originality *in context*, that is, the place of a work in relation to other creativity within the intellectual commons. This might be loosely termed 'situational originality' which, in relation to graffiti writing comes to hold a, literally and figuratively, concrete meaning because, apart from the exhortation to be original, a writer must be seen to be original by being *up* (being visible in the physical commons).

Originality in copyright law, as numerous scholars point out, refers to origination with the author and does not require actual novelty.[61] Writers' insistence on originality-as-novelty within the framework of a 'library of style', the recognition of context, and the attendant prohibition against copying (specifically, against appropriating another writer's style), does not provide an easy parallel with copyright but may suggest an appropriately more stringent basis on which to judge the protection offered.

Personhood and labour can be used to justify both sets of rules as the participants' emphasis on individuality and having one's 'own' style indicate. The concern over passing off another's style as one's own also suggests a close link between copying and the moral right of attribution.[62] What the alternative normative framework of the graffiti writers demonstrates most starkly though is the usefulness of the social benefit justification insofar as it places at the forefront of determinations of both originality and copying the embeddedness of individual works within the broader culture, and adjusts the operation of originality and copying norms accordingly: individual creativity is not an end in itself but part of the flourishing of graffiti culture. With regards to copyright law, the preceding discussion is not intended to suggest that the originality requirement in copyright ought to set the bar so high—by expecting novelty—as to prevent certain works from being granted protection but rather, in assessing infringement, to generously interpret the place of a work in building on the creativity of others. This would

[58] Registered Designs Act 1949, s 1B(1).
[59] CDPA, s 213(4).
[60] Patents Act 1977, ss 2, 3.
[61] See eg Rosati (n 51) 531.
[62] See chapter eight.

include a recognition of the way in which copying, including faithful copying, serves an important cultural function in preserving and propagating creativity. In doing so, copyright might preserve a boundary between the propertised and public domains of the intellectual commons that allow for the production and promotion of a diverse culture.

Originality and the Name

Name and style are linked because the choice of letters used in the tag will dictate a writer's stylistic options. Whereas the preceding section considered originality in terms of the style in which a name is written, this section examines the originality of the name itself. In the 1970s, for example, writers were prepared to change their names 'hoping that a new combination of letters to write might inspire them to create new designs'.[63] It was the writing of a *name* that signalled belonging within the subculture,[64] and this—'getting up' by writing your tag—remains a key motivation of graffiti writers. Having a name distinguishable from that of other writers is therefore important in ensuring there is minimal confusion regarding to whom the fame for getting up with that name should accrue. At the same time, writers tend to seek names that *sound* good as well or that suggest a particular attitude. One writer's advice is to

> [c]hoose a clever name that defies the norm of simple-minded slang. An example of a good name is 'Argue' (RIP). It looks good when written, sounds cool when spoken, and conveys a combative attitude.[65]

Importantly, writers will not normally write someone else's name[66] but rather will need to choose their own and write that. A writer cannot elect to write the same name in a different style: the originality of the style does not excuse copying another's name. Nor should the chosen name be similar to another writer's name. As one writer explained, in the context of confronting another writer who was using a similar tag:

> It's one of the unwritten rules. It's kind of like the respect thing I suppose. You don't copy other people's stuff. It's just a no-no you know what I mean. If you do that you're a toy basically. (Anon14)

Three points with respect to names are discussed here: choosing an original name that is intelligible to others within the subculture; novelty and the use of

[63] Castleman (n 13) 56.

[64] eg in his autobiography Fuzz One remembers starting to write in 1970 in the Bronx: 'I finally came to realize that the name was the really significant thing that made you who you were.' V Fedorchak, *Fuzz One: A Bronx Childhood* (New York, Testify Books, 2005) 17.

[65] Powers (n 6) 145.

[66] 'Don't write … other writer's names': ibid.

common names; and the regulation of derivatives and similar-sounding names. These points demonstrate again, to an extent, a concern with originality as novelty.

Choosing and writing a name performs a similar function to the recognition of stylistic heritage (discussed above) in identifying a writer as a creator within a community of like-minded creators. A writer's exposure to the history of New York graffiti might motivate them to choose a particular name even at the risk of skirting the border between copying and inspiration:

> [T]here are obviously no rules but things like that, obviously you shouldn't be copying someone else's stuff. … [But] I think a lot of the European tag names have come from New York so someone might've seen something in a book when they were younger and chosen that word. … Obviously it's developed and you've done it for years but still the idea might've been you nicked it from somewhere. (Anon27)

Even so, straightforward biting is not acceptable. One writer, for example, accepted that he could not use a chosen name even though he was unaware that another writer was already using it:

> I would feel that someone was trying to steal my name, steal my style. I wouldn't like it. But it happened to me the other way around. I did the same thing as one other guy, the same tag and the same kind of letter and these things are known really quickly so I was told by a friend of mine 'you can't do this, there is already someone doing exactly the same thing'. (Anon8)

The requirement of an original name is therefore effectively an instantiation of the broader prohibition against biting discussed in the first part of this chapter. Cooper traces the prohibition back to 1970s New York, noting that short names became the norm because they were quicker to write and that using another's name was 'disparaged as biting'.[67] This led to the use of numbers to distinguish one writer from another.[68]

In a subculture where it is difficult to find a name that is 'new' this raises the issue of how similar one name can be to another. Thus, choosing an original name within a subculture in which certain names—Scribe is an example[69]—are likely to be popular can be difficult. One writer, when running into this problem decided to have 'one letter removed from [the] tag' (Anon19). As an example, commentators on a graffiti blog discussing a photograph of tags and throw-ups disagreed as to whether the name Tocs was too similar to the name Tox. One commentator stated it was 'quite similar' while another vehemently disagreed saying 'so many tags are different by a letter'.[70]

The crucial question then becomes how similar a name has to be before it is so similar as to constitute copying. One way in which this issue is debated amongst

[67] M Cooper, *Tag Town* (Arsta, Dokument Forlag, 2008) 15.

[68] ibid.

[69] 'There are certain words out there which a lot of people are attracted to … very popular tag which I've seen all over the place for obvious, really obvious reasons is Scribe' (Anon4).

[70] *Raised Alarm*, Friday 8 June 2012 www.raisedalarm.blogspot.co.uk/2012/06/blog-post.html.

writers is in considering whether a tag means that the writer owns the alternative spellings and derivatives of the name. The famous London writer Drax, for example, claims all similar sounding names as his own[71] suggesting it is the sound of a name that matters not merely the similarity of letter combinations. The problem seems to be less about the quantity of the tag that is changed (eg swapping certain letters or numbers) but rather the likelihood that the change will confuse others (and so compromise the original writer's fame). One writer described his attempt to reason with a writer using a similar name as follows:

> [A]nd then other people were confused … and I was going 'look we're in the same business mate, it's like Pepsi and Coke but you know, we're so similar'. … Like I've always changed my name to steer clear and whoever got up in London first I've always respected that. That's how I was brought up within the scene. (Anon2)

This is relevant because, again, the adherence to the norm is explained in terms of respect for graffiti culture which in turn requires respect for others within the scene: the requirement to respect an individual, that is, is derivative of a concern for the culture as a whole, which participants can reasonably be expected to value.

Guarding the originality of names is consistent with the approach to the regulation of creativity via the alternative normative framework of the subculture more generally: individual creativity is protected while attending to the preservation of graffiti culture within the relevant scene. It also protects the scene itself by seeking to preserve the existing fame hierarchy of the subculture in a particular territory. Thus, the norms relating to name originality are concerned with regulating creativity within the subculture's 'bounded commons' in such a way as to recognise that certain brakes on individual creativity are necessary to benefit the subculture as a whole. As the writer above indicates, the territory in which a writer is using a name matters because if that writer wrote the name first, they have priority and it does not matter that the second writer might have independently come up with the same name.[72]

An allegation of biting may lead to a battle[73] for the name even if the copying is purely coincidental. As one participant explained:

> If someone was to use the same name and you know you'd been writing it first that's a violation. That's just like what are you doing, you've seen I write, you're trying to write something so similar or exactly the same, are you trying to make people think … But if it is a coincidence I think you battle for the name. … If you're in the same city, whoever does it better … The other one basically quits or changes their name. (Anon15)

[71] Forsyth (n 7) 60.

[72] This operates in a similar way to patent law priority. See Patents Act 1977, s 5.

[73] For one description of a battle see N Macdonald, *The Graffiti Subculture: Youth, Masculinity and Identity in London and New York* (Basingstoke, Palgrave Macmillan, 2001) 1.

The writer here is affirming the priority rule with respect to the name but, where the apparent copying is merely coincidental, suggests that it is the writer who is the most visible ('better') who gains respect and the right to keep the name by demonstrating their ability to 'get up' consistently. We might speculate that the underlying concern is with identifying the individual who deserves to keep the name, but that—by focusing on the question of who 'does it better'—desert comes to be understood in a way which contributes to the vibrancy of the subculture as a whole.

Furthermore, the justification for the prohibition on biting other writers' names is that to do so is based in part on the appropriation of their personality as embodied in the 'aesthetic presentation'[74] as well as the interference this causes within the hierarchy of the subculture. The writer who copies is seeking to appropriate the original writer's fame. The name and the style in which it is written is about the presentation of the writer themselves—how the writer communicates with others in the subculture—which would explain one participant's insistence that a 'good copy' of his tag would be acceptable (though in practice this is unlikely to occur):

> Like I said, I've got no ownership of the alphabet but if you've got a word and you're writing it you've got an opinion about how those letters should look. (Anon7)

There is also a concern that the poorly executed tag that has been copied will reflect badly on the original writer.[75] For example:

> Anon2 [I]t's the letters and number of my name that sounds similar. If he's out in a club and he says [the name], and some people are thinking it's me. It's just like I was first and now he's come along with a name and number that sounds so very similar so …
>
> M So he gets props for your work?
>
> Anon2 Yeah, sometimes … people think. And I'm almost embarrassed to say who I am now in case … 'cause I think his work's horrible. … Now I have to go through 'well which one are you?' So annoying because for years I didn't have that problem and it was great.

Finally, it is worth mentioning that notwithstanding a personal identification with one's tag, writers may change their name in order to avoid law enforcement or simply because the writer is bored with the old name.[76] In choosing a new name, of course, the prohibition against biting would again constrain the writer's choice of a new name.

[74] Cooper (n 67) 15.

[75] This issue overlaps with reputational concerns mirroring the moral right of integrity: see chapters eight and nine.

[76] 'Sometimes it's to get around the law … I need to write some new letters or I'm going to get really bored' (Anon4).

Copyright *Beyond* Copyright—Marks Without Trade

The norm relating to name originality has a superficial analogue to the originality of literary works in copyright law. An originality requirement may be used to prevent the misappropriation of a name or style by one writer and the obscuring of the first creator. What the graffiti rules suggest is that the relevant investment[77] is not merely one of time (and certainly not of money) but of the writer's effort more generally in building up his/her reputation. The graffiti writer's name is valuable not only to the individual but to others within the subculture in order to distinguish one writer from another and therefore appropriately grant respect to the most proficient writers.[78]

The notion of 'causal connection' between a work and an alleged copy in copyright law as an element of demonstrating that an infringement has occurred[79] is relevant under the graffiti rules but not, perhaps, in the way which might be expected. The writer who had the name first would be expected to prevail regardless and may well have writers higher up in the hierarchy recognise the claim to his/her name. As one writer who had trouble with another writer for writing a similar name observed:

> [S]ome people say we should fight and then if he wins the fight I should even stop [using my name]. … I'm not a fighter. … A lot of top writers are cutting him off. (Anon2)

Needless to say a court examining a copyright infringement claim would be unlikely to order a fight (artistic or physical) to settle such a claim, nor indeed the ostracism of a creator.

Given the norm—though perhaps more honoured in the breach—against two writers in the same scene having the same or very similar tags, the regulation of names within the graffiti subculture has more of an affinity with trade mark than copyright law, albeit without the necessary connection to trade. The concern with confusion and the similarity of names in particular, are more obviously associated with trade mark law concerns. The norm against copying names is from this perspective really a norm to protect the tag as, effectively, a badge of origin: it associates the work on the wall with the creator and in doing so allows the creator to accumulate respect. Moreover, and by contrast to copyright, the norm operates to provide a monopoly to a writer, usually the one who was the first to write a particular name.[80] Even so, the trade mark parallel is not straightforward either

[77] Echoing Ginsburg on 'protect[ing] investment [rather] than creativity' by reference to the 'sweat' standard in (pre-*Infopaq*) UK copyright law: JC Ginsburg, 'The Concept of Authorship in Comparative Copyright Law' (2003) 52 *DePaul Law Review* 1063, 1080.

[78] This is perhaps not so different to the argument made with respect to the social value of attribution more generally. See eg G Lastowka, 'The Trademark Function of Authorship' (2005) 85 *Boston University Law Review* 1171, 1184 on social norms against plagiarism.

[79] As usefully identified in *Designers Guild Ltd v Russell Williams (Textiles) Ltd* [2001] FSR 11 [39] (Lord Millett).

[80] But see exceptions below regarding eg territory.

since tags will not be considered unacceptable simply because the name chosen—for example, 'Scribe'—is not distinctive.[81] The parallel is clearer with regard to acquired distinctiveness[82] whereby an apparently ordinary or common name may nevertheless distinguish one writer from another within a particular scene. In contrast to copyright' law's fundamental concern with creativity, the graffiti rules suggest that 'originality' may spring, after the fact of creation, from the *use* of a work. As such, the graffiti rules seem to import an equivalent to acquired distinctiveness into the graffiti-originality standard.

The regulation of creativity within the graffiti subculture suggests that a system of rules that avoids creating boundaries between discrete but overlapping areas of intellectual property law might be desirable, especially in removing the distinctions between copyright and trade marks. The regulation of creativity within the graffiti subculture, insofar as it represents an empirically grounded response to the difficulties of regulating creativity within the 'bounded commons', suggests that this would be an appropriate response because graffiti creativity requires protection of the kind offered by both rights, namely both to protect a name from copying and to prevent its use in a particular scene (territory). Vaver, for instance, argues for the consolidation of intellectual property rights, for example to avoid offering protection—such as to a logo—under both copyright and trade mark law.[83] As Davis and Durant point out, different justifications are offered for copyright versus trade mark protection with the latter more concerned with 'mundane, materialistic concerns'.[84] Yet in instances concerning, for example, potentially confusing names and ensuing damage to reputation, the prohibition against biting—though arising out of the same concerns which are reflected in copyright law—seems to achieve what trade mark law sets out to do; it enables the name to function as a marker of origin.

Exceptions for Biting

Although being the first to produce a style or come up with a name means that a writer can avoid accusations of copying,[85] other exceptions to the general prohibition exist. This part focuses on four situations in which participants indicated that conduct which would otherwise be treated as biting was in fact acceptable and so not really biting at all: copying in blackbooks (private copying); copying in a

[81] See Trade Marks Act 1994, s 3(1)(b).
[82] Mirroring Trade Marks Act 1994, s 3(1) regarding distinctiveness acquired through use.
[83] D Vaver, 'Reforming Intellectual Property Law: An Obvious and Not-so-obvious Agenda: The Stephen Stewart Lecture for 2008' (2009) 2 *Intellectual Property Quarterly* 143, 156.
[84] J Davis and A Durant, 'To Protect or Not to Protect? The Eligibility of Commercially Used Short Verbal Texts for Copyright and Trade Mark Protection' (2011) 4 *Intellectual Property Quarterly* 345, 348.
[85] One writer recounted '[proving] that he did his piece first' (Anon5).

different territory (with respect to names); acknowledging another writer (shout outs); and copying within crews.

Blackbooks

The expectation that a writer will copy tags or pieces or elements of these in a blackbook (sketchbook) forms part of a broader acceptance that writers need to practise their style before heading to a wall or train. This in turn encourages the development of creativity within the subculture's intellectual commons. The first step in a writer's career will be to learn to tag.[86] One of the ways for a new writer to learn is to copy and practise other writers' style[87] in a blackbook. Copying in a blackbook is associated in particular with learning to write. One participant contrasted the acceptability of copying by writers who are learning with copying by 'established' writers:

> It's like something's your own. When you're learning, when you're first starting you do, you look at other stuff and it's hard not to be inspired by what you like … but then it's quite another to be established … and going 'I'm going to pinch that bit and do that'. (Anon14)

The reason for this difference appears to be that writers account for the need to master a style, which in turn requires a certain amount of copying, but also that the copying in a blackbook is private and only for the benefit of the writer attempting to produce and master an individual style. It is not the writer placing a tag or throw-up in urban space as if the tag was his/her own. The copying in a blackbook does not therefore threaten the status of other writers; writing in blackbooks is not a false claim to their creativity.

This is not to say that there is no interest in blackbook drawings,[88] but rather sharing blackbook writing with others is considered to be qualitatively different to placing a tag on a wall. This can be an exciting experience as a participant recounted a more experienced writer sharing 'his photo album, his sketchbook, everything' (Anon15). The writer said, furthermore:

> So you could say that I bit him but just like when I used to let people copy my style on paper, I suppose he just lets me. I learned from him. (Anon15)

The willingness to share blackbooks suggests that a broad distinction appears to be drawn within the subculture between private and public writing.

Writing in a blackbook, practising styles and letters will not necessarily entail copying something from a wall. It may include, as for the writer above, copying

[86] Regarding bombing and the 'rules, expectations and ethics' of the subculture: Macdonald (n 72) 74–75.

[87] See also, with respect to the acceptability of copying by 'toys', Powers (n 6) 155.

[88] Graffiti publications such as *London Black Book* (no date) indicate that there is.

material that has not been shown publicly. Deazley notes that such undisclosed works will not be part of the intellectual commons.[89] The boundary between disclosed and undisclosed information in the graffiti commons is difficult to draw. If a blackbook drawing is shared amongst a crew it might perhaps be private but what if it is shared at an event such as a graffiti festival by being passed around by participants in a particular territory? Certainly it has not been published nor even placed on the wall for everyone to see—graffiti writers and non-writers alike—as they walk by. But it does nevertheless seem to form a part of the graffiti-specific 'bounded commons' in the sense of being shared and allowing others to be potentially inspired by this work.

Tags, Commons and Territory

While the prohibition against copying another writer's style extends to copying a writer from a different scene or a different time, graffiti writers accept that a writer can use the same name as a writer in a different city. This is the product of the graffiti subculture's organisation into scenes generally meaning the collection of writers and their attendant hierarchies in a particular territory, specifically a city (eg London, Berlin, Brighton) but potentially different parts of the same city (eg East London, West London). However, the names of very famous old school writers would not usually be copied even in different cities.[90] A practical effect of this is that more writers may make use of popular tags:

> [T]here's probably 247 Scribes in the world and then it might also come down to 'are they in the same city or in the same neighbourhood in that city?' It can often come down to geography. It's like, yeah, I'm Scribe in Timbuktu, I know there's a Scribe in LA but you know he's cool, whatever, we're not going to meet each other. And there's ... there's kind of like a case of 'this town ain't big enough for the two of us' ... but this world is. (Anon4)

This territorial exception is implicitly justified on the basis that it protects the writer and their individual style because you're not 'trying to capitalise off the other person's fame' but rather 'make your own name, like your own little bit of history' (Anon27).

The same territorial exception applies to crew names. The crew that was first will use the name (or rather its acronym) in that city or neighbourhood. If a non-crew member is putting up the crew name and 'it's in the same city ... they'd like to know who that is' (Anon8). If there are two crews with the same letters 'we always try to find out who was the first' (Anon8). Just as for individual writers placing their tag, the placement of a crew name is also circumscribed by territorial considerations. Interestingly, one writer, though not overly concerned about how

[89] R Deazley, 'Copyright's Public Domain' in C Waelde and H MacQueen (eds), *Intellectual Property: The Many Faces of the Public Domain* (Cheltenham: Edward Elgar, 2007) 23.

[90] eg a writer recounting his mentor questioning his choice of a name that was very similar to a famous graffiti writer from 1970s New York: Anon15.

territory might circumscribe the acceptability of name copying, still acknowledged the relevance of the prohibition:

> It's geographical, because if there's a crew that exists in another city with the same name and everyone's aware that crew is from that city, you don't really invade each other's space or reputations. (Anon7)

Failing to take into account these territorial limitations is thus a problem because, aside from copying, the new crew writing the same name in the same city may damage the reputation of the original crew.

Writers expect that 'there's nobody locally who does [their tag]' (Anon3). This is shored up by references to the historical importance of demarcation of territory.[91] Using someone's name in their own city—especially their *part* of the city—is even more egregious. This is implied in one writer's response to another writer biting his name when he had used it prior to the alleged copier:

> [B]ut he should respect history … and who was first so obviously he's a got a few of his mates [to] stick up for him but overall a lot of people, he could've done a lot better if he wrote something else … (Anon2)

This poses a particularly interesting problem for writers travelling to other cities. When they do travel, however, there would often be local writers on hand to help navigate the local scene. In any event, one writer described the graffiti rules when writing in another country as 'heightened'. This is because writing in a different territory means being deprived of the information (eg about who is 'up') needed to apply the various rules and exceptions which rely on the making of subtle context-specific judgments. Speaking about writing in a European city two writers observed:

> Anon5 It's almost like the rules are really heightened, like they're amplified, don't kind of … I didn't paint in a hall of fame or anything like that because I didn't want to go over pieces I didn't know and I didn't. It was mostly tagging and the odd piece.
>
> Anon6 The local dudes … not saying that you would, but they would be looking out to make sure you didn't do anything stupid.
>
> Anon5 But the thing is about graffiti that the rules do kind of translate to most cities but depending on what kind of writer you are, depending on your approach to that city.

The locals 'don't take too kindly' to foreign writers 'smashing that town' (Anon5). This is why knowledge of the scene is very important. A local writer could be fine with it or there could be 'trouble' (Anon27). The writer pointed out that just visiting did not count and that the writer could use their name in a different city since they

[91] Though as Anon4 pointed out, the hugely famous writer Seen was one of two writing in New York, however, it would appear that the two were from different neighbourhoods.

were just visiting. As one writer pointed out, in home territory, knowing who is in an area is crucial:

> [I]f you know the scene well enough you'd know who's writing what in your area. If you came to an area and there's a person writing it, it would cause a lot of conflict. [It's] between the two of you whether you keep writing it or whether someone changes it. (Anon18)

However, one participant considered that when a writer goes to a different city 'you just have to change … you should do the right thing and change it anyway' (Anon27). That a writer would change names reveals something not only about the fundamental role of respect underpinning the norms regulating creativity but about the pleasure inherent in the creative process that makes the writer willing to forgo the potential individual benefits of writing their own name.

Shout outs

Copying another writer's tag is acceptable in certain circumstances, including where it is done as a 'shout out' to a fellow writer, friend or family member, or as a memorial. Some writers also mentioned the possibility of granting another writer permission, usually a friend.[92] If a graffiti writer does place another writer's tag on a wall the understanding is that the tag belongs to the original tagger, not the person who merely copied it and put it on the wall, and in any case it would not be written in the original writer's style. One writer explained why he puts up the name of a well-known writer:

> [I] might just put him up to show that I know him and he's got my back. … I want to big him up for doing a lot for the scene. … I put him up next to my piece, I just sort of write the word for him and then it's there and he knows … so you put each other up. (Anon2)

Writers may also put up the name of a writer who has died. In 2012, there were numerous CK1 pieces put up in London in memory of the writer. These memorial pieces are often marked with 'RIP'. This exception—writing the names of writers who have died—and the attendant safeguarding of works by deceased writers, shows perhaps most clearly the way in which the graffiti rules operate within a 'bounded commons' that fuses physical and intellectual space. The respect shown for the dead in the tending of memorial pieces and the creation of works bearing the dead writer's name are what preserves that name within the physical commons and so ensures the name is granted appropriate respect in the intellectual commons as well.

Finally, the homage—a reproduction of significant pieces that form part of graffiti history—is similar to a shout out insofar as the exception which relates

[92] One example, though not one mentioned in the fieldwork interviews, is putting up the name of a graffiti writer who is in prison: Macdonald (n 72) 80.

to homages shows deference to graffiti writers who are part of the history of the subculture. It would not necessarily constitute biting (as the discussion above has suggested) since the writer is not presenting the work as their own. One writer expressed his opinion as follows:

> [I] like the thought process that's gone into it, they've gone out and got the right colours. I wouldn't want to diminish their work. … The difference between like an actual copy, like a replica, [that would be] like a tribute … (Anon7)

The individual labour in this instance has been acceptably used in order to preserve the memory of an important piece.

The operation of the 'don't bite' rule and its exceptions shows these various norms to be attuned to the nature and the needs of the subculture: creativity is regulated as a means of protecting the writers' names, but also in regulating the space—specifically, the territory—of writing. Overall, the 'don't bite' rule reveals a concern with the preservation and promotion of graffiti culture while recognising the need to protect the labour and/or personality underpinning the choice of a name and the production of an individual style.

Copying Within Crews

Similarly to shout outs, writers collaborating on a piece as a crew may put up the names of their fellow crew members. Implicit permission appears to be granted to crew members to use the other members' names. Writers may also use each other's style in their own work but this is more likely to be a matter for negotiation within a crew. One writer recalled writing a letter in the same style as a member of his crew, noting that 'you can almost not tell the difference but we're in the same crew so that's allowed' (Anon15). Letters are 'influenced by people in your crew' (Anon11). Another writer also described copying within crews as acceptable, or rather, inevitable:

> [Y]ou pick up their style and that's accepted or you paint with a crew and the crew has a style so you take part of their style. It's another thing about being in a crew: you can share styles and that's fine. (Anon28)

This does not mean, however, that one crew member putting up a signature element of the other's style will always be acceptable. One writer recounted, for example, that when one writer altered another's character on a crew piece that 'didn't go as well' (Anon2).

One of the justifications offered for allowing copying within a crew is similar to the arguments related to individuality and being 'up'. A crew offers a way of being 'up' with like-minded people. Explaining that people outside a crew cannot put up the name of the crew a writer stated:

> So yet again it's [about] being yourself, having your own name, finding your own style, your niche. … [If you are] down with people or you start, you could be put down in

a crew and be part of it or you could start with your own friends and make your own crew. … [A]ll that goes back to will you last the initial being into it, finding out about it, knowing they're a name you can have and then finding your own space. (Anon27)

The issue of collaboration on pieces also raises a number of other issues including the expectation that a piece belongs to the crew and not the individual writers that worked on it.[93] But the key issue here is the way joint creativity serves, as the writer quoted from above suggests, to provide the individual with a supportive environment that is conducive to developing an individual style.

Copyright *Beyond* Copyright—Exceptions and the Commons

The exceptions to the 'don't bite' rule discussed above—that writers will write their own name in an original style—are notable in that they ameliorate what might otherwise seem to be a rather harsh injunction against copying by a set of exceptions that recognise creativity to be a collective endeavour. In recognising the interests of others, a key parallel emerges between the exceptions in the graffiti rules discussed in chapter six relating especially to fair dealing for research or private study in the UK copyright rules. Fair dealing for research or private study in UK copyright law[94] is echoed in the blackbook exception in the graffiti rules. The graffiti exception, however, is not concerned with the distinction between copying in order to learn (this usually relates to young, inexperienced writers) or practising and otherwise copying the tags or elements of other writers in their blackbooks. At the same time it should be noted that this exception appears to function on the understanding that the writer using a blackbook is not claiming the copied work as his/her own so there are no (potentially) adverse reputational effects for the copied writer.

Instead of applying the research or private study exception, the recently enacted (and more recently, quashed)[95] exception for personal or private use would also have been relevant here. Under section 28B CDPA (echoing Article 5(3)(b) Infosoc Directive) the making of copies for personal use had been permitted and would appear to have covered, for example, the copying of artistic works in blackbooks. However, the exception was narrower than it might have first appeared. The individual writer would need to have acquired an 'initial copy' lawfully and continued to hold it with further copies made for private and non-commercial purposes.[96] Yet this is unhelpful where a graffiti work is placed in a public space and the initial copy is the one made by the writer in a blackbook. In other words, while such an exception makes sense where a consumer purchases a CD and then copies the

[93] eg as demonstrated by putting up the names of crew members who did not contribute to a piece: Anon4.

[94] CDPA, s 29.

[95] *R (BASCA) v Secretary of State for Business, Innovation and Skills* [2015] EWHC 1723 (Admin).

[96] CDPA, s 28B(4).

musical works to their computer, here there is simply the initial copy which—seeing as a reproduction of the original work on a wall or train is made without permission—cannot be said to be 'lawfully acquired' or indeed acquired unlawfully. Furthermore, for graffiti writers it is precisely the point to copy the whole of a work as a means of improving style and it is unclear what a lawfully acquired copy would mean here. Most likely, given that the section 62 CDPA exception for works permanently situated in a public place does not apply to graphic works, graffiti writing (as an artistic work) could not be said to be lawfully acquired.

Clearly then, the subcultural norm provides for a more appropriate regulation of creativity, one that, indeed, ought to be adopted by copyright law. The study of graffiti norms suggests that private study and personal use copying should be broadened out to include wholesale copying of copyrighted material where it is not copied for a commercial purpose and so long as there was no attempt to pass the work off as belonging to the copier. The latter point also reflects a concern with moral rights rather economic rights. The CDPA fair dealing exceptions already make the provision of a 'sufficient acknowledgment'[97] necessary. However, the requirement for a 'sufficient acknowledgment' does not reflect graffiti writers' concerns, in common with other creators, with attribution and reputation.[98] In other words, where the graffiti rules suggest an understanding of copyright-type rules that combine economic and moral rights under the umbrella of (what looks like) 'author's rights' UK copyright law provides a typically common law dualist approach that divides the economic from the moral.[99] This is problematic: exceptions to copyright infringement have a 'moral' dimension—in requiring 'sufficient acknowledgment'—without in fact taking moral rights seriously. The standalone moral right of attribution, for instance, requires certain conditions to be met[100] making the protection it offers weak.

The acceptability of private copying is part of a broader question about how copyright law can enable people to 'interact with texts as well as absorb them'.[101] For graffiti writers, the ability to copy and learn from each other is central to the creative process, especially when they are starting out. It is therefore natural that exceptions to biting relate specifically to copying in blackbooks. In particular, it would seem that, based on the creative process in the graffiti subculture discussed above, a US-style 'fair use' type exception may be helpful. It could combine elements of the existing law on fair dealing with a section 62 CDPA exception broadened out to include two-dimensional reproductions of graphic works but for private, educational or non-commercial purposes only.[102]

[97] eg CDPA, s 30(1).

[98] eg J Silbey, *The Eureka Myth: Creators, Innovators and Everyday Intellectual Property* (Stanford, Stanford Law Books, 2015) 166–67.

[99] See generally P Goldstein and B Hugenholtz, *International Copyright: Principles, Law, and Practice*, 3rd edn (Oxford, Oxford University Press, 2013) 19–21.

[100] Primarily, the requirement to assert the right to be identified in CDPA, s 78. See chapter eight.

[101] Considered in terms of the scope of US copyright law, especially 'fair use': J Litman, 'Lawful Personal Use' (2007) 85 *Texas Law Review* 1871, 1910.

[102] This suggestion is taken up again in chapter ten.

The graffiti rules are closely attuned to what is required for the development of graffiti culture; by contrast it is difficult to argue that copyright rules take a form which is suited to fostering cultural development.[103] Crucially, the exceptions in the graffiti rules take the form that they do precisely because they are part of a normative framework that is highly conscious of creativity as a process taking place in a certain territory and requiring writers to engage in locational creativity. The fair dealing exceptions, by contrast, have often been interpreted so that 'that fair dealing could not be allowed to cut across copyright owners' rights'.[104] Perhaps what is required for the development of culture is an emphasis on private copying whether transformative or not. The recognition of uses, such as the use protected by the blackbook copying exception in the graffiti rules, needs an exception broader than 'fair use' that would enable private copying of the kind that falls within the 'core of ordinary uses of copyright works'.[105]

Conclusion

For graffiti writers, the form of graffiti creativity—writing letters—is inextricably linked to a demand for having an original style which in turn is supported by the need to demonstrate can control. This chapter has examined the graffiti rules relating to originality and biting of both the name and the style in which the name is written. The concept of 'style' was used in this chapter in a number of ways: referring to a form or type of graffiti creativity, the manner in which a word is written and, above all, in terms of having an original style. The preceding discussion has suggested that 'being original' in the graffiti subculture is a process of remaining faithful to the history and culture of graffiti writing while creating something 'new' within the confines of the well-defined form of creativity around which the subculture coalesces.

The chapter has also addressed shout outs (including memorial copying), and copying within crews, and in doing so identified potential grounds for copyright reform especially by considering private copying in blackbooks. The exceptions protect a writer's relationship with other writers in the scene, in particular, the crew. As such, while there are similarities between the graffiti rules and copyright rules on originality and copying there are also significant divergences. The study of the graffiti rules here—especially with regard to the protection of the name—suggests that a strengthening of moral rights would be particularly welcome. The next two chapters will address this point in more detail.

[103] See generally F Macmillan, 'Copyright, Culture and Private Power' (1998) 16(3) *Prometheus* 305, 305–16.

[104] A Sims, 'Strangling Their Creation: The Courts' Treatment of Fair Dealing in Copyright Law since 1911' (2010) 2 *Intellectual Property Quarterly* 192, 223.

[105] R Tushnet, 'Copy This Essay: How Fair Use Doctrine Harms Free Speech and How Copying Serves It' (2004) 114 *Yale Law Journal* 535, 554.

Above all, the graffiti rules discussed in this chapter begin to show what an alternative 'copyright' beyond law might look like, one which takes as its basic value the health of a (sub)culture; one which has a far stronger commitment than does the current regime to the development of culture. Even if there is a lack of consensus as to what culture means, the graffiti rules, in their easy acceptance of private copying for example, suggest that copyright law would do well to map onto the graffiti exceptions to biting. This is in part because the graffiti norms already echo public perceptions about what copying is acceptable, namely that 'personal uses' such as copying within the home are *already* allowed.[106] And since the norms are so closely aligned to what (a certain group of) creators need and expect from rules regulating creativity in order to protect and further their creativity, that copyright law ought to mirror (some of) these norms seems not just sensible, but necessary for the development of an attractive and diverse culture.

[106] Defining personal use as 'a use that an individual makes for herself, her family, or her close friends': Litman (n 102) 1894.

Panel IV

Reputation

8

Moral Rights

Introduction

Graffiti creativity, as the preceding chapters have suggested, is regulated within the subculture's 'bounded commons' in a way that is sensitive to—to use language familiar to copyright lawyers—moral rights concerns. For example, the preoccupation with the originality of the name and the resolution of name disputes show a concern with both attribution—in the sense that one writer ought not to pass their work off as that of another—and, more importantly, the protection of reputation. The first part of this chapter considers the situations in which authors are able to seek redress for interference with their moral rights. It focuses on the public exhibition of graffiti writing, its communication to the public and commercial publication. The second part examines three moral rights that may apply to graffiti creativity as an artistic work: the attribution right, the right against false attribution and the integrity right. It then briefly considers the possibility of communal moral rights protection. While the discussion focuses on the application of moral rights to graffiti creativity within the subculture it is also useful in understanding the moral rights implications of certain interactions by non-writers with graffiti writing. This is relevant, in particular, to the full or partial destruction of graffiti by whitewashing it from walls and the discussion below engages with buffing as well as interference by one writer with the work of another (eg by crossing it out or covering it with their own work). Chapter nine examines the graffiti rules that function as analogues for the copyright rules discussed here, especially the moral right of integrity.

Preconditions for Moral Rights

Assuming there is a work in which copyright subsists, under UK copyright law 'authors' have certain moral rights,[1] the infringement of which is a breach of

[1] Ownership of copyright is necessary for the operation of the economic rights discussed above, such as the right to copy. By contrast authorship, irrespective of ownership, is required to exercise moral rights.

statutory duty.[2] With respect to works created by a sole graffiti writer, it is the writer (as author) who will have been in a position to enforce their moral rights. Where a piece, instead, was created by multiple members of a crew, only those members of the crew defined as authors under the Copyright, Designs and Patents Act 1988 (CDPA) would be able to avail themselves of moral right protection. Notwithstanding that within the graffiti subculture a piece will be treated as originating with the crew (in the sense of representing the crew and helping to raise its profile within the subculture's hierarchy) not all members would necessarily have contributed to its creation and therefore, according to copyright law, would not be authors of it. This is another example of a mismatch between creator expectations and the legal protection offered.

Public Exhibition

The public exhibition of a work gives rise to a potential claim that an author's moral rights of integrity,[3] the right against false attribution[4] and the right of attribution[5] have been breached. The legislative phrasing 'exhibited in public' arguably concerns any public exhibition whether within or outside a gallery. While it seems unlikely that works placed without permission on the exterior walls of buildings were contemplated as constituting 'exhibition', these works are, on the ordinary meaning of the word, indeed exhibited (ie displayed to others). A possible discomfort with non-traditional forms of art exhibition is revealed, somewhat obliquely, for example, in section 80(4)(a) CDPA (the integrity right). The relevant act giving rise to a potential claim—'publishes commercially or exhibits in public … or communicates to the public'—implies that someone is publishing, or exhibiting, or communicating *independently* of the creator. This does not sit easily with the creator themselves being the initial exhibitor of the work on the street where, upon the partial destruction of the work, that work continues to be, unwittingly, exhibited by the owner of the building.

However, the exhibition need not occur in a commercial context although the preoccupations of the moral rights provisions are geared towards the exploitation of works as demonstrated by, for example, the reference to 'dealing' with regards to the right against false attribution. 'Dealing' means 'selling or letting for hire, offering or exposing for sale or hire, exhibiting in public, or distributing'.[6] Exhibition may encompass the exhibition of graffiti as artistic works within a gallery as well as inviting members of the public to, for example, 'live painting'. What is interesting here is that creation—the entire creative process—is

[2] CDPA, s 103.
[3] CDPA, s 80(4)(a).
[4] CDPA, s 84(2)(b).
[5] CDPA, s 77(1). The right is infringed where the artistic work is, inter alia, 'exhibited in public': CDPA, s 77(4)(a).
[6] CDPA, s 84(7).

simultaneously an exhibition. Assuming that such display of the works constitutes public exhibition then, with respect to the moral right of attribution, the right would need to be asserted (discussed further below). In particular, a writer could assert the right to be identified as an author by signing a canvas: the 'part[ing] of possession'[7] with the work will then require the gallery to identify the writer as the author of the work 'on the original or copy, or on a frame, mount or other thing to which it is attached'.[8] Of course, graffiti writers will not ordinarily use a canvas as a material support. Works resulting from 'live painting' on walls may arguably fall into the same category because the signature (this, apart from the piece itself, may include the writer's tag to the side of the piece) is on the wall to which the original artistic work might be said to be 'attached'.[9]

However, where the artistic work is fixed to the outside wall of a gallery, apart from stretching the definition of attachment (the section also refers to a frame or mount), it is difficult to argue that there has been a parting of possession when we are dealing with land (ie part of a building) rather than a chattel. The assumption, explored in chapter four, relating to the artistic work's materiality, is that an artistic work, such as a sculpture, cannot be separated from its material support. The argument might be made that, given the phrase 'into whose hands that original or copy comes'[10] really refers to ordinary possession.[11] On that basis, painting directly on a wall already owned by the gallery would constitute an assertion of the right to be identified as the author of an artistic work that is in the gallery's possession. Still, if the writer is the owner of the copyright in the work but is not its 'first possessor'[12] the signing of the work appears to be of little use when emphasis is placed on the *parting* of possession. Of course, an original on a wall may be parted with where it is cut from the wall and placed up for auction.[13] The difficulties revealed through the application of 'exhibition' to graffiti writing in the context of moral rights seems to point to a different, and more fundamental, issue concerning the conception of the artistic work.

The moral rights provisions, the discussion above suggests, are geared towards the organised and/or commercial exhibition of creativity. Yet the vast amount of graffiti writing is produced without a gallery in mind and in spaces—railway bridges and underpasses, roller shutters, tracksides—that exhibit the works publicly in a way not contemplated by the CDPA. To that extent, moral rights will only be relevant to graffiti writers outside of the 'bounded commons' of the

[7] CDPA, s 78(3)(a).
[8] CDPA, s 78(3)(a).
[9] CDPA, s 78(3)(a).
[10] CDPA, s 78(4)(c).
[11] K Garnett, G Davies and G Harbottle, *Copinger and Skone James on Copyright, Volume 1*, 16th edn (London, Thomson Reuters, 2011) [7-070].
[12] Pointing out that the first owner and the first possessor of a work may not be the same person, eg an employee: ibid [11-22].
[13] See eg M Ryzik. 'Another Banksy Mural to Go From Wall to Auction' *New York Times* 13 August 2013.

graffiti subculture: that is, when they move from the subculture—and therefore its commitment to the identification of writers by their tags and its understanding of appropriate surfaces on which to write—to the relative rigidity of the art world (and, usually, indoors, to closed-in spaces) in which their work is no longer a pure marker of identity within the graffiti scene but, more often than not, a commodity. This sits uneasily with the personhood justifications for moral rights protection—it suggests that the operation of the moral rights provisions is effectively contingent on the works in question being part of the mainstream art world. Yet, to take moral rights seriously in relation to the development of culture must mean also protecting works, such as graffiti creativity, in order to produce a plural culture[14] and so maintain an appropriate boundary between the public and propertised domains within the intellectual commons.

Communication to the Public and Commercial Publication

Aside from exhibition, an alternative way in which a moral rights claim could arise is where a work is communicated to the public or published. Where an artistic work has been communicated to the public or copies of the work have been issued commercially[15] the author may seek to exercise the right of attribution, the right against false attribution and the right of integrity. For graffiti creativity that exists purely within the 'bounded commons' of the subculture, the concept of commercial publication does not readily apply. As chapter ten will show, the position is different with respect to the exploitation of works by the public generally (eg through the publication of photographs of graffiti in coffee table books). Nevertheless, as with the exhibition of works in galleries, writers may also create and sell, in particular, prints or stickers. Graffiti writers would then be in a position to enforce their moral rights where, for example a print is sold without attribution, attributed falsely or if it had been interfered with in such a way as to give rise to an integrity right claim.

The closest the graffiti subculture comes to commercial publication is, arguably, with the publication of graffiti magazines. These might be seen as the logical progression of the trading of photos between graffiti writers either in person or by post. As Snyder puts it with respect to their proliferation in New York in 1989 at the time of the successful 'war on graffiti' on the city's trains:

> The movement found a new medium. Photographs of graffiti made permanent what is essentially ephemeral, allowing writers to view the work of others without attachment

[14] M Iljadica, 'Graffiti and the Moral Right of Integrity' (2015) 3 *Intellectual Property Quarterly* 287.

[15] CDPA, s 77(4)(a). See, regarding issuing copies to the public, CDPA, s 84(2)(a); regarding dealing with infringing copies in the course of business, CDPA, s 84(5). Note that commercial publication includes 'making [the work] available by means of an electronic retrieval system' (CDPA, s 77(4)(a)). Arguably, placing a work on the internet constitutes public exhibition: S Stokes, *Art and Copyright*, 2nd edn (Oxford, Hart Publishing, 2012) 121.

> to a specific place or time. The inclusion of flicks in magazines created a space where graffiti pieces from all over the world ran together to be judged, critiqued, and learned from. This liberation of graffiti from a geographically specific location essentially formed the beginnings of a global community of writers.[16]

In other words, the dissemination of graffiti creativity via, for example magazines (and now the internet) was, and continues to be, an important part of the subculture. Even if the dissemination of graffiti publications is classed as commercial publication—therefore enabling a moral rights claim to be made—a graffiti writer will likely not be in a position to make a moral rights claim regarding, in particular, attribution because this right needs to be asserted (discussed further below). Pages upon pages of photographs of tags, throw-ups and pieces on trains and walls are published without captions. The attribution right is highly unlikely to be asserted independently of a work that is in itself—in the letters of the tag (name)—an assertion of their identity as authors. Of course, for those who can read graffiti writing a caption is unnecessary.

There is a practical reason for the lack of (further) attribution in magazines and blogs as well: these photographs may be submitted anonymously or by others. Furthermore, the risk associated with typing one's tag or real identity with a photograph of one's work is substantial. Thus, even if writers were aware of the attribution right, there would be no incentive to assert it. The same argument applies to the enforcement of the rights against false attribution and integrity. In any event, magazines are exempt from recognising both attribution and integrity rights.[17] By contrast, the communication to the public[18] of graffiti creativity has become more relevant both within the subculture and on its fringes, specifically relating to blogs and similar websites created by graffiti writers and non-writers alike. In both situations the communication to the public mainly occurs with respect to the sharing of photographs of graffiti works on the internet. Nonetheless, it is unlikely that writers would go out of their way to protect their moral rights in works communicated to the public on the internet. As one writer put it in relation to copying, that would require going into the 'named realm' (Anon29). This would make an attempt to vindicate moral rights unlikely except for those graffiti writers who have crossed over to produce works within the art market.[19]

[16] GJ Snyder, *Graffiti Lives: Beyond the Tag in New York's Urban Underground* (New York, New York University Press, 2009) 31.

[17] CDPA, ss 79(6) and 81(4). There is also an exception for the reporting of current events: ss 79(5) and 81(3). But see chapter six—the news reporting exception is unlikely to cover the publications of graffiti in specialist graffiti magazines.

[18] The right to communicate a work to the public is one of the economic rights of the copyright owner (moral rights by contrast refer to authors).

[19] eg BBC News, 'David Cameron presents Barack Obama with graffiti art' 21 July 2010, www.bbc.co.uk/news/uk-politics-10710074.

Attribution, False Attribution and Integrity

Moral rights, broadly speaking, are associated with author's rights ('droit d'auteur') in civil law legal systems in Europe that are concerned, or intended to be, with protecting a creator's personality. Although economic rights—such as the right to reproduce a work discussed in chapter six—may also be justified on the basis of protecting the creator's personality by providing control over a work, moral rights make explicit the link between personality and the work.[20] Moral rights include the attribution or paternity right (the right to be identified as the author of a work) and the integrity right (the right to object to the modifications of a work that would prejudice the author's reputation).[21] This part thus examines attribution, false attribution and integrity and how it might apply to graffiti creativity assuming the preconditions discussed above are met.

The moral rights provisions in the CDPA implement Article 6*bis* of the Berne Convention. The 'right to be identified as the author or director of the work' is contained in section 77 and applies to literary and artistic works.[22] The author must assert his/her right to be identified as the author of the work.[23] Section 80 provides the author with the right 'not to have his work subjected to derogatory treatment'. Two further rights, not required by Article 6*bis* the Berne Convention, are the right against false attribution[24] and right to privacy in private and domestic photographs and films.[25] Suffice it to say at this point that the implementation of the Berne provisions in the UK has been described as 'minimalist'.[26]

The argument usually advanced is that jurisdictions that have been influenced by personhood justifications for copyright, namely Germany and France, offer stronger moral rights protection than common law systems do.[27] France, unlike

[20] Underpinning the argument that creators should have control over it or that interference with the work (as the embodiment of its creator) is interference with its creator. Argument made with respect to artists: Stokes (n 15) 83–4. See generally W Fisher, 'Theories of Intellectual Property' in SR Munzer (ed), *New Essays in the Legal and Political Theory of Property* (Cambridge, Cambridge University Press, 2001) 174.

[21] Berne Convention, Art 6*bis* (1): '[T]he author shall have the right to claim authorship of the work and to object to any distortion, mutilation, or other modification of, or other derogatory action in relation to, the said work, which would be prejudicial to his honour or reputation.'

[22] The other works covered by the section are musical works, dramatic works, works of architecture and film.

[23] CDPA, s 78(1).

[24] CDPA, s 84.

[25] CDPA, s 85.

[26] IA Stamatoudi, 'Moral Rights of Authors in England: The Missing Emphasis on the Role of Creators' (2015) 4 *Intellectual Property Quarterly* 478, 478. See also JC Ginsburg, 'Moral Rights in a Common Law System' (1990) 1(4) *Entertainment Law Review* 121, 125. The requirement to assert the attribution right is indicative of this given that Art 5(2) of the Berne Convention provides that rights will not be subject to formalities: W Cornish, D Llewelyn and T Aplin, *Intellectual Property: Patents, Copyright, Trade Marks and Allied Rights*, 7th edn (London, Sweet & Maxwell, 2010) [12-71].

[27] Fisher (n 20) 174.

the UK, offers a greater range of moral rights protection, too. Alongside the rights of attribution and integrity[28] are the rights to divulge the work and control the manner in which the work is disclosed[29] and also to withdraw the work after it is published.[30] Authors also have a right to access their works[31] whether or not, as in the case of an artwork, they own the physical object embodying the work and whether or not they own the copyright in it (ie since this is independent of their economic rights).

The gulf in protection between France and the UK raises the question of the esteem in which creators are held. As Ginsburg puts it:

> Adoption of moral rights sends a message that a society cares about creation, and about authorship.[32]

Ginsburg argues that in light of the lack of evidence on the effect of moral rights protection, the extent of moral rights protection that ought to be granted becomes a question of social policy.[33] Moral rights provision thus becomes another way of promoting creativity.[34] The attribution right, for instance, serves a public good in giving the public accurate information about who created a work.[35] This fits neatly with the social benefit justification for copyright protection. The encouragement of creativity in order to foster cultural development—promoting 'a vision of a just and attractive culture'[36] and additionally should moral rights apply to graffiti and other subcultural creativity, a plural culture—is supported by moral rights protection. The question is whether the form of moral rights rules is adequate to the task.[37] Yet, as the subsequent discussion suggests, when applying moral rights rules to graffiti creativity a tension is revealed between the preservation of certain forms of culture and the recognition of the reputation or dignity of an individual creator in such a way as to promote a diverse culture that embraces subcultural creativity. The relevant point is that this tension would likely not be resolved in favour of the graffiti writer who is placing works on walls without permission (or legally placing works that exhibit the same style).[38]

On the other hand, when it comes to commodified graffiti creativity—such as canvases or prints sold within the art market—an economic argument can be made

[28] Intellectual Property Code, Art L121-1.
[29] Intellectual Property Code, Art L121-2.
[30] Intellectual Property Code, Art L121-4.
[31] Intellectual Property Code, Art L111-3.
[32] Ginsburg (n 26) 122.
[33] ibid.
[34] ibid 130.
[35] ibid 122.
[36] Fisher (n 20) 175.
[37] On the limited scope of moral rights see Ginsburg (n 26) 130. The difficulty in implementation has been observed in other common law systems. The limited protection offered to artists in the US Visual Artists Rights Act and some state statutes is indicative of this but for a contrary perspective see TF Cotter, 'Pragmatism, Economics, and the Droit Moral' (1997) 76 *North Carolina Law Review* 1.
[38] Iljadica (n 14). Regarding crimes of style see J Ferrell, *Crimes of Style: Urban Graffiti and the Politics of Criminality* (Boston, Northeastern University Press, 1996).

that links the provision of moral rights protection to the public good. Hansmann and Santilli argue with respect to the integrity right that moral rights protection is useful, for instance, in preserving culturally important works from destruction.[39] Furthermore, the protection of a creator's reputation has consequences for the market value of his/her work.[40] An argument based on personality is thus not necessary to justify moral rights protection. At the same time, because moral rights attach to the author this suggests they are about showing respect for the author's effort in making the work.[41] This last point seems to suggest that a labour justification might also be indirectly offered for moral rights protection. The relationship between the regulation of creativity through copyright rules and the protection of reputation chimes with the concern with fame and respect in the graffiti subculture. The remainder of this chapter thus considers how well copyright rules might serve writers' preoccupation with fame and respect if the creativity in question was not regulated within the graffiti subculture's 'bounded commons'. Again, of course, much of the discussion here will apply to the dissemination of graffiti writing by non-writers too.

Moral Right of Attribution

The attribution right[42] in the CDPA applies, in the case of literary works, when 'the work is published commercially' or adapted.[43] In the case of artistic works the attribution right applies to commercial publication as well as public exhibition and the communication of an image of the work to the public or included in a film that is shown to the public.[44] The attribution right is heavily circumscribed. It may, for instance, be waived.[45] A major obstacle to exercising the right is the requirement that, as indicated above, the right be asserted either when copyright in the work is assigned to another, through a signed instrument, or, in the case of artistic works, by being identified on the work itself or something attached to it such as a frame.[46] The requirement of assertion is thus slightly different

[39] H Hansmann and M Santilli, 'Authors' and Artists' Moral Rights: A Comparative Legal and Economic Analysis' (1997) 26(1) *The Journal of Legal Studies* 95, 106.

[40] ibid 142.

[41] C Waelde, 'Moral Rights and the Internet: Squaring the Circle' (2002) 3 *Intellectual Property Quarterly* 265, 266.

[42] CDPA, s 77.

[43] CDPA, s 77(2)(a). This subsection excludes literary works in the form of lyrics and the situations in which the attribution right is triggered are outlined in subsection (3).

[44] CDPA, s 77(4)(a) and (b). Certain three-dimensional artistic works—mirroring the special treatment granted to such works in s 62 perhaps—must also provide attribution to the author (where the assertion requirements are met) when 'copies of a graphic work representing it or of a photograph of it, are issued to the public': CDPA, s 77(4)(c).

[45] CDPA, s 87.

[46] CDPA, s 78(3)(a). See also *Beckingham v Hodgens* [2003] EMLR 18, 75–76 in which a signed written document qualified as an assertion.

depending on whether graffiti creativity is judged to be a literary or an artistic work. Assuming the right has been asserted there are various ways in which the author of the work might be identified. It is difficult to ascertain how assertion and identification may apply to graffiti writing in terms of the ordinary activities of the subculture. Photo sharing and other such non-commercial publication purely within the subculture would, under the copyright rules, need to be accompanied by an assertion in writing.[47] This, however, would be unlikely to occur. This is simply because an attribution right is arguably not needed where the work is also its signature.

When photographs are taken of a work and posted on graffiti blogs, for instance, they are not necessarily captioned. The *LondonCityGraff*[48] blog, for example, consistently posts a wealth of photographs without a title or any identifying information about the writer or the writer's work, such as its location. Since the generation of graffiti creativity is about the granting of fame or respect, other writers can identify the graffiti name from the work. A writer generally does not need to be told who the writer is (not in terms of their personal identity, but rather in terms of their tag) because that is evident from the work itself. Insofar as subcultural creativity generally is concerned with attribution, specifically in the context of plagiarism,[49] such a concern is also evident in the graffiti subculture with respect to biting (copying) of names. Such copying matters because another writer is attempting to pass off the creativity of others as their own, rather than regarding an identification on the work or its copy in a graffiti magazine. As the discussion of name originality in chapter seven indicated, it is the attempt to appropriate another writer's fame that is problematic: the moral right of attribution would be of no help in resolving this type of name dispute.

There is a further reason why the right of attribution does not really make sense in the context of artistic works created by writers in urban public space. There is no feasible way to take advantage of the additional methods of asserting the right to attribution provided in the CDPA. For instance, a writer is very unlikely to assign copyright in their work and include a term regarding attribution[50]—simply, that is not how creativity within a subculture based on the pursuit of fame is understood. By contrast, this is not a problem with paintings on canvas where we might expect the painting to be sold and, potentially, the copyright to be assigned to a buyer. The aim is to be seen in a certain location meaning that the primary subcultural value of the work is bound up in this locational creativity as much as any inherent aesthetic value that the work might hold. Even if the work is photographed there is no easy way for the writer to assert his/her right to be identified

[47] In traditional photo sharing there is no sense that another writer with whom the photographs are shared is being assigned the copyright in the works.

[48] Available at www.londoncitygraff.blogspot.co.uk/.

[49] R Tushnet, 'Payment in Credit: Copyright Law and Subcultural Creativity' (2007) 70 *Law & Contemporary Problems* 135, 155.

[50] See CDPA, s 78(2)(a).

on subsequent copies[51]—for example by asserting the right in an instrument in writing—at least not in such a way that his/her identity would remain safe. Thus, the attribution provisions are limited not only in circumscribing the right but also in assuming that creativity will occur in recognisable ways and in traditional spaces such as galleries.

The impracticality of expecting graffiti writers to assert their rights to be identified as the authors of their works highlights a common criticism of the attribution right. As Teilmann argues, in practice a statement such as 'I assert my right to be identified as the author of this work' is merely a statement of something that appears to have happened and not a 'performative act of "assertion"'.[52] Thus in cases of subcultural creativity, as with creativity generally, it would be sensible to remove the assertion requirement altogether.[53] This would avoid situations where it is impractical to assert the right but also be more sensitive to the process—and indeed to the performative aspect—of graffiti creativity. (The very fact of moving through time and space consolidates, we might even say, asserts, an individual's identity as a writer within a community of writers.)

A further, particular case of impracticality concerns the attribution of joint works. To exist, the attribution right must be asserted individually by the joint authors.[54] Yet authorship of works by crews—where a *crew* is understood within the subculture as the owner of a crew piece (in the sense that reputational benefits accrue to the crew as an entity) regardless of the actual creator of it—does not match the definition of joint authorship in UK copyright.[55] On walls or trains, the crew is identified by its acronym. Some writers may therefore have their name written on the piece separately even if they did not contribute to its creation in the form of shout outs. Moreover, a crew whose work is publicly 'exhibited' on the street will have made no assertion in respect of that work. A writer could use spray paint to put the assertion in writing next to the work on a wall but this does not occur in practice. It is also unclear whether, even if it was to occur, this would qualify as an 'instrument' in writing since a wall is not a document.[56] It is difficult to see, however, why paper should be privileged over brick when the assertion has been made in such a way as to bring it to the attention of everyone who sees the work and may wish to reproduce it.

Nevertheless, there are situations in which graffiti creativity exists within the subculture-specific 'bounded commons' (or perhaps, more accurately, lingers at its borders as is the case with exhibitions of street art and graffiti that attract

[51] A writer could assert the right to be identified with respect to future works ('asserted generally': CDPA, s 78(2)) but this still leaves the problem of bringing that assertion to the notice of others. See Garnett et al (n 11) [11-21].

[52] S Teilmann, 'It's a Wise Text that Knows its Own Father: Some Problems in Paternity Rights' in F Macmillan (ed), *New Directions in Copyright Law, Volume 4* (Cheltenham, Edward Elgar, 2007) 111.

[53] Cornish et al (n 26) [12-71].

[54] CDPA, s 88(1).

[55] See chapter six.

[56] On the point of an 'instrument in writing' see generally Garnett et al (n 11) [11-21].

non-writers) where the assertion of the attribution right is, exceptionally, practicable. The public exhibition of an individual writer's graffiti creativity as an artistic work activates the attribution right when a graffiti writer exhibits, as is increasingly common, in galleries. For example, galleries in London have mounted street art, graffiti and other exhibitions.[57] This includes the sale of works including prints by creators, whether exhibiting a graffiti writing or street art aesthetic or not. In this rather more formal setting, the handover of a signed work to the gallery will be an assertion if, in accordance with section 78(3)(a) CDPA:

> [T]he author is identified on the original or copy, or on a frame, mount or other thing to which it is attached.

This raises a few interesting questions relating to the form of the identification, especially the use of pseudonyms and the intelligibility of the identification to its audience.

The assertion of the attribution right in this way (and assuming it is possible) enables the author to specify how he or she would like to be identified. That the author may specify that a pseudonym[58] should be used is of obvious benefit to graffiti writers. In the case of public exhibition or the commercial issue of copies—this is particularly common with respect to the issue of prints—writers will likely sign their tag (and where applicable the print number).[59] Interestingly, however, the form of identification other than a pseudonym must be a 'reasonable form of identification'.[60] It is not clear what this might cover but at least within the graffiti subculture, the pseudonymous work itself would likely count as a reasonable identification.

It is unclear whether a gallery owner could claim that a writer's assertion of the right to be identified as the author has been met on the basis that the artwork itself is the signature (as suggested earlier in this section). The identification must be 'clear and reasonably prominent'.[61] The problem is that while the tag might be argued to be a 'name' (ie that identified the author) its existence on the canvas would not necessarily indicate that the tag/name refers to its *authorship* to a general audience. Indeed, even within the subculture, where there is a homage or a memorial piece, other writers will understand that the author is in fact somebody else. This is not to say that such an identification is not 'reasonable' but that,

[57] On the relevance of the print to street art see L Dickens, 'Pictures on Walls? Producing, Pricing and Collecting the Street Art Screen Print' (2010) 14(2) *City* 63. On street art, graffiti writing and the art world: L Dickens, '"Finders Keepers": Performing the Street, the Gallery and the Spaces In-Between' (2008) 4(1) *Liminalities: A Journal of Performance Studies* 1.

[58] CDPA, s 77(8).

[59] Perhaps of more use would be protection offered under Intellectual Property Code, Art L113-6 (France) to release the work to the public but to remain anonymous. The writer could thus prevent anyone else from making his/her actual name known. For a discussion see G Davies and K Garnett, *Moral Rights* (London, Sweet & Maxwell, 2010) [12-009].

[60] CDPA, s 77(8).

[61] CDPA, s 77(7).

within the graffiti subculture, identification requires a knowledge of who else is writing and where, in what territory. Such knowledge will be largely inaccessible to non-writers.

This view is supported by the limited case law on the subject, specifically *Hyperion v Sawkins*,[62] which suggests that the work cannot also be its signature. In *Hyperion* the lower court held, and this was upheld on appeal, that the identification must identify the author of the work, not merely name him. In this case Dr Sawkins (found to be the author of a musical work that involved correcting and filling out musical compositions by the composer Lalande) was merely thanked on the defendant's infringing CD.[63] This, the High Court found, was insufficient, stating that:

> The sleeve has to clearly convey Dr Sawkins's authorship to all possible readers and not simply to those who might have some inside or particular knowledge of what to infer from the words that have been used.[64]

The identification relates to both the clear identification of the work's author and, more interestingly, the audience to whom the identification must be intelligible. One argument proceeding from the treatment of attribution in *Hyperion* is that the identification of authorship must be 'clear to all persons who are likely to see the form of identification'.[65] A tag, while visual, may not be identification that is in a 'visually perceptible form'.[66] Though this will, of course, be intelligible to other graffiti writers it will not be perceptible to everyone else who will also see it.

Yet this argument is based on particular assumptions of *who* the audience or beneficiary of the 'clear' identification is. A writer would assume that the author is the person whose tag is on the canvas; a non-writer might not. Similarly, at a more publicly accessible event such as the 'Battle of Waterloo'[67] (a graffiti competition in London) most of the possible readers would understand who the author was but others (PhD students researching graffiti included) would not. Based on *Hyperion*, the work as a form of identification would be insufficient because it requires the abilities of a writer or a graffiti expert to understand graffiti style and decipher the letters that form the name and then connect the name to authorship. Of course, writers—purely in terms of their subcultural activities and not any of their commercial offshoots—would not necessarily be concerned with this. This points to a further difficulty that copyright law has in simultaneously

[62] *Sawkins v Hyperion Records Ltd* [2004] EWHC 1530 (Ch) [85]; and on appeal, *Sawkins v Hyperion Records Ltd* [2005] EWCA Civ 565.

[63] *Sawkins v Hyperion*, first instance (n 62) [84].

[64] ibid [85]. This reasoning was approved by the Court of Appeal: *Sawkins v Hyperion Records Ltd* (CA) (n 62) [69] (Mummery LJ).

[65] Garnett et al (n 11) [11-17].

[66] H Laddie, P Prescott, M Vitoria, A Speck and L Lane, *The Modern Law of Copyright and Designs*, 3rd edn (London, Butterworths, 2000) [13.10].

[67] Writers were judged on '[l]etterform, fill-in, characters, concept, background': Mr Chrome, 'Battle of Waterloo 2 Line-Up' *Chrome & Black*, 1 August 2011 (web page no longer available).

having spatial effects by regulating the consequences of an exhibition in a particular space but poorly equipping authors to protect their works when such exhibition is non-traditional and brings a work to a multiplicity of audiences, willing or not. In general terms, this is another facet of the overlap between the physical and intellectual commons which is appropriately accounted for by the graffiti rules but not by copyright law.

If the tag identifies its author to the people to whom the identification matters—that is, other graffiti writers—why should the identification be intelligible to others as in *Hyperion*? This suggests that where the work is the signature a separate right of attribution is irrelevant; the relevant information is already visible. The hierarchical system in which graffiti writers compete for respect/fame is fundamentally concerned with attribution but without requiring separate attribution of works. The identification of the writer is, in any event, also achieved through the right of reproduction by ensuring that only the author of a tag has the right to reproduce it and therefore is the only author associated with that name. The reproduction right protects the personality of the writer and the authenticity of his/her work though only to an extent. Reverse passing off, discussed in conjunction with the right against false attribution below, would appear to be more relevant to graffiti writers.

Finally, the argument that identification is for the broader public—because there is a social benefit to knowing the author of a work is somewhat shaky with respect to works created without permission where such information will not be provided in a manner necessarily legible to the public, nor will the identification be asserted. The assertion provisions are better suited to the quasi-public space of the gallery than the street. Of course the public can also see graffiti writing on the street but it is not necessarily 'speaking' to them and, arguably, there is therefore little need to identify the author in a way that makes sense to the non-writer. Yet, works may be enjoyed (or not) when they are to be found in public space, so the unexpected public exhibition of graffiti creativity should not be a barrier to finding that the mere exhibition of a work that *is* a name is *also* assertion of the attribution right even if such an assertion is not intelligible to everyone who sees it.

In prizing attribution graffiti writers are not so different from other creators, as empirical studies into this area of copyright law have found.[68] Yet, the emphasis within the graffiti subculture on the *name* and the striving for fame/respect is simply not captured by the attribution right nor moral rights generally. In particular,

[68] eg CJ Sprigman, C Buccafusco and Z Burns, 'What's a Name Worth?: Experimental Tests of the Value of Attribution in Intellectual Property' (2013) available at www.papers.ssrn.com/sol3/papers.cfm?abstract_id=2011403. In practice, however, creators will not necessarily be credited: M Kretschmer, S Singh, L Bently and E Cooper, *Copyright Contracts and Earnings of Visual Creators: A Survey of 5,800 British Designers, Fine Artists, Illustrators and Photographers* (Centre for Intellectual Property Policy & Management, Bournemouth University, 2011) available at www.papers.ssrn.com/sol3/papers.cfm?abstract_id=1780206, 82.

the quest for recognition and the way recognition within the graffiti subculture is attained is not solely to do with the name but also where that name is found (its visibility, the choice of an appropriate surface, etc). Moral rights, as they exist in law, will not, however, protect that aspect of the creative process of graffiti writing; no validation will be granted to an author for being the first one 'up' in a highly dangerous, visible spot; there is no possibility of recognising that a writer in that spot was the first to write their name.

Moral Right Against False Attribution

The right against false attribution is the right of an individual not to have the authorship of a work falsely attributed to them either expressly or impliedly.[69] It forms an interesting counterpoint to the attribution right with respect to graffiti creativity because it indirectly engages with concerns within the subculture over, in intellectual property language, a sort of reverse passing off (ie where one writer copies the name and style of another and thus damages the original writer's reputation, because it is assumed that the named writer is also the author).[70]

As with the attribution right, the right against false attribution may be exercised when a work is issued to or exhibited in public,[71] or communicated to the public.[72] Specifically with respect to artistic works, a person may be held liable for dealing with a work or its copy that has been falsely attributed.[73] A person may be held liable if in the course of business a work has been altered but is presented as unaltered and attributed to the author,[74] or, a copy of an artistic work is 'falsely represented' as having being made by the author.[75] In the case of graffiti writing, writers do have a reputation to protect but within the subculture only.[76] As *Clark v Associated Newspapers*[77] suggests, to show false attribution it is merely necessary to show that the false attribution is clear to the 'notional reasonable reader'.[78] The Patents County Court decision *Harrison v Harrison*[79] referred to the effect of a set of statements in the absence of explicit attribution on a 'reasonable, interested

[69] CDPA, s 84(1)(a). The section refers to dramatic, musical, literary and artistic works.

[70] On reverse passing off generally see L Bently and B Sherman, *Intellectual Property Law*, 4th edn (Oxford, Oxford University Press, 2014) 858.

[71] CDPA, s 84(2).

[72] CDPA, s 84(3)(a).

[73] While 'knowing or having reason to believe' that the attribution is false: CDPA, s 84(5).

[74] CDPA, s 84(6).

[75] CDPA, s 84(8)(b).

[76] The issue of reputation is discussed in more detail with respect to the integrity right in the next section.

[77] *Clark v Associated Newspapers Ltd* [1998] RPC 261.

[78] ibid [273]. The court notes that a more stringent test applies than relates to passing off where 'in order to succeed it is sufficient for the plaintiff to establish that one of those meanings misleads a substantial number of people': [273].

[79] *Harrison v Harrison* [2010] EWPCC 3.

person of average intelligence'.[80] With respect to graffiti it is unclear whether this reader would be a writer or a member of the public at large. However, it would make sense to consider the views of a graffiti writer or that of someone interested in graffiti culture as expert evidence in order to determine whether the attribution was false by, for instance, demonstrating that the work itself could not have been created by the person whose name formed the work because the style was poorly executed.

False attribution is potentially more useful to graffiti writers than the attribution right. A piece being captioned as having been created by a different writer for instance would not be credible because the piece itself is the signature and it clearly spells out a different name to that being captioned. The problem would arise with respect to copying another writer's tag, throw-up or piece, for example, if another graffiti writer decided to write the same name. This may be problematic where the copy is a bad one because it may have a negative effect on the copied writer's reputation within the subculture. The issue here would be at once one of copying as well as false attribution. The copier is presenting the work as if it was created by the other (falsely attributed) writer. If the style was copied as well as the name this would be even more problematic because, given that such a reproduction may not meet the standard of the first writer, there is both a false attribution and a potential integrity right breach.

It seems that in the hypothetical described—one writer copying another's name—there would appear to be false attribution. However, this means leaving aside the difficulties inherent in adopting the reasonable person test (it is unlikely that the test encompasses the ordinary, reasonable graffiti writer). The assumption that the identification was false would appear to require knowledge on the part of a reasonable person that in the graffiti subculture the work is also the author's pseudonym. As with the preceding discussion on moral rights protection in commercial contexts, this small example suggests that, echoing the aesthetic conservatism of the closed list of subject matter, that artistic works are simply not in themselves expected to *be* the attribution of authorship.

Moral Right of Integrity

The right to object to derogatory treatment (the integrity right) implements Article 6*bis* of the Berne Convention albeit in weakened form. Section 80 of the CDPA provides that the author of an artistic work 'has the right … not to have his work subjected to derogatory treatment'.[81] The right applies where such a work is published commercially, exhibited in public,[82] is included in a film[83] and, in the

[80] ibid [55]. The case concerned a purported new edition of a book.
[81] CDPA, s 80(1). The integrity right also applies to literary, musical, dramatic works and films.
[82] CDPA, s 80(4)(a).
[83] CDPA, s 80(4)(b).

case of sculptures, buildings and works of artistic craftsmanship, issues a graphic work or photograph of it.[84] The treatment of the work is derogatory

> if it amounts to distortion or mutilation of the work or is otherwise prejudicial to the honour or reputation of the author or director.[85]

Crucially, the integrity right is dependent on the treatment affecting the author's reputation notwithstanding the presence of the word 'otherwise' above.[86] By contrast, Article 6*bis*(1) offers somewhat broader protection in also referring to 'other derogatory action in relation to' a work.

A distinction between the immaterial elements of a literary work and the embodiment of the immaterial in a physical artwork is evident in the application of the integrity right in the UK to copies of artistic works. Teilmann argues, on the basis of UK case law[87] on this point, that there is reluctance on the part of courts to find the integrity right of an author has been infringed where the derogatory treatment is related to a copy.[88] A further, more general problem here relates to the link between the integrity right and the regulation of space. While the integrity right is conceived of as a question of vindicating individual author interests in maintaining how they present themselves to the world,[89] a concern that is shared by other creators, the application of the integrity right to graffiti writing necessarily implicates other parties. This is not simply a question of addressing what reputation means, although this presents its own difficulties given public perceptions of graffiti as a 'crime of style',[90] but what it means to protect graffiti writing and other forms of publicly accessible works in urban space. This again reveals the relevance of space to the regulation of creativity. The spatial effects of copyright are pronounced in relation to the integrity right as it applies to public display of works because the protection afforded to the author has the potential to prevent interactions with the work by members of the public who may wish to preserve the work (or not).[91] Such interaction may involve the destruction of works but, as has been the case with some street art, an instinct to preserve those works as well.[92]

[84] CDPA, s 80(4)(c).

[85] CDPA, s 80(2)(b).

[86] *Confetti Records v Warner Music* UK Ltd [2003] ECDR 31 [150]: 'the distortion or mutilation is only actionable if it is prejudicial to the author's honour or reputation'.

[87] eg *Pasterfield v Denham* [1999] FSR 168.

[88] S Teilmann, 'Framing the Law: The Right of Integrity in Britain' (2005) 27(1) *European Intellectual Property Review* 19, 22–23. With respect to the relevance of this distinction to fair dealing see F Macmillan, 'Is Copyright Blind to the Visual?' (2008) 7(1) *Visual Communication* 97, 113–14.

[89] In relation to which see generally eg LK Treiger-Bar-Am, 'The Moral Right of Integrity: A Freedom of Expression' in F Macmillan (ed), *New Directions in Copyright Law, Volume 2* (Cheltenham, Edward Elgar, 2006).

[90] Ferrell (n 38). On the application of the integrity right to the destruction of graffiti: Iljadica (n 14).

[91] eg J Coleman, 'Council U-turn in Row over ROA Graffiti Rabbit in Hackney Road' *Hackney Gazette* 10 November 2010.

[92] eg local authorities preserving certain works by covering them with Perspex, mentioned eg in *Creative Foundation v Dreamland* [2015] EWHC 2556 (Ch) [10].

In considering the regulation of graffiti writing as the regulation of creativity within an intellectual and physical commons, it is necessary to consider the spatial effects of integrity right protection as well.

The evidence from the US, where an integrity right scenario has been addressed by the Eastern District Court of New York in *Cohen v G&M Realty*,[93] suggests that moral rights do have spatial significance but that in a contest between parties where a number of interests are represented—those of the creators, the community and the real property owners of a wall—real property rights will trump the moral rights of creators and the members of the public supporting them. Several points are discussed below that touch, impliedly, on this interface between the physical and intellectual commons: the extent to which interference with graffiti writing constitutes 'treatment', whether such treatment can be considered 'derogatory' especially given how reputation is determined in the moral rights case law, and how, by way of comparison to moral rights law in the US, the question of placement without permission might be addressed.

Before discussing treatment as it relates to graffiti creativity, it is necessary to consider the difference between the treatment of the work (as required by the CDPA) and the treatment of its underlying support[94] (this issue applies only to the original work and not its copy). Determining whether interference with support constitutes treatment would appear to be especially relevant in the case of graffiti writing on walls and trains primarily because it does not matter that the wall or train does not belong to the writer. The integrity right applies whether or not the person allegedly infringing the right owns its material support.[95] The intuition that artistic objects such as paintings are somehow special seems to underpin the argument for preventing owners from destroying cultural objects.[96] The psychological basis for this intuition has been confirmed via an empirical research project that measured responses to the alteration of artistic objects—the responses in the study indicated that 'there was something about art' that made alteration morally wrong even if people believed it was legally permissible to do so.[97]

Even so, the type of material support also seems to matter:

> Imagine, however, that the support is not a canvas but the wall of an Italian villa, and that the work is not an oil painting but a fresco fixed on the ceiling of one of the villa's bedrooms. Suppose that the owner of the house decided to paint that ceiling, or to paint a part of it in such a way that the work was partially covered. These variations of the

[93] *Cohen et al v G&M Realty et al* Case No 13-CV-5612 (FB) (JMA) (EDNY 2013). See SM Burke, '5 Pointz Down: The New York District Court Ruling on "Graffiti Mecca"' (2014) 4(3) *Queen Mary Journal of Intellectual Property* 226.

[94] See generally A Waisman, 'Rethinking the Moral Right to Integrity' (2008) 3 *Intellectual Property Quarterly* 268, 270–73.

[95] ibid 268–80.

[96] See JL Sax, *Playing Darts with a Rembrandt* (Michigan, Michigan University Press, 1999).

[97] BA Spellman and F Schauer, 'Artists' Moral Rights and the Psychology of Ownership' (2009) 83 *Tulane Law Review*, 661, 668.

previous setting suggest that, intuitively, we might not be willing to say that the owner should always be prevented from having his property painted.[98]

These issues with respect to the material support of a work become even more pronounced in relation to property in public space, raising the issue again of the conflict between individual moral rights as against both private property rights and the interests of the public in interacting with works in public space.[99] With respect to graffiti where a piece has been partially whitewashed, the argument could be made that it is clear to the public, as the work's audience, that there has been a modification of the support and not the work.[100] On this basis the argument could be made that there has been no treatment of the work but merely its support. This in turn suggests that, after all, copyright must concern itself with space by considering the placement of an artistic work, that is, *where* the physical embodiment of creativity occurs not merely on *what*. For graffiti writers, it would matter that only the support was treated because this would interfere with the locational aspect of creativity. For example if the work was cut from the wall without harming the work itself, the power of that work will arguably be diminished by its changed context.[101]

The next question is whether one writer going over another's work either by partly obscuring it with a new work, crossing it out or tagging it, going over it completely so as to destroy the work (this also applies to the 'buff')[102] would constitute 'derogatory treatment'. Two preliminary questions arise: first, whether these actions amount to the 'treatment' of the original artistic work and second, whether the treatment is derogatory. A further question also arises regarding the wording of section 80—specifically, the interpretation of 'otherwise prejudicial'—namely whether a treatment needs to be prejudicial or whether it is sufficient to show an 'alteration' or 'distortion' whether or not it is also prejudicial.[103] Suffice it to say that given the difficulties in demonstrating harm to reputation, the more favourable interpretation for graffiti writers is the latter as the discussion below, using the graffiti piece as the example of an artistic work, shows.

Even assuming that this fine distinction between the support and the work can be made, it would not alter the result of two of the scenarios mentioned above with respect to the treatment of graffiti, namely going over a piece with a new work or

[98] Waisman (n 94) 269.

[99] Regarding how individual moral rights challenge collective creativity and experience of the work, see P Loughlan, 'Moral Rights (a View from the Town Square)' (2000) 5(1) *Media & Arts Law Review* 1.

[100] Applying to graffiti the argument in Waisman (n 94) 285. A similar point is made in J Griffiths, 'The UK's Integrity Right and Freedom of Expression' in J Griffiths and U Suthersanen (eds), *Copyright and Free Speech: Comparative and International Analyses* (Oxford, Oxford University Press, 2005) 239.

[101] T Aplin and J Davis, *Intellectual Property Law: Text, Cases and Materials* (Oxford, Oxford University Press, 2009) 141.

[102] eg local authorities whitewashing graffiti.

[103] *Delves-Broughton v House of Harlot Ltd* [2012] EWPCC 29 and *Tidy v Trustees of the Natural History Museum* (1995) 39 IPR 501 suggest the latter is the correct interpretation but this is not settled. For the contrary view see eg *Confetti* (n 86) and *Pasterfield* (n 87) indicating that the alteration or distortion must be prejudicial.

crossing the piece out. Both appear to be instances of treatment by alteration.[104] More problematic is the question relating to whether this treatment is derogatory. The graffiti writer's 'reputation' is an obvious hurdle and *Confetti Records v Warner Music*[105] is helpful on this point. The case concerned the use of a musical work as a backing track for a rap. Although the author of the first musical work did not raise the issue, the court found that there was no infringement of the integrity right. Two points stand out in applying the reasoning in the case of a graffiti writer seeking to demonstrate infringement for going over.

First, the prejudice to the author's reputation is an objective test.[106] The graffiti writer could not simply argue that he or she was hurt by the alteration to the piece. In *Confetti Records v Warner Music* no evidence was provided that the treatment was prejudicial.[107] In a case relating to graffiti writing, evidence could be called from graffiti experts. This might include graffiti writers working legally. More difficult to answer is what reputation would mean in this context. *Pasterfield v Denham* is more useful here insofar as it suggests that it does refer to 'reputation … as an artist'.[108] Yet, even if evidence in the case of a graffiti writer were adduced that crossing out or partially covering a piece was prejudicial to the writer's reputation 'as an artist', the illegality of the creativity may be indirectly brought to bear because it would be difficult to show that the writer has a 'professional' reputation[109] as an artist. This would not be possible unless the writer also creates works legally (and this assumes again that the writer would be prepared to reveal his/her actual identity by suing for infringement of the moral right).

This in turn suggests that the concept of reputational damage as something adjudicated by the public response to the treatment is particularly problematic for a graffiti writer especially if:

> Evidence should normally be adduced that some members of the public do, or would be likely to think less of the author or director because of the treatment.[110]

Existing reports into public associations with graffiti writing as indicative of violence, danger and 'visual pollution'[111] suggest that very few writers are likely to be found to have a reputation that could be prejudiced by an alteration to their work.

[104] eg the reduction in size of a work and the change of colours: *Tidy* (n 103).

[105] *Confetti Records* (n 86).

[106] This is implied in *Confetti Records*: Davies and Garnett (n 59) [8-040]. *Confetti Records* (n 86) [150]. *Pasterfield v Denham* (n 87) [182] makes this clear by stating that 'it is not enough that the author is himself aggrieved'. Compare the more author-friendly approach in the Canadian case *Snow v Eaton Centre* (1982) 70 CPR (2d) 105.

[107] *Confetti Records* (n 86) [157].

[108] *Pasterfield v Denham* (n 87) [182].

[109] The narrower meaning of reputation can be implied from *Harrison v Harrison* (n 79) [64]: Davies and Garnett (n 59) [8-038].

[110] Garnett et al (n 11) [11-45].

[111] eg summary of responses to graffiti in R White, 'Graffiti, Crime Prevention & Cultural Space' (2001) 12 *Current Issues in Criminal Justice* 253, 258–59.

On the other hand, if other writers and, potentially, graffiti aficionados are asked, evidence could be led that the treatment was prejudicial because of the reputational damage suffered in the context of the fame hierarchy in the subculture. This leads to the second point, namely the relevance of the author's presentation to the public to date. Apart from the lack of evidence, the judge in *Confetti Records* was not prepared to infer prejudicial treatment from the use of violent lyrics.[112] It is unclear whether one writer's reputation could be inferred from the way in which other writers style themselves (ie as bombers or vandals).[113] It is even more problematic to assume that the reputation of the writer must be assumed from the prevailing public view of the writer as vandal and thus lacking any kind of reputation that could be damaged. Indeed, it is difficult to speak of graffiti writers as having a reputation outside of the graffiti subculture at all. To that extent, the moral right of integrity appears to privilege certain forms of creativity that might be described as traditional or market-based over others that challenge these established orders. Graffiti writers are thus likely to have difficulty objecting to the derogatory treatment of the work, whether the (partial) destruction was instigated by a writer or someone else such as a property owner.[114]

The meaning of 'honour' is no less significant. It appears to refer to the author's self-worth and dignity.[115] This lessening in emphasis away from the more outward-facing definition of 'reputation' (relating to the esteem in which the author is held) is potentially useful with respect to graffiti writing because the reference is to honour *or* reputation.[116] A writer could therefore argue that notwithstanding his/her reputation as a vandal, the alteration to the piece is prejudicial to his/her honour. Showing prejudice to the writer's honour, because it does not necessarily depend upon an assessment as to how the public might perceive the writer, would be the better option for graffiti writers by focusing on their dignity as authors. As Ginsburg has said, protecting moral rights shows that a 'society cares about creation, and about authorship'.[117] Protecting the individual integrity of an author may also therefore serve a social benefit in producing, or at least signalling the importance of, a diverse local culture.

Although the focus in this chapter has been on the application of moral rights rules to interaction with graffiti creativity within the subculture it is important to

[112] *Confetti Records* (n 86) [153]–[155].

[113] Where a group styled themselves as gangsters in a music video there could be no prejudice arising from violent lyrics: ibid [160].

[114] Note that property owners may avail themselves of the defence in CDPA, s 81(6)(a) regarding 'avoiding the commission of an offence' if compelled to destroy the work pursuant to a local authority notice (eg one under the Localism Act 2011, s 127).

[115] Arguing that infringement of the right could be found even when the reputation of the author is not affected: E Adeney, 'The Moral Right of Integrity: The Past and Future of "Honour"' (2005) 2 *Intellectual Property Quarterly* 111, 117–19; 130. See also Davies and Garnett (n 59) [8-037].

[116] The words may be discussed separately based on a close examination of the official French text of Art 6*bis*: Adeney (n 115) 122.

[117] Ginsburg (n 26) 122.

address the issue of the destruction of works by non-writers. This may of course relate to, for example, the destruction of a work by one writer by covering it entirely and replacing it with their own piece. It is also relevant to the 'buff', that is the extent to which graffiti writers could seek redress via moral rights when their works are destroyed by property owners or local authorities. While destruction may amount to the 'treatment' of a work[118] the graffiti writer would still have the difficulty of demonstrating it was derogatory.[119]

By contrast, the protection offered to 'works of recognized stature' in the US's Visual Artists Rights Act (VARA)[120] specifically provides protection against the destruction of a work. Yet even if such a right existed in the UK it would not provide an adequate solution to the destruction of graffiti creativity either within the subculture, when one writer goes over another's piece, or in providing redress against a property owner or local authority for buffing the work if, as under VARA, the *stature* of the work matters. Graffiti writers would then be faced with the same problems raised above regarding their reputation as the street artists in *Cohen v G&M Realty*[121] found out.

Given that 'recognized stature' is meant to function as a 'gatekeeping mechanism',[122] by giving weight to social attitudes and 'common sense', graffiti writing is unlikely to be protected. Certainly, regardless of the sympathy shown to a group of street artists in declining to make an order to prevent the destruction of works at the 5Pointz site in New York, the court in *Cohen* predictably privileged real over intellectual property rights and, indirectly, the rights of private property over public or community wishes in relation to this important cultural space.[123] With respect to one of the claimants—Lady Pink, a famous writer mentioned in *Subway Art*[124]—while the court agreed the work may be of 'recognized stature', there was a difficulty in demonstrating reputation because the importance of Lady Pink's specific work ('Green Mother Earth') was not evident in the expected forms of documentation such as in scholarly publications[125] that would ordinarily be used to evidence stature.

As the US case *English v BFC*[126] indicates, works placed without permission are even less likely to fare well. The case did not concern graffiti writing but rather murals and sculptures placed without permission and together forming the

118 Suggesting that destruction can be treatment: *Harrison v Harrison* (n 79) [60].

119 Iljadica (n 14) 275. But see, arguing destruction cannot be prejudicial and is therefore not part of the integrity right, Waisman (n 94) 273, note 18. See also Garnett et al (n 11) [11-47].

120 17 USC § 106A (a)(3)(B).

121 At the time of writing the matter had not gone to full trial.

122 *Carter v Helmsley-Spear* 861 F Supp 303 (SDNY 1994) 325.

123 Albeit with regret on the judge's part: *Cohen* (n 93) 23, 27. On the significance of the redevelopment see J Heathcott, 'The Bold and the Bland: Art, Redevelopment and the Creative Commons in Post-Industrial New York' (2015) 19(1) *City* 79.

124 Pictured in M Cooper and H Chalfant, *Subway Art* (London, Thames & Hudson, 1984) 68.

125 *Cohen* (n 93).

126 *English v BFC&R East 11th Street LLC* 97 Civ No7446 (HB) (SDNY 1997). Upheld on appeal, though the court did not discuss the VARA ground: *English v BFC* 1999 US App LEXIS 23697.

'Mural Garden'.[127] The lot where the sculptures and mural were placed was due to be developed. In rejecting the 'recognized stature' claim under VARA the court observed:

> Defendants *rely on common sense* and on Botello v. Shell Oil Co., 229 Cal. App. 3d 1130, 280 Cal. Rptr. 535 (Ct. App. 1991), in which the California appellate court noted in passing that that state's moral rights statute applied only to 'art that is affixed or attached by arrangement with the owner. It *obviously does not apply to graffiti*, which lacks these characteristics …' 280 Cal. Rptr. at 537 n.2 (citation omitted). This is a compelling argument, for otherwise parties could effectively freeze development of vacant lots by placing artwork there without permission. Such a construction of the statute would be constitutionally troubling, *would defy rationality and cannot be what Congress intended in passing VARA*. [Emphasis added.][128]

That it is 'obvious' that graffiti would not be protected is a view consistent with the case law on the 'recognized stature' provision. *Carter v Helmsley-Spear* emphasises that:

> The phrase 'recognized stature' is not defined in VARA. In light of the preservative goal of this Section, however, the recognized stature requirement is best viewed as a gate-keeping mechanism—protection is afforded only to those works of art that art experts, the art community, or society in general views as possessing stature.[129]

The fate of a particular work would then rest on which of these groups' views—experts, the art community or society—or some combination of them were considered in determining stature. For example, evidence from graffiti experts could be led that a certain graffiti piece is highly significant to the subculture (insofar as graffiti writers could be said to form an 'art community'). Equally, evidence might be led to the contrary. Even if the works were placed with permission the graffiti writers may suffer from the association of graffiti style with crime.[130] Indeed, the court in *Cohen* referred to graffiti writing, by contrast to street art, in less than complimentary terms.[131]

When, as under VARA, the outcome of a moral rights claim effectively turns on the location of a work (ie privileging property owners and the broader social requirement of building more housing),[132] the court is indicating that placement will be one of the key factors determining the extent of protection offered and not the work itself.[133] Crudely put, it places the protection of real property ahead of

[127] The court decided it was unnecessary to determine whether the garden as a whole was an artwork because VARA would not apply either way: *English v BFC* 1999 US App LEXIS 35242 9–10 (Baer J).

[128] ibid 11 (Baer J).

[129] *Carter v Helmsley-Spear* (n 122) 324–5.

[130] See Ferrell (n 38).

[131] Describing graffiti writing as 'distasteful' in the same case: *Cohen* (n 93) 10–11.

[132] ibid 27.

[133] Making the general point: SK Katyal, 'Semiotic Disobedience' (2006) 84(2) *Washington University Law Review* 489, 551.

intellectual property and hence potentially also ahead of creativity and cultural development. Considering whether the UK integrity right applies to graffiti (but the same issues arise in the application of VARA) indicates that the placement of the work in question matters because placement without permission will potentially affect a court's assessment of the reputation of the author, quite apart from any questions that might be raised with respect to the subsistence of copyright in graffiti since a refusal on the basis of illegality would remove the writer's ability to raise a moral rights claim.[134]

Moral Rights and Communal Creativity

It is useful here to return to an aspect of graffiti creativity—its communal nature—in order to consider what kind of moral rights protection might appropriately be offered to collective creativity. As some participants observed, the problem with the commodification and exploitation of graffiti creativity is not simply that it is harmful to the individual creator whose work is commodified, but also that it constitutes an exploitation of the culture as a whole.[135] Yet there is no means by which graffiti writers as a community might enforce their moral rights in the culture which they collectively produce and sustain. Thus for example, those participants who criticised the commodification of graffiti culture[136] would find no recourse in moral rights for protecting graffiti culture as a whole from undesirable exploitation because moral rights rules make the author the object of protection. This is important because there are a number of reasons for which it will often make little sense to discuss graffiti creativity in relation to an individual creator when graffiti writers themselves (as chapter seven has shown) are highly aware of their indebtedness to, and place within, a wider graffiti culture to which they consider themselves to belong and which is worthy of protecting as an end in itself. The difficulty here is not that moral rights might not attach to works of joint authorship, they plainly may.[137] Rather graffiti culture as a whole cannot be kept from the kind of exploitation graffiti writers might be inclined to find objectionable: by exploiting the subculture in general—the aesthetic which defines it and which, being within the subculture's 'bounded commons', no individual 'owns'—rather than some particular work within it, the party exploiting it evades any restrictions moral rights rules might impose.

Although discussing a different form of creativity with highly developed understandings of authorship, Simone's research into copyright law as it applies to Indigenous creativity shows that, in general terms, copyright law is incapable of

[134] Illegality is considered in chapter four.
[135] See chapter ten.
[136] In chapter five.
[137] CDPA, s 88. See chapter six.

accounting for collective creativity via standard joint authorship tests.[138] A similar failure may be seen in the apparent willingness to introduce communal moral rights legislation in Australia before postponing and effectively abandoning the plan.[139] A fundamental question arises here about the protection and promotion of graffiti culture, and indeed other forms of creative production that relies upon shared aesthetic references, via a copyright system geared towards the protection and (via moral rights) the concern with the authenticity of individual expressions. A difficulty identified in relation to Indigenous creativity[140] would also apply to any attempt to remedy this lacuna as it applies to graffiti: the problem of determining who speaks[141] for creators and for the shared culture which defines them. Community-based moral rights protection does not seem likely to be introduced in the UK yet it is exactly this kind of protection which may be needed in order to preserve the collective creativity of subcultures such as those comprised of creators producing writing in public space.

Conclusion

This chapter has examined the applicability of copyright rules on moral rights to graffiti creativity. It included a discussion of two situations—public exhibition and communication to the public—that would enable graffiti writers to enforce their moral rights. As the discussion demonstrated, particularly with respect to the assertion requirement, the moral rights rules are ill-suited to the regulation of graffiti creativity. In particular, the integrity right is problematic because it appears to be based on an assumption that artistic works are created within the mainstream art world in which works are exhibited, bought and sold and in which artists have reputations that might be damaged through the 'treatment' of their work. The analogue to the integrity right—the prohibition on going over another writer's work—is, by contrast to moral rights protection, attuned to graffiti creativity as a collective endeavour. This is discussed in the next chapter.

[138] D Simone, 'Dreaming Authorship: Copyright Law and the Protection of Indigenous Cultural Expressions' (2015) 37(4) *European Intellectual Property Review* 240.

[139] ibid 249, note 92.

[140] Only insofar as Indigenous creativity also raises issues of collective recognition for the creative process; this is not to suggest that this creativity and graffiti writing are equivalent.

[141] K Bowrey, 'Alternative Intellectual Property' (2006) 6 *Macquarie Law Journal* 65, 65.

9

Graffiti Rules—Don't Go Over

> The rules of the game are really important. You gotta respect writers who display superior skills or who have been in the game a long time. Never go over a piece unless you are putting up a better piece. You can put a piece [over] throw-ups, you can put throw-ups over tags. But never tag over a throw-up and never throw-up or tag over a piece. (Anon26)

Introduction

Graffiti writers aim to make their name visible with a view to achieving fame within the subculture; any interference with a tag when it is written on a wall has a potentially deleterious impact on their subcultural fame. It is unsurprising then that, alongside norms regulating the originality and copying of names and styles, a norm would evolve to protect the continued visibility of the name in a given location within the physical commons of the graffiti subculture. This chapter examines the relevant graffiti rule—that which states 'don't go over'—as it relates to the full or partial destruction of tags, throw-ups and pieces within the graffiti subculture. This rule, it is argued, broadly parallels the moral right of integrity in that it gives effect to an underlying concern with the reputation of, and respect for, the original creator. This chapter thus considers, first, the circumstances in which interference with another's graffiti writing is acceptable, taking into account factors such as effort, status and territory.

Interference with another writer's work may also be a response to a breach of the norms within the subculture. However, to complicate matters, such interference may also be a manifestation of subcultural politics rather than a response to a prior breach mirroring, in broad terms, remedies for copyright infringement. The second part of this chapter therefore considers 'going over' as a sanction for breaking the graffiti rules, including for biting (copying), but also as an expression of subcultural politics, in particular the dislike of one writer by another writer, or disagreement between writers (beef).

Norm Against Interference

This first part of the chapter discusses the fieldwork data on the circumstances in which it is acceptable to go over another writer's tag, throw-up or piece: these are effectively exceptions to the fundamental subcultural rule against the interference with works—'don't go over'. It considers the importance of the hierarchy of style (piece over a throw-up, throw-up over a tag) and the expectation that works by more skilled or highly respected writers—usually relating to pieces that have stood the test of time—will be left alone regardless of such considerations of hierarchy. Memorial pieces, already discussed with regard to copying that serves to memorialise a writer in chapter seven, are discussed again here, as is the appropriateness (or not) of interfering with pieces that are faded or have been dogged (tagged). Underpinning the norm against interference are concerns with both placement and territory, and in particular with the appropriate way to approach writing in a different city and within that city's scene, as well as respect for other writers. A somewhat understated justification for this set of norms was provided by one writer: 'but then people feel very strongly about their artwork' (Anon23).

To understand the significance of the hierarchy of style to the norms against interference it is necessary to briefly revisit the issue of subject matter. Specifically, creativity within the subculture is concerned primarily with the writing of letters but that not all expressions that contain letterforms may be described as graffiti *writing*. Apart from the expectation that graffiti writers write letters, the writing takes particular forms in the same way perhaps as the types of artistic works (eg paintings, drawings) are categorised in copyright law. The three main types of graffiti creativity, as indicated previously, are: the tag (written name), throw-up (larger, name written in eg 'bubble letters') and piece (larger again, distinguished by complexity of angles, colours, etc). The dub and production are more complex forms of the throw-up and piece respectively. The wildstyle, too, is a type of piece.

The three main types of creativity are highlighted here because they require different amounts of effort to execute and this is one of the factors in determining the acceptability of going over. The tag, for instance, can be written in seconds while a writer may spend many hours working on a piece. This does not necessarily make the tag easier to write—the effort expended by the graffiti writer earlier in the creative process in developing and practising a style over a number of years is considerable.[1] Nor are the creators of more complicated works (ie pieces) necessarily better respected than taggers; as chapter one indicated, there are different methods for acquiring fame within the subculture. Placement and the volume of

[1] See chapter seven regarding can control.

works created is also important. Being 'up' by consistently bombing (prolifically writing tags) will gain a graffiti writer respect whether they also engage in piecing or not.

Before addressing skill and the hierarchy of style of in more detail it is useful to revisit the historical foundation of the 'don't go over' rule. As with much else in the graffiti subculture the rule has its roots in New York train writing. A writer at that time in New York needed to make the decision whether, in order to be seen, it was necessary (and appropriate) to go over someone's work when they were standing in the yard.[2] As one writer put it:

> This is all old school graffiti stuff, in the old days you would pick up on these rules or risk getting a bit of a slap when you were caught up with by the established writers. (Anon26)

The rule, having arisen when space was scarce on the outside of trains, is arguably far less important today simply because there is more space—primarily on walls—on which to write. Given the difficulties London writers face in painting overground trains (let alone tube trains) writers will always have a clean carriage on which to write:

> [W]ith respect to trains [piecing] over an existing piece would be deliberate when there's space elsewhere. I don't really think that's been relevant since New York basically because trains have never had that kind of coverage. (Anon6)

This is less true of some popular walls where writers may find it more difficult to find a blank space; a lack of space is likely to be acute in halls of fame. In certain spots, such as a hall of fame, faced with a wall already heavily covered with graffiti writing, a writer will need to make a decision about whether to go over another writer. Yet in certain respects the hall of fame is not a very good example because writing in these spots carries an expectation that the writing will be short lived. The existence of such a rule made more sense before the New York trains were buffed prior to running.

Finally, it should be noted that, as with the other graffiti rules within the subculture's 'bounded commons', the participants queried the extent to which they were adhered to in terms of the familiar old school/new school divide. Participants also raised the (only partly related) problem of younger writers not yet knowing the rules and needing to learn them. In the context of going over one writer said:

> Age wise I'm new school, mentally I'm a lot more old school than a lots of the guys my age so I respect a lot of the older stuff, a lot of the guys don't, it doesn't matter to them. … [T]hey cap an old school piece that shouldn't be capped not because they're against that person but because they're ignorant to the rules. (Anon26)

The rules about which pieces should or should not be interfered with—namely not to go over a 'better' work whether in terms of style or status—have the effect

[2] Regarding limited space on trains see M Cooper and H Chalfant, *Subway Art* (London, Thames & Hudson, 1984) 29. On the history of graffiti writing see chapter one.

that, as the above extract suggests, knowledge of the scene and of any given writer's place in it is a necessary element of determining the acceptability of going over in a particular situation.

Style, Skill and Respect

The norm against interference was summarised as a 'basic rule' by one writer who stated: 'don't go over [something] better than you' (Anon27). The references to 'you' or 'mine' in place of 'going over your work' or 'going over my work' by other writers suggests the extent to which going over is taken as an offence against the writer *personally* because their writing is effectively treated as indivisible from them. The writer is 'disrespecting the artist and the piece' (Anon26). This is why, for instance, seemingly extraneous information matters. Factors (alongside the form or skill of the graffiti writing *itself*) that may be considered in determining the acceptability of going over, are another writer's place in the subculture's hierarchy, or the respect for the other writer regardless.

The recognition of skilled writing, or the recognition of skilled writers, also means recognising the effort and the danger of producing the work. As one writer explained in response to a follow-up question about why it would be disrespectful to disregard the hierarchy of style:

> Throw-ups go over tags, pieces go over throw-ups. It's one of those things everyone learns ... It's about time as well. The more time you spend and the more colours you use in in an illegal environment the danger escalates, so the longer you're there, the longer it takes to execute. The danger goes up so the more colours you use the bigger balls you have and it's showing off. If you go on a road and it's full of throw-ups and you manage to do an eight colour top to bottom full craziness then you show everyone up. (Anon11)

This extract reflects a generally accepted (if not always respected) rule: a throw-up goes over a tag, a piece goes over a throw-up. This point was brought up for example by two writers who described the hierarchy of style as 'tag—throw-up—piece—wildstyle' (Anon5 and Anon6). Similarly another participant stated: 'A throw-up goes over a tag and a piece goes over a throw-up' (Anon13). Yet as Anon11 above suggests, the amount of labour (time) expended on the execution of a work is relevant in interpreting the rule.

Beside the labour expended on the writing, the perceived value of the writing itself also matters here. Unlike copyright law, which does not take into account aesthetic quality, graffiti creativity is consistently judged in terms of its aesthetic quality and/or effort required to write, whether in terms of can control or technique, or placing the writing in a dangerous but highly visible space. As two participants stated:

> Anon13 If you can't beat it don't go over it. If there's a wall, if you turn up and the wall's full and it's a wicked piece and you know you can't beat it then don't go over it.

Anon14	Walk away.
Anon13	If you go over it with a piece of shit, do you know what I mean.
M	Yeah I do, I do.
Anon13	If you're just starting out and whatever and you go I'm going to paint over this and you're no good.

As discussed in chapter seven, 'having style' matters when the writer is seeking fame and respect. This also explains why the hierarchy of style may not apply in favour of a toy writer. Still, that does not mean that all older or more experienced writers will go over the work of younger ones. One participant explained that he would be more inclined to paint with 'passionate' young writers who 'show a lot of interest' and would 'never go over them' (Anon18).

Quite apart from the hierarchy of style and the skills involved the status of the writer also matters. The position of the writer within the scene dictates that the work of a well-respected writer who is consistently 'up' will not be interfered with, regardless of the relative stylistic merits of the letter writing. For example one writer said: 'no matter how good I am I would never go over [a king].' (Anon19). Similarly, even if the writer contemplating going over is more skilled, where the piece is of value to the subculture—especially where it has survived for a long time and is by a well-respected writer—it would not normally be gone over. One writer explained this as follows:

> Yeah, yeah, if you're, generally, if you're going over someone it should be better than what's already there but then, as I've said, you could have something nostalgic that's there for 20 years and [has] some history then that shouldn't be gone over. (Anon27)

There is an implicit concern here with the preservation of graffiti culture by ensuring the continued existence of the piece in the physical commons. Ensuring its continuing existence *also* cements its position within the subculture's intellectual commons. The writer continued:

> Generally, if you're painting on tracksides or whatnot you have to do something that's better than the existing piece but even then there's no rules, that person could still, like, want to kill [you] for going over them. (Anon27)

The final point the writer above makes relates to writers taking offence at going over. It suggests that even where a writer goes over another when it is apparently acceptable to do so—because something 'better' is replacing it—this may be interpreted as disrespectful. Such an action may in turn prompt destruction in retaliation. This is discussed further in the second part of the chapter, below, on sanctions.

Skill and effort are at the heart of the determination of the hierarchy of style. However, it is possible to invert the hierarchy of style so long as the new work is *better*. One writer went so far as to dispute the relevance of the hierarchy of style as the fundamental basis on which the determination of what 'better' means saying the hierarchy is:

> Not relevant anymore because it's about reputation. If someone goes over a full colour with two colour then [the] person doesn't go over it [even] if it is better. Two colour things can be better. (Anon29)

A throw-up could be produced with more technical skill than a poorly executed piece even though the former is more straightforward to execute than the latter. Thus, while indicating these rules were irrelevant, the writer above nevertheless acknowledged the importance of both reputation (fame) and history noting that 'you can do a wildstyle over older and better things and you'll lose everything you've got' (Anon29). In other words, a writer may seek to take advantage of the key exception to the norm against interference—don't go over unless you are putting up something better—and so, for example, go over a throw-up with their own technically proficient, large-scale piece. However, this exception does not apply where the writing in question, even if apparently less skilled, is a high status work.

There is a tension at play in the responses. While acknowledging, to an extent, the operation of a norm against interference with higher status works, the same writer professed not to care about the rules saying that he was 'not bothered' (Anon29) by someone going over his work. In part he saw this as an acknowledgment that it is more difficult to regulate writing in a scene as big as London's. By contrast in a less populous city:

> [They] believe in throw-up goes over a tag, piece [goes over] a throw-up but in London it all goes over everything. But that comes from in [a small city], everyone knows everyone and [it's] easier to establish a hierarchy. (Anon29)

A different participant described the problem instead as a conflict between old school writers and some young, new school writers:

> [These] guys don't particularly know what they're doing, they don't know the locals, they don't know the people and they're going over someone who's been putting in work since like the mid-70s or the 80s ... whereas if you're of the old school mentality you'd see the piece, you know their persona and go 'I've got respect, I'm not going to mess with his stuff' and so I'll leave him and I'll go over somebody else. (Anon27)

The, somewhat tricky, exception to the respect shown to old pieces and famous writers is that writers may go over pieces that are faded or have been dogged. Yet this will not necessarily stop the other writer from feeling aggrieved. One participant recounted his own experience as follows:

> [O]ne of the first pieces I did was going over. It was going over a piece that was... that had been dogged out so they'd put a lot of tags over, so. ... And that's a circumstance, if that was the only space on the wall at the time then that was ok. There was another time I went over a piece of somebody who wasn't particularly up, I thought at the time, I thought he was just a... somebody from another city. And they looked quite faded and it was probably one of the worst dubs on the wall so I just said well I have to [go] over this [one]. ... I actually met the guy [*laughs*] about a year later ... and he was not

> too happy but fortunately I knew a lot of people he did and he was ok with it in the end. (Anon3)

Thus, the difficulty lies in determining the extent to which the piece has been dogged and whether the status of the writer of the piece may demand that it should be left alone notwithstanding its current condition.

That the permissibility of going over 'depends on context' (Anon5 and Anon6) should be obvious from this discussion, and is best illustrated by the approach to memorial pieces. Such pieces should be left alone *irrespective* of the skill or identity of their creator, as neither of these factors matter in this particular instance: they are trumped by the imperative to memorialise. One writer recounted incredulously the great disrespect shown to a deceased writer whose 'rest in peace memorials were getting capped' (Anon18). The same non-interference principle applies to the pieces created by any late writer:

> [I]f there's a piece done by someone who died, especially in the action of doing graffiti, people will show respect … I mean often you'll have new jack writers who come along and they'll go over something stupidly. But for people who are involved in the movement they'll go 'oh that guy, even if he wasn't good it's like he did die doing graffiti' which happens unfortunately regularly and they'll show respect and leave it even though we know we can do something better there … Even a tag, you know. You don't go over tags and pieces by people who are dead. It's disrespecting the dead. I don't think that's cool in any culture really. (Anon4)

Respect for the individual who contributed to the culture is again invoked to determine the acceptability of going over; the norm is not underpinned by a standalone concern with respect for an individual. And, in the respect afforded to the dead, like the respect afforded to 'personal' private property,[3] the underlying justifications for the graffiti rules are revealed to be, perhaps surprisingly, conservative in their preoccupations.

Finally, another participant observed that once a writer has committed to going over that it is more respectful to cover the entire piece:

> [Y]ou could go over it disrespectfully and not cover it all and make a mess or make a mark over it where it's clearly visible that you've gone over something. That's more of an act of aggression but my goal would be to cover the spot. … [A line] is more aggressive and disrespectful to the person's time and energy spent to create the piece. It's more disrespectful to do a few lines over it or write something over the top rather than reclaim the space as a whole and paint something large. (Anon11)

This writer tied the issue of respect closely to the use of a space and in so doing suggested the existence of a link between space and the labour of individual writers as an implicit part of the 'don't go over' rule. Another writer disagreed noting that if it 'overlaps another slightly' (Anon15) then this is fine. Of course there is a

[3] See chapter five.

difference between going over a piece with a piece and simply lining it, which is a clear sign of disrespect.[4]

Placement, Territory and Commons

The placement norms discussed in chapter five focused on situations where writers must choose the surface on which they write, without taking into account what happens when a wall—and this is predominantly an issue for walls rather than trains—is already covered with graffiti. As with the other graffiti rules, such contextual factors—the space on the wall (or trackside, or train) and the territory (ie a particular city's scene)—serve to modify the operation of the 'don't go over' rule. This is particularly relevant to the treatment of writers visiting from another city. In short, the norm against interference is useful in encouraging writers to be cautious in how they approach a particular spot as well as how they approach writing in a city, or part of a city, other than their own: abiding by the norm lessens the potential for disagreements to arise.

Going over was described by participants as a last resort. The expectation is that if there is a space on a wall the writer will put up their tag or piece or throw-up in the space without encroaching on another writer's piece. Thus, the next question after considering the placement of writing on the spot itself such as whether it is public or 'personal' property, is to consider the other tags or throw-ups or pieces that are there. One participant described going to great lengths to avoid going over on a trackside in order to 'create space':

> [A]nything that you can see from the tracks is basically fair game and that's where it's nice as well 'cause there's tons of space on the tracks even, with everything being buffed for the Olympics … There's still tons of space and that's all part of it, going that little bit different … When we [the crew] first started we didn't want to go over anyone we liked or had been inspired by but knew we had to create space for ourselves … or we'd go above [higher]. (Anon27)

Territory as a factor in determining whether or not going over is acceptable may relate not only to a spot but also to a particular urban neighbourhood, a train or underground line or to an entire city. One writer described the attitude of some, exceptionally territorial, writers as follows:

> [Some writers say] 'I go over people if they're in my neighbourhood. I go over people if they're on my line, they know it's my fucking line' and people take ownership and they're just militant about it. (Anon4)

[4] See eg N Macdonald, *The Graffiti Subculture: Youth, Masculinity and Identity in London and New York* (Basingstoke, Palgrave Macmillan, 2001) 211.

Thus writers from other cities may cause problems simply by painting the wrong surface altogether so as to make it unsafe for local writers. An example given was of a crew of writers

> coming over and hammering the tubes and then basically people saying 'you've basically ruined it for us because you've come, painted every night for a week, they've installed a load of new security and stuff and we can't paint' kind of thing. (Anon6)

To avoid a situation like this, as with belonging in the graffiti subculture generally, it is crucial for a writer to understand not only who else is 'up' but *where*. To know, for example, that a yard has been claimed a writer would 'need to understand the scene and history or else [they] will be gone over' (Anon5 and Anon6). A writer needs to 'earn [their] place in the city and it doesn't happen overnight, it shouldn't happen overnight' (Anon5). This position is not limited to London, but applies in other cities as well, as one writer explained:

> If it's in my city I think I know pretty well all the people and if I don't recognise anybody or I know it's a kid or someone less experienced or who's done it quickly just for covering the surface I think I can go on top of him. (Anon8)

As a writer on the receiving end of going over in a different city explained, as a non-local he 'wouldn't be upset if any of my stuff [was gone] over' (Anon11). Echoing this, another participant said, with respect to going over in particular spots, that 'London just doesn't sort of observe these rules as well' (Anon23). However, the internet and the 'international thing' (Anon6) makes it 'harder to pinpoint out-of-towners' (Anon5). This suggests that while the graffiti rules are transnational in their application across numerous global cities—all of these having been transplanted from the US[5]—the size and complexity of the global subculture makes the rules difficult to enforce.

Copyright *Beyond* Copyright—Spatialised Moral Rights

The graffiti rules are the product of certain modes of belonging and a form of creativity that is highly dependent on movement through space. The norm against interference is based on a consensus, however limited, on what it means to be a 'good' writer and therefore what it means to contribute to graffiti culture. Going over and the circumstances in which it is acceptable provides a qualified parallel to the integrity right discussed in chapter eight. The norm against interference, which seeks to safeguard graffiti creativity from adverse reputational effects, is a self-consciously spatialised form of 'moral rights' that is beyond copyright. In relation to graffiti creativity this norm relates to how the writer is viewed both literally (on the street) as well as within the scene when a tag, throw-up or piece is partially or completely obliterated. The rights of attribution and against false attribution

[5] On which see chapter one.

are subsumed into the prohibition against biting because the writer is evident from both their name and style: reproduction of the name or style also calls into question who created the graffiti writing. This section thus contrasts the 'don't go over' rule and the moral right of integrity, especially in relation to the destruction of works. It then revisits questions raised earlier in the book regarding the importance of protecting an individual's name by linking that discussion to broader questions on the role of moral rights protection in 'authenticating' creativity.

Going over, for example by lining another's tag, is at least superficially similar to the concept of mutilation in section 80(2)(b) of the Copyright, Designs and Patents Act 1988 (CDPA). However, unlike the integrity right, the norm against interference goes further than mutilation to regulate the *destruction* of the work. The applicability of the integrity right to destruction is a possibility considered only fleetingly in the relevant case law.[6] Turning to the integrity right, the first difference is that while, under the integrity right, the mutilation of a piece, for instance, may be derogatory there is usually no possibility of confusion as to who made the alteration to the piece. When a piece is tagged the writer is clearly identified; the specialist (ie graffiti) audience *knows* that the original writer did not tag the piece. To that extent, the alteration is not necessarily prejudicial to the writer's reputation but it certainly is an affront, broadly speaking, to the writer's *honour*. That affront, however, is the product of a hierarchical subculture to which fame and respect are central.[7] This is different to, for example, the facts in *Tidy v National Trustees*,[8] where the artist argued that the treatment of a drawing was prejudicial because it affected how the audience for his work would view him as an artist (since in that situation the audience may well think the cartoonist made the change).

The graffiti rule appears to mirror the prohibition against the destruction of 'works of recognized stature' under VARA[9] more closely than it does the UK integrity right. The US's legislation is based on the work as the embodiment of the artist, and moral rights as necessary for the protection of the artist's dignity.[10] The 'recognized stature' provision is concerned specifically with 'societal loss'.[11] Specifically, the desire to protect works that are significant—those that have '*stature*'—within the subculture depends on a *recognition* that where these works are by very well-known writers and/or have survived for a very long time these works must be protected as (sub)culturally significant. In that way, the norm against interference would seem to be based on the promotion of social benefit (ie by preserving graffiti creativity and culture).

[6] See *Harrison v Harrison* [2010] ECDR 12 [60].

[7] Going over effectively acts as a challenge to the wronged writer to punish the offending writer and restore their respect (as the discussion below regarding going over and beef between writers suggests).

[8] *Tidy v Trustees of the Natural History Museum* (1998) 39 IPR 501.

[9] 17 USC §106A(a)(3)(B).

[10] Reference to HR Rep No 101-514, 15 (1990) in the moral rights case *Martin v City of Indianapolis* 192 F 3d 608; 1999 US App LEXIS 20886 611.

[11] See eg reference to House Report in *Carter v Helmsley-Spear* 861 F Supp 303; 1994 US Dist LEXIS 12207 52–59.

At the legal level, moral rights protection may potentially step in to protect creativity that cannot be protected as a trade mark.[12] What moral rights protection arguably protects is the personality of the creator or, more accurately, the persona or brand of the creator.[13] The effect of a derogatory treatment is thus linked to reputation, that is, how the creator is perceived (and how that derogatory treatment influences the perception), rather than to the creator's experience of feeling personally injured by the treatment. The integrity right thus protects the author as the brand that encapsulates the relationship between different works. The difference between the writer and an artist brand or a company brand is that the creativity need not be commercial in order to be fully protected within the relevant normative framework for regulating creativity. The graffiti subculture's norm against interference provides protection within its 'bounded commons' that is stronger than the equivalent protection provided under copyright law. In the subculture the name functions akin to a brand. The norms against interference is thus directed not simply to the integrity of an individual work but—akin to trade mark law[14]—the dilution of the writer's reputation. This is compounded by the identification of writers not only with a particular name but also a particular style or stylistic twist that might be described as the writer's 'trade mark style'.[15]

There is undeniably a 'personal' quality to graffiti creativity that is not necessarily evident in all forms of creativity protected by copyright. In particular, there is a linguistic conflation of the person and the work—writers will refer to *someone* being 'up' (eg 'he's all city', 'he gets up'). This suggests that it is difficult to say that graffiti creativity is an expression '*by* the self, not necessarily *of* the self'[16] because the whole mode of being in the subculture involves the assumption of a new self or persona of which the work is a clear emanation. The tag is necessarily *of* the graffiti-self. The 'personality' standard is not explicitly part of the originality test[17] (though arguably post-*Infopaq* personality is more important given the emphasis placed on an individual making creative choices)[18] but the norm against interference suggests that, perhaps, the regulation of originality and the regulation of interference with a work ought to be considered as a breach of the same norm, that is as breaches that damage the personality (ie dignity, reputation) of the creator. Such a reformulation at EU or UK level does not seem likely but it is worth considering that the monist approach to copyright found in

[12] P Masiyakurima, 'The Trouble with Moral Rights' (2005) 68(3) *Modern Law Review* 411, 431–32.

[13] See C Lury, 'Portrait of the Artist as a Brand' in D McClean and K Schubert (eds), *Dear Images: Art, Copyright and Culture* (London, Ridinghouse, 2002)

[14] See Trade Marks Act 1994, s 5(3).

[15] The notion of the 'artist as a brand' is by no means confined to graffiti writing. See Lury (n 13) 317; 320–23.

[16] LK Treiger-Bar-Am, 'The Moral Right of Integrity: A Freedom of Expression' in F Macmillan (ed), *New Directions in Copyright Law, Volume 2* (Cheltenham, Edward Elgar, 2006) 134.

[17] See ibid 133–34.

[18] On which see chapter six.

Germany[19] more closely resembles graffiti writers' approach to their own creativity in that reproduction and moral rights breaches are not categorised as different species of breach. Rather, moral and economic rights are inextricably linked so that economic rights may be used to protect moral rights and vice versa.[20]

Another aspect of any rethinking prompted by such a consolidation of norms relating to copying and reputation would be to allow for the creation of a spatialised moral rights regime so that reputational effects are determined not only by reference to the work but also via a consideration of *where* the work is found. This would allow, in particular, for considering reputational damage in the context of a certain territory (ie the specific city's scene). In the language of section 80(2)(b) CDPA this would mean asking only whether the author has been prejudiced[21] rather than also requiring a finding that a work has been distorted or mutilated. The interference with the work on a wall in the physical commons matters not only because the material work has been interfered with (by being crossed out on a wall) but because its visibility in the physical commons in turn affects the creator's body of work—and hence their reputation—in the subculture's intellectual commons. A system of moral rights taking the concerns raised by graffiti writers with regards to reputation seriously would need to be fundamentally re-thought.

Furthermore, in light of the dematerialisation of the work in EU copyright law which requires subsistence and reproduction to now be dealt with differently,[22] then this must also have an impact on moral rights. In other words, graffiti writing or indeed any other creativity must be considered independently from its material support so the only question we ought to ask is whether reputational damage, or damage to dignity, has occurred where there has been some form of interference with the creativity regardless of whether that interference has a *material* basis (eg lining a work on a wall). The question could instead be whether, echoing the notion of a taking of an original part (ie intellectual creation) which we encountered in chapter six, the interference is an interference with the author's personality as embodied by the work, such as to damage their dignity or reputation. This would mean, for example, that leaving a work untouched but removing it from its location—for example, by cutting a graffiti piece from a wall—might come to be seen as a moral rights breach. Even though the work itself remains unchanged, the interference with the locational creativity manifested within the work presents an affront to the dignity of the creator.

[19] See generally P Goldstein and B Hugenholtz, *International Copyright: Principles, Law, and Practice*, 3rd edn (Oxford, Oxford University Press, 2013) 20–21.

[20] E Adeney, *The Moral Rights of Authors and Performers: An International and Comparative Analysis* (Oxford, Oxford University Press, 2006) 222.

[21] The wording in CDPA, s 80(2)(b) leaves open whether there needs to be a distortion or mutilation as well as prejudice. See chapter eight on the interpretation of 'otherwise' in this subsection.

[22] See J Griffiths, 'Dematerialization, Pragmatism and the European Copyright Revolution' (2013) 33(4) *Oxford Journal of Legal Studies* 767.

Another way of looking at the norm against interference is that it serves to protect a creator's dignity *as an author*, and means their work ought not to be interfered with because to do so may interfere with the name as a marker of authenticity. This is very similar to the argument that the relevance of moral rights lies in granting accurate information about the provenance of works that is useful to creators and the general public alike.[23] The norm against interference might, in its focus on the preservation of the name and its identification of a writer within the subculture's hierarchy, be viewed as indivisible from the norm against biting. At heart then this graffiti rule might be conceptualised as a norm to protect the personality of the creator, and to confirm the authenticity of their works.

To return briefly to attribution and the use of pseudonyms, the correct identification of the author is important to determine the provenance of creative output. The link between moral rights, trade marks and their corresponding relevance to the protection of reputation are perhaps better conceptualised, with respect to graffiti writers at least, as concerns over authenticity. There is a certain similarity between the writer and the way in which the relationship between all of a writer's works is similar to the relationship between the products of a brand: 'the relations between products are the site of intense affective mediation'.[24] The difference perhaps for graffiti writers is in the desire to protect the existence of a work in a *physical* site as well as its immaterial manifestation within the intellectual domain of the 'bounded commons'. The norm against the copying of another writer's name is concerned with the continued visibility, in a certain location, of an existing identification of a creator and the authentication of their creativity.

Sanctions and Subcultural Politics

When looking at a piece or throw-up on a wall that has been tagged or lined, or where a piece has gone over a throw-up, the lay viewer, without a working knowledge of the subculture, will not be able to tell whether it constitutes an example of permissible or impermissible going over. Is the piece over a throw-up an example of the hierarchy of style in action or is it impermissible because the throw-up was by a highly respected writer? For example, is a tag over a piece an indication that the writer of the tag is new to the city, is it punishment for biting, or do the creators of the tag and piece simply dislike each other? This part concentrates on the two latter questions, examining, first, going over as a sanction for the breaking of the graffiti rules and, specifically, as a sanction for biting. The part then considers going over as an indication of beef between two writers, illustrating the point via a discussion of the well-known Banksy/Robbo war.

23 See H Hansmann and M Santilli, 'Authors' and Artists' Moral Rights: A Comparative Legal and Economic Analysis' (1997) 26(1) *The Journal of Legal Studies* 95.

24 Lury (n 13) 323.

Going Over and Other Sanctions

Before continuing, however, it is important to introduce the three main (potential) consequences which might result from biting (or indeed the infringement of any of the graffiti rules), or as a consequence of graffiti 'politics' more broadly. These are: dialogue between (and gossip amongst) writers, violence and going over. As one participant put it: 'It could be violence or it could be dialogue' (Anon4) and going over, too, might be considered a form of violence against the writer. Similarly, going over might be considered as another way of talking. A neat overview of these sanctions was provided by one participant:

> Or I'm going to talk to that person and tell them what I think and maybe you have a dialogue about it but it could go either way. It could be pure street justice or it could … you could talk about it and figure out the differences. … Or you can have that communication by writing on each of his stuff. (Anon4)

Where the particular situation concerns a crew this means that all crew members might, as guardians of each other's reputations, sanction other writers for an affront against an individual crew member.[25] A sanction likely to be employed by an individual writer or crew is gossip—inflicting reputational damage—but, equally, a writer may decide to confront the alleged infringer and seek to resolve their differences through dialogue. It is *talking* to which we now turn.

Some participants (though not all of them) recounted talking to other writers as a way of resolving disputes. Regarding copying another writer's name, for example, one writer explained that usually you would want to speak to someone because they might be a toy[26] and not know the rules or not know that the name they are putting up is actually someone else's tag. A writer gave the example of a toy writing a more established writer's 'common word' tag:

> A lot of the time it's them being a toy and they don't know. They've just started and they've picked a common word, it's a cool word, I'll pick that. If they are just a toy you go and talk to them and tell them nicely. (Anon 27)

Biting was described as being 'frowned upon' by another writer too who prefaced his comment by noting that if he had given permission or the copy had been made by a 'good friend' it would be fine but if:

> [It's] someone you don't know and they did it that's really messed up. … It shows that you're not even, you're not even attempting to create your own style, you're just flat out living off someone else, you know, you're not even putting any effort in. That's just

[25] eg M Halsey and A Young, '"Our Desires are Ungovernable": Writing Graffiti in Urban Space' (2006) 10(3) *Theoretical Criminology* 275, 291.

[26] eg during fieldwork I saw a tag on the wall that had been gone over with the word 'toy'. A new tag was placed next to it.

> laziness. It's stupid. Yeah, I'm sure it's been done a lot of times but it's definitely frowned upon, it's not cool. (Anon4)

The reasons for the writer's disapproval mirror the concerns identified in chapter seven regarding biting. In short, 'you get no respect for it' (Anon14). There is no respect afforded because rather than developing an individual style advantage is taken of the labour of another writer, a practice which in turn harms the development of graffiti culture as a whole. This type of situation may then lead to gossip about the offending writer.

While there was a clear sense that dialogue or gossip played an important part in the subculture, both as a way of learning about what was going on and who was 'up' but also, indirectly, as a means of shaming wrong-doers, there was some disparity amongst participants as to the extent to which they considered that violence also played part. It seemed, however, that the writers who seemed to be more deeply involved in the subculture, were more likely to mention violence as a (potential) aspect of writing. As one writer put it:

> If your attitude is 'I don't like the rules about not going over people, I'm going to go over a lot of people' then you've got to have not just the strength of mind but actual strength to probably get in a lot of altercations. (Anon4)

Similarly, another participant, in response to a question about how a writer would know what the rules are, said: 'Because if you went over something or tagged on it you would have the shit kicked out of you' (Anon14). Another writer echoed him saying: 'You could get beat up' (Anon13). Even so, overall there were relatively few examples given of writers resorting to violence in response to biting or the breach of another graffiti rule; violence was discussed in the abstract, rather than in relation to real-life happenings.

Regarding the example of a toy writer above and the importance of engaging in dialogue, the writer continued saying that after talking with a writer:

> Anon27 They get it straightaway. Sometimes you know they might be a toy but they might be big or they might think they're strong, you know, whatever and they say 'no, you stop writing that' and then, yeah.
>
> M So what happens then? You start crossing them out?
>
> Anon27 You beat them up.
>
> M Does it work?
>
> Anon27 Yeah.

As the above extract suggests, violence, or rather the threat of violence must also be considered alongside as a relevant consequence albeit a secondary one.

Most importantly, notwithstanding the above discussion of dialogue and violence, the participants concentrated on going over as the appropriate response to a breach of the graffiti rules, primarily in terms of where and against whom it was appropriate to interfere with another writer's work. An example of such a situation would be where one writer has copied another. For two writers, explaining why it is 'wrong' to copy and the consequences for it rested on the personal nature of their style and tag. A writer could feel confident that copying had occurred because it would be 'obvious' since each writer's style is unique (Anon3), while remaining within graffiti's stylistic constraints. The extract below returns to the fieldwork data considered in chapter seven regarding copying and identity:

Anon13	It's your personal identity… so you don't do it.
Anon14	You get no respect for it.
Anon13	And if I see any I'd go over it now … I'd still go over it.
Anon14	I would as well.
Anon13	Even to this day. It's just a rule [don't bite]. It's rules.

As the above extract suggests, and as a number of other participants suggested in discussing going over alongside dialogue for instance, one of the concerns with biting is that one writer is attempting to damage the personality (reputation) of another.

At the core of the kind of personal animosity that may give rise to going over may be a breach of a graffiti rule. Few participants mentioned going over as being a consequence for biting specifically but instead concentrated on the broader issue of going over as a result of personal animosity or dislike. It could be that the writer does not like another's 'strand of ethics' or, where the writer is a purist, that the other writer is a 'boring public muralist' only doing legal work (Anon4). In such a situation, a breach of the norm against interference—such as going over a long-standing piece by a famous writer—may result in going over but then evolve into a much bigger dispute (discussed below).

In the context of the regulation of creativity within the graffiti-specific 'bounded commons' which collapses the distinction between the physical and intellectual commons it makes sense that 'street justice' (Anon4) for breaking the norms would take place in the physical commons in the form of violence against the creator or their work. Indeed, it demonstrates that the regulation of creativity is simultaneously the regulation of space: at the very least the consequences of breaking the graffiti rules are inscribed on the city's walls. The penalty is material and highly public which is perhaps unsurprising given the role of gossip as an alternative consequence that is based on shaming. Since their subcultural norms exist apart from society's official (legal) rules—and the normatively thinner conception of creativity on which they are based—graffiti writers, through their own system of rules and sanctions create their own commons in order to fill the gap left by their forbearance of copyright protection but also to protect the normatively richer conception of graffiti creativity and culture.

Going Over and Beef

Going over another writer is 'starting trouble' because it's a way of saying 'I'm better than you' (Anon19). As shown above, an exception to the norm against interference is replacing a work with something stylistically superior, for instance. However, as might be expected, there will, even in a community with a common sense of its own culture, be disagreement as to what exactly 'better' means. This can escalate into a war or, the closely related form of competition, the battle in which writers destroy the offending writer's work and seek to make their own as visible as possible.[27]

An example of going over as both a source and aspect of beef was the apparent dispute between Banksy and Robbo. The war was covered in the Channel 4 documentary *Graffiti Wars*[28] and widely commented on in graffiti and street art media.[29] Robbo had placed a colourful piece bearing his name ('Robbo Inc.') on a part of wall on the Regent's Canal in 1985. Although the piece had been dogged with numerous smaller tags in the meantime, it had not been gone over completely. In 2011 Banksy allegedly went over almost the entire piece by painting the figure of a man papering it over. Robbo went back to paint 'King Robbo' so it seemed that the Banksy character was painting the phrase. The war is relevant in particular because of the discussion it generated; a discussion that demonstrated the continued relevance of respect and hierarchy in the graffiti subculture (and, especially respect towards graffiti writers such as Robbo who were active from the early days of the London graffiti scene). Indirectly, the war demonstrated the continued relevance of the graffiti rules and especially of the rule against going over older, better works. As one participant put it:

> And the fact that he went over Robbo was like very very important. Pioneering in the London scene and when Banksy incorporated Robbo's artwork even if it was ruined, interference with his artwork was seen as very very disrespectful to someone who was there before him and kind of helped to create the scene that he's now living off in a big way. There's all kinds of ... it's offensive to graffiti artists on a lot of levels. (Anon4)

The view of participants was generally negative towards Banksy for going over the piece though some noted that both Banksy and Robbo gained publicity from the events which followed. One participant also argued that while it may have been alright for Banksy to go over the work, he should have asked for permission to do so (Anon9).

Strictly speaking, this was not solely a graffiti subculture war and an argument can be made that it was evidence of a broader animosity towards street artists on

[27] See in context of the broader account of going over as well as dissin' in J Ferrell, *Crimes of Style: Urban Graffiti and the Politics of Criminality* (Boston, Northeastern University Press, 1996) 87–92.

[28] Channel 4, *Graffiti Wars*, aired 14 August 2011.

[29] eg M Battersby, 'The gloves are off: Graffiti legend King Robbo has resurfaced to settle a score with Banksy' *The Independent*, Thursday 21 April 2011.

the part of graffiti writers,[30] but in fact since Banksy was formerly a graffiti writer, his disregard for the rule against going over caused serious consternation. It led to 'Team Robbo' tagging and altering a large number of Banksy's works, especially along Regent's Canal (since Robbo's longstanding piece had also been placed on Regent's Canal).[31] The war escalated to Robbo and his supporters changing other Banksy works around London by, for instance, adding slogans insulting Banksy or placing Robbo's tag on Banksy's works. A reaction that captures the extreme of condemnation was as follows:

> I hated him [Banksy] and then thought I'd give him a chance but then when he went over that Robbo piece … Ok, he's made his money, I don't blame him, I'd do the same. But to try and claim some respectability back, he's purposely gone over a piece of history and I think that's fucking bang out of order. (Anon14)

There was some debate over whether Robbo's piece had been dogged and was faded to such an extent that going over was justified but Robbo's status as a king within the subculture made this argument more difficult to sustain. A more moderate response to the war also emphasised the importance of history in terms of going over:

> [Y]ou don't know the history. A little bit like with Robbo and Banksy on the canal, that was 25 years yet [the piece] had been gone over. But he shouldn't have gone over it, it was a bit of art that was there 25 years ago … (Anon27)

This particular example was only used by a few participants, but the extent of internet discussion[32] about it makes it a good study of going over. The example shows what it means for going over to be both deeply *personal* (because it is directed at the work of an individual writer whose work is defaced or destroyed) and highly *public* (because the interference is visible to other writers and the public at large). It is very evidently the flip-side of the subcultural preoccupation with visibility as a means for building a reputation within the subculture. It also suggests again that a defining feature of regulating creativity with the subculture's 'bounded commons' is its spatialised operation: going over hurts because it interferes with the work but—in offering a material record of a sanction—also publicly shames the writer alleged to have breached a graffiti norm.

[30] Participants differed on this point but there was consensus that street artists did not necessarily know the graffiti rules and thus seemed to suggest that they were outside of their 'jurisdiction'. Graffiti writers who were highly engaged in the subculture were more likely to think it was fine to go over street artists. One of the reasons provided was the lack of effort by 'lost art students' (Anon29) who create paste-ups (wheatpaste posters) that can be put up in a couple of seconds, showing no style and the action itself being of no personal cost to the street artist in terms of potential danger.

[31] See J Fuertes-Knight, 'My Graffiti War with Banksy by King Robbo' *Sabotage Times*, 1 August 2014 www.sabotagetimes.com/life/king-robbo-archive-interview-my-graffiti-war-with-banksy.

[32] eg commentator quoted in Dr Funky, 'Anonymous Says "Hating Banksy"' *Street Art Is Dead* www.streetartdead.blogspot.co.uk (web page no longer available).

Copyright *Beyond* Copyright—Damage and Damages

Chapter one indicated, with respect to graffiti writers' motivations, the aim is to 'get up'. The graffiti rules discussed in chapters five and seven with respect to placement and originality in particular have the effect of protecting a writer's reputation as they 'get up'. That is, other writers may lose respect for a writer who tags 'personal' property or who bites another writer's tag. The latter is especially important; it suggests a blurring between reproduction rights and moral rights in the sense that the problem with copying is the appropriation of the copied writer's personality. Yet the relationship between graffiti creativity and identification with the writer is made explicit for instance when writers say that *an individual* is 'up'. They do not say that their tag is up, though literally that would seem to be more correct. This apparently minor linguistic emphasis points to a strong identification between the writer and their creative output and may perhaps explain why the sanction for a breach of the graffiti rules is either damage to the work or damage to the writer. Punishing the person (bodily violence) or punishing the artwork (as the embodiment of the person by going over it) effectively amount to variations on a single theme.[33]

The unavailability of a useful analogue within copyright law to the sanctions for going over and for breaking other graffiti rules suggests again the difficulty—an insurmountable obstacle perhaps—that copyright law and its potential reform is faced with in providing meaningful remedies for the infringement of the moral rights of subcultural creators.[34] Graffiti writers want protection for their creativity. As the next chapter will show, this includes copyright protection and the remuneration for exploitation that it potentially provides. Fundamentally, however, graffiti writers create and regulate their creativity within a 'bounded commons' because copyright law does not meet their needs as creators—this goes as much for the remedies available as it does for the rules which regulate creativity.

Conclusion

This chapter has considered going over as both a rule preventing the destruction of other writers' works and as a sanction. The evident concern with

[33] This argument has some affinity with the notions of punishment fitting the crime on the body with the difference here that the graffiti work against which the punishment is focused on the work as the extension of the writer's body. See generally M Foucault, *Discipline and Punish: The Birth of the Prison*, A Sheridan (trans) (Midddlesex, Penguin Books, 1982).

[34] Thank you to Andreas Phillippopoulous-Mihalopoulous for making this point on the limitations of copyright.

reputation provides a parallel to the moral right of integrity while moving beyond it to consider the integrity not only of a certain creator but of the scene itself. It shows that reputation and status play a major role in determining appropriate and inappropriate changes being made to other writers' works but also that the best way for graffiti writers to protect themselves is via rules that are attentive to the materiality of the work and the space in which it is found in a way that copyright law plainly cannot be (or at least does not try to be). The chapter also considered going over as sanction for breaking the graffiti rules, alongside sanctions for biting including shaming and violence. As with the empirical findings in chapters five and seven, notions of hierarchy, respect, appropriate placement and territory were recurring themes. Above all, perhaps, the concern with going over—both as one of norms within the alternative normative framework of the subculture and as a sanction—shows the depth and seriousness with which creativity in the subculture is treated.

The next chapter ventures outside of the confines of the graffiti subculture to consider what non-writers may and may not do with the graffiti creativity that is visible when wandering down the street, staring out of a train window or, occasionally and unexpectedly (and only if we are very lucky) seeing a train with a piece on its side pull in as we are standing on the platform.

Panel V

Interactions

10

Graffiti Rules and Copyright Law

> [I]f you don't want people to see it then I don't think you should put it places that people are going to see it. (Anon6)

Introduction

The visibility of graffiti in public spaces means that questions about how graffiti creativity is regulated cannot be confined to the subculture alone. To date there have been no reported UK cases dealing with the use of graffiti creativity without permission, though with the growing commercialisation of graffiti writing and street art it does not seem unthinkable that such a case will reach the UK courts as it has in the US.[1] Thus where preceding chapters examined the regulation of creativity within the graffiti subculture and were then contrasted with the alternative normative framework revealed by the fieldwork data, this chapter looks outwards from the subculture. It considers the regulation of the uses of graffiti creativity by non-writers. While chapters four, six and eight applied copyright law to graffiti creativity as it occurs within the subculture, those discussions pointed to potential infringements of moral and economic rights that may occur where non-writers use or exploit graffiti creativity. Rather than revisiting these arguments this chapter returns to certain themes developed in chapter two to consider the *space* of graffiti creativity, specifically the impact of its public placement on the rules regulating its use both within the graffiti subculture's alternative normative framework and within copyright law.

The chapter begins by discussing the interface between copyright and real property law and then examines the operation of section 62 of the Copyright, Designs

[1] On copyright infringement, see *Williams et al v Roberto Cavalli SpA et al* CV 14-06659-AB, 2015 US Dist LEXIS 34722 Central District Court of California, 12 February 2015. On 'recognized stature' moral rights protection, see *Cohen v G & M Realty* No 13-CV-5612 (FB)(JMA) Eastern District of New York, 20 November 2013. See also another copyright infringement complaint, *Tierney v Moschino* CV 2:15-cv-05900 (filed 5 August 2015 in the Central District Court of California, Western Division) and *Daniel Reece v Marc Ecko Unltd et al* 10 Civ. 02901 (SDNY) 2011 US Dist Lexis 102199. Similarly, in rejecting an application for summary judgment in *Michael Tracy v Skate Key, Inc.* 697 F Supp 748; 1988 US Dist LEXIS 11617, the court considered the reproduction of a graffiti piece as a logo on merchandise.

and Patents Act 1988 (CDPA) which provides an exception to copyright infringement for certain works located in public places by allowing two-dimensional reproductions of three-dimensional works. The chapter then considers expectations within the graffiti subculture about the reproduction and dissemination of (publicly placed) graffiti writing. Considering the interaction between the graffiti rules and copyright law in this way provides an opportunity to reflect upon the lessons that might be drawn for copyright law—that is, how to make copyright, especially the copyright exceptions, more sensitive both to the space in which creativity occurs and the needs of creators.

Copyright and Public Placement

This part considers the relevance of public placement in copyright law. Rather than examining all of the relevant aspects—the most obvious point would be to discuss the meaning of a place open to the public in relation to the infringement of the right to play or perform a work in public[2]—it focuses instead on the interface between real property law and copyright, the control of the material object with respect to exhibition, and the operation of section 62 of the CDPA. This part first considers the issues relating to the exercise of control over the material support of an artistic work by addressing, in particular, the implications of cutting graffiti writing from land (ie a building wall) and seeking to sell the chattel (ie the piece of a wall that embodies the artistic work).

Land, Chattels and Copyright

If it is accepted that graffiti writers own the copyright in their works, the placement of the works on a wall nevertheless implicates the rights of owners of real property of which a wall is a part. As discussed in chapter four, the subsistence of copyright is not dependent on the ownership of the material support[3] of the work such as a chattel (eg a canvas) and this point may be usefully extended to the ownership of walls or other parts of 'land'.[4] Although the point has not been raised in a UK court with respect to graffiti writing specifically, it was raised in *Creative Foundation v Dreamland*[5] in relation to a stencil. The case concerned the consequences for the tenant of the relevant property who had cut out the stencil from the wall in order to sell it. The author of the stencil was unknown but it had

[2] CDPA, s 19(1) but note that this applies to literary, musical and dramatic works only.

[3] K Garnett, G Davies and G Harbottle, *Copinger and Skone James on Copyright*, vol 1, 16th edn (London, Thomson Reuters, 2011) [5-68].

[4] Law of Property Act 1925, s 205(I)(x) defines land to include 'buildings or parts of buildings'.

[5] *Creative Foundation v Dreamland* [2015] EWHC 2556 (Ch).

been attributed to Banksy making it potentially highly valuable; indeed, the court noted its 'aesthetic and economic'[6] significance. This may usefully be extended to graffiti writers—the mere fact of using another's material support, such as a building wall, does not make the real property owner the first owner of copyright in the work.[7] There was no suggestion in *Creative Foundation* that the chattel belonged to the author.

The claimant, as an assignee of the property owner (landlord) in the title of artwork as well as the legal action, sought the delivery up of the work in order to display the work for the benefit of the public in Folkestone.[8] The court, in a summary judgment, agreed that the landlord had the better claim and made the order sought. The case was not decided on the basis of the public benefit that the delivery up of the work might bring; the judgment turned on the interpretation of a term in the lease requiring the tenant to keep the property in 'substantial repair and condition'.[9] Yet although *Creative Foundation* is not a copyright law case—as Arnold J observes, 'I am not concerned with the copyright in the artistic work, which *prima facie* belongs to Banksy' (emphasis in original)[10]—it is interesting precisely for showing that when it comes to the public placement of works copyright claims may not be the most advantageous means of safeguarding artistic works.[11]

Furthermore, no arguments were made by the parties regarding the moral right of integrity.[12] This is interesting for two reasons, both of which hinge on the methods (on which the parties agreed) by which the repair obligation could have been met: by painting over the mural, by chemical cleaning or abrasive cleaning, or by cutting it from, and then repairing, the wall.[13] So, Creative Foundation might have argued that Dreamland was effectively prevented from complying with the obligation to repair because to do so would potentially constitute a 'derogatory treatment' (assuming the destruction could constitute a 'treatment' under section 80 CDPA).[14] This brings into play a second issue. Dreamland might plausibly have sought to argue in response that it chose the only method of complying with the repair obligation that *also* ensured that the artwork was preserved from

[6] ibid [43].

[7] Historically, commissioned sculptures pass copyright to the commissioner when certain formalities are met *unless* the sculpture is made to a model where the creator's name and the date has been placed on the model and subsequent copies: *Blaine's Laws of Artistic Copyright* (Albernale Street, John Murray, 1853) in L Bently and M Kretschmer (eds), *Primary Sources on Copyright (1450–1900)* www.copyrighthistory.org, 45. Thanks to Maurizio Borghi for the citation.

[8] *Creative Foundation* (n 5) [1], [4].

[9] ibid [15].

[10] ibid [2].

[11] M Iljadica, 'Street Art Belongs to the Freeholder' (2016) 11 *Journal of Intellectual Property Law and Practice* 2.

[12] Arnold J suggests this would have been an argument that the claimant might have made: *Creative Foundation* (n 5) [24].

[13] ibid [28].

[14] See chapter eight.

the type of treatment—tagging the stencil—that would constitute an alteration or distortion.[15] Yet this in turn assumes that removal of street art, which might be plausibly described as site-specific, from its original location is not in itself a derogatory treatment of the artistic work.

Considering the way in which the real and intellectual property rules intersect with respect to street art is useful for revealing the different interests—the author, the public, the owner of the freehold, the owner of the leasehold—intersecting in the physical commons which, as chapter two indicated, is discussed here as an amalgam of both public and privately owned property that is physically (eg a street) or visually (eg a billboard or trackside) accessible. The ramifications of this, in particular how public interests might be best taken into account, are discussed in the final part of this chapter but before that it is worth considering what recourse, if any, a graffiti writer might have to object to the removal of their work from a wall and its subsequent sale. *Creative Foundation* raised the prospect of an integrity right claim. Beyond moral rights, the distribution right and exhaustion of rights as well as the resale right are potentially relevant.

Considering distribution and the exhaustion of copyright brings up again the question of the extent to which copyright law treats artistic works as im/material[16] especially since the EU harmonisation of copyright has accelerated the dematerialisation of the work into a 'recorded form and … immaterial essence'.[17] This might be seen, albeit indirectly, in the *Art & Allposters*[18] judgment of the Court of Justice of the European Union (CJEU) which, while concerning the exhaustion of rights, provides some insight into the conception of the work at play in EU copyright law.[19] The CJEU subsequently noted with respect to reproduction:

> [A] replacement of the medium, as was carried out in the case in the main proceedings, results in the creation of a new object incorporating the image of the protected work, whereas the poster itself ceases to exist. Such an alteration of the copy of the protected work, which provides a result closer to the original, is actually sufficient to constitute a new reproduction of that work[20]

Of course, the ink—at the instant between being removed from the medium of the poster and placed on the new medium of the canvas—is the very material of the expression but there is no work until it adheres to a surface. That new surface

[15] The different aspects of the destruction of graffiti and the engagement of moral rights are beyond the scope of this chapter but see M Iljadica, 'Graffiti and the Moral Right of Integrity' (2015) 3 *Intellectual Property Quarterly* 266.

[16] See chapter four.

[17] J Griffiths, 'Dematerialization, Pragmatism and the European Copyright Revolution' (2013) 33(4) *Oxford Journal of Legal Studies* 67, 770.

[18] Case C-419/13 *Art & Allposters International BV v Stichting Pictoright* [2015] ECDR 8.

[19] Advocate General Cruz Villalòn's Opinion draws attention to Allposters' argument that it is necessary to differentiate between the 'corpus mechanicum' (the *material* work) and the 'corpus mysticum': *Art & Allposters International BV v Stichting Pictoright* [2015] ECDR 7, Opinion of AG Cruz Villalòn [37].

[20] *Allposters* (n 18) [43].

is therefore a new embodiment. It is thus an infringement of the copyright in the artistic work insofar as the distribution right relates specifically to the ability to control the initial object in which the artistic work had been incorporated.[21] Of course, the exhaustion issue will be unlikely to come up in the context of graffiti writing except where, for instance, a poster depicting graffiti writing is sold and a similar ink-removal technique is used.

Hypothesising about a different situation in which graffiti was either cut from a wall and that chattel was sold or where, by some means for lifting spray paint from a wall a poster or canvas was then sold, the graffiti writer may be able to claim an infringement of the distribution right. Section 18(1) CDPA refers to the issuing of copies of a work (which also means the 'issue of the original')[22] and Article 4(2) Infosoc Directive refers to 'the original or copies of the work'. Arguably, the freeholder in the *Creative Foundation* type of scenario has infringed the distribution right of the author by placing the chattel embodying the work on the market without the author's consent *unless* the author's placement of the work on the public wall in itself constitutes the issuing of the work to the public. On the face of it this does not seem to be correct; certainly the graffiti writer is not selling or in any sense offering the work for sale but merely exhibiting it. This position is consistent with *Peek & Cloppenburg SA v Casina SpA*[23] in which the CJEU said that a display of a work did not engage the distribution right. (The graffiti writer as author would retain, in any event, the other relevant economic rights such as the reproduction right.)

A related argument might be raised by the owners of a building in the above situation and that is that upon placing a work on a wall there was an implied assignment of the copyright in the work to the real property owner. If that was the case then the distribution of the original work, its copies and the other dealings with the work such as reproduction might also be unproblematic. However, the case law on this point tends to address situations where works are commissioned[24] and a contract exists between the author and commissioner of an artistic work. It is instructive also to note the German approach to this in *Re Pictures on the Berlin Wall*:[25]

[21] *Allposters* echoes the dissent in the Canadian case of *Galerie d'Art du Petit Champlain v Théberge* [2002] 2 RCS. The majority judgment provides the contrary view in determining that a copy is not made when ink is transferred in this way. Note, however, Mr Theberge's comments when giving evidence: 'it is once again a dilution of my work; it is an abusive commercialization of my work, without authorization; it is a manipulation of the work because, in many cases, my signature does not appear on the reproduction; it is an anonymization' (351). The better argument in cases where the material support has been substituted is that such an action is a breach of the moral right of integrity (assuming such a right exists within the relevant jurisdiction).

[22] CDPA, s 18(4). The concept of exhaustion does not privilege sale but rather refers to a change in ownership, and even potentially an offer to sell: L Bently and B Sherman, *Intellectual Property Law*, 4th edn (Oxford, Oxford University Press, 2014) 151.

[23] Case C-456/06 *Peek & Cloppenburg SA v Casina SpA* [2009] ECDR 9.

[24] As in *R Griggs Group Limited v Evans* [2003] EWHC 2914 (Ch). Normally an assignment must be made in writing: CDPA, s 90(3).

[25] *Re Pictures on the Berlin Wall* (Case I ZR 68/93) [1997] ECC 553.

> [A] further distribution of an original work is permissible if it is put on the market by passing of title, with the consent of the person entitled to distribute the work … The putting of the Wall pictures on exhibition to the public, contrary to the appeal court's view, does not constitute a passing of title in this sense.[26]

Finally, it is useful to consider, although it is not clear how this might work in practical terms, that the resale of a chattel bearing graffiti writing that had been removed from a wall and sold at auction could bring *droit de suite* into play as well. So, if the leaseholder in *Creative Foundation* above had been successful in auctioning off the work and the work was then sold again, and perhaps increased in value, the author could rightfully expect a proportion of the 'resale royalty'.[27]

Public Exhibition

The discussion of distribution above points pretty clearly to a gap in the protection of artistic works in the UK: the distribution right does not seem to cover exhibition and yet there is no exhibition right that mirrors the public performance right. While it is an infringement to perform works in public, this applies to literary, dramatic and musical works only;[28] artistic works are not protected in an equivalent way. Indeed, making works available for 'the purpose of exhibition in public' is specifically excluded from the ambit of the rental and lending rights.[29] By contrast, Germany recognises such a right as does the US;[30] in France, the right to exhibit a work is captured by 'représentation' (roughly, performance).[31] While it is an infringement to communicate artistic works, amongst other categories of work, to the public there is no economic or moral right to control the public exhibition of a work in the UK.

Unless a piece or throw-up for example is considered a literary work—but as chapter four indicated, the artistic works category is the better fit—the author of a piece of graffiti writing could take advantage of protections relating to the public dissemination of the work both in relation to public showing of the material works and its reproduction and dissemination on the internet for instance. What this means is that, in a situation where graffiti is cut from a building and exhibited elsewhere there would be no breach of the author's economic rights with respect to the exhibition and, in any event such a right might be said to have been exhausted at the point at which the author publicly displayed the work on

[26] ibid [15]. The Bundesgerichtshof did note, however, that upon the first display of the work, the exhibition—but not the distribution—right could be exhausted: [18].

[27] Artists' Resale Right Regulations 2006 (SI 2006/346).

[28] CDPA, s 19(1). 'Performance' includes 'visual or acoustic presentation': CDPA, s 19(2)(b).

[29] CDPA, s 18A(3)(b).

[30] P Goldstein and B Hugenholtz, *International Copyright: Principles, Law, and Practice*, 3rd edn (Oxford, Oxford University Press, 2013) 329.

[31] Intellectual Property Code, L 122-2. See generally Nomos, 'France: Copyright—Towards the Consecration of an Exhibition Right' (2003) 14 *Entertainment Law Review* 6, N46.

the street. In practice, graffiti writers are de facto exhibiting their work publicly by placing it on a wall—there is no third party forcing the exhibition of their work. This is not the case when their work is cut from a wall. The only possible recourse for the author in such a situation would be to make the, admittedly difficult, argument that the exhibition of the chattel was a moral rights infringement (ie a derogatory treatment).[32]

The Section 62 Exception

The CDPA contains an exception in section 62[33] to copyright infringement where certain artistic works are reproduced as graphic works. It is limited to a small range of works: namely buildings, sculptures, models for buildings, and works of artistic craftsmanship 'permanently situated in a public place or in premises open to the public'. As such it is unusual in addressing directly the relevance of public placement to the regulation of creativity by copyright law. Pursuant to section 62(2), to avail oneself of the defence these works may be reproduced only as a graphic work, film, photograph or broadcast. The section itself was not discussed in Parliament but more general observations were made in the House of Lords debate on the CDPA, for instance that 'a balance has to be struck between the creators of intellectual property and the public who use that property'.[34] Thus, on the face of it, a person may photograph a street scene that includes a public sculpture but not a graphic work such as drawing on an advertising billboard, graffiti writing or street art. It seems then that, since section 62 does not offer a defence for the reproduction of graphic works located in a public place (assuming that such works could be said to be permanently situated, which is unclear) this exception does not apply to graffiti writing. Therefore, graffiti writers have *more* protection than do authors of commissioned public sculptures.

There appears to be an underlying assumption in section 62 that art works belong in certain spaces and not others, that is, that graphic works will be found in art galleries and not on streets. Section 62 implicitly reflects an expectation that the kinds of artistic works to be found in public space and appears to reject a conceptualisation of graffiti as 'public art'.[35] The scope of the section suggests that Parliament only contemplated traditional works of public art of a kind—such as commissioned sculptures for public squares—that are expected to be found in

[32] See also, regarding the lack of a 'performing' right for artistic works and the moral right of attribution, Bently and Sherman (n 22) 155, note 104.

[33] An equivalent defence may be found in the potential, though not mandated, list of exceptions in the Infosoc Directive, Art 5(3)(h). Note also of relevance to graffiti writing, the incidental inclusion exception in CDPA, s 31 which would presumably cover the 'background' inclusion of graffiti writing. See K Garnett, 'Incidental Inclusion under s. 31' (2003) 25(12) *European Intellectual Property Review* 579.

[34] Viscount Eccles, Hansard, HL Deb, vol 489 col 1492 (12 November 1987).

[35] I am grateful to Fiona Macmillan for this point.

public spaces notwithstanding that graffiti writing had already been transplanted to the UK by the time the CDPA came into effect. The section can be understood as part of the law's difficulties more broadly with artistic works that take non-traditional forms or in the case of graffiti writing are legally 'out of place'.[36]

It may, at first, seem that where there is graffiti on a building that the graffiti writing (ie the artistic work) comes within the scope of the exception on the basis that a building is defined to include 'part of a building or fixed structure'.[37] If someone takes a photo of the building wall that happens to be adorned with a painting then taking the photograph would, following this line of argument, not be an infringement by reproduction. However the section 4(1) definition of artistic works distinguishes between graphic works and works of architecture, suggesting that a graphic work ought to be distinguished from a 'part' of a building. It would be stretching the definition of a 'part' of building to include a painting on its external wall. When a section of a building is photographed, copyright (if it subsists) will not be infringed in the wall (insofar as the wall or section of the building forms a protectable 'part of a building') but will nonetheless be infringing the reproduction right of the author of the artistic work fixed to that wall. As Kingsbury notes, graphic works could 'at best be covered by implication'[38] under such an exception but that it is unlikely. Indeed it seems an odd omission to list the types of works covered by section 62—sculptures, works of artistic craftsmanship, buildings—when simply referring to 'artistic works' would have been sufficient. The exclusion of graphic works would appear to be deliberate in circumscribing the operation of the exception.

One explanation—referring to section 73, the equivalent provision in the New Zealand Copyright Act 1994—for the exclusion of graphic works is that the person reproducing the work can only ever make a derivative (two dimensional) work not a competing (three dimensional) work.[39] Thus, one could take a photograph of a sculpture but not re-create it in three dimensions. The exception appears to have tourists in mind, yet as a New Zealand case on section 73, *Radford v Hallensteins Bros Ltd*[40] demonstrated, commercial reproductions are also acceptable:

> To the extent that s. 73 does speak it does so plainly. It sets out to allow members of the public, including players in the market, to copy in two-dimensions sculptures permanently in the public domain and even for profit; and it does so by setting aside any

[36] See T Cresswell, *In Place/out of Place: Geography, Ideology, and Transgression* (Minnesota, University of Minnesota Press, 1996) 31. The 'public' quality of graffiti is also being recognised via 'creative city' initiatives which is at odds with the criminalisation of graffiti: C McAuliffe, 'Moral Geographies of the Creative City' (2012) 34(2) *Journal of Urban Affairs* 189.

[37] CDPA, s 4(2).

[38] A Kingsbury, 'Copyright Law, Designs Law, and the Protection of Works on Public Display' (2007) 15 *Waikato Law Review* 78, 84. Noting that if a work has an underlying drawing, the exception is ineffective (83).

[39] ibid 82.

[40] *Radford v Hallensteins Bros Ltd* CIV 2006-404-004881 (unreported, Keane J, 22 February 2007). A sculptor sued a clothing chain that had printed images of a sculpture by the artist onto t-shirts.

copyright in the work that the author might otherwise enjoy. However s. 73 is interpreted, that clear policy is not for compromise.[41]

The High Court was critical of arguments that copyright was infringed in the underlying drawings for the sculpture.[42] Finding that copyright could be infringed in the underlying work would make the section ineffective because sculptures will usually 'fully realise'[43] an underlying work. The court also emphasised permanent placement as one of the factors that made it acceptable for members of the public to photograph the sculpture.[44] The notion of social benefit, perhaps even of cultural and economic development is thus addressed by looking closely at the *space* of a work (we might say, the physical commons) not merely the work itself.

Graffiti Writers' Rules for Non-writers

The sharing of graffiti creativity (and also street art) on the internet, in books and documentaries[45] is widespread. While such uses may be acceptable to graffiti writers, other uses—which the interview data suggest are usually unremunerated—such as reproducing works on clothing or selling canvases and/or posters, pose greater difficulties. This commodification problem presents, effectively, a question about regulating creativity at the border of the subculture's 'bounded commons' and the broader intellectual commons. The norms within the subculture are directed internally towards the regulation of creativity within the 'bounded commons' yet they shape expectations about how graffiti creativity ought to be regulated outside of it. Two key themes emerge from the data considered below: the appropriateness of private copying of publicly placed works, and the acceptability of non-commercial versus commercial copying and sharing of graffiti creativity by those outside of the graffiti subculture.

Approval (or Tolerance) of Sharing

Graffiti writers accept that their work will be reproduced and disseminated. Such interactions include taking photographs of the works and sharing these on social media, posting them on graffiti and/or street art blogs, placing them on canvases,

[41] ibid [35].
[42] ibid [36].
[43] ibid [37]. With respect to s 62, in tracing the origin of the section to the Copyright Act 1911 Burrell and Coleman show that the original incarnation of the provision referred not only to sculptures and buildings but also impliedly to the underlying drawings but this was omitted, perhaps overlooked, in the subsequent incarnation of the provision in the Copyright Act 1956, the precursor to the CDPA: R Burrell and A Coleman, *Copyright Exceptions: The Digital Impact* (Cambridge, Cambridge University Press, 2005) 233–34.
[44] *Radford* (n 40) [34]–[39].
[45] eg Channel 4, *Graffiti Wars*, aired 14 August 2011.

exhibiting photographs in art galleries or reproducing them in books. This section considers the interview data in which graffiti writers discussed the acceptable and expected—given the works are placed in public—uses of their work. The subsequent section discusses the limitations that are placed—or rather that graffiti writers wish to place—on the myriad interactions a non-writer might have with graffiti writing.

The main point to note here is that the expectations about use were based primarily on the *location* of graffiti works. It is the fact of public placement that determines the graffiti writers' general position whereby it is acceptable for people to take photographs of graffiti creativity. Yet graffiti writers do not assume that copyright law must apply to their creativity. Although the participants interviewed were aware that such legal rules exist, a question along the lines of 'do you think your work is/ought to be protected?' usually elicited silences and expressions of confusion. The participants did not consider that copyright law might apply to their work because it is in public, because 'you stole the space to make it' (Anon5). At the same time, and as the next section indicates, it was made clear that this did not mean that graffiti writers felt, in all circumstances, that they should be denied remuneration.

Participants articulated an awareness that when their work was in public it was not only their interests as creators that mattered. There was an awareness that the physical situation of a work must change how that work can be used. As a writer asked: 'if you do it in a public place how can you then comment when it's in the public?' (Anon27). Unlike section 62 CDPA, pursuant to which three dimensional but not two dimensional artistic works in public places may be photographed, for instance, the graffiti writers seem to adopt an extended version of the same reasoning. One participant placed the responsibility on writers to refrain from making the work public rather than expecting the public to refrain from copying the work when it was freely available:

> Once you put it out there, that's the whole … you don't want it to be public, you don't put it on something that's public … half the point of graffiti is for it to get seen and if you don't want people to see it then I don't think you should put it places that people are going to see it. (Anon6)

This in turn suggests that while the norms regulating graffiti creativity are internal to the subculture and act to legitimise graffiti writing within its 'bounded commons' and to develop graffiti culture specifically, there is an implicit recognition amongst writers that their creativity is exposed in such a way as to make some level of concern with non-writers' use of graffiti creativity inevitable.

What graffiti writers appear to grasp intuitively is that they create public art (if indeed graffiti writing may be defined as a type of public art, this position is contested)[46] which is different to other art. Public art is public because it demands

[46] eg graffiti writing or street art may be conceptualised as 'pure, unmediated expression and the most natural manifestation of public art' or as 'defacement, destruction, and an anathema to a "civil" society': R Schacter, 'An Ethnography of Iconoclash: An Investigation into the Production, Consumption and Destruction of Street-art in London' (2008) 13(1) *Journal of Material Culture* 35, 36.

attention beyond the merely personal. The significance of public art lies not in the form of the artistic object in question but rather the space in which it finds itself, and, by extension the nature of the public or publics contemplating the object.[47] This is understandable given the explanations for graffiti writing given by one of the participants quoted earlier in the book that graffiti writing offers an alternative to those who 'can just pay' (Anon21). This view—that graffiti is a form of public art that challenges the commercialisation of public space—remained unarticulated amongst the majority of participants but this is not to say that participants were insensitive to the impact graffiti has on the public.

A further reason was given by some participants for why copying and sharing was expected and even desirable: acknowledgment by the public. Copying means that 'someone appreciated it' (Anon3), even if individuals dislike it. Yet at least one writer expressed a desire for a greater quality of recognition by encouraging the public to appreciate the more complex pieces common in legal spots:

> Even when you're in an argument with the public you need to at least be able to say look we've got these sort of really good spots, there's great artwork, you know … [T]o sort of help give the movement some kind of long term gain you do need some areas of sort of established art like you've got the cans tunnel in Waterloo. (Anon23)

The public placement—and hence public accessibility—of graffiti writing is not viewed as a threat but a means by which graffiti creativity gains recognition. This would not be the position of all writers of course, but even writers who profess to write only for themselves and/or for others within the subculture are aware of the perception of graffiti writing amongst the broader public. Public access is in any case the by-product (or price) of seeking the development of creativity in the subculture itself. The writer quoted above continued by saying:

> So I think it's important to have these long running spots that build up a sort of history. If you're out of town, you know somebody, you can go and visit and sort of click into what's happening … (Anon23)

This is not to say that individuals within a subculture are unaware that their creations are potentially protected by copyright—certainly, some graffiti writers are aware that copyright law might apply to their works. Such concerns were usually expressed in relation to the commercialisation of their work (discussed below). Copyright law was not always mentioned as a means of enforcing these rights but it was indicated by the majority of participants (graffiti writers and street artists) that such an appropriation warranted a remedy in monetary form. However, what writers think of as 'copyright' is a right to acknowledgment of their moral and not simply economic ownership of creativity.[48] It needs to be reiterated, however, that

[47] See generally L Moss and E Norman, 'Space for the Individual: An Alternative Taxonomy of Public Space?' (2000) 1(3) *Public Art Journal* 32, 34.

[48] This echoes findings regarding fan fiction, that attribution is crucial whether or not the author is happy for their work to be released: R Tushnet, 'Payment in Credit: Copyright Law and Subcultural Creativity' (2007) 70 *Law & Contemporary Problems* 135, 165.

none of the above discussion negates the findings in chapter seven, namely that the copying of another writer's name or style is prohibited. Moreover, although it was not a point raised by participants themselves, it seems unlikely that public placement would give non-writers the right to claim the work as being their own. Rather, to reiterate, members of the general public sharing graffiti is acceptable because it further exposes a writer's tag.

Although it is understood that placing works in public space changes the logic of what might be done with them, this does not mean that any and all reproductions are acceptable. It is accepted that members of the public may decide to take photographs and share them on various websites because this is a non-commercial activity; it involves the mere dissemination of photographs of graffiti writing. This makes sense in light of writers' preoccupation with the documentation of graffiti writing. One writer echoes the idea that copying can be a positive in terms of making a writer more visible:

> [T]he currency is fame and if someone else is out there taking photos of your work 'cause they like it you go "wicked they like my work". They might publish it so more people will see it. (Anon4)

Thus, a graffiti and street art blog that is updated by a non-graffiti writer would be considered acceptable even if one writer expressed scepticism that an outsider could really capture the scene virtually:

> [The blogger] is just kind of reporting on stuff that's already happened, that people know about. Just go out in the street and see it. (Anon6)

Crucially, for at least one writer, the problem that arises with respect to reproductions on the internet is not the fact of the reproduction but the seeming attempt by the non-writer to speak for the subculture:

> [Y]ou have to have earned your wings and perhaps if the same blog was written by someone who had been part of the scene or used to publish zines or magazines or been a longstanding participant in the community then it would be taken more seriously and they might offer more insight because they know the artists and they have access to the artists. But to just all of a sudden turn up with this blog and kind of just spread all this information and contact all these people and … it's almost as if because it's on the street people feel that they own a part of it [the scene] or they own the right to talk about it and pass comment on it … (Anon5)

This objections must be viewed in light of the more general objections raised by some participants on the potentially corrosive impact of the communication of graffiti creativity on the operation of recognition within the subculture by producing 'cheap fame'.[49]

The above explanation of graffiti creativity affects its creator by imposing an interpretation on the work by an outsider—this is at odds with the practice of

[49] See chapter one.

graffiti within the community of writers. This critical response seems to be at odds with the views expressed by other writers about giving up 'rights' to work in public space. The difference might be explained, at least in terms of reproductions on the internet as between reproduction that occurs outside the subculture and reproductions that occur on its fringes where it appears, as in the above example, that someone is attempting to gain unearned access into it by publicising works on the internet rather than walking on the street and seeing walls as a graffiti writer might. For another writer, posting the photograph was merely an issue of appreciation:

> If someone took a photo of my painting and put it on the internet that means they like it so much to do that which is quite nice so why should I care? (Anon13)

Returning to the argument that there is implied permission to copy when the work is in public space another writer continued by saying:

> But if it's in public how can you moan at that? If it's there for everyone to see how can you moan that someone's taking if you don't want no one to see it ... (Anon14)

Following on from the above, the vulnerability of graffiti writing to buffing means that writers both accept the transient nature of graffiti and are inclined to document it.[50] This is significant because the copies of the graffiti work, including those placed on the internet by members of the public, come to be considered to be 'as good' as the original work. The materiality of artistic works is thus de-emphasised but without losing sight of the creative process that produced the original material work. A photograph of a wall that has been digitally manipulated to include a tag is useless without this antecedent process.

Participants were aware that taking photographs was crucial to preserving their work (though not all were concerned with this, some were concerned instead only with the pure act of creation) which ties in neatly with graffiti writers' sense of a practice developed by its shared cultural history. The expectation that graffiti writing on a wall or train surface will be transient is deeply ingrained. One participant referred to graffiti writing as 'totally temporary' (Anon29). Another stated: 'unless you get good photos you don't get anything from it' (Anon18). It is irrelevant whether they or someone else takes the photograph so long as it is preserved.

Therefore, the underlying justification for allowing such reproductions is that there is a link between physical public space and the virtual public space of the internet that makes their creation and dissemination acceptable. Although in the graffiti subculture it is the physical commons that is of fundamental importance to the creation and preservation of a fame hierarchy, when situating themselves in the broader culture graffiti writers (though not all graffiti writers) accept the

[50] The documentation will not necessarily be of one's own work. eg the fieldwork suggested that this applies to 'bombers' ('bombing' refers to extensive coverage of a space with graffiti writing, especially with tags) in particular though this contention did not come from the writers in question themselves. In these situations others will document the tags as numerous flickr streams encountered during the fieldwork indicate.

reproduction of the work and its sharing with others, as a given. This is perhaps the most interesting point. The arguments made are not that there is a licence, that is, the individual writer feels that he or she is giving the public permission to copy, but rather that the *space* of the creativity determines that the public may reproduce and share the work virtually. The graffiti work is both in intellectual *and* physical space and this change in perspective—beginning with the space rather than with the creator—presents an opportunity to set aside the notion of an implied licence or assignment of copyright and begin by asking what the space, and the broader development of culture, demands. In any event, any implied permission does not generally extend to commercialisation. As the discussion below indicates, the unease with the *commercial* exploitation of *one's own* creativity is of great concern for graffiti writers.

Disapproval of Commercial Copying

Notwithstanding the acceptance of the sharing of graffiti by members of the public, there was a keen awareness of how graffiti creativity should be used outside of the subculture beyond mere sharing. Participants did not state that *anything* might be done with their work despite comments such as '[you] give up all rights to have a say' (Anon27). Instead, writers *do* object to commercial exploitation despite the public nature of the work being copied. A clear distaste emerged in the field interviews for the commercial exploitation of graffiti creativity without credit or payment being given to the graffiti writer. For example:

> It's all the intellectual property that's been ripped off and sold on so yeah, I mean just because it's street it doesn't mean it shouldn't be illegal for someone to [sell copies]. And I'm sure you could fight it in court. … But it's also the fact that they know that a lot of people wouldn't put up a big fight with it so it's like taking candy from a baby. (Anon18)

In short, the prevailing view was that 'if somebody's making money off your work then that's wrong I think' (Anon14). The writer was speaking in the context of a 'company doing printed canvases'. It would be too hasty then to assume that graffiti writers are unaware of the potential economic rights associated with producing works even if not all of the same writers were against all forms of commercial exploitation of their work.

Writers are aware that even if those people making commercial reproductions wanted to ask permission they may not be able to do so and writers themselves will be reluctant to reveal their names in order to enforce their copyright. Yet this does not excuse the commercial exploitation of graffiti creativity. One writer, commenting on the publication of one of his pieces in a book, explained in conversation:

M	So it wouldn't bother you if someone went out, they took a photo and they put it in a book?
Anon4	No, it's happened loads of times.

M Ah ok.

M	Nobody asks you?
Anon4	No 'cause they generally don't know who you are.
M	Ah ok.
Anon4	The thing [that] does get kind of irritating is you know that there's people making a lot of money out of your culture and that's where it kind of doesn't match up.

This leaves writers with a certain difficulty because they are still forced to forbear existing copyright law protections even when they are suffering economic harm. As one participant said regarding a clothing company that had copied his work:

> [The company] has copied an idea of mine and made a t-shirt they sell in their shops, also places sell photographs of my streetwork printed onto canvas. There's nothing that can be done about that. (Anon26)

After being asked about what would happen if someone took a picture of his graffiti writing, put it on a canvas and started selling it in a gallery, a writer responded that 'if it did happen I'd go to the gallery and cross it all out' (Anon15).[51]

One writer offered a nuanced view of the appropriateness of commercial uses of graffiti that mirrored the reasons offered for distinguishing between appropriate and inappropriate placement on commercial premises[52] whereby a distinction was drawn between large corporations and small business owners. The writer recounted seeing copies of his work being sold at Spitalfields market in London. He talked to the seller without revealing his identity and felt pleased that the work was there though the writer acknowledged that this was not everyone's attitude:

> [I]t's nice to remain anonymous and not let him know that he's taken a picture of your work. I know people who would want to take the photographs there and then, it's mine, I'm taking it, but I'd be like, what are you doing, it was in a public place that's like the guy's photos. … I can understand people wanting to take pictures of stuff and try to sell it for their own little company. (Anon27)

By contrast, the co-option of graffiti creativity by advertisers and brands was of particular concern to some writers as is the underpayment of writers when they are commissioned to create works:

> [T]hey'd do it for nothing, they'd do it for paint, they'd do it for tins of beer and a sandwich, like. I'm kind of cynical 'cause I think half the problem with graffiti writers is that they just want to write their name … if they get to do [that] whenever, wherever, however, then it's cool and it's good and that leads to a lot of exploitation. And that that leads to a lot of diluted stuff out there and it's a shame, just doing a piece for whatever brand or TV show, Good Morning or whatever just for the paint or just for the profile

[51] A photography exhibition documenting graffiti in London, 'London Walls' at London's ICA, 23–27 February 2011 did not, by contrast, appear to attract the ire of graffiti writers presumably because it served a documentary function.

[52] See chapter five.

> and just to be out there is counter-productive and it's, it has a negative effect. You have to value your work and I don't think that a lot of graffiti writers see it as being [valuable]. It's not a commodity, it's an art form and I don't, it's important that I'm not interpreted as saying it's a commodity. It's an art form and artists are paid for their artworks and they have been forever and graffiti artists should see themselves as artists in that way. (Anon5)

A further justification for this approach both implicitly and, for the writer above, explicitly, is that graffiti style ought not to be treated as a commodity. The problems with exploiting graffiti creativity are *both* that the individual writer will not be remunerated *and* that it is exploitative of the subculture as a whole. The exploitation is not here merely of the work but of the very practice of graffiti writing as a process that, as shown in chapter two, engages the body of the writer and the movement through a particular space to produce a work: graffiti writing is a creative practice not merely a creative output. Yet this expansive approach to creativity also means that it is difficult for writers to prevent the commercial exploitation of the practice of graffiti writing, that is, where the cachet of the subculture is exploited rather than any one individual work (such as through the adoption of graffiti letter styles). Even if their copyright in the final work is respected, writers cannot protect the experience of pleasure of creating the work and belonging to a community that are part of the process of creation.[53] Moreover, while the primary motivation is personal and focused on getting up, the objection to commercial exploitation fits into a subsidiary motivation for writing as an indirect form of resistance: '[It is] my continuing protest at [the] police state and surveillance society, and corporate control' (Anon26). The suggestion that graffiti writing might function as a form of resistance is considered in broader terms in the Conclusion. This next part turns instead to a discussion of public placement and the effect it has on the operation of copyright law. It considers, in particular, what copyright might look like if the underlying approach taken was that of the graffiti writers by putting space first.

Graffiti Rules *for* Copyright

This part considers the extent to which the rules which exist within the graffiti subculture which have been identified over the course of this book, but especially those discussed in this chapter, travel outside of the 'bounded commons' of the graffiti subculture and suggests that writers' expectations about their creativity—specifically the acceptability of copying—reveal points of similarity and difference to copyright law as it as and, perhaps, as it ought to be. It is intended

[53] See also, regarding process, in the context of contemporary music and dance, C Waelde and P Schlesinger, 'Music and Dance: Beyond Copyright Text?' (2011) 8(3) *SCRIPTed* 257, 257–91. See chapter two.

therefore to be a contribution to the ongoing conversation on the reform of copyright[54] on which arguments have often been presented, perhaps more eloquently, elsewhere.[55] Rather than presenting a general programme of reform, this part instead highlights some of the points of relevance raised in the 'copyright beyond law' sections of the preceding empirical chapters and in the discussion of graffiti writers' expectations above. A consideration of such matters in turn involves a return to a discussion of the motivations underpinning the alternative normative framework within the graffiti subculture, and allows for a consideration of how, if at all, these observations might translate into a set of principles for repurposing copyright law in a manner sensitive to community and space. This in turn, it might be hoped, would enable copyright law to promote (and more successfully) the production of culture.

The discussion of the norms regulating creativity within the graffiti subculture's 'bounded commons' suggests it is easier to demonstrate how to regulate creativity in a way more closely aligned with the promotion of culture where the norms help to constitute a culture in which there is some level of agreement on who belongs within the community and what it means to be a creator within it, as well as a well-defined (and limited) sense of what is the activity being regulated by the relevant norms. The difficulty with considering possible changes to copyright law is how to regulate creativity within the intellectual commons when there is no, or little, agreement on who constitutes the 'community' or what kind of culture a normative framework might wish to promote—where the rules are those of a polity as a whole rather than some self-selecting subculture which is both within it and transcends it. That is, one key difficulty with seeking to promote and develop culture within copyright law—a difficulty avoided to a large extent by graffiti writers—is the lack of a coherent view held by all creators nor a common goal to which everyone can be said to subscribe and in pursuit of which the rules can then function.

[54] The most recent report on copyright reform in the UK was I Hargreaves, *Digital Opportunity: A Review of Intellectual Property and Growth.* UK Intellectual Property Office, May 2011. At the EU level there is the *Public Consultation on the Review of EU Copyright Rules* (2014) www.ec.europa.eu/internal_market/consultations/2013/copyright-rules/docs/consultation-document_en.pdf, and more recently see *European Parliament resolution of 9 July 2015 on the implementation of Directive 2001/29/EC of the European Parliament and of the Council of 22 May 2001 on the harmonisation of certain aspects of copyright and related rights in the information society* (2014/2256(INI)). This is an ongoing conversation in other jurisdictions too: Australian Law Reform Commission, *Copyright and the Digital Economy*, Final Report, ALRC Report 122 (November 2013). On the Australian proposal see I Alexander and M Fraser, 'Copyright Reform in Australia: Asking the Right Questions' (2014) 6(1) *Journal of Media Law* 8. For a theoretically informed account, including of the role of private ordering, see S Dusollier, 'The Commons as a Reverse Intellectual Property: From Exclusivity to Inclusivity' in HR Howe and J Griffiths (eds), *Concepts of Property in Intellectual Property Law* (Cambridge, Cambridge University Press, 2013).

[55] eg regarding the US but of broader relevance, J Litman, 'Real Copyright Reform' (2010) 96 *Iowa Law Review* 1, 1–55. More recently, regarding EU copyright law reform, C Geiger at al, 'The Resolution of the European Parliament of July 9, 2015: Paving the Way (Finally) for a Copyright Reform in the European Union?' (2015) 37(11) *European Intellectual Property Review* 1.

In particular, the literature on public art shows that one of the crucial difficulties with determining the appropriate interaction of the public with works of publicly accessible art reveals a question to which there is no easy answer: which public?[56] With copyright reform, the problem is even greater, for copyright lays down rules which (at least purport to) apply to *all* publics. The problem to be addressed then is first whether it is possible to suggest copyright rules without having a sense of who is the public at any given moment and—if it is not—to then adopt a set of copyright rules that might accommodate the shifting and fracturing of the various publics who are now or might in the future be bound by them. One way of surmounting this difficulty is to take as our starting point neither the work itself nor even the public, but rather the work's place in the physical and/or intellectual commons.

Drassinower[57] argues, amongst other things, that the reproduction of works is problematic because it compels the author to speak against their wishes.[58] The study of graffiti writing—but also billboards and other forms of publicly placed copyrighted works—complicates this proposition to portray such works as a form of *compelled listening*, of *compelled viewing*. This in turn suggests a more nuanced approach needs to be taken to the use of such works by members of the public, who do not necessarily choose to consume them. Indeed, as Borghi suggests, 'the act of speaking publicly in one's own name not only does not prevent, but actually encourages others to speak in their own name on the same subject.'[59]

Assessing 'appropriate' interaction with works might therefore take place with specific reference to the expectations of use which arise from a consideration of the space in which they are found.[60] The space where a work is found matters because it subtly shapes responses to the work, and what might be done with it. Seeing a painting on a wall, for example, might reasonably lead an individual to photograph it, as the participants above indicated was fine. The question for copyright law is whether to allow this apparently natural response—to photograph the work—but nevertheless to disallow its exploitation. The participants above would certainly expect such a curb on exploitation because, while they might be happy to have their speech disseminated, its *exploitation* forces them to speak in a way not chosen by them.

[56] See generally B Hoffman, 'Law for Art's Sake in the Public Realm' (1991) 17(1) *Critical Inquiry* 540. The controversy over the removal of a Richard Serra sculpture in a public square in New York is emblematic of this. For an overview see JC Ginsburg, 'Moral Rights in a Common Law System' (1990) 1(4) *Entertainment Law Review* 121, 125–26. Perhaps the only true work of public art is Anthony Gormley's rotating cast of members of the public atop the fourth plinth in Trafalgar Square in 2009 *One & Other* (www.antonygormley.com/show/item-view/id/2277) literally taking the public as its subject.

[57] A Drassinower, *What's Wrong With Copying?* (Cambridge, Mass., Harvard University Press, 2015).

[58] ibid 113 referring to 'compelled speech'. Similar arguments can be made using the work of Kant eg M Borghi, 'Copyright and Truth' (2011) 12 *Theoretical Inquiries in Law* 1. See also A Barron, 'Kant, Copyright and Communicative Freedom' (2012) 31 *Law and Philosophy* 1.

[59] Borghi (n 58) 19–20.

[60] Admittedly such an approach may work less well with respect to virtual space.

Reflecting this sort of spatially oriented consideration of appropriateness which emerged in the interviews with graffiti writers, three related suggestions are made here. First, that UK copyright law ought to introduce a public placement exception which avoids ambiguities by also covering underlying works and that such an exception should exclude commercial uses of publicly placed works unless such use is incidental.[61] This would amount to sanctioning existing, typical reproductions of street scenes that are then posted on social media.[62] While the relatively recent introduction of new exceptions to copyright—such as the quotation exception and private copyright exception (quashed in *BASCA*)[63]—in the UK is welcome, it seems preferable for the exceptions to be broadened out beyond parody and quotation so as to cover non-commercial reproduction and communication.[64] The lack of clarity as to the expansiveness of the exceptions points to a second, catch-all suggestion that has been made repeatedly elsewhere: the introduction of a US-style fair use defence to copyright infringement. The third suggestion is that such an exception should be paired with stronger moral rights protection than is currently offered in order to bring copyright rules more closely in line with creators' desires to be acknowledged as authors. This adds up to a set of suggestions that are intended at once to strengthen the ability of non-authors to use works but also provides stronger protection to authors regarding commercial uses and to enforce their moral rights.

Revising the Public Placement Exception

In relation to the first two points, the suggestion that flows from an examination of the regulation of creativity in the graffiti subculture is that the matter of purposely placing works on public display ought to trigger the operation of a new version of the section 62 CDPA exception which would allow these work to be lawfully reproduced for non-commercial purposes. Section 62 already tracks, to an extent, graffiti writers' own expectations about the uses of their work discussed above: certain reproduction and dissemination is expected, even welcomed, because the work is located in a public space. Yet rather than developing an implied licence or assignment point—that is, that any publicly placed work automatically is 'free' to use—instead there is a need for a functional equivalent to section 62 that covers both underlying drawings and, significantly, both two dimensional and three

[61] See CDPA, s 31.

[62] This is not without its problems in particular because of the potential for sharing an image in degraded form thus engaging the moral right of integrity: C Waelde, 'Moral Rights and the Internet: Squaring the Circle' (2002) 3 *Intellectual Property Quarterly* 281. There is the additional problem of social media sharing by companies eg as part of a commercial endeavour.

[63] *R (BASCA) v Secretary of State for Business, Innovation and Skills* [2015] EWHC 1723 (Admin).

[64] Arguably the quotation exception (discussed below) might serve this function, however it would not excuse the use of a work in its entirety: L Bently, 'Exploring the Flexibilities Available to UK Law', response to Hargeaves Review, [29] note 3.

dimensional works. Such an exception would exempt from copyright infringement the innumerable people who currently take photographs of graffiti writing, street art, and other works, and share these on the internet.

One way of reconfiguring the existing section 62 exception in response to such sharing is to replace it with the equivalent exception in the Infosoc Directive.[65] Indeed, Burrell and Coleman favour the inclusion of the Infosoc Directive exceptions, as worded, into UK law.[66] Certainly the wording of Article 5(3)(h) is potentially more expansive in referring to the 'use of works, *such as* works of architecture and sculpture, made to be located permanently in public places' (emphasis added).[67] Such a direct transposition would be helpful insofar as it might encompass two as well as three dimensional works in public places, although the difficulty remains regarding the potential commercial exploitation of such works.[68]

If a new version of section 62 was expanded to cover two dimensional works—thus allowing for 'competing' two dimensional works to made, additional protection would need to be granted to authors. Such additional protection would include attributing the work and ensuring that the scope of the new section was narrowed so as to exclude commercial uses. The principles that apply to orphan works may be useful here in helping to determine the scope of the limitations on the reproduction and dissemination of works that are publicly placed.[69] Of particular interest is the requirement to perform diligent searches prior to reproducing and/or making works available.[70] This would be relevant, for example, in relation to the publication of street art and graffiti books. As one participant above identified, it is difficult to gain permission, even where the artistic work is a name/signature that points to the identity of the creator, because the creator cannot, or does not want to be, found. Of course one might expect the tag (name) to be included along with a note explaining, perhaps, the city in which the work was photographed. The inclusion of such information would, a diligent search having failed to find the author, present a way of acknowledging and preserving graffiti creativity. Such preservation would track graffiti writers' own expectations

[65] But it is worth noting that, in any event, the rights relating to publicly placed works seem to be rarely enforced. See E Rosati, 'Are EU Policy-Makers Fighting the Right Copyright Battles' (2015) 10(9) *Journal of Intellectual Property Law & Practice* 651.

[66] Burrell and Coleman (n 43) 300.

[67] Another problem raised here is that, buildings excepted, it may be difficult for a member of the public to determine whether a work is permanent.

[68] See reference, echoing concerns of participants, to commercial reproduction: 'Considers that the commercial use of photographs, video footage or other images of works which are permanently located in physical public places should always be subject to prior authorisation from the authors': European Parliament (n 54) recital 45.

[69] On orphan works see generally M Borghi and S Karapapa, *Copyright and Mass Digitization* (Oxford, Oxford University Press, 2013) chapter 4.

[70] Directive 2012/28/EU on certain permitted uses of orphan works. The Directive is already limited in the protection it provides to museums and other institutions that may seek to digitise their collections: Bently and Sherman (n 22) 55.

and experiences: the 'photo culture' describe elsewhere in this book is a particular example. The exclusion of commercial reproductions may be more problematic because of the problems in distinguishing between commercial and non-commercial uses when works are disseminated.

The bigger problem here is that a diligent search rule would—akin to the rules operating in relation to orphan works—depend on the existence of a set of sources that those seeking to reproduce the works would need to check; certainly there would not appear to be an obvious source for checking the identity of pseudonymous graffiti writers and street artists.[71] This brings us back again to the introduction of a fair use defence where elements such as the nature of the use can be more sensitively taken into account. It might allow for full reproductions of works for non-commercial purposes while allowing for the possibility of certain reproductions that are commercial, such as the publication of books which serve an archiving function, to nevertheless fall within the exception (eg the sale of subculture-specific books documenting graffiti writing culture).

Introducing 'Fair Use', Making Use of Quotation

There is a long-standing literature on the nature and scope of 'fair use' in the US.[72] Scholarly arguments regarding the introduction of a US-style fair use standard have also been made in the UK.[73] This section is concerned with the aspects of graffiti writers' 'rules for the public' and how these might be reflected in the adoption of a fair use defence in the UK, or indeed reflected in the broad interpretation of the new quotation defence.

The fair use defence offers a high level of flexibility that is largely absent from the application of existing UK exceptions to copyright infringement even following the most recent expansion of the exceptions to include, amongst others, fair dealing for quotation in certain limited circumstances. In contrast to such circumscription, the scope of 'fair use' is appealingly open in providing a defence to copyright infringement by reference to a non-exhaustive list of factors: the 'purpose and character of the use'; 'the nature of the copyrighted work'; the amount of the work taken; the effect of the taking on the work's market.[74] It is not entirely

[71] The guidance on diligent search for fine art is unlikely to help. See Intellectual Property Office, *Orphan Works Diligent Search Guidance for Applicants: Still Visual Art* (2015) www.gov.uk/government/uploads/system/uploads/attachment_data/file/474403/orphan-works-still-visual-art.pdf. Thanks to Maurizio Borghi for this point.

[72] eg P Aufderheide and P Jaszi, *Reclaiming Fair Use: How to Put Balance Back in Copyright* (Chicago, University of Chicago Press, 2011); W Patry, *How to Fix Copyright* (New York, Oxford University Press, 2011); R Tushnet, 'Copy This Essay: How Fair Use Doctrine Harms Free Speech and How Copying Serves It' (2004) 114 *Yale Law Journal* 535; NW Netanel, 'Making Sense of Fair Use' (2011) 15 *Lewis & Clark Law Review* 715.

[73] R Burrell, 'Reining in Copyright Law: Is Fair Use the Answer?' (2001) 4 *Intellectual Property Quarterly* 361; W Dnes, 'Should the UK Move to a Fair-Use Copyright Exception?' (2013) 44 IIC *International Review of Intellectual Property and Competition Law* 418.

[74] 17 USC §107(4).

surprising then to find that the defence has been flexible enough to be exported to other jurisdictions, including Israel and South Korea, where it has been shaped into doctrines sensitive to the cultures in those countries.[75] In Australia, for example it was ultimately recommended for inclusion by the Australian Law Reform Commission.[76]

The task here is to consider the way in which the graffiti rules point to the adoption of fair use as an appropriate avenue of reform. This is because the malleability of the fair use defence presents a potentially more sensitive means of promoting the social benefit approach to copyright protection (ie the promotion of culture). A useful way of conceptualising the fair use defence is to follow Howe in adopting a stewardship, rather than a liberal, model of copyright law under which 'the copyright owner is a "steward" of the copyright work and holds the copyright in the work for the benefit of the community as well as themselves.'[77] In other words, the fair use defence may serve as a bulwark to protect community interests in creativity and culture. This stewardship model is arguably reflected in the rules regarding copying within the graffiti subculture. Graffiti writers seek to promote their own creativity and their position within the hierarchy but also to recognise that their works are benefitting the development of graffiti culture meaning that copying is, in certain circumstances, to be expected.[78] This approach has the benefit of enriching the graffiti-specific intellectual commons (eg in promoting innovations in the development of letter styles).

A study of the graffiti norms presents further support not only for the introduction of fair use but also for the potential introduction of a broader set of factors to be taken into account in determining fairness. One of the key factors in making reproduction and dissemination of works acceptable, and constituting a potential fair use factor, is the public placement of the works. Returning to Howe's model of copyright in which 'need' is identified as a relevant factor,[79] the space where graffiti writing, and indeed other forms of creativity visible in urban public space, is found arguably makes the taking of photographs a necessary freedom for an individual to have when in that space. On the other hand, this is perhaps expanding the concept of a 'need' far beyond the kinds of specific *dealings* that are currently permitted in UK copyright law. For instance, the fair dealing defences circumscribe dealings with works to those dealing that are 'fair' for a particular purpose such as criticism and review or parody[80] rather than an inchoate desire

[75] P Decherney, 'Fair Use Goes Global' (2014) 31(2) *Critical Studies in Media Communication* 146. See also O Fischman Afori, 'An Open Standard "Fair Use" Doctrine: A Welcome Israeli Initiative' (2008) 30(3) *European Intellectual Property Review* 85.

[76] ALRC (n 54) 13, 87ff.

[77] HR Howe, 'Copyright Limitations and the Stewardship Model of Property' (2011) 2 *Intellectual Property Quarterly* 183, 204.

[78] See chapter seven on exceptions to biting.

[79] Howe (n 77) 212. One example given is the need for students to be able to copy work as part of their studies.

[80] See CDPA, s 30.

to contribute to the promotion and production of culture. Such defences do not account for the reproduction of a whole work simply because an individual went for a stroll, a work seemed beautiful to them and they wished to share their pleasure in seeing it by communicating it to the public via social media. This is not to say that the introduction of a fair use defence would necessarily allow for such reproductions[81] but it might make it possible.

Whether or not the 'free' *movement* of the public through the physical commons ought always to allow for the 'free', albeit (as the graffiti writers above stress) non-exploitative, *uses* of works in the intellectual commons is a matter to be determined by taking into account factors other than space (eg the provision of acknowledgement, or not). However, a more generous allowance being made for the uses of publicly accessible works makes sense in the context of a desire to effect the development and promotion of a plural culture. In introducing *space* as a relevant factor—in the sense that being able to reproduce and communicate publicly available creativity is recognised as necessary to the production of, and participation in, culture[82]—a non-prescriptive 'fair use' norm is perhaps best placed to address the difficulties inherent in seeking to promote the public interest.

Samuelson, for example, points to the usefulness of 'fair use' in the promotion of public interest principles.[83] In particular, Samuelson draws attention to the Hargreaves report which also recommended the introduction of 'fair use' in the UK but also the flexibilities inherent in adopting the list of exceptions within the Infosoc Directive.[84] The Hargreaves report describes fair use as

> offer[ing] a zone for trial and error, for bolder risk taking, with the courts providing a backstop to adjudicate objections from rights holders if innovators have trespassed too far upon their rights.[85]

Although the introduction of the exception was not ultimately recommended, the report highlighted the benefit of adopting a fair use exception because of the flexibility it had offered in the US context in responding to changes in technology.[86] More generally, the benefit of such an exception is that it allows courts to take into account the particular facts and circumstances in which copyright works are used without being explicitly constrained by the existing fair dealing categories of uses in UK copyright law. Hugenholtz and Senftleben[87] argue for the introduction of a halfway house between what they term the 'open norm' of US style fair use and

[81] See *Gaylord v United States* 595 F 3d 1364; 2010 US App LEXIS 3915 (2010) in which fair use did not provide a defence to the reproduction, on postage stamps, of a publicly placed sculpture.

[82] See chapter two.

[83] See also P Samuelson, 'Justifications for Copyright Limitations & Exceptions' (2014) available at www.papers.ssrn.com/sol3/Papers.cfm?abstract_id=2476669.

[84] ibid 34–35.

[85] Hargreaves (n 54) 44.

[86] ibid 47.

[87] PB Hugenholtz and M Senftleben, 'Fair Use in Europe: In Search of Flexibilities' (2012) available at www.papers.ssrn.com/sol3/papers.cfm?abstract_id=2013239, 9.

the existing exceptions along the lines of the model Wittem Code.[88] The Wittem Code, for instance, combines the three-step test[89] for the application of copyright exceptions and limitations with a list of acceptable uses that are left open-ended via a reference to comparable uses.[90] This includes model article 5(2)(1)(d) on use for quotation which may cover the whole of a work,[91] making it a particularly flexible exception.

A recent addition to the suite of defences in the CDPA is the defence in section 30 (1ZA) of using a quotation from a work for criticism, review or otherwise. This appears to be a welcome broadening out from mere criticism and review but as with that fair dealing defence, it must also be accompanied by a 'sufficient acknowledgement', the dealing must be 'fair' and the work—our concern is with graffiti writing as an artistic work—must have been made publicly available.[92] It is the third point that raises questions about what it means for a work to be publicly available, specifically whether this would include the public placement of works on walls or trains. Of course for a graffiti writer, as the discussion of visibility in chapter one indicated, a big part of the creative process is to make sure their name is seen. It is not clear that placement on a wall constitutes 'making available' expect perhaps by defining such placement as the 'exhibition'[93] of the work.

A further question relates to what 'quotation' means in the context of an artistic work. If a writer adopts a certain stylistic element (a part of the work) from another writer, as is likely, given the existence of a shared history and culture, this might be described as fair because it is beneficial to the promotion of culture. (This in turn requires us to assume that a subcultural benefit can be equated with cultural benefit more broadly though, given the chilly legal reception of graffiti writing, this cannot be taken as a given.) Bently and Sherman suggest that fairness may require something akin to quotation marks but that other 'conventions … will have to be invoked.[94] From the perspective of graffiti writers, however, such a convention is unnecessary if participants in graffiti culture understand that 'quotation' or some amount of taking is part of the creative process rather than something to be treated as exceptional or prima facie illegitimate.

Yet for all of the likely benefits of fair use, or perhaps even a semi-open list of exceptions (or a very broad interpretation of quotation), it is worth remembering Burrell's caution that even the introduction of a fair use defence will not suffice

[88] Wittem Group, *European Copyright Code*, www.copyrightcode.eu.

[89] Berne Convention, Art 9(2). Infosoc Directive, Art. 5(5) provides—and indeed echoes participants' expectations—that the exception is used in 'special cases', that it does 'not conflict with normal exploitation', and that it does not 'unreasonably the legitimate interests' of the copyright owner. See also R Arnold and E Rosati, 'Are National Courts the Addressees of the InfoSoc Three-Step Test?' (2015) 10(10) *Journal of Intellectual Property Law and Practice* 742.

[90] European Copyright Code, Art 5.5 refers to 'Any other use that is comparable to the uses enumerated in art 5.1 to 5.4(1)'.

[91] ibid note 50.

[92] See Bently and Sherman (n 22) 239.

[93] CDPA, s 30(1A).

[94] Bently and Sherman (n 22) 241.

unless courts interpret it in a way that respects users' interests.[95] A recent case on the use of musical works by The Beatles—which necessitated the application of UK as well as US copyright law to the facts at issue—included a consideration of US fair use by Arnold J as the following extract indicates:

> The fair use doctrine has often been criticised as indeterminate and unpredictable. Over the last decade, however, work by scholars such as Pamela Samuelson, Barton Beebe and Matthew Sag has demonstrated that what at first blush may appear to be an amorphous mass of individual decisions can be analysed and categorised in the same way as other areas of common law (negligence, for example). Prof Jaszi cited an article by Neil Weinstock Netanel, 'Making Sense of Fair Use' 14 Lewis & Clark L. Rev. 715 (2011) which, building on the work of these earlier scholars, provides a helpful overview of the doctrine as it is currently interpreted and applied. Nevertheless, the doctrine remains flexible and fact-sensitive.[96]

This suggests that the exception might be introduced without giving rise to excessive uncertainty as to what is and is not permitted conduct.

It is, furthermore, worth considering how graffiti writers' beliefs about the re-use of their works could inform a broad copyright exception for private use of works made publicly available by an author (discussed briefly in the context of copying in blackbooks and copyright reform in chapter seven). The discussion of the interview data above on graffiti writers' expectations relating to the uses and sharing of their creativity by third parties suggest that such a norm already exists within the subculture. This points to a further advantage of a broad fair use exception: it allows the copyright law system to take into account internal group norms (here, writers' own uses of works and their expectations about others' uses of those works) to determine whether a particular use is indeed 'fair'. This occurs already in relation to the guidelines issued by libraries regarding what constitutes appropriate reproduction of a work.[97]

The question then becomes whether the graffiti rules discussed in this book, but especially those in this chapter, are a form of custom that could be taken into account in determining whether the use of graffiti writing as an artistic work was a fair use. A relevant aspect here would be the expectation that publicly placed works will be shared. This seems to echo a principle developed under common law copyright of the 'implied' permission for use of works performed in public. An example of this may be seen in the reference to 'implied' permission for the use public speeches in *Walter v Lane*.[98] There was no assumption that any public

[95] eg Burrell (n 73) 387.

[96] *Sony/ATV Music Publishing LLC & Another v WPMC Ltd & Another* [2015] EWHC 1853 (Ch) [100].

[97] See, in the US context, JE Rothman, 'The Questionable Use of Custom in Intellectual Property' (2007) 93(8) *Virginia Law Review* 1899.

[98] 'Copyright is the right of multiplying copies of a published writing. There is no copyright in a speech although delivered on a public occasion, and on the other hand there is no copyright under the statute in a piece of writing until it has been published': *Walter v Lane* [1900] AC 539, 550 (Lord Davey).

speech would be unprotected but rather protection was offered under the then-current copyright legislation for speeches and lectures only if (and Lord Roseberry failed to do this) notice of the speech was given in advance and in writing, and more importantly there was no 'common law copyright' protection because it was given 'in public, and indeed in the presence of newspaper reporters, thereby impliedly authorising further publication.'[99] (As such what was at issue in the case was a reporter's copyright which, famously, was found to subsist in the record of the speech.)[100] The application of a similar rule via the use of the graffiti rules as custom—that material placed in public may be shared unless it is somehow disclaimed—might be useful here. To make such a move would be to revive a nineteenth-century idea about the publication of a literary work as 'a gift to the public'[101] albeit in connection with debates over perpetual copyright at common law. This notion of a 'gift' is useful in that it echoes some graffiti writers' (and indeed street artists') conception of their own creative practice as an act of giving art to the public.[102] On this point, certain dicta from *Millar v Taylor* are useful in drawing a clear analogy between public placement and the production of commons:

> For, when an author throws his work into so public a state that it must immediately and unavoidably become common, it is the same as expressly giving it to the public. He knows, before he publishes, that this will be the necessary consequence of the publication: therefore he must be deemed to intend it.[103]

Of course, in order to be workable, this may require some form of symbolic communication with the public to the effect that reproduction and dissemination for non-commercial purposes is acceptable. But then the world of intellectual property law has already developed a series of such symbols (eg ©) so may quite well cope with another. The difficulty would remain in relation to subcultural creativity, such as graffiti writing, that creators might nonetheless exempt themselves from legal frameworks for the regulation of creativity.[104] (It is not in any event

[99] NP Gravells, 'Authorship and Originality: The Persistent Influence of Walter v Lane' (2007) 3 *Intellectual Property Quarterly* 267, 269.

[100] *Walter v Lane* (n 98).

[101] Quoting Yates J in *Millar v Taylor*: B Sherman and L Bently, *The Making of Modern Intellectual Property Law* (Cambridge, Cambridge University Press, 1999) 28.

[102] The argument is *not* being made here that in placing their works in public that graffiti writers are impliedly dedicating their work to the public domain—on which see P Johnson, '"Dedicating" Copyright to the Public Domain' (2008) 71 *Modern Law Review* 587—nor that such a dedication ought to be recognised.

[103] *Millar v Taylor* (1769) 4 Burr 2303, 233–34 (Yates J).

[104] Graffiti writers do not, and are not likely to, append Creative Commons and Licence Art Libre notes to their works but I found during fieldwork that some works will carry the © symbol. On the difficulties of applying such licences to artistic works see J Farchy, 'Are Free Licenses Suitable for Cultural Works?' (2009) 31(5) *European Intellectual Property Review* 1. As a general proposition, it is the promotion of community-sensitive copyright licences that may be more appropriate for creators working within specific communities. As Dussolier says: 'To some extent, Creative Commons can be said to provide a useful answer to the needs of some communities of creators who might consider sharing as the normal way of disseminating their creation, whether artistic, informational, scientific or

intended to suggest that graffiti writers are somehow abandoning their copyright when publicly placing works.)[105]

The problem here is that, as has been identified in relation to the use of custom in the US for determining the fairness of 'fair use', looking to the graffiti rules as custom may have the opposite of the intended effect: graffiti writers may, in tolerating reproduction and certain communication to the public of their works and considering such uses fair, effectively be granted less protection than the author of a different kind, and differently placed, artistic work. As Rothman shows, embracing custom is not without its perils.[106] In the absence of new UK or EU copyright rules adopting fair use and the steadily growing amount of empirical copyright research into the practices of different creative groups, it is relevant to consider whether customary practice might be integrated into the determination of existing fair dealing claims, especially the new quotation exception. To do so would provide for a more sensitive determination of copyright claims; determination in a way which can, potentially, take into account the peculiarities within communities of creators. The difficulty lies not in recognising such practices but rather that, having taken them into account, the principles extracted from the practice about 'fairness' would become ossified and no less inflexible that a close-ended copyright exception. Indeed, the kind of 'optimal' normative frameworks within specific communities—Rothman refers to Ellickson but this would apply equally to graffiti writers—would not necessarily be reflected in the production of 'optimal IP rules' more generally.[107] Taking the rules within the 'bounded commons' of the graffiti subculture where the rules are recognised by a self-selecting group and where the group as a whole is oriented towards specific forms of creative production, it is entirely possible that such rules can never be optimal over the field of cultural production as a whole. What they can do, as indeed this chapter attempts to do, is suggest an alternative, a reconsideration of copyright as it is.

In the absence of the introduction of fair use, the best option may be the further, more flexible, interpretation of existing limitations. In the wake of *Deckym*,[108] for instance, the European Copyright Society has called for full harmonisation of copyright limitations and exceptions in the EU in a manner that emphasises

functional': S Dusollier, 'Scoping Study on Copyright and Related Rights and the Public Domain' World Intellectual Property Organisation publication available at www.wipo.int/edocs/mdocs/mdocs/en/cdip_4/cdip_4_3_rev_study_inf_1.pdf, 56.

[105] On abandonment see E Hudson and R Burrell, 'Abandonment, Copyright and Orphaned Works: What Does It Mean to Take the Proprietary Nature of Intellectual Property Rights Seriously?' (2011) 35(3) *Melbourne University Law Review* 971.

[106] JE Rothman, 'The Questionable Use of Custom in Intellectual Property' (2007) 93 *Virginia Law Review* 8, 1899–1982.

[107] ibid 1954–55.

[108] Case C-201/13 *Deckmyn v Vandersteen* [2014] ECDR 21.

both certainty and flexibility[109] but which nevertheless falls short of the full-blown introduction of fair use. In the meantime, the quotation exception provides an opportunity to be grasped.

Strengthening Moral Rights

The empirical chapters suggest (especially insofar as they relate to uses of graffiti by the general public) that graffiti writers are concerned with both the desire to communicate and to have their dignity as creators recognised. For this reason, any rethinking of copyright would need to include a strengthening of moral rights to reflect this desire for dignity and recognition via, in particular, the attribution and integrity rights. The copyright rules that ought to give effect to graffiti writers' concerns ought to pay at least equal attention to integrity, the attribution of authorship as to economic ownership.[110] At the very least, to redress the relative weakness of moral rights as compared to economic rights, this would require a removal of the assertion requirement from the attribution right if not making such a requirement a crucial component in determining whether a use is fair (or indeed as a condition of any form of non-commercial or private reproduction).[111]

In particular, it is possible for fair use, much as with the interpretation of the scope of the quotation exception, to protect the moral rights of creators, albeit indirectly. The determination of what is 'fair' could take into account not only the way in which a certain use might affect the market for a work but also the extent to which the creator's dignity has been respected.[112] To that extent, and notwithstanding that the scope of fair use may be narrowed by judicial interpretation, the introduction of an open exception such as fair use presents an appropriate means by which to promote the development of culture.

Conclusion

This chapter has suggested that there is an overlap in terms of approaches to public placement of works between graffiti writers' expectations and copyright.

[109] C Geiger et al, 'Limitations and Exceptions as key Elements of the Legal Framework for Copyright Reform in the European Union—Opinion of the European Copyright Society on the Judgment of the CJEU in Case C-201/13 Deckmyn' (2015) available at www.papers.ssrn.com/sol3/papers.cfm?abstract_id=2564772.

[110] This echoes the argument in Tushnet (n 48) 165.

[111] Such a requirement is already part of existing fair dealing defences, eg the 'sufficient acknowledgment' requirement in the defence of fair dealing for the purposes of criticism, review and news reporting: CDPA, s 30(1).

[112] Indeed, US fair use may be viewed as a substitute for lack of moral rights. But see DS Ciolino, 'Rethinking the Compatibility of Moral Rights and Fair Use' (1997) 54 *Washington & Lee Law Review* 33.

Indeed, the graffiti writers' approach—notwithstanding the fraught relationship of graffiti creativity and real property—is perhaps surprisingly conservative, in that it seeks, in a straightforward fashion, nothing more than compensation for the reproduction of works. The surprising thing here is not that graffiti writers regulate creativity, though such a discovery is exciting in and of itself, but rather that the study of alternative copyright norms provides support *for* the continued existence of copyright, albeit in an occasionally modified form, rather than for its wholesale abolition.

The continued commodification of graffiti culture makes it probable that the UK courts, or other EU Member State courts, will at some point need to consider some of the difficult points rehearsed in this book relating to subsistence and infringement of copyright in graffiti writing. This chapter suggests that when they do, copyright ought to be enforced to its fullest extent so as to aid graffiti writers as authors of copyrighted works and, in turn, to meet graffiti writers' own expectations of how their works should be treated. Alongside this, the disconnect between graffiti writers' expectations about how their works should be used and what copyright law in its present state is able to offer them ought to point policy makers in the direction of copyright reform aimed at creating a body of law which is, much more than at present, sensitive to space, and especially to the public placement of works not simply in determining appropriate uses but in taking spatial factors (the locational creativity discussed in chapter two) into account in determining the subsistence of copyright.

The focus of the final part of this chapter has been an argument for the introduction of simultaneously broader and narrower exceptions to copyright infringement. The suggested reforms are directed towards the protection of culture in that they foreground the *space* of creativity, rather than taking the inherent qualities of a work or the claim that its creator is inherently worthy of protection as a starting point. The suggestions made are not about balancing the interests of a creator and a potential user but rather about recognising that the space where creations are found necessitates accommodations to be made by both. In the meantime, when a graffiti case comes before a UK court, it seems likely that that court will have no choice but to apply to graffiti a body of copyright law which is neither as rich nor as sensitive to the creative process as would be one which took heed of the alternative normative framework which prevails within the subculture's 'bounded commons'.

Finally, the empirical data considered here as well as the data considered in the preceding empirical chapters might lead us to conclude that applying the 'universal' norms of copyright to a subcultural practice will usually provide suboptimal results. The attempt to 'scale up' subcultural copyright-like norms are equally likely to be suboptimal. The focus on the graffiti rules means that the book has highlighted particular aspects of the creative process—its movements, its pleasures and spatial realities—and this process and the normative framework that has evolved to support it is not neutral towards the good. But these very aspects make it antithetical to copyright law which must, in applying to creative production more generally, be (at least on the face of it) neutral as to the exact 'good' that copyright seeks to promote. This is so even when we adopt the social benefit approach in which the public interest is paramount, if largely undefined.

The graffiti rules might thus be conceptualised as a communitarian model of 'copyright beyond law' which places it immediately at odds with a liberal model of what creativity is and how it ought to be protected by copyright law.[113] It must therefore be considered that what is needed for the health of the intellectual commons and the production and promotion of an attractive and diverse culture is not the discovery of a totalising set of norms that might apply to all creativity but for the recognition of the need to nurture and promote a plurality of normative frameworks that, in their flourishing, will bring about that diverse culture.

[113] I am grateful to Paul Scott for discussion of these and related points.

Conclusion

The introduction to this book opened with the claim that 'Graffiti breaks every rule but within itself still has rules' (Anon29). The subsequent chapters have demonstrated that creativity within the graffiti subculture reflects a set of rules relating to the production, the placement and the content of creativity within the subculture's 'bounded commons'. First, graffiti writers must paint letters (a point that serves to distinguish them from street artists). Second, graffiti must be placed in highly visible places such as trains, tracksides, large corporate and public buildings, but not on 'personal' property such as houses and cars. Third, graffiti writing styles must be original, and copying is prohibited except in particular situations, such as private copying in a writer's blackbook or where implied permission is given to write a fellow graffiti crew member's tag. Fourth, graffiti writers generally must not alter or destroy the work of other writers, though such destruction will be acceptable in a narrow range of circumstances such as where one places a bigger, more stylistically advanced work over it. Fifth, graffiti writers not only accept but in fact expect that members of the public will reproduce and share their work. They believe, however, that such dissemination should be non-commercial.

The regulation of creativity within the subculture's 'bounded commons'—a set of rules running both parallel to, and beyond, copyright—suggest a distinct form of regulation, an alternative to copyright, for the promotion and protection of creativity and culture. The graffiti rule relating to letter writing is analogous to the subject matter requirement in copyright law; rules regarding appropriate placement are analogous to the public policy exceptions for copyright subsistence and the enforcement of copyright; the originality and prohibition of copying rules are analogous to originality in relation to subsistence of copyright, and infringement by reproduction; finally, the prohibition of alteration and destruction is analogous to the moral right of integrity in copyright law.

These parallels also show how and why copyright might be thought lacking as regards the regulation of creativity within a discrete, highly motivated community of creators. The fact that graffiti writers belong to a discrete subcultural community and strongly self-identify as members of that community means that the graffiti rules cannot easily be compared to copyright rules which necessarily affect disparate creative communities and so must be (mostly) neutral about the forms of creativity which they encourage and protect.[1] The lack of parallels in particular instances suggests that copyright law is ill-suited to regulate particular, especially subcultural, forms of creativity. This is perhaps unsurprising given that graffiti creativity occurs within a particular space (ie public streets, tracksides and the like) operating in a particular territory (usually a city which, in turn, overlaps with the subculture's scene). For example, the lack of a direct parallel between 'going over' (destruction of works) as a sanction versus damages for copyright infringement is relevant because it suggests the potential impossibility of copyright law providing remedies that are equally meaningful for very different forms of creativity and in line with the economic and non-economic expectations of a variety of creators. As such, contrasting the graffiti rules with copyright law in the empirical chapters (chapters five, seven and nine) was significant in identifying the limitations of copyright law and explaining how graffiti creativity comes to be beyond copyright altogether. The identification of parallels also contributed to the existing intellectual property and social norms literature while contributing an additional perspective to the existing sociological literature on graffiti writing.

Alongside a discussion of these parallel graffiti rules, this book has demonstrated that copyright law can, and does, apply to graffiti writing. The application of copyright law to graffiti writing has also brought into focus a number of limitations and difficulties within copyright law, especially its shortcomings in recognising the process-oriented nature of creativity and the space in which it occurs. In particular, these issues include: copyright's privileging of the 'work' over the creative process, the extent to which an author's dissemination of works in public spaces should imply permission to copy, the relevance of distinguishing between the material work and its digital copy, the importance of moral rights, the link between copyright and trade mark law, and, more broadly, the role of copyright in producing public space (discussed further below).

Apart from the analysis of the empirical data, the application of copyright law to graffiti creativity showed that graffiti writing can be protected by copyright notwithstanding that considerations of public policy may potentially prevent the enforcement of that copyright in certain circumstances. While graffiti creativity is unlikely to be an original literary work, it meets the criteria for an original artistic work and of being the author's 'own intellectual creation'. Furthermore, insofar as the graffiti writer is an author, he/she may have certain moral rights which, for a number of reasons including the assertion requirement and the difficulty of recognising the reputation of graffiti writers, may be difficult to enforce. Although graffiti writers could seek redress for copyright infringement (such as where one writer copies another writer's work) the empirical findings show that they forbear

[1] Which is not to say that copyright rules are neutral on aesthetics regardless of the requirement to protect graphic works 'irrespective of artistic quality' in CDPA, s 4(1)(a). This attempt at providing an objective standard is flawed in asking judges to determine how a work is 'normally' made: A Barron, 'Copyright Law and the Claims of Art' (2002) 4 *Intellectual Property Quarterly* 368, 385.

copyright protection in favour of the graffiti rules. Instead of copyright, graffiti writers adhere to a parallel set of norms that are highly attuned to the history, culture and hierarchy of the graffiti subculture. Yet this does not mean that graffiti writers ought not to gain the full benefit of copyright protection where they are in the position to avail themselves of such protection (eg where non-writers reproduce their work for commercial purposes). Instead the argument made over the course of the book is that not only can copyright law apply to graffiti but that the insights gained into the regulation of graffiti creativity provides an insight into copyright law and its complex relationship to creativity.

The discussion below returns to some of the themes that have emerged over the course of the book. The first part considers the extent to which the graffiti rules converge with and diverge from copyright law before considering briefly how graffiti rules might be used to bolster existing justifications for copyright. The second part considers the broader consequences of the argument made over the course of the book, namely that the graffiti rules are a normative framework for the regulation of creativity that is *beyond* copyright law.

Convergence and Divergence: Justifying Copyright?

This book has explored the way in which the regulation of creativity within the intellectual commons may serve the production and promotion of culture. In the graffiti subculture, creators—who make an active choice to participate in that subculture—are incentivised to *write* in order to gain fame. Similarly, insofar as copyright law is concerned with incentivising creativity for social benefit, the subject matter rules identify the types of creativity that are considered useful to economic and/or cultural development and so attract the protection of the law. Both the copyright and the graffiti rules outlined in this book grapple with the problem of categorising certain forms of creative output as objects of regulation at the expense of others. Even if, for copyright law, this is not a matter of being wedded to a particular theory of art, it may be the inevitable result of treating creative outputs as property.[2] This points to a more significant divergence: that is, between copyright law's commodification of creativity[3] and the graffiti rules' treatment of writers' creative output as an extension of the writers, or rather, of their alter egos. Biting (copying) a writer's name or style is problematic because it is the appropriation of that writer's labour but also of his or her personality.

[2] A Barron, 'Copyright, Art, and Objecthood' in D McClean and K Schubert (eds), *Dear Images: Art, Copyright and Culture* (London, Ridinghouse, 2002) 291–92.

[3] See eg F Macmillan, 'Copyright, Culture and Private Power' (1998) 16(3) *Prometheus* 305, 307.

The loss suffered when a writer's tag is copied, for instance, cannot therefore be captured in monetary terms because it is a personal not a pecuniary loss. Instead, the biting may have an impact on the writer's status.

Another point of divergence between the two sets of norms which emerged in the research relates to originality. An originality standard within the graffiti-specific commons arises out of a complex interplay of a number of factors including the 'newness' or individuality of the expression, the demonstrating of skill, and the territory in which the name or style is inscribed on a wall or train. A novelty requirement in copyright law akin to that found in design law or patent law would likely mean that fewer creations would be protected by copyright. Yet in the graffiti subculture, standing apart and being the first to create a style is a crucial means of gaining respect. In a subculture that values individual expression as a form of personal branding, the hierarchy would function less effectively without such a stringent originality requirement. Moreover, this suggests that the regulation of creativity in alternative normative frameworks, such as that of the graffiti subculture's 'bounded commons', produces a set of rules that are highly attuned to the needs of the creative community in question. It does not therefore recognise boundaries of the sort that divide artistic and literary works (copyright law), inventions (patent law) and marks of origin (trade mark law).

The defences to copyright infringement provide further parallels. The justifications for a fair dealing type of defence in both copyright law and the graffiti rules suggest an attempt to balance the accessibility of works (for cultural and subcultural development respectively) and the potential damage (monetary and fame-based respectively). However, the graffiti rules, by allowing private copying, operate more flexibly. This may be the result, at least in part, of accepting that the attempt to gain fame as an individual writer is pursued while being attuned to the group's historical and cultural constraints. Belonging requires writers to copy others in their blackbooks so that they can develop their own style in order to eventually contribute to the subculture's 'library of style'. Similarly, as with copyright law, the graffiti rules are concerned with the integrity of the work and the effect of its alteration on its author's reputation. In the subculture's 'bounded commons', however, interference with the integrity of a work is, arguably, treated more seriously than it is in UK copyright law.

Parallels and divergences between copyright rules and graffiti rules also exist with respect to the justifications offered for the protection of creativity. The empirical data showed an overlap between labour, personhood and cultural development justifications in the graffiti rules, with a particular focus on social benefit justifications in light of the broader question as to the appropriate regulation of the intellectual commons in order to promote a diverse culture. Differences lie in how these justifications were translated into the graffiti rules and these differences suggest that copyright law would benefit, first, from a more expansive approach to creativity and second from a re-examination of the relationship between creativity and space (discussed below).

The empirical research confirmed the findings of some existing empirical studies into alternative norms which suggest that 'nonfinancial motivations'[4] lie at the heart of creative production. The line between the two justifications was not always clear. Overall, the reasons offered by writers for producing works suggested that a change in emphasis away from the economic and toward the personal (ie strengthening non-economic rights) in copyright law would better reflect both the desires of creators and the reality of how and why (at least certain types of) artistic works are produced. In eschewing monetary rewards, creativity *within* the subculture both honours graffiti's collective roots at the same time as celebrating the individuality of creative output. Tagging is similar, perhaps, to the writing of monks in that it is an 'act of claiming or declaiming a culture's authorities'.[5] It is this acute awareness of the debt to past creativity that produces the graffiti writer's expansive conception of authorship. It also challenges the narrow conception of authorship in copyright law which having identified an 'author' sets the stage for the commodification of the 'author's' creativity by granting the 'author' a property right.[6] By contrast, the graffiti rules stem from an acknowledgment of moral rather than economic ownership[7] of creativity. At the same time, graffiti writers acknowledge that where a non-writer uses their creativity they should, rightly expect monetary compensation for it when it is used for commercial purposes.

In particular, the regulation of creativity within the graffiti subculture brings into sharp relief existing questions in the literature about copyright and economic power and, especially, the commodification of creativity. The protection of creativity through copyright suggests that modern copyright law is based on neoliberal assumptions, treating as it does creative outputs as the 'propertisable [result]' of individual effort.[8] Yet this again has the effect of producing a narrow definition of creativity and potentially marginalising cultural development (especially of the type not susceptible to easy commodification) notwithstanding the aims of the Berne Convention.[9] This may be seen in the difficulty which copyright

[4] D Fagundes, 'Talk Derby to Me: Intellectual Property Norms Governing Roller Derby Pseudonyms' (2012) 90 *Texas Law Review* 1093, 1145.

[5] MB Ross, 'Authority and Authenticity: Scribbling Authors and the Genius of Print in Eighteenth-Century England' Collectivity' in M Woodmansee and P Jaszi (eds), *The Construction of Authorship: Textual Appropriation in Law and Literature* (Durham, Duke University Press, 1994) 232. The writer, unlike the monk who is 'a translator or medium of authority' (233), is the writer and promoter of his/her own persona.

[6] See F Macmillan, 'What Might Hans Christian Andersen Say About Copyright Today?" in H Porsdam (ed), *Copyright and Other Fairy Tales: Hans Christian Andersen and the Commodification of Creativity* (Cheltenham, Edward Elgar, 2006) 89.

[7] Making a similar point regarding fan fiction: R Tushnet, 'Payment in Credit: Copyright Law and Subcultural Creativity' (2007) 70 *Law & Contemporary Problems* 135, 165.

[8] CJ Craig, *Copyright, Communication and Culture: Towards a Relational Theory of Copyright Law* (Cheltenham, Edward Elgar, 2011) 11.

[9] This is part of a broader argument about the effects in particular of US multinationals. See P Drahos, with J Braithwaite, *Information Feudalism: Who Owns the Knowledge Economy?* (London and New York, The New Press, 2005).

law encounters in protecting traditional knowledge because it is the product of community rather than individual creativity.[10] As Barron explains, by adopting Habermas's notion of the 'lifeworld', for the law and economics approach, and often copyright theory generally, the 'lifeworld' is 'invisible except as an environment for economic activity'.[11] The graffiti rules provide a tantalising look at what an alternative form of regulation, treating creativity as a process undertaken within a community of creators, might look like.

However, the privileging of economic concerns may in part be an issue with the *form* and interpretation of copyright rules, for example, the extent to which exceptions and defences to copyright infringement are sufficient in encouraging the consumption and creation of new works, rather than the substance of copyright protection generally. Examining graffiti creativity as if copyright rules were applied within the subculture provides a new perspective on subsistence, infringement and defences, offering a useful insight into the limitations of copyright as it attempts to deal with a creative process that is both before and beyond copyright.[12] This is especially important in relation to the vexed issue of how incentivisation and reward for creation, or the recognition of an author's personhood, might be reconciled with the goal of providing a social benefit in terms of the propagation and development of culture, in this case, the graffiti subculture. As Barron suggests, albeit in the context of a discussion of Kant, graffiti writers' approach to creativity, including their highlighting the importance of pleasure and community, might also point to

> an alternative vision of what 'copyright' law could be: a regime of cultural/communication rights, unequivocally detached from the institution of property.[13]

The graffiti rules suggest not only the way in which non-economic factors might be integrated into 'copyright-like' rules but also how this might serve to delineate the border between the propertised and non-propertised domains in the intellectual commons in a way that is conducive to the promotion of culture. Chapter ten offered some suggestions for copyright reform based on the graffiti rules. But these suggestions work within copyright as it is; they would not necessarily produce the hypothetical 'regime of cultural/communication rights'. Such a regime is arguably produced via the graffiti rules specifically because the rules operate within a community that has a common aesthetic language and a consensual cultural goal (ie to 'get up' by writing a name in an individual style and in doing so to strengthen the

[10] J Gibson, *Creating Selves: Intellectual Property and the Narration of Culture* (Aldershot, Ashgate, 2006) 103. See also M Blakeney, 'The Protection of Traditional Knowledge Under Intellectual Property Law' (2000) 22(6) *European Intellectual Property Review* 251.

[11] A Barron, 'Copyright Infringement, "Free-Riding", and the Lifeworld' in L Bently, J Davis and JC Ginsburg (eds), *Copyright and Piracy: An Interdisciplinary Critique* (Cambridge, Cambridge University Press, 2010) 124.

[12] The book has adopted the wording of C Waelde and P Schlesinger, 'Music and Dance: Beyond Copyright Text?' (2011) 8(3) *SCRIPTed* 257.

[13] A Barron, 'Copyright and the Claims of Art' (2002) 4 *Intellectual Property Quarterly* 368, 401.

subculture by participating in the creative activity which defines it). We are left to consider the extent to which the very existence of an alternative 'copyright' challenges our conceptions of creativity and space. The next part thus turns not to a further examination of what reforms the graffiti rules might suggest *for* copyright but rather to the relationship *between* the graffiti rules and copyright law.

Space, Pleasure, Resistance

Perhaps the easiest, or most relevant, way to reflect upon the meaning of creativity before considering its regulation within the graffiti subculture specifically, is to simply begin with the experience of creators. In line with experimental music and dance, graffiti has been described in this book as being 'beyond copyright'.[14] The *practice* of graffiti writing is beyond copyright because it rejects copyright law's narrow conceptualisation of creativity as the *work* (as opposed to a process that may or may not include the production of a work in which copyright subsists). The empirical research revealed an alternative normative framework operating to support this creativity as a form of 'copyright beyond law'. Two aspects of the regulation of creativity must be highlighted: creativity as a process that is concerned with space, pleasure and community belonging, and the manner in which the regulation of creativity in turn serves as a form of resistance by generating an alternative regulation of space.

Creativity, Space and Pleasure

The empirical study of the graffiti rules offers a window into a form of creative regulation that breaks down the borders between rules, space, action and emotion. Writers are motivated by the love of writing. The fieldwork data suggested that it is difficult to discuss graffiti creativity without also considering what writing means to the graffiti writers themselves, that is as something they experience through their bodies, through their movement. Many participants emphasised the feeling of creating a work. This encompassed the selection of an appropriate place to paint as well as the (pleasant) feeling of danger in doing so. In particular, the importance of placement for graffiti writers calls into question boundaries between physical and intellectual space and in so doing highlights the difficulty of copyright law in accommodating notions of space (except abstractly as public domain) and creativity as a process. Thus the 'graffiti rules' hold a mirror up to copyright law by identifying similar concerns and justifications but then go further to suggest a

[14] Waelde and Schlesinger (n 12).

different way in which creativity can be regulated that fully embraces both creative practice and the space in which the creativity occurs.

Creativity and creative space may be understood as a series of networks, in particular in the context of the argument that creativity needs to be incentivised in order to produce economic growth.[15] This 'relational mapping' indicates that government policy needs to take into account both physical spaces as well as communication between creators when seeking to encourage creativity.[16] Although such 'relational mapping' does not address copyright law, it suggests how, in seeking to uphold moral standards and/or the public interest, both space and community might be taken into account to determine appropriate levels of copyright protection. One of these ways was suggested in chapter ten in relation to the introduction of fair use.

As with the graffiti rules relating to placement, the empirical findings relating to biting (copying) also demonstrate that the rules and attitudes to copying are embedded in an awareness of graffiti writing as a fundamentally spatial practice. The empirical findings suggest that it is difficult, if not unwise, to discuss the operation of any rules to regulate creativity without acknowledging their spatial effects. The key insight to be gained from the empirical findings discussed in this book regarding appropriate placement is that the protection of graffiti creativity is more than a negotiation between 'getting up' (visibility), respect for 'personal' property and the desire to make a political statement: it suggests that the regulation of individual creativity has the capacity to re-order space. The norms regarding appropriate placement in particular offer a competing, albeit non-legal, set of norms for determining what, and where, creativity can be experienced in public space.

This brings us back to the discussion of the subculture-specific 'bounded commons' (combining both the physical and intellectual commons) within the broader intellectual commons. The interesting parallel to be drawn between copyright rules and the graffiti rules is that they both grapple with how to define the boundaries in the intellectual commons between material that is free to use and that which 'belongs' to an individual. The graffiti subculture's commons is additionally concerned with regulating the territory of graffiti creativity. In doing so the graffiti rules heed, in a way that copyright law does not, Cohen's suggestion that:

> [A]n account of artistic and intellectual creativity must situate creative practice within the material and spatial realities that constrain it.[17]

[15] RC Granger and C Hamilton, 'Re-spatializing the Creative Industries: A Relational Examination of Underground Scenes, and Professional and Organizational Lock-in' (2010) 3(1) *Creative Industries Journal* 47, 48.

[16] ibid 57.

[17] JE Cohen, 'Creativity and Culture in Copyright Theory' (2007) 40 *UC Davis Law Review* 1151, 1177.

Drawing a parallel between the graffiti rules on placement and the copyright rules on immorality/public policy provides a way of thinking about how copyright law might take into account these 'spatial realities' as well as the notions of community and belonging that form the foundation of the graffiti rules. If space is socially produced[18] then the interpretation of laws, including copyright law, also 'actively *produce* space' (emphasis in original).[19] The parallels between legal and non-legal rules discussed in the empirical chapters suggest that the practice of graffiti writing and its attendant rules challenge the range of acceptable actions in public space. By contrast, copyright law tacitly restricts movement, not least in the brake placed on copying (eg photographing) certain two dimensional works that are visible to the public.

Graffiti Rules as Resistance

One writer, after a long discussion of the graffiti rules' historical origins and importance to the subculture, wondered why there rules existed at all to regulate an illegal activity: 'Fuck the rules. I thought graff was meant to be a revolutionary activity' (Anon4). The point, of course, is that it is. Demonstrating the existence of an alternative set of norms that are 'beyond copyright' is not merely confirmation that creativity can and does flourish without copyright law but rather shows what a radically altered copyright might look like. Revolutionary need not mean 'no rules', but rather 'better rules'; rules which make room for and reflect that which copyright, because it cannot, does not. Graffiti creativity and the graffiti rules are 'revolutionary' in their awareness of space. Graffiti writing does not challenge existing legal rules by addressing the 'art or crime' dichotomy but more fundamentally by addressing 'the limits of public space'.[20] The regulation of graffiti creativity within a 'bounded commons' suggests that another type of regulation of creativity is possible and so too is another type of urban space.[21]

The graffiti rules serve to protect the work, the practice of writing and the community of writers. Moreover, they provide an appropriate means of legitimising and regulating graffiti creativity within a hierarchical subculture. This 'bounded commons' presents an alternative set of principles on which to base rules regulating creativity and, even if these rules may not necessarily be capable of being 'scaled up' to suggest avenues for the reform of copyright law, the 'bounded

[18] There is a vast literature on the subject. See especially eg H Lefebvre, *The Production of Space*, D Nicholson-Smith (trans) (Malden, MA, Blackwell Publishing, 2009).

[19] N Blomley, *Law, Space and the Geographies of Power* (New York, Guildford Press, 1994) 45.

[20] See AM Brighenti, 'At the Wall: Graffiti Writers, Urban Territoriality, and the Public Domain' (2010) 13(3) *Space and Culture* 315, 328.

[21] Echoing J Austin, 'More to See Than a Canvas in a White Cube: For an Art in the Streets' (2010) 14(1) *City* 33, 44.

commons' itself functions as a form of political resistance—a means by which to say that some creative practice 'counts', even if the legal system, whether implicitly or explicitly, suggests otherwise.

The notion of graffiti writing as resistance (which is the implication of the argument in this section and of the quotation above) occurs frequently within the academic literature on the subject.[22] For example, Brighenti observes:

> [S]een from the outside, the writer in fact 'touches' something that belongs to all, something that is public, like a wall in a street or a train's façade, and, by doing so, he or she renders visible a number of questions about the norms and the rights, about the *law*—pluralistically conceived (Macdonald, 2006)—that defines the nature and the register of social interaction in public spaces. [Emphasis in original.][23]

In particular, the 'graffiti rules' emphasise that creativity is dependent on the reworking of existing creative expression in order to further the culture of the group as a whole. They demonstrate clearly the sort of substantive normativity—the non-neutrality about the forms and purposes of the creative process—without which a creative subculture could not be said to exist.

Similarly, in an empirical study of graffiti writing in Sydney focusing on writers' use of space McAuliffe observes:

> I am suggesting here that by paying attention to the moral geographies of creative practice we can reveal interesting schisms between the way we are seeking to regulate creativity in the city and the operation of the creative city. And further, that the unsanctioned presence of creativity in the city is not merely subject to a moral framing from without, but also contributes to the continuous production of new urban moral codes…[24]

The empirical study in this book suggests that rules regulating graffiti culture are not merely rules for creating an intellectual commons but rules forming part of a counter-regulation of urban space that is necessary for graffiti writing to flourish. Re-framing the graffiti rules as an alternative form of copyright regulation in public space suggests the worth of exploring the spatial aspects of copyright rules in more detail. Perhaps, a discussion of graffiti and copyright law must also entail a discussion of law, aesthetics and the 'right to the city'; to truly understand what it means when a graffiti writer says, 'the whole city was destroyed and it looked great' (Anon2).

In other words, a creative activity that is, in terms of the criminal law, destructive may be viewed instead as the production of sites of resistance: graffiti writing provides an insight into how the city is ordered.[25] The location of each discrete

[22] See especially J Ferrell, 'Urban Graffiti: Crime, Control, and Resistance' (1995) 27 *Youth and Society* 73.

[23] Brighenti (n 20) 327–8.

[24] C McAuliffe, 'Moral Geographies of the Creative City' (2012) 34(2) *Journal of Urban Affairs* 189, 192.

[25] See especially chapter five.

piece of graffiti writing suggests the presence of an overlapping site that perhaps find an echo in the idea of a place that 'juxtapos[es] in a single real place several spaces, several sites that are in themselves incompatible'.[26] The alternative ordering present within the graffiti subculture (by comparison to copyright law regulation of creativity) is suggesting the existence of another physical and intellectual commons where creativity is regulated differently. The operation of the rules regulating creativity is intimately tied to space including, amongst other things, the operations of sanctions whether through 'street justice'[27] or the destruction of works. This in turn suggests that space, or rather the rules producing it, could be differently constituted. Graffiti writers are inscribing on walls and trains the possibility of a different city.

The question that follows is: what kind of city? Can a city be remade via the regulation of creativity within a 'bounded commons'? Or, if not, then what of the possibility that the city is remade via the regulation of creativity within a plurality of such subcultural commons and their overlap and interaction? These possibilities must be considered because if the argument made in this book about the existence of an alternative normative framework within a subculture-specific commons (one that collapses the distinction between a physical and an intellectual commons) is correct, then the implications of the operation of these norms reaches further than what it might say about the shortcomings of copyright. Indeed, it is worth considering the extent to which the existence of the rules—to return to a point briefly made in chapter two with respect to community and 'commoning'[28] is indicative of an assertion of the right to the city which transcends any rights that might be recognised, or even be capable of recognition, by the law. The territorial aspects of writing become expressions of resistance, as does the act of writing itself. If nothing else, as some participants pointed out themselves, their writing is free in an urban landscape overrun by advertising and other commodified creativity.

As Young puts it, 'Is it possible … to think of the actions of graffiti writers and street artists as pointing to another kind of commons?'[29] While the question is asked specifically in the context of the legal geography literature, including on the meaning of the 'right to the city', it is equally apt when posed with regards to the regulation of creativity in the intellectual commons. It would seem arguable that in collapsing the distinction between the physical and intellectual commons that the graffiti rules present, or begin to present, a 'spatialized normativity'[30] that is

[26] Comment from Foucault in relation to the theatre as heterotopia: M Foucault, 'Of Other Spaces', J Miskowiec (trans) (1986) 16(1) *Diacritics* 22, 25.

[27] See chapter nine.

[28] D Harvey, *Rebel Cities: From the Right to the City to the Urban Revolution* (New York, Verso, 2012) 73.

[29] A Young, *Street Art, Public City: Law, Crime and the Urban Imagination* (Abingdon, Routledge, 2014) 56.

[30] J Ploger, 'Foucault's Dispositif and the City' (2008) 7(1) *Planning Theory* 51, 67.

an assertion of the 'right to the city'.[31] In relation to motivations considered in chapters one and two it is worth highlighting for instance the resistance to the commercialisation of space. This links neatly to Layard's observation (in relation to the semi-public spaces of the shopping centre) that public space has, through property, planning and other forms of legal regulation, 'aggregate[d] a collection of previously heterogenous and diverse sites into a single unified and homogenous legal whole'.[32] So what might be seen here—with respect to the analysis of the graffiti rules as a form of resistance—is the same anxiety relating to the commodification and homogenisation of the intellectual commons playing out in the physical urban commons as well. This interface between the physical and intellectual domains is explained by Brighenti as follows:

> The public is therefore the arena where territories are created: the public domain, that is, public space and public sphere at the same time, a zone of convergence and tension between the material and the immaterial. And, as Iveson (2009, p. 242) suggests, 'to address a public is to address a horizon of strangers.' From this perspective, graffiti writing and its longitudinal approach to walls assumes its full significance: not as a subcultural practice among others, or as a personal search for the thrill (although these perspectives are certainly legitimate and important aspects to develop a good description of the practice at stake), but as a radical interrogation of public territories, a questioning of the social relationships that define the public domain.[33]

This interface between the physical and intellectual commons is encapsulated in Young's conception of the '*public city*, whose existence is organized around a *commons of the image*' (emphasis in original).[34] The graffiti-specific 'bounded commons', in offering a parallel to copyright rules, also offers a glimpse into a way of regulating creativity that respects the public interest and enriches the intellectual commons more broadly by encouraging public interaction with creativity.

If commodification and the suppression of potentially diverse and plural expressions leads to the production of a bounded commons, it is perhaps easy to see how the marking of physical public space produces a new (overlapping) commons too. Section 62 of the Copyright, Designs and Patents Act 1988 (CDPA), for example, provides perhaps the most obvious starting point[35] for considering the political potential of regulating creativity in new ways by placing the space where creativity is found at the centre of determinations of whether the uses of the creativity are acceptable or not.

[31] See generally eg D Mitchell, *The Right to the City: Social Justice and the Fight for Public Space* (New York, Guilford Press, 2003). A relatively thin discussion of space is provided in this book, but in highlighting that copyright law leaves much of the spatial politics associated with it unexpressed, it is intended, simply and in broad terms, to articulate the problem.

[32] A Layard, 'Shopping in the Public Realm: The Law of Place' (2010) 37 *Journal of Law and Society* 412–14.

[33] Brighenti (n 20) 329.

[34] Young (n 29) 57.

[35] See chapter ten.

Yet, given the glacial pace of copyright reform, the further question that occurs is whether, and how, copyright law might take into account the dynamism of creativity—as the creative process of producing graffiti suggests, creativity is both spatially (as the placement norms show in particular) and temporally (as, for instance, demonstrated in the accumulation of fame over time) contingent. This is not to suggest some fanciful, even if desirable, overhaul of copyright but rather to consider how the alternative normative framework within the graffiti subculture might usefully interface with copyright law in the legal domain. The preceding chapter suggested, for instance, that graffiti rules and practices might be brought to bear in interpreting existing copyright rules.[36] The same might be said of all those others norms which regulate subcultural creativity, whether or not they have yet come to the attention of scholars. Indeed, the ability of the graffiti rules to shed light on the appropriate *legal* regulation of creativity makes the identification and understanding of alternative frameworks of regulation increasingly urgent.

Where Next?

The creative process in the graffiti subculture is not incentivised by copyright law: graffiti creativity flourishes despite copyright forbearance. In keeping with the existing literature on alternative normative frameworks, the graffiti rules highlight the shortcomings of existing copyright rules in dealing with the complexities of creativity and suggest particular reforms for the intellectual property system as a whole. These include introducing private and non-commercial copying exceptions, fully embracing the 'intellectual creation' test through the removal of the closed list of subject matter, and removing the assertion requirement from the attribution right. However, the existence of a parallel framework for regulating creativity also calls into question the extent to which copyright law serves to entrench corporate power[37] and weakens the development of alternative communities and power structures that may challenge the operation of copyright law and the socio-political assumptions to which it gives effect. By contrast, in regulating both creativity and space through notions of appropriate placement, the graffiti rules also provide hints of an alternative copyright system, or at least one in which the relationship between copyright rules and space is made manifest.

This book has been pervaded by a tension—it has sought to demonstrate both that copyright law applies to graffiti writing and that it is largely irrelevant within the subculture. Yet understanding the parallels between the graffiti rules and copyright law as regimes for the regulation of creativity produces a picture of an alternative 'copyright' to show what rules that were highly sensitive to the needs of

[36] On the role of custom in 'fair use' determinations see chapter ten.
[37] See eg Macmillan (n 3).

creators and the broader culture would look like. The underlying concern of this book has been to demonstrate the existence of 'copyright' *beyond* law—that is, graffiti rules that both mirror and exceed the regulatory potential of copyright—and what we might learn from such non-legal means of regulating creativity. The study of the graffiti rules points to the aspects of creativity that are lost in the copyright case law or at least abstracted out of consideration by the courts: the importance of pleasure and the potential for belonging.

While copyright rules might yet be improved, and while there may or may not exist an optimum set of rules for the protection and promotion of creativity, any changes will not reach the creative process engaged in to produce particular works (much less enhance it) where creativity is part of a broader subcultural endeavour. Moreover, transposing graffiti rules into copyright law would offer no guarantee that the law would come to operate so as to produce a just and diverse or plural culture; the graffiti rules 'work' because a thick notion of culture is shared by those who bring themselves within the 'jurisdiction' of the rules. The graffiti rules cannot, therefore, be used instrumentally as a tool to 'improve' copyright. The account offered in this book does, nevertheless, provide support for existing calls for reform (discussed in chapter ten). At the very least, and perhaps paradoxically, the application of copyright law to graffiti and the existence of an alternative normative framework that is like, but beyond, copyright within the subculture's 'bounded commons' confirms the relevance of copyright law, and amounts in fact to a call for the continuing existence of copyright or something like it.

Above all, we might continue to reflect upon what the rules regulating creativity are and ought to be. Perhaps what matters, ultimately, is that the relationship between copyright law and the graffiti rules is not to be viewed as one where, in imperial fashion, copyright law absorbs alternative normative frameworks with a view to improving itself. Rather the empirical study suggests a need for the tolerance, indeed promotion, of a multitude of 'bounded commons' and their norms within the socially unified intellectual commons as a means of promoting an attractive, plural culture.

INDEX

www.ingramcontent.com/pod-product-compliance
Ingram Content Group UK Ltd.
Pitfield, Milton Keynes, MK11 3LW, UK
UKHW020134290926
15471UKWH00003B/474

9 781509 927944